ROBERT E. PEARY
AT THE NORTH POLE

ISBN 978-0-914025-20-7

Published by

Starpath Publications

3050 NW 63rd Street, Seattle, WA 98107

Manufactured in the United States of America

www.starpathpublications.com

ROBERT E. PEARY AT THE NORTH POLE

A REPORT BY
THE FOUNDATION FOR THE PROMOTION OF THE ART OF NAVIGATION
REAR ADMIRAL THOMAS D. DAVIES, USN (RET)
PRESIDENT

DIRECTORS
THOMAS D. DAVIES
ALLAN E. BAYLESS
ERNEST B. BROWN
TERRY F. CARRAWAY
MEREDITH B. DAVIES
G. DALE DUNLAP
ROGER H. JONES
JOHN M. LUYKX

ELOISE E. DAVIES, J.D. EDITOR
DOUGLAS R. DAVIES, J.D. CONSULTANT

DECEMBER 11, 1989

Acknowledgement

In the preparation of this report the Foundation has been the recipient of a great deal of generous and helpful assistance from a large number of people. While we would like to acknowledge each individually it is not feasible to make a really comprehensive list. We are therefore expressing our thanks to the staffs of the below-listed organizations, all of whom provided us with significant and important information.

National Geographic Society
Naval Historical Center
Navy Civil Engineer Corps-Seabee Museum
New York Museum of Natural History
Peary-MacMillan Arctic Studies Center of Bowdoin College
Ohio State University, Polar Center
National Aeronautics and Space Administration
American Geographical Society
Rutgers University
Naval Polar Oceanographic Command
Scott Polar Institute
National Oceanographic and Atmospheric Administration
Chemung County Historical Society
George Eastman House Museum of Photography
Office of Naval Research
Defense Mapping Agency
National Archives, Civil Reference Branch
The Explorers Club of New York
U.S. Naval Institute
Arctic Institute of North America
Naval Oceanographic Command
State of Maine, Bureau of Parks and Recreations
Johns Hopkins University
Bucksport Historical Society
Library of Congress

The photograph of Admiral Peary was provided by Commander Edward Peary Stafford. Other photographs are from the collection of the National Geographic Society.

Contents

INTRODUCTION

On September 6, 1909, then Commander Robert Edwin Peary announced from Indian Harbor, Labrador, that he and the five members of his polar party — his assistant, Matthew Henson and the four Eskimos, Ootah, Egingwah, Seegloo and Ooqueah — had reached the North Pole on April 6, 1909. In the terse language so typical of him, Peary telegraphed American news services, "Stars and Stripes nailed to the Pole!" Peary's claim was formally recognized by the Congress of the United States, the National Geographic Society, and a number of American and foreign geographical societies, and he has since gone down in history books as the "discoverer" of the North Pole.

From the beginning, however, some persons have been skeptical of his achievement. The earliest assaults on Peary's credibility came in the press during the period immediately after he returned home. To a significant extent, the hostility was attributable to a bitter controversy between his supporters and those of his affable former surgeon, Dr. Frederick Cook, who had since turned arctic explorer in his own right. A few days before Peary announced that he had won "the last great geographical prize, the North Pole, for the credit of the United States," Cook had telegraphed from the Shetland Islands that he had reached the Pole, accompanied by two Eskimos, nearly a year earlier on April 21, 1908. Cook was then enroute from Greenland to Copenhagen, Denmark, where he would be accorded a tumultuous welcome and cordially received by the Danish King.

A surprising majority of the American people chose to believe Cook, who did not contest Peary's claim but charitably asserted that "Two records are better than one." Peary angrily responded that Cook had handed the public "a gold brick." Such remarks would lead the author-explorer Peter Freuchen to comment: "Cook was a liar and a gentlemen, Peary was neither." Eventually, Cook's claim would be completely discredited, but Peary would never recover from the blow that Cook had dealt him. When the University of Copenhagen rejected Cook's claim, *The Nation* astutely observed:

As for Peary himself he has been defrauded of something that can never be restored to him ... False as it had proved, the claim ... has dimmed the lustre of the true discoverer's achievement. He will receive the full acknowledgement that his work merits, in the form of recognition from scientific and other bodies and of a sure place in history; but the joy and acclaim that should have greeted him at the triumphant close of his twenty-three years quest can never be his.[1]

The prognostication was wrong in one respect. Robert E. Peary would not enjoy the "sure place in history" for which he seemed destined when the verdict against Dr. Cook was rendered.

In 1911, Peary, then a captain in the Civil Engineer Corps of the United States Navy, presented his proofs of his attainment of the North Pole to a sub-committee of the House of Representatives' Naval Affairs Committee that had under consideration a bill to recognize his achievement of the Pole by bestowing upon him the "Thanks of Congress" and retiring him with the honorary rank and pay of a rear admiral. In the end the measure, which had already been passed by the Senate without controversy, cleared the House by a large majority. In the course of the sub-committee's hearings, however, -Peary had been mercilessly pilloried by a vociferous minority, led by Congressman Macon of Arkansas, who questioned the authenticity of his celestial observations, which showed him to have reached the near vicinity of the Pole, of his diary entries, of the photographs he brought back, and of his bathymetric soundings.

In 1916 Peary's critics again held sway during the floor debate on a House bill, sponsored by Representative Henry Helgesen of North Dakota, which would have rescinded his honorary promotion to the rank of rear admiral. As in the earlier sub-committee hearings, his behind the scenes antagonists were Cook partisans, a handful of enemies within the community of arctic explorers, in particular Army General Adolphus Greely, and certain U.S. Navy line officers who resented the promotion to flag rank of an officer who had never commanded a naval vessel. With Helgesen's death in 1917, the Congressional controversy subsided, but the successive acrimonious debates left the explorer sorely wounded in the American public's esteem.

The questions raised in 1911, and again in 1916, have since formed the basis for innumerable anti-Peary books and articles published during an era in which it has become altogether too popular to debunk our American heroes.[2] We dare say that today, as the result of one-sided negative publicity unsupported by any new or conclusive evidence whatsoever, the majority of the American people again disbelieve Robert E. Peary.

---

[1] *The Nation*, New York, Vol. 89, No 2321, Dec. 23, 1909, p. 616; cited in *Peary*, William Herbert Hobbs, p. 426.

[2] The first critical book was published in Peary's lifetime by merchant seaman Captain Thomas Hall, *Has The North Pole Been Discovered?*. This was followed by the Reverend James Gordon Hayes' vituperative *Robert E. Peary*. Then in 1973 came Dennis Rawlins' *Peary At The North Pole: Fact Or Fiction?* which, because the author is an astronomer, was heralded as a scientific expose of Peary's claim. The most recent addition to the list is British author-explorer Wally Herbert's *The Noose Of Laurels*, published in England and in the United States in 1989, which expands upon a *National Geographic Magazine* article of September, 1988.

In 1988, Baltimore professor of astronomy Dennis Rawlins, author of *Peary At The North Pole: Fact or Fiction?* (1973), made national headlines by announcing in the *Washington Post* that he had discovered a long-suppressed document containing calculations by Peary which proved that the explorer had faked his claim and had been nowhere near the Pole. At the request of the National Geographic Society, the Navigation Foundation looked into Rawlins' contentions and discovered that he had misinterpreted an inconsequential document containing undated calculations which, as Rawlins' has since admitted, have no bearing whatsoever on whether Peary reached the North Pole.[3]

The Navigation Foundation's task did not end, however, with our examination of that spurious document. We had been instructed by Mr. Gilbert Grosvenor, President and Chairman of the National Geographic Society, to conduct a thorough review of all available navigational evidence to determine what light could be shed on the entire eighty year old controversy surrounding Admiral Peary's claim to have reached the North Pole in 1909. As it turned out, our inquiry led us far afield from strictly navigational issues; we found ourselves foraging also into the fields of arctic oceanography, bathymetry and forensic photography (photogrammetric analysis).

The ultimate question addressed in this our final report is whether Peary arrived at his intended goal or whether he faked his journey. We realized with a jolt at the beginning of our inquiry that there is no middle ground. Even his critics concede that the celestial observations Peary claimed were taken near his polar camp, Camp Jesup, on April 6 and 7, 1909, place him within a few miles of the Pole. The technical correctness of these observations, which were first evaluated by a board of navigational experts appointed by the National Geographic Society to pass upon Peary's claim, and have now been scrutinized by our own navigational experts, eliminates any possibility of his having innocently mistaken his most northernmost position. He was either an out-and-out imposter like Dr.Frederick Cook, or a genuine American hero who deserved the honors bestowed upon him in his lifetime, and now deserves far more respect than he has been accorded by the media. We feel that the time has come to determine for once and for all how Robert E. Peary should go down in the history books.

Our findings and conclusions, which may startle skeptics who have long since dismissed Peary's claim of having "nailed the Stars and Stripes to the Pole" as a hoax, are summarized immediately below.

---

[3] What Rawlins took to be calculations for compass variations were in fact the serial numbers on Peary's chronometer watches! The document in question was a time sight that Peary used to determine a correction for his chronometers and perhaps to determine longitude by Chauvenet's "transport of chronometers" method. Although one can only speculate as to the time and location of the shot, it plainly was not taken at Peary's farthest north camp in April, 1909, as Rawlins claimed. See the Navigation Foundation's interim report in Appendix A.

SUMMARY AND CONCLUSION

We, the directors of the Navigation Foundation, are pleased to report that we have unanimously concluded that Robert E. Peary, Matt Henson and their four Eskimo companions reached the North Pole on April 6, 1909. Our analysis of the data Peary brought back from his journey — his celestial sights, his diary, his ocean soundings and his photographs — has convinced us that their final camp, named Camp Jesup, was no more than five miles from the Pole, allowing for some inaccuracy in their instruments. Thus our study confirms the decision of the original three-man committee of experts appointed by the National Geographic Society in 1909 to examine and pass upon Peary's claim.[1]

Our conclusion is based upon a year of intensive research by members of the Foundation who have combed through 225 cubic feet of papers at the National Archives, and have reviewed materials from the archives of the American Geographical Society, the National Geographic Society, the Explorers Club of New York, the Library of Congress, the Smithsonian Institution, the Peary-MacMillan Arctic Studies Center at Bowdoin College, Maine, and many other public and private institutions. In addition, we have had access to bathymetric and other data provided by government agencies, including the Department of Defense Mapping Agency, the Naval Observatory, the Office of Naval Research, the Naval Oceanographic Office, the Navy Polar Oceanographic Command and the NOAA Snow and Ice Data center.

---

[1] The decision of that original committee has been criticized over the intervening years as rendered with undue haste after a single appearance by Peary at which he presented his proofs, and after a cursory examination of his instruments. Our extensive research of the Peary collection in the National Archives revealed that this criticism is unwarranted. Individual members of the committee that was comprised of Henry Gannett, geographer of the United States Geological Survey, Admiral Colby M. Chester, a navigation expert, and O. H. Tittmann of the Coast and Geodetic Survey, corresponded with Captain Robert Bartlett, the skipper of Peary's ship, the *Roosevelt*, and expedition members Donald B. MacMillan and George Borup, all of whom submitted their logs for the committee's examination. Also Peary's celestial observations were examined with care. There was no need for more than a cursory look at Peary's instruments. On his polar journey he used only the basic navigational instruments, such as chronometers, sextants, compasses and paraphernalia for use with the artificial horizon, with which they were all familiar. From Gannett's testimony it is clear that they understood Pear's navigation methods.

To our surprise we found that remarkably little new information relating to Peary's claim has been introduced in the succession of critical books and articles that have appeared in the seven decades since the explorer's death in 1920, and few new issues have been raised since the Congressional hearings of 1911 and 1916. We determined that in our study we would not merely scrutinize the charges that have been brought against him by those who label his claim a hoax, but that we would examine the proofs he brought back from his journey in the light of all applicable scientific data and techniques. We have now done so, as is explained below.

At the outset, however, in **Part I**, "Peary's Role in Arctic Exploration," we review the story of Peary's life and his achievements against the background of what had been accomplished by courageous arctic explorers who had preceded him. In their day we must realize that these men were tantamount to the astronauts of the 1960's whose goal was to reach the moon. We touch upon Peary's early explorations in Greenland, which took him over the great interior ice cap to the uncharted east coast of northern Greenland, and eventually enabled him to determine the insularity of Greenland. And we take note of his early futile attempts to reach the North Pole via bases in northern Greenland or Ellesmere Island, one of which nearly cost him his life and did cost him the loss of eight toes. Though the experience might have deterred a less determined explorer, Peary persisted and in 1906 established a new "farthest north" record of latitude 87-06, which meant that he had come closer to the top of the world than any explorer before him.

Then finally in 1909, on a journey in which fortune smiled on him by favoring him with good weather, relatively smooth ice surfaces, and few open water leads, he claimed to have reached the Pole at last. He came home, however, to find that most Americans had already accorded the honor of being first at the Pole to his rival, Dr. Frederick Cook. When the Cook-Peary controversy was finally resolved, Peary emerged as the sole contender for the prize. Though he eventually attained public recognition and the honors he deserved, his enjoyment of them was diminished by the ensuing battles with hostile Congressmen, spurred on by his enemies, among whom was General Adolphus Greely whose own arctic expedition had ended disastrously. The story of Peary's life and career is therefore one of bitter irony.

In **Part II**, "Peary's Navigation," we show that the explorer's method of navigation, which he described to the Congressional committee as "dead reckoning" corrected by noon observations of the sun, was entirely adequate for polar latitudes. It was, in fact, the method used by Roald Amundsen on his successful trip to the South Pole in 1911. There was no need for longitude observations and none were taken — a factor which has evoked unwarranted criticism from persons who have not grasped his techniques. His method called for finding the direction of the Pole from the sun as often as feasible. By always heading straight for the Pole itself, however he had been diverted, he compensated as he went along for the effects of ice drift, changing magnetic variation, and detours to the east or west due to open water leads and unsurmountable pressure ridges. His was a zigzag course with his heading intermittently corrected to true north, not a beeline up a given meridian.

Peary's compass always pointed to the magnetic pole and not true north. However, he was able to set his compass course by the sun, which, when visible on the trip north, lay exactly due south at "local apparent noon," the moment at which the sun reaches its highest altitude above the horizon. To make an observation for apparent noon, he used a sextant to measure the angle between the sun and the horizon. Since the frozen Arctic Ocean with its ice ridges does not provide a clean horizon, he used an instrument called an artificial horizon — a small wooden pan covered with glass and filled with liquid mercury. The mercury acts as a perfectly level mirror, and the sextant measures the angle between the sun and its reflected image.

When taking a sun sight, he would note the time of culmination on his watch, and it is important to note that the time indicated by the watch did not have to be the "correct" time. Much has been made of the fact that the *Roosevelt*'s chronometers were fast when Peary set his watches from them upon starting for the Pole. We have determined that the most probable error of the watches was less than one minute, but whatever the error was, it did not matter, since the time of the sun's maximum altitude determined the time of local noon. Whatever his watch read when the maximum altitude was achieved was regarded as local noon on subsequent days when noon sights were not taken, but the direction of the noon sun was used whenever it was visible. We are persuaded that Peary's system of navigation was adequate to get him to the near vicinity of the Pole, without taking longitude observations along the way.

We also examined the patterns of ice drift in the Arctic Ocean, and the expedition members' accounts of winds and ice movements experienced, and concluded that Peary was able to maintain a relatively direct course to the Pole up the 70th meridian. We determined that the initial drift westward noted by the explorer Wally Herbert, in his *National Geographic Magazine* article (September 1988) and in his book, *The Noose of Laurels* (1989) was offset by a subsequent rapid eastward movement of the ice that he apparently overlooked.

Herbert's conjecture as to Peary's track (which places him west of the Pole for his entire journey) is based upon a westward drift of the ice just north of Cape Columbia of about 20 miles in the first three days, caused by easterly winds. He asserts that from the outset of the polar assault Peary was always west of where he thought he was because he had failed to take this phenomenon into account. However, Herbert overlooked the fact that after returning to the land base for supplies, expedition members Ross Marvin and George Borup recorded that westerly winds (also noted by Peary) were moving the ice rapidly back eastward. To their surprise the outbound trail, which earlier had been driven 15 miles west of Cape Columbia, had drifted back almost to its original position. We have thus concluded that during the entire northward trip, Peary would have experienced only a slight westward drift due to the net effect of the wind.

Moreover, available modern data indicates that he would have experienced a slight *eastward* ice movement as he got closer to the Pole. In sum, from our study of ice drifts caused by winds and currents, we think that the net effect of ice movements within the time span of Peary's polar journey was negligible.

Since Peary's critics have unanimously denounced as "faked" the celestial observations he brought back from the Pole, we minutely examined those sights for mistakes that a faker would be likely to make. Our examination led us to conclude that the sights are indeed genuine, as determined by the National Geographic Society's board of experts in 1909. Among other things, the pattern of "random scatter" — the fingerprint of the field observer — is completely consistent with other sights Peary made on previous expeditions. In short, we are satisfied that the observations of the sun that Peary took over a period of 24 hours after arriving at his northernmost camp,

Camp Jesup, were not faked, and that he was essentially where his sights showed him to be when he "nailed" the Stars and Stripes to the Pole.

In **Part III**, "Peary's Sledging Speeds and Distances," we consider the critics' contentions that the speeds and distances Peary claimed to have attained on his final dash to the Pole and back, when his sole witnesses were Henson and the Eskimos, are incredible. As for the distances in controversy, we specify them, as did Peary, as "nautical miles made good." The polar party covered about 270 miles (excluding excursions Peary made at the Pole) round-trip from 5 a.m. April 2, when they departed from Camp Bartlett (where Captain Bartlett turned back) to 30 minutes after midnight on April 10, when they returned to the same camp after spending 30 hours in the vicinity of the Pole.

Peary covered the distance to the Pole in five marches averaging about 27 miles per march, at an average speed of about 2.5 miles per hour. Peary's return trip, from 4 p.m. on April 7 to 12:30 a.m. on April 10, is more frequently the basis of skepticism. This trek was made in three forced marches of about 45 miles per march, following the party's old trail and using previously built igloos, totalling about 48 hours of sledging at an average speed of about 2.8 miles an hour with nine hours of stops for food and rest. Peary's rapid progress on the return trip was attributable more to the duration of his extended marches than to the small increase in speed. Both factors are understandable when one considers that every hour of delay increased the party's chance that their southward travel would be hindered by winds that would obliterate the trail or open leads that could be slow to freeze over, leaving them to face starvation on the ice.

We examined the distances and speeds of a number of sled travellers in the Arctic, including Peary himself on his earlier expeditions. From the accumulated data, it is clear that skilled drivers of dogs and sledges have often maintained or exceeded the claimed speeds of Peary's polar party; thus we do not consider them incredible. To give but one example, Gunnar Isachsen, captain of the *Fram* under the Norwegian explorer Otto Sverdrup, wrote in *Geographical Review* in 1929: "On our sledging trips we were not content with marches under 15 miles. We often made 20 to 30 miles, and marches of over 30 miles were not rare."

Speed in sledging is determined by a number of variables — the ability and determination of drivers, the strength of dogs, the configuration and weight of sledges and, of course, ice conditions. Peary's Eskimo drivers were unsurpassed; Ootah's sledging skills had made him a hero among his people, and Matt Henson, after long years in the Arctic, was almost his equal. The north Greenland dogs were conceded to be superior to those of other Eskimo tribes. Peary's dogs for the final dash were the pick of 133 that had started the trek and were well fed in preparation for the final assault.

Except for Peary's own accounts in his journal — which reported better than usual ice conditions for the last five marches — we cannot know what ice conditions were at the time. But Will Steger reported that on his 1986 trek to the Pole in Peary's footsteps, he encountered a smoothing of the ice and the presence of north-south leads that provided an improved surface for sledge travel in the near vicinity of the Pole. Similarly, Colonel Gerry Pitzl, navigator on Ralph Plaisted's snowmobile expedition to the Pole in 1968, reported that for the last two weeks before reaching the Pole travel was "practically unrestricted ... In many cases the lead direction was north, affording us the luxury of effortless travel."

Lastly, while on the subject of Peary's speeds and distances, we note that his critics who place him 50 miles east, west or south of the Pole as a result of his alleged miscalculated distances combined with faulty navigation, have failed to explain why upon discovering his error when he took his observations at Camp Jesup, he did not continue on for those relatively few additional miles. To assume that this persistent and fearless explorer would have turned back when so close to achieving his lifetime goal, even though he had supplies enough for approximately another forty days, in favor of faking observations upon his return to the *Roosevelt* makes no sense whatsoever. Yet that he did just that is the untenable premise upon which the "hoax" theory espoused by Dennis Rawlins and Wally Herbert, among others, rests.

In **Part IV**, "Peary's Soundings," we analyze the measurements of the ocean depths taken by Peary on his trek from Cape Columbia (on the northern coast of Ellesmere Island at the 70th meridian) to the Pole, and find that they contribute significantly to the question of where his course lay. These data were of no help to Peary in proving his case in 1909, since a profile of the Arctic Ocean in the vicinity of the 70th meridian did not exist. Now of course it does.

The Defense Mapping Agency made available to the Foundation a number of relevant bottom depths obtained by U.S. submarines operating under the arctic ice, and these were used to refine a chart of the area issued by the Office of Naval Research. A computer-generated model based on these data shows that if Peary's track was close to the 70th meridian, he would twice have crossed over a major feature of the ocean bottom, the Lomonosov Ridge, during the trek to the Pole. Sure enough, a series of deep-shallow-deep soundings by Marvin indicates that the party passed over a southern leg of the ridge. A later sounding made by Bartlett at 87°-15' north indicates that they were over the canyon just west of the ridge. And a sounding by Peary at 89°-55' indicates that the ridge had been crossed again. We realize that some of the soundings showing "no-bottom" are less informative than they might be. Yet taken together, the series of soundings shows that Peary was essentially on the track he claimed he was on enroute to the Pole. At least the soundings rule out one of the suggested tracks that Wally Herbert defines in his *National Geographic Magazine* article, which happens to be the *single* track he decided was the correct one in his book.

In **Part V**, "Shadows on the North Pole Photographs," we present the results of our final and most conclusive examination of the data Peary brought back from the Pole — the photographs taken near Camp Jesup. Since an inadequate attempt by merchant captain Thomas Hall in *Did Peary Reach The Pole?* (1917), no one has attempted to analyze Peary's photographs; accordingly, our efforts represent new evidence.

Techniques of photographic analysis that were pioneered during World War II developed into a fine craft afterward with the advent of satellite observation. One technique, called photogrammetric rectification, can produce the angle of the elevation of the sun from shadows in pictures. The angle can be compared with the sun angle calculated from the *Nautical Almanac* to confirm a specific location and time. There are, however, certain prerequisites that must be met. There must be shadows that begin and end within the frame of an uncropped negative; there must be a horizon to determine the orientation of the camera; and the focal length of the camera must be known. Thus not every photograph can be analyzed, but we found that several from Peary's North Pole collection could be.[2]

The technique is one based on simple perspective. Imaginary lines drawn through each object and the end of its shadow would be, in the real world, parallel to the sun's rays. Such lines drawn on a two-dimensional picture converge at a vanishing point (often outside the picture). This vanishing point is also the point at which a ray of sunlight through the camera would cast a shadow of the camera. Thus the vanishing point defines the angle of the sun's rays relative to the optical axis of the camera, which may be pointing up or down, as shown by the horizon.

The mathematical method used to fix these relationships is spherical trigonometry, much like that used in the reduction of a navigation sight. The *Nautical Almanac* gives the declination of the sun at the Pole for the date, and the time (taken from Peary's account of his activities at the Pole) tells which meridian the sun is on. The altitude of the sun measured from the photograph is used to establish a rough "line of position."

We were able to analyze several pictures taken in the vicinity of Camp Jesup and concluded that they place Peary within four or five miles of his reported position and certainly no more than fifteen miles away.

We regard the photogrammetric analysis of the photographs as the most innovative and significant contribution thus far made to the dispute over the attainment of the Pole because while sights can, at least in theory, be faked, the natural shadows in the photographs cannot be falsified. To quote Captain Hall: "Shadows are nature's witnesses. They never lie and they testify on other subjects besides that of altitudes"[3] Here since they place Peary and his party in the near vicinity of the Pole, they reinforce our conclusion that the sights are genuine.

In **Part VI**, "Ancillary Matters," we digress to consider some of the extraneous matters that critics have raised in their efforts to prove that Peary faked his attainment of the Pole. We address oft-repeated allegations (1) that Peary's 1906 "farthest north" record is dubious, and may also have been faked; (2) that on the 1906 expedition he faked the discovery of non-existent new land, which he called "Crocker Land," in order to be able to name territory after a financial backer, George Crocker; (3) that his 1909 diary entries are suspiciously incomplete or irregular; and (4) that he deceived his faithful Negro assistant, Matt Henson, about the location of Camp Jesup, thereby making it easier to pull off his hoax of having attained the Pole.

To summarize: *First*, we determined that Peary *did* set a new "farthest north" record in 1906 by reaching latitude 87°-06'. He brought back a photograph which we assumed was taken at that latitude in the early afternoon of April 21 — on the basis of his account in his *Nearest The Pole* — that when subjected to the photogrammetric technique we utilized in analyzing his Camp Jesup photographs showed him to be at least at latitude 87°-06' or perhaps a little further north. In short, we used forensic photography.

---

[2] Establishing the focal length posed an initial problem because the only Peary camera we found was the 1906 camera at the National Geographic Society. With the help of the International Museum of Photography in Rochester, New York, however, we determined the focal length of the type of camera Peary was using.

Second, we are persuaded that Peary honestly believed that he had seen distant "new land" when he viewed "Crocker Land" because he told a member of his expedition, Dr. Wolf, of having seen it, as Dr. Wolf records in his diary. He did not, as his critics claim, first mention his discovery upon his return to the United States. If he believed in the existence of "Crocker Land" there is nothing reprehensible in his having named it for George Crocker who was a sponsor of the 1906 expedition. He followed a common practice of explorers from time immemorial. We believe that what Peary actually saw was either a mirage or a floating ice island as other persons have speculated.

Third, we discount the discrepancies with regard to Peary's diary that have led critics to speculate that it was fabricated in whole or in part, these include: (1) the lack of a destination (which presumably would have read "the North Pole") on the cover; (2) some pages left blank on the return trip; and (3) the fact that the entry "The Pole at last!!!" is written on a loose page. We found that the incomplete cover is typical of virtually every journal of Peary's that is preserved in the Archives. One must bear in mind that his diaries were never intended for publication but as an aid in preparing books or articles; accordingly proper form was of little concern to him. As for the missing pages on the return journey, we accept Peary's explanation to the Congressional committee that he was sometimes "too busy" to write in his diary. We know that he was racing for the safety of land, and keeping a complete diary was necessarily secondary to survival. As for the loose page on which he scribbled his "The Pole at last!!!" entry, we offer two possible explanations. First, that he tore the page from a notebook similar to the diary notebook — from which he tore pages to send messages to expedition members — that perhaps was closer at hand. Or, second, that he intentionally scrawled the dramatic entry which, unlike the rest of the diary, *was* intended to be published, on a separate sheet of paper. If indeed he faked his 1909 diary, it seems to us that he would have filled in the blank pages, would have completed the cover destination, and would have made sure that all the pages were attached.

Fourth, we are distressed by the allegations of critics Rawlins and Herbert that Peary deceived Matt Henson as to the location of Camp Jesup while he formulated Machiavellian plans for deceiving the world as to his discovery of the Pole. The claims are premised on innocuous but unreliable ghost-written accounts of Henson's experiences at the Pole which can be construed to suggest that relations were strained between Peary and himself at the end of the journey. We do not pretend to know whether this was true or not, but even if it was, it affords no basis for presuming that Peary was engaged in carrying out a sinister plot. As for ourselves, we remain convinced that Peary, Matt Henson and the four Eskimos went to the Pole together, just as they all maintained for the rest of their lives.

In **Part VII**, "Peary's Track," which concludes our report, we present in graphic form our version of how Peary and his party proceeded from Cape Columbia to the Pole. The track integrates the information we developed with regard to ice movements during the early part of the trip, Peary's method of navigation, and his and other expedition members' celestial observations and soundings.

In sum, in the light of all the data we accumulated and assimilated, we feel that we can say categorically that Peary realized his lifelong goal of attaining the Pole on the last of his many expeditions. Certainly we turned up no evidence to the contrary.

We should also like to say that after perusing hundreds of boxes of Peary's private papers, his correspondence and his journals, we are convinced of the man's integrity. We can appreciate Roald Amundsen's statement: "I know Admiral Peary reached the Pole. The reason that I know it is that I know Peary."[4]

We sincerely hope that this report will help to set the record straight and perhaps put an end to the long process of vilification of a courageous American explorer.

---

[3] *Has The North Pole Been Discovered?*, p. 150.
[4] *My Life As An Explorer*, p. 225.

Part One

PEARY'S ROLE IN ARCTIC EXPLORATION

*"Show me a hero, and I will write
you a tragedy."* —F. Scott Fitzgerald

A. Peary's Early Career [1]

Robert Edwin Peary was born in Cresson, Pennsylvania, on May 6, 1856. His forebears had resided in Maine for many generations but his father, Charles Peary, and his mother, Mary Wiley Peary, had moved to Pennsylvania to join Charles' brothers who were there engaged in manufacturing barrels from Allegheny Mountain timber. Within two years of his son's birth, Charles died of pneumonia, and Mary took the boy, whom she called "Bertie," to Portland, Maine, to be raised among her family. In Maine, Peary grew to be a tall, slender, broad-chested and auburn haired young man, and an avid outdoorsman who enjoyed sailing on Casco Bay, hiking in the White Mountains, and collecting and mounting wild life specimens. He excelled academically in school, but preferred his individual outdoor pursuits to team sports. He was devoted to his mother, as she was to him, and he tended to be something of a loner, developing a reticence that would stay with him for life.

In the summer of 1873, Peary enrolled at Bowdoin College in Brunswick, Maine. When he graduated four years later, he stood second in his class, was a Phi Beta Kappa, and had distinguished himself in the field of civil engineering. Shortly after his graduation, he purchased a seventeen acre uninhabited island in Casco Bay, named "Eagle Island," with the vowed intention of someday building a home there.

---

[1] Peary's life story, as told here, is primarily based upon John Edward Weems' definitive biography, *Peary, The Explorer And The Man* (1988 Ed.) For further details see Peary's *Northward Over The "Great Ice"* (1898), *Nearest The Pole* (1907), and *The North Pole* (1910); and see William Herbert Hobbs, *Peary* (1936); and Fitzhugh Green, *Peary, The Man Who Refused To Fail* (1926).

Peary worked for a time for the U.S. Coast and Geodetic Survey in Washington, D.C. before joining the United States Navy as a civil engineer with the rank of lieutenant. In 1884, he conducted a survey of a potential route for a canal across Nicaragua connecting the Atlantic and the Pacific Oceans. This surveying of tropical swamps required the skills in finding positions by observations of the sun that he would later use in the Arctic.

While working in torrid Nicaragua, Peary dreamed of achieving fame by becoming an arctic explorer. He had written to his mother when he was twenty-four years old: "I don't want to live and die without accomplishing anything or without being known beyond a narrow circle of friends. I would like to acquire a name which would be an 'open sesame' to circles of culture and refinement anywhere, a name which would make my mother proud and which would make me feel that I was the peer of anyone I might meet." (Letter dated August 16, 1880; Weems, p. 3)

In the summer of 1886, Peary obtained a six months leave of absence from the Navy during which he travelled to Greenland on the steam whaler *Eagle*, landing at the small Danish station of Godhavn. There he and a young Danish official, Christian Maigaard, took a boat north to a tiny outpost at Ritenbank, and from there made a sledging reconnaissance trip inland onto the uncharted great central ice cap to about 7525 feet above sea level and 120 miles from their starting point. At this time only the fringe of the gigantic 800,000 square mile area of Greenland was known to settlers, possibly only about 5,000 miles along the southwest edge. Peary returned home filled with a desire to explore the unmapped inland area further and to reach the eastern coast. He realized that if Greenland extended far out into the Polar Sea, as many scholars suspected, it might provide a feasible route to the North Pole.

In 1887 Peary returned to Nicaragua to continue his work there, this time on leave from the Navy and employed by "The Maritime Canal Company" as second in command to its chief engineer, A. G. Menocal. He was placed in charge of about forty-five engineers and one hundred laborers, many of whom were picked up in Jamaica, quite a responsibility for so young a man. With him when he left on this assignment was a youthful Negro manservant he had recruited in Washington, D.C., Matthew Henson, who would later accompany him to the Arctic. During the next seven months as the proposed canal was located under Peary's direction, four thousand miles of lines were surveyed in extremely difficult terrain. In 1902, however, the work came to naught when a government committee appointed to decide between the proposed Nicaraguan and Panamanian routes decided on the latter.

Upon his return from Nicaragua, on August 11, 1889, Peary married Josephine Diebitsch, the tall, handsome and spirited auburn-haired daughter of a scholar with the Smithsonian Institution. Earlier he had written of Jo: "That she loves me I know, that she can make me happy I think; that she would hamper me less than any woman I have met or am likely to meet I am confident. Still I shrink from voluntarily chaining myself, and hate to submit my last fairest dream to the cold light of prosaic daily life." (Undated observation from journal; Weems, pp. 75-76) Six weeks after the marriage his dream of being the first man to cross the Greenland arctic icecap was shattered when he learned that a young Norwegian, Fridtjof Nansen, had sledged across the icecap at the narrow southern part, trekking from east to west.

---

[2] A chart showing Peary's travels in Greenland and on Ellesmere Island is provided in Figure I-1.

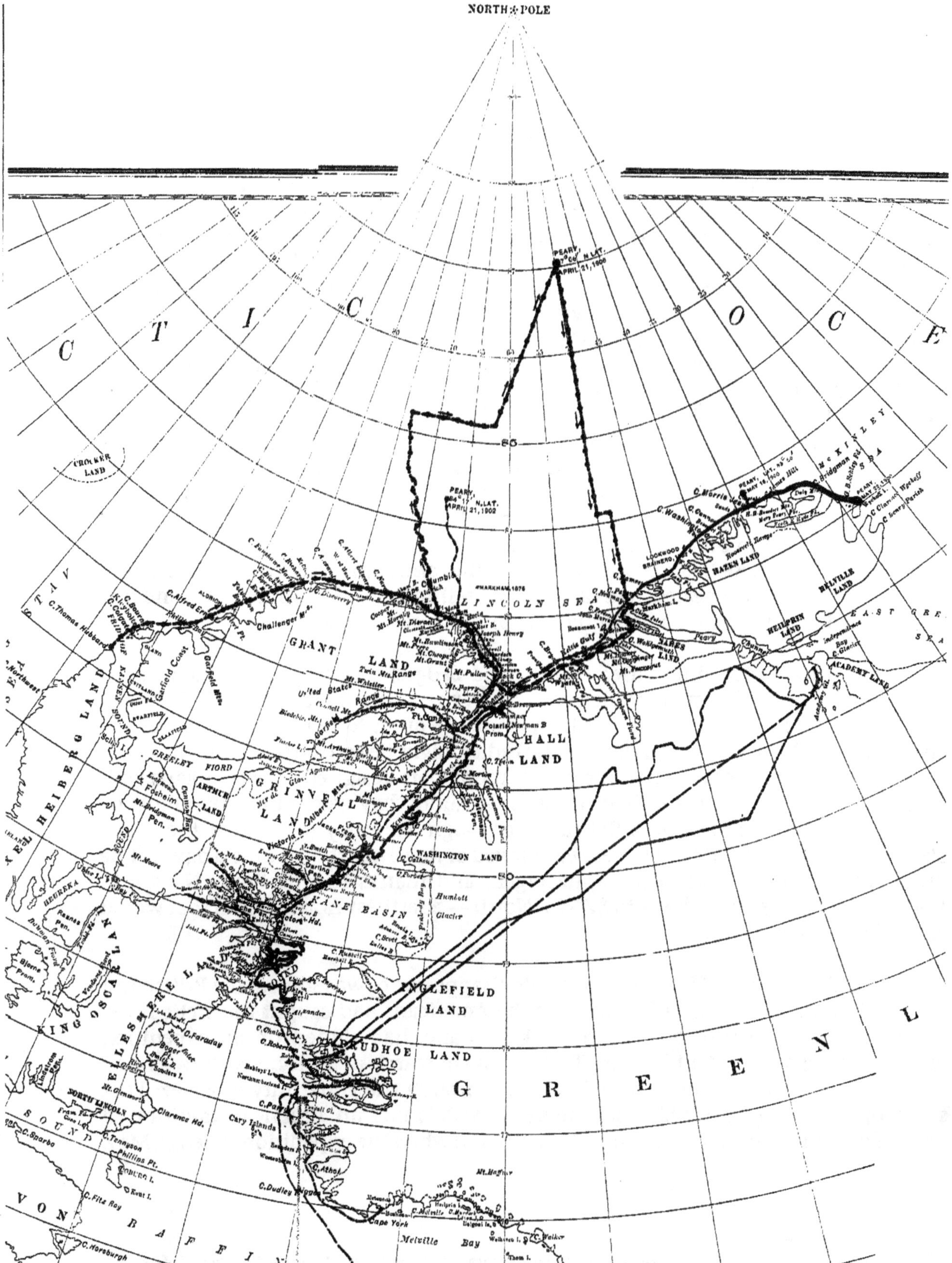
NORTH POLE
CROCKER LAND
LINCOLN SEA
GRANT LAND
GRINNELL LAND
HALL LAND
WASHINGTON LAND
KANE BASIN
INGLEFIELD LAND
PRUDHOE LAND
HAZEN LAND
HEILPRIN LAND
ACADEMY LAND
MELVILLE LAND
GREELEY FIORD
ARTHUR LAND
Challenger Mts.
Garfield Coast
C. Thomas Hubbard
C. Columbia
Humboldt Glacier
Cary Islands
NORTH LINCOLN
Clarence Hd.
C. Sparbo
C. Horsburgh
Cape York
Melville Bay
C. Dudley Digges

Peary was by no means the first athletic and ambitious young man to have caught the "Arctic fever." A distinguished line of explorers had proceeded him and his contemporary, Nansen.

B. The Arctic Dream [3]

1. Early 19th Century Arctic Explorations

The earlier nineteenth century arctic explorers, such as England's Sir John Franklin, were not so concerned with finding the North Pole as with finding a navigable northwest passage to Asia. True, Franklin himself sailed in the *Trent* from Spitzbergen in 1818 in a failed effort to reach the Pole. But Franklin's last and most famous quest came in 1845, when he sailed for the Canadian North in two ships, the *Erebus* and *Terror*, in search of a northwest passage. Somewhere in those waters his two ships disappeared without a trace. Dozens of ships, British and American went in search of him, many on missions financed by Lady Franklin. There were discovered on Beachey Island in 1852 the headstones of three sailors, one of whom had died "on board her Majesty's ship *Terror*." That indicated to the searchers that the ships had not been wrecked at the time the seamen were buried, but were only missing. Five years later an Englishman, Captain Leopold McClintock, found a written message in a cairn on King William Island which told of the expedition's fate. After being beset on the ice for eighteen months, both *Erebus* and *Terror* had gone to the bottom. The surviving crews — 105 men in all — had set out south for the mainland dragging boats and supplies. (One of these boats as well as three bodies and some relics were found later.) Sir John, the message revealed, had earlier died on shipboard of natural causes and had been buried at sea. At last Lady Franklin's mind was set to rest.

McClintock's expedition used man-hauled sledges, adopting a technique developed by another Englishman, William Parry, on expeditions in 1819 and 1827. Parry's 1827 expedition was notable in that he forsook the quest for a northwest passage to try for the North Pole, hoping a route to the Indies might lie across the top of the world. Parry's sledges were actually flat-bottomed troop boats designed as amphibians with detachable wheels and metal shod runners. On shore they were pulled by sailors by means of horsehair ropes. On a flat run over rough ice, Parry found that the heavy sledges, dragged by fourteen bluejackets, moved at no better than a mile a day. Yet he and his men started north from Spitzbergen, and thanks to true Royal Navy grit, trekked over the open polar sea to 82°-45' North — a farthest north record that would stand for half a century.

After the mystery of Sir John Franklin's disappearance was solved, the British lost interest in arctic exploration, but by then the Americans had caught the arctic fever. A frail Philadelphia surgeon, Dr. Elisha Kent Kane, had signed on an expedition commissioned by President Zachary Taylor to go in search of Sir John with two brigs, *Advance* and *Rescue*. The brigs were furnished through the generosity of a New York shipping merchant Henry Grinnell, thereby establishing an American tradition of privately financed arctic exploration. In command when the expedition sailed in May,

---

[3] For a rollicking account of "the heroic age of polar exploration," see John Maxtone-Graham, *Safe Return Doubtful*, Charles Scribner's Sons, New York (1988). We are indebted to Mr. Maxtone-Graham's work, among others, in the brief summary provided here.

1850, was Lieutenant Edwin DeHaven. The Americans passed the winter in the Arctic hobnobbing with British ships engaged in the search for Sir John. Among them was Lady Franklin's own schooner, *Felix*, in command of Sir John Ross. The Americans returned in September with no discoveries to report, but for Kane, this had been an important indoctrination.

In 1853 Kane returned in command of his own expedition of seventeen men, in search of Sir John's missing sailors, on *Advance*. He wintered at 78-38 North in a harbor on Greenland's coast he named Rensselaer Bay, further north than any vessel had wintered before. Kane was convinced that some of Sir John's party clung to life somewhere in the unexplored Smith Sound region. Adopting the Eskimo style of travel with dogs and hickory sledges, and the Eskimo custom of dressing in furs, Kane sledged northward up the coast until all but six of his dogs had died of the dread disease the Eskimos called "piblockto." During the summer of 1854, he bartered for more dogs from the Eskimos, lightened his sledges and sent sledging parties out again. Taking his cue once more from the Eskimos, his sledgers carried only a tent, a fur sleeping bag, pemmican and a portable stove. On two separate sledge trips, Kane explored both the eastern and western shores of "Kane Basin." Two of his sailors, including the ship's surgeon, Isaac Hayes, left the *Advance* and sledged seventy miles to "Grinnell Land" (named after their patron) on the Canadian shore and back. Another two-man expedition, which included an Eskimo, set Kane's farthest north record of 80-33 North, short of Parry's record but the best yet for an American.

During the second winter in the Arctic, rations were tight, fresh meat a scarcity, and many of the men developed scurvy. Eight of them, the healthier half of the ship's complement, led by Hayes, decided to walk south leaving Kane with the invalids. But in December the dissidents were back, starving and crippled, rescued by Eskimos. Kane, in a turnabout for a chronic invalid, alone remained healthy throughout the winter, perhaps because only he ate boiled rats. Though the game caught ashore amounted to no more than a few hares, the shipboard rats were plentiful.

In May 1855, the *Advance*, held fast in the ice, was abandoned. Kane and his men set out south toward Melville Bay in small boats and by foot, hugging the Greenland shore. Game was plentiful in the spring season, and fortune smiled upon them. After an eighty-eight day trek they were picked up by a Danish sailing vessel. On their return to America, Kane was lionized in New York. He published a dramatically illustrated book telling the story of his adventures that caught the fancy of the American public. Sadly he died two years later, at age thirty-seven, of the rheumatic fever that had plagued him all his life except for those years in the Arctic.

Isaac Hayes, Kane's dissident surgeon, next led an American expedition along the so-called "American route" up Kane Basin. He claimed to have sledged to a farthest north of 81 degrees, on May 18, 1961, but the record is in doubt because his cairn has never been recovered.

The acknowledged successor to Kane's mantle was Charles Francis Hall. Shortly after Kane's funeral, Hall, a Cincinnati publisher, obtained funding from Henry Grinnell and left his home and family to follow the lure of the Arctic. He had no ship of his own but sailed cheaply on whalers, and lived for a time with the Eskimos. Along King William Land's western coast, he found many artifacts of the Franklin castaways. From these it appeared that Franklin's men had carried away impossible burdens; they were encumbered even by useless ship's silver and many books.

In 1870, Hall obtained government backing ($50,000) and was given a tug, *Polaris*, to conduct an expedition of his own. By now he had given up the hunt for the Franklin sailors and set his hopes on attaining the Pole. His mixed crew of ordinary seamen and civilian scientists, along with a drunken ship's captain, gave him trouble from the start; some jumped ship before the vessel sailed from New London, Connecticut. Hall set his course northward through "Kennedy Channel," entered "Hall Basin," then passed through "Robeson Channel" — thus "sandwiching his name among those of two U.S. Secretaries of the Navy." (Maxtone-Graham, *Safe Return Doubtful*, p.41) Miraculously, those northern waters were free of ice; unobstructed the *Polaris* steamed boldly into the polar ocean (Hall called it the "Lincoln Sea"), achieving on August 30, a northing of 82°-11', only 34 miles short of Parry's ancient record. In the winter of 1871, he took refuge at an anchorage in an inlet along Greenland's coast to which he gave the colorful name, "Thank God Harbor."

Six weeks later, Hall succumbed to a mysterious violent illness after drinking a cup of coffee , leading some of his crew to believe he had been murdered. When his frozen body was exhumed from a shallow grave in 1968, a forensic scientist determined that he had ingested a prodigious amount of arsenic before his death. It seems probable that he was poisoned; yet since arsenic was a Victorian medication, it is possible that he consumed an overdose of the poison inadvertently. A year later, the *Polaris* sank in a storm, leaving nineteen castaways on the ice, nine of whom were Eskimos. Food ran short, but thanks to the Eskimos' hunting ability, and the complex of igloos they constructed, all survived. Eventually, after untold hardships, one group of castaways was rescued by a sealer, skippered by Isaac Bartlett, whose nephew would captain Robert Peary's ship in 1906 and 1909. Another group was picked up by a whaler. All made it back to New York safely except for Hall himself.

2. Later British and American Expeditions

In 1872, the Royal Navy got back into the fray by forming an Arctic Committee of the Royal Geographic Society to promote arctic discovery. What prompted the move was that in 1871, two Austrian officers, Lieutenant Julius von Payer, of the Army Engineers, and Lieutenant Karl Weyprecht of the Imperial Navy, had hired a small vessel to explore Novaya Zemblya, that long, caterpillar-shaped island extending north from Russia's arctic coastline. They had encountered open water and were convinced that perhaps an entire *northeast* passage might be possible. The news was greeted in Austria with such enthusiasm that a full scale expedition was mounted by public subscription. The steamer *Admiral Tegetthoff* was provisioned for three years and sailed in June, 1872, with a crew of twenty-one sailors and mountaineers. This time instead of open water there was pack ice in the region of Novaya Zemblya. After a year of being beset, for two months the ship was slowly worked within three miles of shore. Then von Payer and Weyprecht disembarked onto new arctic terra firma which they named Franz Josef Land, after their emperor.

In 1875, Captain George Nares, of the Royal Navy, in *Discovery*, explored the vicinity of Cape York and wintered on the western shore of Hall's Basin at what he named "Discovery Bay." He sailed north during the summer, surpassing Hall's latitude of 82°-11' North, and in September, sought a new winter anchorage on the virgin coast along Ellesmere Island. His backup ship, *Alert*, was moored at a new record, for a ship, 82°-30' North, eighty miles north of the *Discovery*. Within weeks, Lieutenant Pelham Aldrich's dog sledge *Challenger* (named for the warship Nares had commanded), would surpass Parry's northern mark of 82°-45' North.

Nares divided his men into divisions, and parties set out to sledge between the ships, experimenting with fifty sledge-dogs picked up in Greenland. But they had made the mistake of making pets of the dogs while they were kenneled aboard ship, and found they would not work when put ashore. Accordingly, old fashioned man-hauling won out, and British disillusionment with dog-sledging was implanted.

During the winter on the *Alert*, the expedition's health seemed sound; flanks of salted beef provided meat, claret was served in the wardroom, and a cup of lime juice laced with rum was passed out weekly to all hands. In April, 1876, two sledging parties set out in high spirits from the *Alert*, one led by Lieutenant Albert Markham for the Pole, the other led by Aldrich to proceed west along the coast. From the *Discovery*, far to the south, Lieutenant Beaumont would lead a party across Hall Basin to investigate Greenland's northern shore. Everything presaged success.

As it turned out, the men of all three divisions suffered grievously — in some cases fatally — from scurvy, a plague that had presumably been eradicated from the Royal Navy since Nelson's time when a daily ration of rum had been prescribed for all hands. (From then on Navy seamen had been called "limeys.") In the case of the Nares expedition, unfortunately, the early symptoms of the devastating disease, "stiffness of the hamstrings," was attributed to man-hauling. Markham's division gave up first; on May 10, he stopped at what would be their northernmost camp at a world's record 83-20-26. A desperate retreat began the next morning with many invalided men hauled on sledges; one died before the ship was reached. Aldrich's division persevered to a new west longitude, 85-33 West. On the return he and another dragged six invalids. Ironically, the severest toll was taken from Beaumont's division, which had supposedly benefitted from the more southerly based *Discovery's* game enriched diet. Two of his men died before the party staggered back to Discovery Bay.

Shaken by the epidemic, Nares sailed for home. A message sent to the Admiralty from Ireland read: "Arrived at Valentia. *All well. Pole impracticable.* No land to northward. Otherwise voyage successful. Highest latitude 83-20 ..." The ships were serenaded with "Home, Sweet Home" when they entered Portsmouth Harbor, and Nares journeyed to Windsor Castle where he was dubbed Sir George Nares. Later there would be an official inquiry, but Nares professed ignorance of the symptoms of scurvy and no heads rolled.

Meanwhile, the Kane and Hall expeditions were followed by two other American expeditions, both commanded by scholarly young officers, Lieutenant George Washington DeLong of the Navy, and Lieutenant Adolphus Greely of the Army. DeLong had fallen in love with the Arctic when he served aboard the *USS Juniata* off Greenland, and volunteered to command the *Little Juniata* which went in search of the *Polaris*. His lovely wife, Emma, claimed he had caught "the polar virus." Backed by a millionaire publisher, James Gordon Bennett, Jr., Delong sailed in the *Jeannette* in July, 1879, from San Francisco. He hoped to proceed to the Pole through the Arctic's back door between Alaska and Siberia. After a long passage north through the Siberian and Alaskan ice packs, the *Jeannette* became imprisoned at a latitude in the low seventies. DeLong was stopped before he had begun: "Truly this is not a pleasant predicament," he wrote in his journal. The *Jeannette* remained imprisoned for the next twenty three months, resisting the crew's frantic efforts to dislodge her. On June 13, 1881, her starboard side caved in and she sank to the bottom of the sea. By then she had drifted with the ice pack north of Wrangel Island.

The crew took to their launches, after six weeks reached uncharted "Bennett Island," and struggled over its ice foot to "Cape Emma," a barren basalt beach covered with driftwood and game. It was their first landfall in two years. Then they passed on, sometimes sledging and sometimes sailing, through the New Siberian Islands where at last they were free of the ice pack. By a cruel stroke of fortune, their three boats, navigating through unobstructed waters, were struck by a gale and became separated. Chief Engineer George Melville's party, in a whaleboat, made it safely to shore and eventually to civilization. One cutter with two officers and six sailors on board was lost. DeLong's party was grounded in the mouth of the Lena River, where it flows into the Siberian Sea, in a delta neither solid enough for marching nor deep enough for navigation. They struck out on foot in knee deep mud, hoping to find enough game to ward off starvation. DeLong sent two men, seamen Noros and Nindemann, ahead to seek help from the Lena Delta's Eskimos. The sailors, who were scarcely less debilitated than their comrades, eventually reached an Eskimo settlement. But when they begged for help for their comrades, the Eskimos either did not understand them or were of no mind to travel in the winter season. The two settled down in an infested hut, where George Melville found them weeks later.

In the spring, with the seamen to guide them, Melville and a party of Eskimos sledged to DeLong's last camp where they uncovered the bodies of their leader and his men. DeLong's journal listed the order of deaths; his had been the last. One page had been torn out; Melville surmised that DeLong had intended to use it for a letter to Emma but it was never found.

A sequel to the *Jeannette* tragedy had yet to be written. In the summer of 1881, Lieutenant Adolphus Greely was in command of an Army detachment of twenty-five men at Fort Conger (named by him for Senator Omar Conger of Michigan) on the shores of Lady Franklin Bay, within a stone's throw of Nares' *Discovery* anchorage of 1875. Their presence at Fort Conger resulted from the United States' commitment to the work of the International Polar Commission, founded through the efforts of the Austrian explorer, Weyprecht, to coordinate scientific observations from eleven nations. No other station was so far north as Discovery Harbor. Behind the choice of the location of Conger was the idle notion that the post might provide a jumping off place for a journey to the Pole.

Greely maintained his post for two successive years, gathering meticulous scientific data. He and his party occupied a relatively commodious pre-fabricated insulated hut, sixty by seventeen feet, and were well supplied with food and fuel. Greely was not a sledger, but Lieutenant James Lockwood, his second in command, travelled along Greenland's northern coast to 83°-23' North, surpassing Sir George Nares' record. This was the high point of the expedition; then came a debacle.

By the end of August, 1883, no relief ship had appeared to reprovision the detachment at Lady Franklin Bay, though this was not for want of trying. During the first summer, the *Neptune* had been able to navigate no further north than Cape Hawkes. During the second summer, the *Proteus* had been crushed by ice and sunk just north of Smith Sound. The Army officer in charge left inadequately marked cairns of supplies at Littleton Island and fled south, taking the lion's share with him. Before the summer's end, Greely determined to evacuate his camp and head south for Cape Sabine. His steam launch, *Lady Greely*, was loaded with coal and three small boats in tow carried forty day's worth of provisions and the expedition's meteorological data. As the flotilla chugged toward Sabine Island, it became all too clear why relief had not been forthcoming; Kennedy Channel was clogged with ice. By September, just north of the 79th parallel, all four boats were hopelessly beset, dragged back north by successive ebb tides. Greely abandoned the heavy *Lady Greely,* and the other loaded boats were sledged across the pack to land. The party would spend the coming winter at Sabine, on bare subsistence rations, far from the comforts of Fort Conger.

Discipline became an increasing problem as the supply of rations dwindled. During below freezing temperatures the party was camped in an abandoned stone hut, roofed over with an overturned whaleboat. Back in the States, jarred by the loss of the *Proteus,* the government dithered over whether to send a relief expedition. One was finally authorized, thanks largely to the efforts of Lieutenant Greely's indomitable wife, Henrietta. George Melville advocated a quick September rescue, but whether a ship could have reached Sabine before the ice closed was debatable. In the spring a Navy expedition was mounted under Commander Winfield Scott Schley. Meanwhile, at Sabine, deaths had set in. Lieutenant Lockwood was among the first to succumb to malnutrition and scurvy. Men had begun to steal each others rations, and in June, Greely ordered one offender, a Private Henry, shot. On the same day the party's doctor, Dr. Pavy, committed suicide. After that, death became commonplace. On June 20, Greely wrote in his journal, "When will this life in death end."

On June 22, Commander Schley and a rescue party, arriving by launch, came upon Greely's collapsed tents. Inside they found Greely, clothed in a filthy dressing gown, on his hands and knees groping for his pince-nez. Seven men out of his original twenty-five had survived, though one would die on the homeward voyage. When the living had been transported on stretchers to the launches, Schley, over Greely's strenuous objections, began to gather up the bodies of the dead, buried and unburied. Back in New York, autopsies performed on the cadavers revealed identical incisions and mutilations. A conclusion of cannibalism was inevitable. This was perhaps the darkest chapter in American exploration.

3. Two Significant "Farthest Norths"

The Norwegian, Fridtjof Nansen, was an extraordinary man of many talents — a doctor of zoology, an artist, a humanitarian, a diplomat, and a crack skier, speed skater and expedition leader. He was also a handsome man, tall and blonde with piercing blue eyes and a luxuriant mustache. In the spring of 1881, Nansen joined the crew of the *Viking* on a six months sailing expedition into Arctic waters. For twenty four days the ship was beset in the pack along Greenland's eastern coast, and he spent hours examining intriguing unexplored mountains through a telescope. His fascination with Greenland led him to plan an expedition across the interior ice cap from east to west, hoping to gain a foothold on the perilous uninhabited eastern coast, and to arrive at a spot on the sparsely settled west coast where he could pick up a ship. He enlisted three other Norwegians for his party, and would later add two Lapps. Second in command would be Otto Sverdrup, a sea captain who would become a famous explorer in his own right.

Having committed himself, Nansen spent the winter of 1887-1888 in the mountains behind Bergen, testing sledges, tents and wool clothing. In addition to the sledges, which the men would pull themselves, he planned to take skis and snowshoes. Since his first problem in Greenland would be to get ashore with his supplies, he had a special amphibian boat built, not unlike Parry's of years earlier. He also experimented with pemmican, ordering a special blend from Denmark. In addition, he designed his own cooking stove, based on equipment used by Greely's expedition.

In the spring of 1888, Nansen was ready, and had contracted with a sealer to get his party near the eastern Greenland coast. The party disembarked on July 17 in two boats, their own specially built one and a ship's boat. Both were packed to the gunwales with instruments, skis, rations, sledges, and a tent — everything the six-man expedition would need to cross the icecap. The two boatloads of men started rowing for the shore, but were caught on the off-shore ice, where they spent the next week and a half battered by surf spray. Their position was perilous. Finally they were able to land at Cape Tordenskjold, far south of where they wanted to be. By then it was the end of July; the brief Arctic summer was half over, but Nansen was determined to go on. The first 300 miles were spent rowing their boats north up to Umivik Fjord, which they reached on August 10. Then at last they abandoned the boats and prepared for the ascent of the icecap. They travelled at night, when the snow was packed hardest, and were soaked by an almost endless deluge of rain. For three days they were confined to their leaky tent by a storm. Finally on the night of August 22, Nansen realized that the most difficult climb was behind. Progress improved and marches of ten miles per day became standard.

Toward the end of the trek Nansen realized that to reach Godthaab, where the journey would end, the party would have to cross water. They improvised a boat — a sort of coracle — from their tent floor laced with willow branches, and relayed men by twos across open ponds. The six men waded ashore at Godthaab on October 3, 1888, where they were greeted by Danish officials and a curious crowd of Eskimos. It was this adventure, which Nansen incorporated into his book, *The First Crossing Of Greenland*, that Peary had learned of while he himself harbored thoughts of returning to Greenland with a serious expedition of his own.

Nansen's greatest achievement, however, was still ahead of him. He determined to aim for the Pole, and to reach it he seized on a plan that was unorthodox but simple. He would commit a vessel purposely to the Siberian ice and let the transpolar current carry her across the top of the world. Monumental patience would be required (more it turned out than Nansen possessed), along with a ship that was especially constructed to withstand the pressure of the ice pack. He sketched plans for an egg-shaped hull with an ungainly three-to-one length to beam ratio, its ovoid flanks sheared so that lateral ice thrusts would be deflected and not pierce or crush the planking. King Oscar and the Norwegian parliament fell in with the plan, and the vessel was built and christened the *Fram*. Its skipper would be Captain Otto Sverdrup.

During the winter of 1892-1893 elaborate preparations were made for a three year voyage. Finally, the *Fram* sailed from Norway's capital city, Christiania, on June 24, 1893. On July 12, the ship entered Tromso through a summer blizzard to take on cold weather clothing — reindeer cloaks and wolfskin parkas, with fur inside and out — and food for over thirty dogs. On July 20, Tromso accorded a heartfelt send-off. Then, after a last Norwegian stop at Vardo, around the far side of the North Cape, the *Fram* headed east across the Barents Sea. She would not be seen again in Norway for three anxious years.

The *Fram* threaded her way through Yugor Strait, making a stop at Khabarova, a Samoyede settlement, to pick up thirty four huskies. At last in September, 1893, as intended, the *Fram* became thoroughly embedded in the Siberian ice pack. From then on, she became not so much a ship as an Arctic station. The men settled down to gymnastics, polar bear hunts and scientific projects that kept them occupied for an entire year, but the constant enemy was boredom. Sometimes in the arctic moonlight Nansen would ski away from the ship and look back to see his vessel in splendid glittering isolation. Meanwhile the ship crept north; at the end of September, 1894, she had progressed 189 miles as the crow flies. By mid-December she was at 82-30, having surpassed the northern record for a ship established by Nares on the *Alert*. Nansen hoped for 84 or even 85 North by spring, but he did not plan to stay around.

In November he had announced that in February he would leave the ship for a try at the Pole. A question to be decided was who should go with him. He would have liked his staunch friend, Sverdrup, but the two agreed that Sverdrup's duty was to stay with the *Fram*. In the end his choice was Hjalmar Johansen, his meteorologist, a gymnast and a superb skier. Typically, Nansen's plan was fraught with risks. The two would make a dash for the Pole and return south to Franz Josef Land. They planned to travel by dog sledge and to carry kayaks on the sledges as well as food and fuel supplies.

When they finally took off on March 14, 1895, with their dogs hauling three heavily loaded sledges, they found that the going over the sea ice was rough and physically exhausting. Their mileages were far less than Nansen had anticipated. On April 8, 1895, they stopped at 86-14, their farthest north and a new world's record. Here they turned back, seeing nothing but pressure ridges ahead, and realizing that their return distance to land would be considerably greater than the distance they had come from the ship. Ironically, when they did so conditions improved and their progress picked up. Pressure ridges and leads ran parallel to the west-southwest course they followed, and there was almost no necessity for heaving sledges over barriers. They burned their third sledge as their food supplies diminished, but the diminution in loads was offset by attrition in dogs.

After weeks of southerly progress, land still eluded them. Both men forgot to wind their watches on the same day, so no longitudinal observations could be made. June came on, and progress was hampered by open leads, necessitating detours. Their rations ran low, but fortunately game became plentiful. When at last they spotted land, they took to their kayaks on August 5, after reluctantly killing their two remaining dogs. They arrived at Franz Josef Land still enjoying the warm weather, but with the realization that they would have to hole up for the winter. For this they constructed a stone hut barely large enough to contain the two of them, where they remained from September until the sun returned at the end of February—an almost intolerable period of stagnation for a man of Nansen's temperament. They resumed marching southward when the spring weather permitted, but not until June 16 did they come upon a hunting party of two Englishmen who welcomed them back to civilization at Cape Flora.

Once back on Norwegian soil, where he received a hero's welcome, Nansen was overjoyed to learn that the *Fram* had arrived at Vardo and was proceeding to Tromso. He and Johansen joined Sverdrup there, and all sailed together to Christiania. The Norwegian Polar Expedition had returned intact.

Nansen's farthest north would be surpassed by an expedition of 1899 -1900, led by Commander Umberto Cagni of the Italian Navy, representing the incapacitated Duke of the Abruzzi, Prince of Savoy. The Duke, an accomplished mountaineer who had intended to lead the expedition himself, was incapacitated from an accident that had cost him two amputated fingers. Cagni and his assault party, consisting largely of Italian mountain climbers with no sledging experience, started from Rudolph Island in Franz Josef Land and achieved a latitude of 86-34 North. During much of the journey they were sledging across level ice, but they were delayed for days at a time by open water. Their expedition proved once more that ice conditions vary from year to year in the arctic regions. As one author has observed: " The Arctic Ocean could be navigable, frozen smooth, or, most likely, chaotic." (Maxtone-Graham, p.153)

C. Peary's Greenland Expeditions

In the summer of 1891, on a leave of absence from the Navy, Peary made his first serious expedition to Greenland accompanied by Jo, who would become the first white woman to endure the harsh arctic winter. The other members of the party were Eivind Astrup, an athletic young Norwegian; Dr. Frederick Cook, a genial surgeon and ethnologist; Langdon Gibson, an ornithologist; John Verhoeff, a youthful sportsman who contributed financially to the expedition; and former valet, Matthew Henson. The trip was marred early on by a shipboard accident on the *Kite* when the vessel's tiller struck and broke Peary's leg just above the ankle. Dr. Cook set the fracture and Peary insisted upon remaining in Greenland rather than returning home. He was brought ashore at Whale Sound strapped to a board, and with Jo's help supervised the construction of a lodge which would be named "Red Cliff House" because of the hue of the cliffs behind it. There the party spent the winter in becoming acquainted with the Smith Sound Eskimos, some of whom lived at the headquarters.

Peary's 1891-1892 experience in Greenland would prove invaluable in that he would learn to dress like an Eskimo in warm but light windproof furs of bear and sealskin (fitting almost skin tight but ventilated at the waist); light water-tight boots lined with grass; soft birdskin shirts; and foxtail ringlets that protected the head and most vulnerable parts of the body. He also learned the value of laying in a fresh supply of meat during the hunting seasons; thus scurvy would never become a factor in his expeditions as in Kane's and Greely's. He came to understand the Eskimos (though not to speak their language with the fluency acquired by Henson), and how to induce them to work for him, and to provide him with dogs in exchange for lumber for sledges and boats, needles, knives, metal tools and cooking utensils. And, most important, he won their confidence; to them he was "Pearyarksuah," or "Big Peary," a man endowed with the strength and hunting skills that they respected and admired.

In May, 1892, Peary, Astrup, Cook and Gibson took off on a sledging party inland, leaving Henson and Verhoeff at the lodge with Jo. The doctor and Gibson turned back early after several days of experiencing blinding snowstorms. Peary and Astrup continued on across the ice cap heading for the northeast corner of Greenland. Progress was agonizingly slow. They encountered crevasses necessitating a long detour, ran into a second severe snowstorm that stopped them for forty-eight hours, and ascended a steep slippery surface that gave men and dogs bad falls. On the descent from the ice cap they very nearly starved before they stumbled upon a herd of musk oxen grazing in a moraine above Independence Bay (so named in honor of the day, July 4). Peary shot two of the animals and men and dogs gorged on the fresh meat before continuing on eastward, hoping to get a distant view of the coast to the north.

On the descent from the inland ice, the party arrived at a high plateau dropping off in a wall almost four thousand feet high which Peary named "Navy Cliff." Looking down toward Independence Bay as he stood on this cliff, Peary glimpsed a deep cleft that he mistook for a channel, leading him to believe that he had established the insularity of Greenland. On a sketch map he made upon his return he dotted in a channel to separate the nearer plateaus he observed from those extending far beyond.[4]

On July 21, Peary and his party turned back; he then had only enough pemmican to feed two men and six remaining dogs for the estimated twenty day return trip. On August 4, a party from Red Cliff met them 5 miles from "Red Cliff House" to tell them that the *Kite* had returned. Peary's trip had proved not only his stamina but his navigational ability; although he had been able to get only three observations on the return journey, his dead reckoning had brought him within these few miles of his destination. (Weems p.126)

Tragedy struck the expedition shortly before the *Kite* sailed for home when Verhoeff disappeared while on an exploratory mission of his own. Search parties discovered his footsteps leading to the edge of a crevasse; Peary left a year's supply of food in a cache in the unlikely event of his return, but the young man did not reappear and is presumed to have fallen to his death.

In January, 1893, Peary astounded the American public by announcing that he intended to return to Greenland, again accompanied by Jo who was expecting a baby in September. He wished to take Dr. Cook along, but the doctor decided not to go and was replaced by a Dr. Vincent. Eventually the eleven man party Peary assembled included repeaters Astrup and Henson and an enthusiastic young novice named Hugh J. Lee; there was also a plucky Scotch nurse, Mrs. Susan Cross, for Jo.

Peary expected that eight men divided into several teams would travel from the west coast northeastward across the ice to Independence Bay, and that a three-man team, including himself, would continue northward along the coast toward the Pole. He planned to rely upon dogs as sledge animals, but as an experiment he took eight burros from Santa Fe, New Mexico. This proved to be a mistake for the burros could not tolerate the cold climate and ended up as food for the dogs.

When on August 5 the *Falcon*, skippered by a Newfoundlander, Captain Harry Bartlett, arrived at "Bowdoin Bay" in Inglefield Gulf, Peary selected a site for his headquarters which he called "Anniversary Lodge." There Jo delivered a baby daughter, named Marie Ahnighto, quickly dubbed "the Snow Baby," on September 12, 1893. Through the winter months when the moon was shining, entire Eskimo families journeyed from far-away villages to get a look at the fairest child they had ever laid eyes on.

---

[4] This striking gap, which has since been shown to be a depression not submerged by the sea, into which Peary showed a series of four glaciers descending, later became a subject of controversy. "Peary Channel" was used in an attempt to discredit Peary by showing that he was an incompetent and unreliable geographical observer. In 1895, Mylius Ericksen with his mapmaker Hagen, reached the vicinity of Navy cliff from the eastward and discovered that the depression immediately beneath the cliff was not a channel but an extension of one of the glaciers Peary had drawn. Though the two men perished, a map made by Hagen was recovered.

When the first Thule expedition under Danish Explorer Knud Rasmussen crossed North Greenland in 1912, Peter Freuchen, his second in command, coming from the westward as Peary had done, stood on Navy Cliff and gained the same impression as had Peary that he saw a channel. In 1925, Dr. Lange Koch, a later Danish explorer, wrote that Peary was fully justified in mistaking the depression for a channel. (Hobbs, p. 13) Today even Peary's severest critics are willing to concede that "Peary Channel" was an understandable mistake.(Rawlins, *Peary At The North Pole: Fact Or Fiction*, p.46)

On March 6, 1894, Peary and seven of his party, along with five Eskimos, set out with twelve sledges and ninety dogs across the inland ice. Trouble developed by March 10, when Lee became infirm with a frozen toe, and Astrup with stomach trouble. Both were returned to Anniversary Lodge by Peary and George Clark, one of his strongest men, who then dashed back to rejoin the main party. On March 22, the party met with horrendously bad weather; furious headwinds hurled drifting snow on their shelter, pinning them down for twenty four hours. Another expedition member suffered frostbite and was sent back to the lodge in the company of Dr. Vincent. Peary realized that any member who had to return later would be forced to travel alone and on skis; he could spare no more men, sledges or dogs for ambulance service.

When the depleted main party continued on, travel became even more difficult. Sledges were broken up and dogs weakened and died and were fed to others. Then the rabies-like disease known to the Eskimos as "piblockto" struck and further diminished the dog pack. On April 10, at a point 128 miles from Anniversary Lodge, Peary turned back, since a try for the Pole was by then out of the question. In support of a future effort, he cached most of his pemmican and fuel supplies at his last camp, and deposited other supplies in a smaller caches closer to the lodge. By the time the lodge was reached on April 20, two more men were suffering from frost-bitten feet, and Peary and another were afflicted with snowblindness.

Peary's next project was an intriguing one. For decades arctic explorers had been hearing rumors of an "iron mountain," which he suspected was a meteorite, some-where near Cape York. On his 1891-1892 expedition he had obtained some informa-tion from natives with the intention of someday locating the site. Now with the promise of a rifle he bribed a young Eskimo to act as a guide, and on May 16 set out to the south accompanied by Hugh Lee. When the party encountered heavy snow-storms their guide took off, but they picked up another at a small Eskimo village. This young native described to them three "saviksue" — great irons — of varying sizes located on an island in Melville Bay. The smallest was called "the Dog," he said, the middle sized one, "the Woman," and the largest, "the Tent."

The threesome was beset by more snowstorms and reached the island only after crossing the rugged bay ice by stepping from one ice cake to another. They found the meteorite called "the Woman," because of its resemblance to a seated cross-legged woman seamstress, and the Eskimo guide explained how it had once served as a source of iron for making knives. For many years, however, the Eskimos had obtained their knives from sealers and whalers in exchange for furs and walrus tusks. Peary did not take time to look for the other two meteorites but scratched a rough "P," on "the Woman," left a record of his discovery in a cairn, and crossed back to the mainland with great difficulty.

The journey back to Anniversary Lodge was made at break-neck speed because Lee, who was never strong, became ill from eating rotten walrus meat obtained at an Eskimo village. Lee later estimated that three final marches made with little sleep and no food on June 2nd-3rd, 3rd-4th, and 5th-6th covered about sixty-five miles each. (From Hugh Lee's diary, Weems p. 146)

On August 20, 1894, the *Falcon* returned to Bowdoin Bay and six days later Jo, baby Marie and most of the expedition members were on their way homeward. Only Peary, Matt Henson, and Lee elected to stay behind to make another attempt at crossing the great ice cap in the spring of 1895. The trip appeared doomed, however, when in October they discovered that a heavy snowfall had buried the small supply cache left at 26 miles from the lodge the previous spring. Poles nine feet high were buried leaving visible only a foot, or had disappeared altogether. It was too late in the season to go looking for the main cache at 128 miles away, but they suspected that this too was buried. Though these supplies — particularly the pemmican and alcohol — were critical to Peary's logistic planning, he declined to give up his plans for the coming spring. The party renewed their fall hunting trips to stock up on extra frozen deer for the men and walrus meat for the dogs, and Peary convinced himself that he would again find musk oxen upon reaching Independence Bay.

On March 31, 1895, Peary wrote a farewell letter to Jo, and on April 1, he departed with Henson, Lee and four Eskimos on yet another trek across the treacherous ice cap. On the outward trip at 128 miles from the lodge, they searched in vain for the missing main cache. Peary then explained to the Eskimos that in going on across the ice cap, he was gambling on finding game on the east coast, and that they were free to turn back. They prudently elected to do so and departed with some of the sledges and dogs. One carried a second letter from Peary to Jo which concluded poignantly, "In the event of mishap, no human can help find or reach us." (Weems, p. 158)

Peary, Lee and Henson proceeded with three sledges, forty-two dogs, and a precariously low supply of rations. Peary in the lead managed to drive his dogs in a northeasterly course across the rugged ice without landmarks to guide him, and Henson and Lee followed. Soon, however, Lee became ill and was forced to ride on his sledge, slowing progress. While he was sick, the forty-two dogs proved too much for Peary and Henson to handle; the entire pack broke loose at feeding time and in the ensuing melee gorged themselves upon the precious walrus meat. Then a blizzard struck, forcing the party to camp for forty-eight hours. When travel resumed Lee's toe had become frozen, and morphine was administered to ease the pain.

By May 5, all the food allowed for the outward journey had been consumed, dogs had been killed to be fed to other dogs, and the party was still short of Independence Bay. On the following day, they camped on the ice cap more than five hundred miles from Anniversary Lodge and assessed their situation. They were now reduced to eleven exhausted dogs and faced with manhauling their sledges — a task that would be impossible for the invalided Lee. Fortunately on the next day, leaving Lee at their camp, Peary and Henson located and shot several musk oxen. The three men and the dogs ate the fresh meat until their stomachs were full, and more meat was cut up for the return trip. The homeward journey was nonetheless a nightmare — Lee became so weak that he was close to death, more dogs died, and the men themselves were reduced to eating dog meat after the supply of musk oxen was exhausted. At the end three half-starved men made it back to Anniversary Lodge with just one dog remaining.

For Peary, this journey exploded the notion that the North Pole could be reached by crossing the inland ice and proceeding northward up the east coast of Greenland. His two journeys to Independence Bay had convinced him that the smooth icy highway to the Pole he had hoped to find there did not exist.

One positive result of the trip was the discovery, from the vantage point of the ice cap, of a towering mountain some seventy miles due north which Peary named Mount Wistar (for General I. J. Wistar, President of the Philadelphia Academy of Sciences). Five years later he would sight the mountain from another point and through his intervening observations establish beyond any doubt the insularity of Greenland. (Weems, p. 163)

Peary had failed again and was in low spirits when the relief ship *Kite* arrived to evacuate him, Henson and Lee. He was not cheered by a letter from his mother which concluded: "If you have not accomplished all you had hoped to do, do not be disheartened; take a cheerful view of your failure. *Many* have failed." (Weems, p. 167) Despite everything that had gone wrong, he was not ready to write off the attainment of the Pole as an impossible goal.

Peary was disappointed that the *Kite* was not bearing Jo and Marie, but Jo's brother, Emil Diebitsch, was aboard with news of the family. Emil proudly reported that after Jo had vainly petitioned the Navy to send a relief ship for her husband, she had solicited funds for the charter of the *Kite* by writing and lecturing on life in the Arctic — tasks that did not come easily for her.

While the *Kite* was available, Peary had it proceed to Melville Bay where he picked up the meteorites "the Dog," found to weigh 1000 pounds, and "the Woman," found to weigh 5500 pounds. He visited "the Tent," but upon observing its gigantic size, decided to let it remain where it was until another day.

In the summer of 1896, Peary returned for "the Tent" with the *Hope* — a vessel of only 307 tons — but a threat posed by the pack ice forced the vessel to flee without accomplishing its mission. Then in the following summer, "the Tent," which weighed 90 to 100 tons, was hoisted aboard the small but sturdy *Hope* by an astounding feat of engineering. The meteorites were put on display in the American Museum of Natural History and later sold to the museum for a reputed price of $40,000.

In 1897, the American Geographical Society awarded Peary a gold metal for establishing the insularity of Greenland by determining the convergence of its northernmost coastlines, and in the following year the Geographic Society of London conferred a similar award upon him. The world was beginning to take the explorer seriously despite the failure of his most ambitious projects.

D. The American Way To The Pole

After giving up on finding a route to the North Pole by sledging up the east Greenland coast, Peary began seriously to consider the feasibility of forcing passage by ship as close to the Pole as possible through the ice-jammed strait lying between the west coast of Greenland and Ellesmere Island. He would establish a base at the northern tip of Greenland or of Ellesmere Island and make an "assault" on the Pole from there. If this feat of navigation could be accomplished, he would be able to commence the sledging journey two or three hundred miles further north than he could otherwise expect. He was realistically prepared to devote several years to the task, living largely off the game to be found on the land. He called this proposed route to the Pole the "American way" because of its having been explored by Kane, Hayes, Hall and Lockwood.

All that stood between Peary and his dream was money, a ship powerful enough to crash through the ice of the northern seas, and another leave of absence from the Navy. A five-year leave was obtained, over the objections of the naval establishment, by the intervention of President McKinley at the behest of a prominent Republican.

A philanthropist, Morris Jesup, and a group of well-to-do businessmen formed the "Peary Arctic Club" to raise money, and a London newspaper magnate donated a steam yacht, the *Windward*. All of this, of course, was in the established tradition of American arctic exploration which had never been government subsidized beyond the sending out of occasional relief expeditions.

Since the *Windward* had to be outfitted with new engines and Peary was in a hurry to return north, on July 3, 1898, he sailed on the little *Hope*, taking with him only Henson and a doctor, Dr. Dedrick. He left in such haste because he had learned that the Norwegian explorer, Otto Sverdrup, was planning to lead an expedition in the *Fram* to the same regions he intended to visit. Since both expeditions would be sledging expeditions, and would draw upon the limited dog supply of the Smith Sound Eskimos, practical considerations as well as questions of priority in discovery were involved. Peary wrote to the Peary Arctic Club: "The appropriation by another of my plan and field of work necessitated the charter of an auxiliary ship if I did not wish to be distanced in my own domain." (Hobbs, p. 198, n. 5)

The *Windward* arrived in Etah, Greenland, not long after the *Hope*, and with Peary, Hensen and Dedrick aboard commenced a crossing of Kane Basin. Five days later the vessel was stuck fast for the winter near Cape D'Urville, far south of Peary's intended goal. Sverdrup's expedition, which had found it impossible to push the *Fram* northward as intended through the ice of the Kane Basin had gone into winter quarters west of Buchanan Bay, and Sverdrup had abandoned the announced plan that would have brought him into competition with Peary; he would focus instead upon a Greenland mapping survey. The two headquarters were about seventy-five miles apart, and the two explorers' once accidentally met near Sverdrup's base. Sverdrup invited Peary in for coffee, but the invitation was rather curtly refused; Peary still harbored ill-concealed resentment of what he regarded as the Norwegian's "poaching" on "his domain."

Peary concluded that with the *Windward* as far south as she was, his best bet for carrying out his plan was to find Fort Conger, Greely's headquarters of fifteen years earlier, and use it as an advance base. This would entail unloading his supplies at Cape D'Urville and sledging them in shifts to Conger, 250 miles distant, travelling by moonlight in the months between October and February. From Conger, he hoped to be able to launch an assault on the Pole in March, after the return of daylight, and be back before warming weather brought about the breakup of the Arctic Ocean ice.

With this plan in mind, Peary, Henson, Dr. Dedrick and four Eskimos began transporting supplies from the *Windward* toward Fort Conger in October, depositing them securely in abandoned native stone igloos along the coast. December arrived before Peary was ready to complete the journey all the way to Fort Conger, which had not been visited since Greely's disastrous retreat south to Camp Sabine. He was by then impatient to see whether usable supplies had been abandoned by Greely's party, and whether the building was habitable. On December 20, he, Hensen and the doctor sped northward, knowing that travel would be feasible only within the eleven days of moonlight.

Travelling proved tortuous over the ice foot, however, and by the ninth day the party had covered only half the distance. Food was low, and a freezing wind blinded the men and their dogs. Some of the Eskimos, numbed with cold and fearful of venturing any further, were sent back to the ship with the weakest dogs. The last part of the trip was made in total darkness, men and dogs stumbling over the jagged ice. Yet somehow, Peary managed to find Fort Conger by the "feel" of the shore. They arrived in blackness on January 6, 1899.

Inside there was an eerie scene. In the kitchen partially consumed tins of biscuits, tea and coffee were scattered about, testifying to a hurried departure. In the men's quarters, dishes remained on a table, left just as they were following a meal before the camp was deserted. Fortunately the food supplies had not spoiled, and there was even fuel for the stove. After the half-starved party had consumed some of the preserved food and tea and partially warmed up, Henson or an Eskimo helped Peary take off his "kamiks," or boots. To Peary's horror, the toes on both his feet were so badly frostbitten that he knew amputation would be required to prevent gangrene. Using primitive methods and medications, Dr. Dedrick removed parts of seven toes.

Then began the darkest period of Peary's life. For six weeks he lay at Fort Conger snowbound and unable to walk. Under such helpless conditions he wrote in heavy pencil on the wooden wall beside his bunk a favorite quotation from Seneca: "Inveniam viam aut faciam" — "I shall find a way or make one." The forced inaction was so unbearable to him that he decided to head back to the *Windward* at all costs. Returning light in mid-February, though dim, provided some consolation and rendered the landscape faintly visible. So, lashed to a sledge, and tended by his men, on February 18, Peary left Conger. On February 28 he reached the *Windward*, physically shattered but clinging to his dream. The difficult journey of 250 miles over the rugged shore ice, with the burden of the crippled man, had been completed by Peary's team in eleven days (an average of over 22 miles each day). Aboard the ship, on March 13, Peary underwent another operation on his feet, leaving him with only the little toes on each foot.

Without waiting for the stumps of his amputated toes to fully heal, but with crutches and still a dead weight on his sled, Peary made a remarkable series of trips to move his supplies up to Conger. On one trip, for example, on April 19, with 10 Eskimos, 50 dogs and 7 sledges, he set out from Cape D' Urville for Conger and arrived ten days later, having averaged 25 miles per day.

On May 23, the return to the ship began, with Peary bearing the Greely expedition's abandoned records from Fort Conger. Then on August 2, 1899, the ice loosened its grip on the *Windward* and she proceeded southward to Etah. There a relief ship, *Diana*, arrived with Herbert L. Bridgeman, Secretary of the Peary Arctic Club, bearing a letter from Jo announcing the birth of a second daughter, Francine, the previous January. Jo lamented that in his long absences life was slipping away from them both, to which Peary replied: "You are right, dear, life is slipping away ... More than once I have taken myself to task for my folly in leaving such a wife and baby (babies now) for this work. But there is something beyond me, something outside of me, which impels me irresistibly to the work..." (Peary, *Northward Over The Great Ice*, v. 2, pp. 69 - 70) When Bridgeman learned of Peary's amputated toes, he futilely urged him to come home, but Peary was determined to stay on and try for the Pole again in the spring.

After the *Diana's* departure, Peary, Henson and Dedrick remained at Etah, the Greenland Eskimo village he had chosen as his headquarters. He retained his advance base at Conger, however, and despite his bad experience of the previous year, took advantage of the periods of winter moonlight to transfer supplies in stages from Etah to Payer Harbor (across Smith Sound near Camp Sabine) to Conger. When he arrived at Conger on March 28, 1900, he was cheered to find that his Eskimos had shot 28 musk oxen near the place; his food supply benefitted and his morale was given a much needed lift. He began to feel that the men of General Greely's party who had starved to death at Camp Sabine would have survived had the General decided to remain at Conger and taken advantage of the game at hand.

In April, Peary was undecided whether to strike out for the North Pole by way of Cape Hecla, about one degree of latitude north of Conger on Ellesmere Island, or to cross frozen Robeson Channel and try from the northern tip of Greenland. He decided to cross the channel, and with Henson and Dedrick, made a trip up the North Greenland Coast venturing into an uncharted region. He rounded the northernmost portion of Greenland at a point he named Cape Morris Jesup, and pressed southward toward Independence Bay. The trip did not get him close to the Pole — indeed his small party was ill equipped for an assault on the Pole — but it gave him his first experience over the Arctic Ocean ice; until now he had been more of a glacial specialist.

On May 22, the party returned to Conger and spent the summer and autumn in hunting. Unknown to Peary, the *Windward* had arrived at Etah in August with Jo and Marie aboard and had missed him there. The Eskimos had reported that he was at Payer Harbor, but, of course, he was not there either. Outside Payer Harbor the ship had narrowly escaped being broken up in a storm, and had become imprisoned in the early-freezing ice. Thus while Peary relaxed at Conger, his wife and child and a host of his friends remained little more than two hundred and fifty miles to the south experiencing a harrowing winter.

On board the *Windward* when she journeyed northward from Etah were a number of Eskimos including the pretty young Allakasingwah — or "Ally" — with hers and Peary's baby son. According to Weems, "the woman innocently boasted of her relationship with 'Pearyarksuah,' not realizing the enormous difference in mores." (p. 190). Jo is said to have been stunned by the revelation that her husband had fathered the child. Yet Peary had long ago written in his journal that American explorers spending long months in the Arctic should be expected to take native wives, and certain of Jo's letters indicate that she was not entirely unaware of his relationships with Eskimo women. Now genuinely hurt, however, she wrote Peary in a letter to be delivered whenever communications could be established, "You will have been surprised, perhaps annoyed, when you hear I came up on a ship ... but believe me had I known how things were I would not have come." (Letter dated August 28, 1900; Weems p.190)

But Jo was a warm hearted and compassionate woman. When "Ally" became seriously ill, she made the Eskimos promise that if the mother died, her baby would not be strangled as was the Eskimo custom. "Ally" recovered, however, and brought up this little boy and another with the knowledge that they were Peary's sons. [5]

Peary did not receive Jo's letter telling of the *Windward's* arrival until the following spring. Though the ship's passengers surmised that he was wintering at Conger, no Eskimos could be induced to make the treacherous trip north on their own

---

[5] See S. Allen Counter, "Descendants of the Expeditions," *National Geographic Magazine*, September, 1988. The existence of these children, when publicized by Dr. Cook, would shock Victorian concepts of morality and make it all the more difficult for Peary to defend his claim against his critics.

for any promise of reward. Meanwhile Peary was spending his coziest winter in the region. He had demolished Greely's sizeable lodge and constructed from the timber three small cabins for Dr. Dedrick, Henson and the Eskimos, and himself that provided privacy and were easier to heat. Some personnel problems developed, however, for Dedrick was jealous of Henson and demanded that he, not Henson, be considered Peary's second-in-command insofar as the Eskimos were concerned. More than once he threatened to resign from the expedition, but he could not well leave in mid-winter.

On April 5, 1901, the entire party set out directly north from Ellesmere Island with Peary, Henson and one Eskimo in a "polar team" and the disgruntled Dedrick and the other Eskimos in a "support team" that would turn back after several marches. On the eve of departure Peary wrote his mother: "Hardly an hour, certainly not a day, has passed that I have not longed for you, and Jo, and my babies. I have been *very* foolish and *very very* selfish, and yet I know that you have forgiven me, for you have been with me so many times and averted trouble [for] me ... Repeatedly I had the most vivid dreams of you. I know you are watching over me." (Letter dated April 4, 1901; Weems pp. 194 - 195)

After eight days, Peary turned back upon reaching the jumbled sea ice at Lincoln Bay. He must have been merely testing this route and his "support party" concept, since his small team was not readied for pressing on to the Pole. Later that month, after returning to Conger, he encountered a group of Eskimos from the *Windward* sent in search of him. They brought mail bringing him news of Jo's arrival the previous summer, and the death of their second child, Francine, who had lived only seven months before succumbing to a childhood illness. Jo's brother Emil had written a letter stating: "Jo has had more than her share of sorrow and trouble, but has borne everything with fortitude ... I hope for both your sakes that your task will soon be finished and that you will attain the summit of the earth and hear for all the rest of your days the praise of the applauding world." (Letter dated July 9, 1900; Weems, p. 1996)

After reading his mail, Peary went south and was reunited with Jo and little Marie on May 6, 1901, his forty-fifth birthday. At summer's end, on August 4, the relief ship *Erik* arrived bringing more sad news — a letter from a relative telling Peary of his mother's death. Mary Peary had died believing that her son had perished in the Arctic; she had not received his last letter. Peary's grief was overwhelming, as his diaries show, but he elected to stay on for another attempt at the Pole in the spring of 1902.

Dr. Dedrick had resigned by this time, and Peary attempted to send him home on the *Erik*. The doctor jumped ship, however, and took up residence in the Eskimo village of Annoatok, declaring that he would be available to Peary in case of need. That autumn at Payer Harbor an epidemic in the nature of dysentery struck the Eskimos and six perished. Peary nursed the victims himself, declining to send for "the crazy doctor," who may or may not have been able to help them.

Peary spent the ensuing winter of 1901 - 1902 at Payer Harbor, but again sledged supplies to Fort Conger during the full moons for he planned to leave for the Pole from the northern tip of Ellesmere in the spring.

On April 6, 1902, Peary, Henson and four Eskimos left Cape Hecla, a distant far-northern point of Ellesmere Island, and began to struggle across the perilous ice of the Arctic Ocean. By then he had already been in the field for a month and had covered 400 miles of arduous sledging in temperatures ranging from 35 degrees below zero to almost 60 degrees below. On April 20, he turned back, having encountered rubble ice that exhausted men and dogs and broke up sledges. He wrote in his diary: "The game is off. My dream of sixteen years is ended ... I have made a good fight but I cannot accomplish the impossible." (Peary diary, April 21, 1902; Weems p. 199)

On May 3, he reached Conger in time for his forty-sixth birthday, then proceeded to Payer Harbor. In August the *Windward* returned, again bearing Jo and Marie. This time Peary accompanied them back to the United States where he was acclaimed for his arctic work. Rejuvenated by the accolades, he wrote to Herbert Bridgeman: "I am as strong as ever in my belief that the Pole can be secured by a determined effort at the Smith Sound gateway ... and that it ought to be done and secured for this country. I am more than willing to throw such energies and experience and ability as I possess into the work for two more years, if sufficient funds can be obtained to insure a first class equipment, it being understood that the first and foremost item of such equipment is to be a powerful ship, the best of her class." (Letter December 22, 1902; Weems, p. 201)

When it came to securing another leave of absence from the Navy, Peary now had a powerful friend and kindred soul in the White House, Theodore Roosevelt. Peary's proposal was approved by the Peary Arctic Club, which came up with money to construct for him a special ice-breaker that would be named the *Roosevelt*. To meet the additional costs of another expedition, he took to the lecture circuit. With Henson dressed in furs and commanding a team of Eskimo dogs to add atmosphere, their performances in the best Chatauqua tradition drew large audiences. Neither the tears of Marie, who complained that her father's long absences were making "an orphan" of her, nor the birth of a son, Robert, Jr., on August 29, 1903, could now forestall Peary's planning for another try at the Pole. (Weems, pp. 203 - 204)

While in the United States, Peary underwent another operation on his feet; a renowned Philadelphia surgeon improved his mobility by providing a cushion of flesh pulled over the stumps of the amputated toes. Thereafter he learned to walk with a sort of slide and never limped, but this was accomplished only by stern self-will.

By 1905 the *Roosevelt* had been designed by Peary himself and constructed to his specifications. The vessel was only 184 feet long while its breadth was 35 1/2 feet; with this stubbiness she could turn and twist her way through ice jammed waterways. The draft load was only 16 feet, allowing her to work close to shore. Her thick and tough wooden sides were egg-shaped, enabling her to rise when squeezed by the ice. Inside, the hull was heavily trussed and braced to withstand the tremendous pressures of the ice pack. In contrast to his previous polar ships, she was built as a steam vessel with auxiliary sails. Jo christened her in March, 1909, by breaking a bottle of champagne encased in a block of ice across her bow, and she sailed from New York on a sweltering July 16, 1905.

The master of the *Roosevelt* was a profane thirty year old stocky Newfoundlander, Robert A. Bartlett, who had first sailed as a mate with Peary in the *Windward* in 1898. Members of the polar expedition included Ross G. Marvin, a young professor from Cornell University; Dr. Louis J. Wolf, a surgeon; Charles Percy, chief cook and steward; and, of course, Matt Henson.

After putting in at Etah, where the ship took on water, coal and supplies, more than fifty Eskimo men, women and children, and more than two hundred dogs,

Bartlett set his course north. The ship was nipped and pounded by ice floes until, on September 5, 1905, she was made fast in the ice at the foot of Cape Sheridan, to the north of Fort Conger but not as far north as Peary had hoped to get. All that winter everyone aboard was kept busy preparing for the polar assault, including the Eskimo seamstresses who fitted each man out in custom-tailored furs.

On February 19, 1906, the supporting parties for the North Pole endeavor began leaving the ship for Cape Hecla. There Peary planned to divide the group into five or six teams that were to move onto the sea ice from Cape Moss, about twenty miles from Hecla, and take stations about fifty miles apart along a direct route to the Pole. Supplies would then be relayed between stations to an advanced base on the ocean ice as far as 300 miles from Cape Moss, from which Peary's team would make a dash for the Pole and back. Throughout the operation, the trail would be kept open, and igloos would be erected at convenient locations for repeated use.

The plan was ingenious but it did not work. Parties stacked up at leads where they were held up for days at a time waiting for them to close, or the water to freeze over. Detours around impassable ice became necessary, usually at the cost of losing the trail ahead. On March 26, Peary's division caught up with three other divisions, all of them halted before a wide lead that Peary dubbed the "Big Lead," or the "Hudson River." For six days the lead held them there around the 84th parallel before the young ice acquired sufficient strength to allow men, dogs and sledges to cross on April 2. Three days later, a blinding blizzard forced them to throw up a shelter they named the "Storm Camp," and there they huddled for another six days.

When the storm finally broke, Peary realized the futility of adhering to his plans for shuttling supplies across the ice to an advance base and determined to set out with lightly loaded sledges on a "dash" northward with Henson and six Eskimos. With supplies depleted by the long delays, and driven far to the east of his original course by the storm, he now had no realistic hope of reaching the Pole but hoped to establish a new "farthest North" record. "The first march of ten hours," Peary wrote, "myself in the lead with the compass, sometimes on a dogtrot, the sledges following in Indian file with drivers running beside or behind, placed us thirty miles to the good, my Eskimos said forty." (*Nearest The Pole*, p.131) The next march brought them to a closed lead, which they were able to cross. The going continued to improve, though there were many leads to be crossed or circumvented.

On April 18, Peary realized that with dwindling supplies and dying dogs he could not go on much longer. Then on April 20, a forced march was made, continuing with only a few hours rest until noon on April 21, 1906. A sun observation showed that the party had arrived at latitude 87-6, a new "farthest North" which bettered by thirty two miles the existing record of 86-34 established by Cagni in the expedition of the Duke of the Abruzzi. The tired men hoisted flags from the summit of the nearest pinnacle, took photographs, left a bottle containing a brief record of their achievement, and headed back southward without even making camp.

Peary knew he would have to make his way back via the north coast of Greenland, for an observation confirmed that he had drifted far to the east as a result of continued strong westerly winds. Again the party was held up at the "Big Lead," which had become so wide and black and threatening that Peary changed its name from "the Hudson" to "the Styx." Lack of provisions made camping there impracticable, so Peary turned eastward hoping to find a safe crossing. On the following day, the party attempted to cross on a bridge of half-congealed rubble ice that gave under their weight, so they scrambled back to the north bank and built a temporary shelter, killed and ate some of the dogs, and waited. One day two Eskimo scouts reported that they had found a film of young ice a few miles from the camp that might be crossable on snowshoes. Peary decided to take the chance and the party crept across slowly, spread out far apart with Panikpah, the lightest of the Eskimos taking the lead. Peary writes: "Once started, we could not stop; we could not lift our snowshoes. It was a matter of constantly and smoothly gliding one past the other with the utmost care and evenness of pressure, and from every man as he slid a snowshoe forward, undulations went out in every direction through the film encrusting the black water. The sledge was proceeded and followed by a broad swell. It was the only time in my Arctic work that I felt doubtful as to the outcome..." (*Nearest The Pole*, pp. 144 - 146) After they had crossed, they discerned that the lead was widening again — they had barely made it to the southern side.

During the next few marches the party stumbled southward until in the distance the welcome sight of the mountains of Greenland came into view. Peary recognized a promontory he had seen in earlier days, and set his course for it. Nearby, he felt certain he could find hare and musk oxen. En route they came upon one of their support teams, led by Charles Clark, a fireman from the *Roosevelt*, so near starvation that the men were subsisting on their spare skin boots. Clark's Eskimos were certain that the drift of the ice had been westward, and they were headed in the wrong direction for the ship. As the combined parties pushed onward to the coast, they did find musk oxen, and all reached the vessel by late May.

When he was sufficiently rested, Peary set out to explore the north coast of Ellesmere Island. From a peak on the northern end of Axel Heiberg Land, he thought he saw uncharted land far to the northwest. This land, which Peary named "Crocker Land," after one of his financial backers, apparently was a mirage. When eight years later the explorer Donald B. MacMillan went in search of "Crocker Land," he could not find it. He did, however, observe an optical illusion of land which he attributed to a mirage or "loom" of the sea ice peculiar to the polar region.[6]

On August 24, the *Roosevelt*, sadly in need of repair, broke free from her imprisonment in the ice and headed southward, creeping among the floes from crack to crack. It was mid-September, however, before her escape was assured. This was none too soon because by then the expedition was threatened with the unwelcome prospect of wintering over without resupply. On Christmas Eve the ship arrived in New York. Jo Peary, who was at the dock to greet her husband, hoped that this time he was home for good. She had written him: "Think of it, home and to stay ... Just think, life is nearly over and we have missed most of it." (Letter dated May 18, 1906; Weems p. 226)

But for Peary, life still meant one more chance at the Pole. At a party honoring him for his attainment of his "farthest North," attended by President Roosevelt, he told a National Geographic Society audience: "The true explorer does his work not for any hopes of reward or honor, but because the thing he has set out to do is a part of his being, and must be accomplished for the sake of the accomplishment. And he counts

---

[6] Like the nonexistent "Peary Channel," the nonexistent "Crocker Land," would be held against Peary by his critics. Because he had named the land for a financial backer, he would be accused of deliberately perpetrating a hoax to secure financing for future expeditions rather than given the benefit of the doubt of having made an innocent error. We deal with "Crocker Land" as an ancillary matter in Part VI of this report.

lightly hardships, risks, obstacles, if only they do not bar him from his goal." (*National Geographic Magazine*, Vol.18, 1907, p. 57)

E. The Pole At Last!

Peary was eager to return to the Arctic for one last try at the Pole in the spring of 1907, but his plans were thwarted by delays in repairing and refitting the *Roosevelt*. He did not believe he was too old at age fifty-two; though he knew that the many years in the north had taken their toll on his physical strength, he felt that the loss was more than compensated by the accrual of knowledge and experience over those years. He had come to feel that he "owned" the so-called American route to the Pole up the narrow waterway between Greenland and Ellesmere Island to Cape Sheridan, then from northernmost Grant Land directly across the Arctic Ocean, and this was the route he intended to use again.

Thus Peary was annoyed, but not greatly concerned, when he learned of a journey into northernmost Greenland contemplated by his former surgeon, Dr. Frederick A. Cook, backed by a wealthy sportsman, John R. Bradley. Dr. Cook had earned a favorable reputation as a polar explorer by serving in the Belgian Antarctic expedition of 1897 - 1899 that included among it members Roald Amundsen, later to become the first man to reach the South Pole. Yet Peary considered the doctor a lightweight and not a serious contender for the Pole.

What might have aroused Peary's suspicion was that recently Dr. Cook had made a dubious claim of being the first climber to ascend Mount McKinley — a claim that was then being investigated by the Explorers Club of New York because of allegations of a hoax. Friends tried to warn him that Cook was capable of perpetrating a similar hoax where the North Pole was concerned, but Peary did not heed them. While he was still waiting for his ship to be readied, Dr. Cook quietly slipped away.

For his 1908 - 1909 expedition, Peary planned to use the methods, equipment and supplies that had worked for him in the past, and to hope for better ice conditions than he had encountered in 1906. There would, however, be some important modifications. He would leave the north coast of Grantland at Cape Columbia instead of Cape Moss, would keep his support teams closer together, would establish a major supply base north of the "Big Lead," and would cache emergency supplies in Grantland and in northern Greenland in case the advance party was cast either eastward or westward by the ice movement before returning from the Pole.

Ready to sail with him on this eighth arctic expedition was the most able team Peary ever assembled: Ross Marvin, the reserved and competent civil engineer and Cornell University professor who had been with him in 1906; George Borup, an athletic and enthusiastic recent Yale graduate; Donald B. MacMillan, a Bowdoin College graduate like Peary and a boys' school athletic instructor; Dr. J. W. Goodsell, a stout and hearty surgeon; and, of course, the loyal, skilled and resourceful Matt Henson. Master of the *Roosevelt* was again the robust Newfoundler, "Captain Bob" Bartlett.

President Roosevelt himself came aboard to inspect the ship that bore his name before it sailed from New York in the broiling afternoon of July 6, 1908. He shook hands with every crew member, inspected every cranny, including the engine room (without concern for his immaculate white linen suit), and pronounced everything "Bully!" "I believe in you, Peary," he said in making his good-byes, "and I believe in your success — if it is within the possibility of man." (*The North Pole*, p. 27)

In Etah Peary found "his" Eskimos on hand to greet him, and came across the trail of Dr. Cook. In fact, he found Dr. Cook's supplies that had been left in the care of an assistant, Rudolph Franke, who was suffering from an injured leg and scurvy and begged to be permitted to return to civilization on Peary's support ship, the *Erik*. Not very graciously, Peary arranged for Franke's transportation, and stationed two seamen to take custody of the supplies that Franke signed over to him. Cook himself was said to have struck out northwest with several Eskimos many months earlier, and some believed all had perished on the ice by this time.

On August 18, the *Roosevelt* steamed northward and again hammered her way up to Cape Sheridan, arriving on September 5. That autumn was crammed with activity — hunting, acclimatizing the new arctic hands, recording tidal and meteorological observations, readying equipment, and transporting provisions by moonlight to Cape Columbia, the point of departure for the planned assault on the Pole. Cape Columbia was situated at longitude 70 degrees, somewhat further west on the Ellesmere Island coast than Cape Hecla, Peary's previous point of departure.

On February 22, Peary left the ship. By then the expedition teams had transferred all the supplies for the Polar journey to a base at Cape Columbia which they named "Crane City," after a financial backer. On February 28, Peary and Bartlett climbed a mountain and gazed northward over the polar ocean. The sea appeared to be a forbidding jumble of ice, but Peary was relieved that he could see no open water. He remarked to Bartlett that conditions appeared to be much more favorable than in 1906.

This was Bartlett's day of departure with his pioneer party that was assigned the job of breaking the trail, and as soon as the light was sufficient for travelling, he left. He had been instructed to limit his advance to 10 miles a day because his heavy sledge loads would require careful handling over the rugged ice piled against the shore. Two hours later George Borup took off with his team; his instructions were to make three marches, drop his supplies, and return to Crane City for another load. The men and dogs of the main party were scheduled to move out with Peary the following day.

Peary awoke before daylight on March 1, and heard the sound of a fierce wind blowing outside his igloo; when he went outside, he discovered that it was coming from the east. The sky was clear, but the ominous wind would open leads in the polar sea, and eventually bring bad weather. At 6:00 A.M. Henson and his Eskimos left, following the trail made by Bartlett and Borup. Peary's and the other divisions left a few hours later. After a day of rough going because of the extreme cold and wind chill, they reached Bartlett's first camp and found two igloos prepared for them. On the trail they encountered Eskimos coming from the other direction with empty and broken sledges headed back for Crane City.

The second day began cold and cloudy and the wind continued to blow from the east. The divisions of the main party began leaving at about 6:30 A.M., with Peary's division coming up in the rear. By taking this position, Peary saved himself for the final stages of the assault on the Pole insofar as possible, and at the same time made sure that the expedition was proceeding as planned and without stragglers. Before the day was over, he had caught up with all his divisions, with the exception of Bartlett's and

Borup's, stranded at an open lead. The Eskimos built four igloos and the party camped by the lead.

Before daylight on the third morning, a thundering grinding noise told Peary that the ice was coming together. The divisions turned out and hurried their sledges across the rafting ice. All crossed safely, but on the other side they found no sign of Bartlett's trail, and Peary feared that the lateral movement of the ice had carried the trail with it. In about two hours, however, one of the Eskimos found the track and footprints indicating that Borup had turned back to Crane City for more supplies. Peary sent Ross Marvin after him, bearing an urgent message to bring extra fuel since some fuel tins had broken open in rough sledging. Peary would learn later that Borup had lost his trail back, missing the main party at their second camp, but had picked it up again a little further on. By March 4, Borup had reached the base, reloaded his sledges, and was ready to start out again when Marvin arrived bearing Peary's urgent message to bring extra fuel. On the morning of March 5, Borup and Marvin travelling together were held up by an open lead stretching east and west that would open increasingly over the next five days. On March 7, Borup observed the sea ice drifting eastward. "The Lord only knew where the trail was," he wrote later, "we didn't." (Borup, *A Tenderfoot With Peary*, p. 162.) By the end of the fifth day of waiting, the two of them feared that Peary was ninety miles out and they would never catch up with him unless he too had been held up by open water.

Meanwhile, many miles out on the ice, Peary had observed a change in the weather on March 4, the day that Marvin had joined Borup at Crane City. "The sky was overcast, the wind had swung completely around to the west during the night, there were occasional squalls of snow, and the thermometer had risen to only nine degrees below zero." (*The North Pole*, p. 224) Though Peary could see an ominous black band of vapor indicating an east-west lead ahead, for the time being Bartlett's trail was easy to follow and they made good progress.

Peary's concern increased when he came upon an igloo built by Bartlett's Eskimos, and found a note informing him that the captain was camped about a mile further north, held up by open water. His main party soon reached Bartlett's camp and found an unwelcome sight that brought back memories of the 1906 expedition, "the white expanse of ice cut by a river of inky black water, throwing off dense clouds of vapor which gathered in a sullen canopy overhead." (*The North Pole*, p.225) The width of the lead was approximately a quarter of a mile, and it extended perpendicular to his course as far as he could see from the highest pinnacle in the area, but Peary was relieved that there was no sign of lateral movement in either direction.

On March 5 (while Borup and Marvin were stopped by open water to the south), Peary noticed that the lead was narrowing somewhat and young ice was forming, but then it reopened wider than ever. Five days passed while the lead blocked further advance and Peary listened for the sound of dog teams arriving from the south.

At daylight on March 10, Borup and Marvin looked out of their igloos and were amazed to find that the lead by which they were camped had frozen over during the night. They had broken camp and were preparing to cross when they saw two Eskimos with sledges and dogs approaching from the northern side. Surprisingly, the Eskimos reported that the trail to the north was within a mile to the west of Borup's and Marvin's camp — that it was intact and they would have no difficulty in finding it.

On March 11, the lead detaining the main party finally closed and Peary prepared to push forward while opportunity afforded without waiting for the rear party to catch up. He left a note for Marvin: "Have waited six days. Can wait no longer. We are short of fuel." (Weems, p. 255, n. 39) On that day's march the main party made good at least twelve miles north and crossed the 84th parallel.

On the following day, Peary estimated another twelve miles made good despite frequent delays caused by cracks, narrow leads and rough ice. On March 13, after covering yet another twelve miles, he had just given orders to make camp when one of his Eskimos shouted: "Dogs are coming." As the dogs drew nearer, Peary recognized Seegloo, who had been sent ahead by Marvin to say that he and Borup were not far behind and bringing an extra thirty gallons of alcohol in addition to the usual provisions.

On March 14, after the main party had been on the ice about two weeks, Dr. Goodsell turned back at about 84°-29', and shortly met up with Marvin and Borup headed north. A few hours later, as Peary described the scene, Marvin and Borup and their four Eskimos came "swinging in, smoking like a battle ship squadron" and carrying the precious fuel. (Peary diary, March 14, 1909)

MacMillan, suffering from a frozen heel, proceeded only a short distance further than Dr. Goodsell before Peary sent him back. This was a sharp disappointment to Peary who had hoped to take the able MacMillan many miles further. It was a tribute to Peary's training and managerial skills that these two novices, along with another, Borup, had already passed the "farthest north" of every preceding arctic explorer except Fridtjof Nansen and Umberto Cagni. Left in the main party now were sixteen men, twelve sledges and one hundred dogs.

On the same day that MacMillan turned back, March 15, Borup suffered a terrifying accident in which his dog team and sledge very nearly fell into an open crack between two hunks of floating ice. With quick thinking and almost superhuman strength, he grabbed the traces and pulled the struggling animals out of the water along with the sledge and its precious supplies.

Five days later, on March 20, Borup turned back from 85°-23' north. Next, on March 26, Marvin turned back at 86°-38' north. Before doing so, he handed Peary a signed statement giving the results of celestial observations he had taken on March 22 and March 25. As Peary said goodbye he cautioned the young professor: "Be careful of the leads, my boy." (Weems, p. 258)

The divisions led by Peary and Hensen continued on, still following the trail blazed by Bartlett. At the end of the day's march they caught up with the captain just as he was shoving off on another leg of his pioneering stint. The next day, March 27, brought dazzling sunshine, and after a six hour march Peary estimated that they had crossed the 87th parallel. On March 28, they came upon Bartlett and his men camped at an open lead. Not wishing to waken the sleeping men, Peary ordered his Eskimos to build igloos one hundred yards distant. Later, he was wakened by a groaning of the ice and was aghast to see a narrow lead of black water running between his and Henson's igloos and Bartlett's. By good fortune, a few hours later the ice raft upon which Bartlett was drifting crunched against the ice where Peary stood and Bartlett and his men debarked as it lay along side like a boat against a wharf. Again, a disaster had been averted.

All the next day, March 29, the lead blocked progress, but on March 30, the water froze over and the entire party hurried across on young ice. On that day the three divisions travelled together and made good an estimated twenty miles. Bartlett was in a somber mood, because according to Peary's game plan, the next march was to be his last. On that day, March 31, Peary surmised that they had made good another twenty miles and were near the 88th parallel.

The next morning, April 1, Bartlett took a celestial observation which put the party at 87°-47' north by his calculations. He signed a memorandum of his observation in which he stated: "I leave Commander Peary with five men, five sledges with full loads and forty picked dogs. Men and dogs in good condition. At the same average as our last eight marches, Commander Peary should reach the Pole in eight days." (Weems, p. 263, n. 53) With that, Bartlett turned south and Peary continued north. Later Peary wrote: "I felt a keen regret as I saw the Captain's broad shoulders grow smaller in the distance." (*The North Pole*, p. 268)

Peary's party was now reduced to Hensen and himself and four Eskimos. He intended to crowd his marches from here on to reduce the number from the eight Bartlett had mentioned to five of at least twenty-five miles each, weather permitting. On April 2, Peary reported in his diary: "Going the best and most equable of any day yet." He estimated thirty miles covered but decided to be conservative and call it twenty-five.

On April 3, Peary called for a forced march, and afterward estimated that in ten hours he covered twenty miles and was "halfway to 89 degrees."

On April 4, the party "hit the trail before midnight, after a short sleep." With the weather holding clear, and "the going even better," they estimated another twenty five miles made good.

On April 5, Peary recorded: "Over the 89th!" In ten hours, he rejoices, they had again made good "twenty-five miles or *more.*"

Peary was back on the trail before midnight, and at 10:00 A.M. on April 6, the stripped down party, led by Henson, stopped at what would be its northernmost camp. As Peary unloaded several small bundles from a sledge containing flags he was carrying with him (including a silk taffeta flag Jo had made for him years ago), Henson asked what this camp would be called. "This my boy, is to be Camp Jesup," Peary replied, "the last and most northerly camp on earth." (Henson, *A Negro Explorer At The North Pole*, p.132)

Peary had Henson build a snow shield, a semi-circular arrangement of snow blocks two tiers high, to protect him from the flying snow drifts while he took a celestial observation utilizing his sextant and an artificial horizon. Henson heated a pan of mercury and brought it to him. Peary filled a trough with the mercury, stretched out on his stomach on a musk ox skin, and held the sextant to his eye. Using the reflection of the sun in the mercury, he determined its elevation and wrote down figures for a set of observations. Such observations were hard on his eyes and they blinded him temporarily. He was able, however, to complete his calculations and he figured his latitude at 89 degrees 57 minutes 11 seconds, about 3 nautical miles from the Pole.

Henson saw Peary square his jaw. "I could see that he was satisfied," Henson said. "Feeling that the time had come I ungloved my right hand and went forward to congratulate him." (*A Negro Explorer At The North Pole*, p.135) Just at that moment Peary pressed his hands over his aching eyes. He did not see Henson's extended hand but went directly into his igloo, asking Henson to wake him in four hours so he could take further observations from various locations. (Weems, p. 269)

Peary wrote later: "The accumulated weariness of all those days and nights of forced marches, insufficient sleep, constant peril and anxiety seemed to roll across me all at once. I was actually too exhausted to realize at that moment that my life's purpose had been achieved." (*The North Pole*, p. 287)

When he awoke after four hours, Peary took out his diary and entered: "The Pole at last!!! The prize of three centuries, my dreams and ambitions for twenty years. *Mine* at last. I cannot bring myself to realize it."

When Peary went outside he saw that the sky was overcast, preventing a 6:00 P.M. observation. He loaded a sledge with instruments, his artificial horizon paraphernalia, a tin of pemmican and a few skins, and with Egingwah and Seegloo journeyed north for about 10 miles to take a midnight reading. This observation showed him to be beyond the Pole.

He returned to Camp Jesup and at 6:00 A.M. April 7, took another series of observations at right angles to those already made there. From these he calculated that the camp was within 4 or 5 miles from the Pole.

Once more Peary left the camp, this time to sledge 8 miles toward the Pole to be sure of passing near it. Then he returned for another series of observations at noon. These observations resulted in a latitude of 89 degrees 58 minutes 37 seconds.

Peary had satisfied himself: "I had now taken ... thirteen single, or six and one half double, altitudes of the sun, at two different stations in three different directions at four different times. In traversing the ice in these various directions ... I had allowed approximately ten miles for possible errors in my observations, and at some moment during these marches and countermarches I had passed over or very near the point where north and south and east and west blend into one." (*The North Pole*, p. 291)

Before leaving Camp Jesup, after spending about 30 hours in the vicinity, Peary planted the American flag on a pinnacle and posed his men for photographs. Each held one of the special flags Peary had brought for the occasion — Jo's handsewn flag, a Navy League flag, the colors of Peary's Delta Kappa Epsilon fraternity, and a Daughters of the American Revolution flag. Henson then led the Eskimos in joining in three cheers; Peary doubted that they knew why they were cheering since to them the North Pole was no different than any other spot on the arctic ice, but they responded with enthusiasm. Afterward he placed a message in a glass jar recording his arrival at "90 North Latitude, North Pole, April 6 1909," though he knew that the chances of its ever being found were virtually nil.

At about 4:00 P.M. on April 7, the party started south, headed for their last camp on the upward journey. Peary was determined to waste no time on the Arctic Ocean ice while the weather held good, but he did stop to take a sounding after about five miles. He lost a large portion of his sounding wire after reeling out to 1500 fathoms and finding no bottom, and abandoned his reel.

From there the party hurried on in three forced marches with infrequent short stops for food and rest. Exhausted by his arduous efforts on the northbound journey, and his frenetic activity in the vicinity of the Pole, and suffering a severe attack of "quinsy" (an inflammation of the throat or tonsils), Peary rode on his sledge for much of the return trip. But fortune smiled on the party. When they reached the camp where Bartlett turned back shortly after midnight on April 9, Peary wrote in his diary: "From here to the Pole and back has been a glorious sprint, with a savage finish. Its results [are] due to hard work, little sleep, much experience, first-class equipment, and good fortune as regards weather and open water."

On April 22, the party reached the firm ice of Grant Land and the Eskimos shrieked with delight. Ootah exclaimed: "The devil [Tornarsuk] is asleep or having trouble with his wife or we should never have come back so easily." (Weems, p. 273, n.71)

The following day Peary relaxed in Crane City and wrote: "My life's work is accomplished. The thing which it was intended from the beginning that I should do, the thing which I believed could be done, and that I could do, I have done. I have got the North Pole out of my system ... I have won the last great geographical prize ... for the credit of the United States, the service to which I belong, and my family ... I am content." (Peary diary, April 22-23, 1909; Weems p. 275, n. 71) He then hurried on to the *Roosevelt*, arriving on April 26 to be greeted and congratulated by "Captain Bob" Bartlett.

From the Captain, Peary learned to his intense sorrow of the death of Ross Marvin who had, the Eskimos said, broken through treacherous young ice and drowned on the return journey.[7] He sent off letters to Borup and MacMillan, who were away taking meteorological observations along the Greenland and Grantland Coasts, and laying in emergency supply caches which might be needed by Peary on his return journey, that his mission had been successful and the supplies would not be needed. Then, for the next few weeks Peary rested in his cabin while waiting for the spring break-up of the ice to free the *Roosevelt*.

Before the return voyage was begun, Borup and MacMillan trekked one last time to Cape Columbia where they erected a memorial to Marvin, and a monument in the form of a guidepost designed by Peary commemorating his attainment of the Pole.

F. The Cook-Peary Controversy

Late in July, 1909, the *Roosevelt* began nudging her way southward. On August 8, at Cape Chalon on the Greenland coast, Peary learned from the Eskimos that Dr. Cook had returned to Greenland. At Etah there was more news of Cook; he had told the Eskimos there that he had been to the North Pole, and had thereafter disappeared. Peary had Henson question the two Eskimos who had set out with the doctor on his northward trek and they were told that Cook lied about his attainment of the Pole. The

---

[7] Years later one of Marvin's Eskimos, Kudlookto, when on the verge of being converted to Christianity, confessed to murdering Marvin, but many persons knowledgeable in the ways of the Eskimos, including MacMillan, did not believe him.

Eskimos stated that they had never ventured out of the sight of land on sea ice, and had gone no further north than Axel Heiberg Island.

Peary did not rush back to civilization to stake out his claim as he might have done had he taken Cook's claim seriously. Instead he stayed in Greenland to conduct walrus hunts so as to provide a winter meat supply for the Eskimos; this he owed them because they had neglected their hunting to support his polar venture.

Finally, at the end of August, Bartlett took the *Roosevelt* southward and from Indian Harbor, Labrador, Peary sent off a series of telegrams announcing his attainment of the North Pole on April 6, 1909. "Stars and Stripes nailed to the Pole!" he informed the news media and his backers. Unbeknownst to him, a few days earlier, from Lerwick, in the Shetland Islands, Cook had announced that he had reached the North Pole on April 21, 1908, a full year earlier. By this time Cook was en route to Copenhagen, Denmark, where he would be given a tumultuous welcome and be received by the King.

When Peary learned of Cook's hoax, he fired off several telegrams to the newspapers warning them that they were being sold "a gold brick." Unfortunately, much of the media and the American public perceived Peary's denunciation of Cook as a display of petulance at having been robbed of priority. Cook, on his part, did not question Peary's claim; he professed to be delighted at the latter's success, and magnanimously stated that "two records are better than one." Such tactics induced the explorer and author Peter Freuchen to remark: "Cook was a liar and a gentleman, Peary was neither." (Weems, p. 282, n. 2)

Backers of Peary were eager to have Cook present proofs of his claim but he procrastinated. He first said he had left his instruments with the sportsman, Harry Whitney, who had occupied his quarters at Etah, but Whitney, who had returned on the *Roosevelt* with Peary, denied having had them. Later Cook agreed to submit his observations to the University of Copenhagen, but instead he presented only a typewritten narrative account of his alleged journey. At this point the committee that had been appointed by the university to examine his proofs rule against him. Then three days after the Copenhagen decision, the Explorers Club in New York dropped the name of Doctor Cook from its rolls for his failure to have produced proof of his Mount McKinley claim which a prolonged investigation had revealed to be a hoax.

Peary was profoundly hurt by the public sentiment against him and remained in seclusion on Eagle Island. For a long while he refused to produce his own records for study by experts for fear that Dr. Cook would learn from them how to fake data to put to his own use. Eventually, however, Peary submitted his records and instruments to a committee appointed by the National Geographic Society which consisted of Henry Gannett, geographer of the United States Geological Survey; Admiral Colby Chester, one of the foremost navigators in the United States Navy; and O.H. Tittmann of the Coast and Geodetic Survey. When the committee unanimously ruled in Peary's favor, after examining him and studying his observations, his soundings and his photographs, one would have expected the American public to be satisfied. Yet some persons remained skeptical because the National Geographic Society had sponsored Peary and honored him for his prior achievements. Also, the seeds of skepticism had been sewn by the bitter Cook controversy and a certain cynicism with regard to the claims of both explorers had crept in.

Following the decision of its committee, The National Geographic Society bestowed a specially struck gold medal upon Peary for his attainment of the Pole, and awarded the prestigious Hubbard medal to Captain Bartlett. Sadly, Matt Henson, being a Negro and regarded as Peary's lackey rather than his most valued assistant, was overlooked. The Royal Geographic Society of England also awarded Peary a gold medal, even before examining his claims. Later, after his data had been submitted, the Society reaffirmed the award.

Peary's navigational data was subsequently scrutinized by two experts retained by him, both analysts of the Coast and Geodetic Survey, Hugh C. Mitchell and Charles R. Duvall. After an intensive examination of his celestial observations they agreed that Peary "probably passed within one and six-tenths geographic miles of the North Pole." (From their "Computations of the Observations," National Archives.

In April, 1910, Peary and his family sailed to Europe where he lectured before large audiences in the European capitals, London, Rome, Vienna, Budapest, St. Petersburg, Paris, Brussels, Antwerp, Dublin and Edinburgh. For a brief time, Jo and Marie basked happily in their husband's and father's fame after the long dreary years of his absences. But Peary himself was happy to return at the end of the tour to the family residence in Washington, D. C. and his beloved summer home on Eagle Island, near Harpswell, Maine.

On Eagle Island Peary lived the life he cherished, enjoying freedom from society and closeness to nature. He had no telephone, nor even a pier; the only access was by a pebble beach reached by a small boat. The living room of the house that he had begun constructing in 1904 was dominated by a triangular fireplace designed to throw heat in all directions. Next to it was a sunroom that faced the Atlantic Ocean and afforded a spectacular view of the wild sea. Both rooms were adorned with Peary's wild life trophies, fox skins and heads of polar bear and musk ox, and birds that he had mounted in his college days. There were two stone turret-like rooms that he called his "bomb-proofs," one of which he used as an office and the other for storing his medals and other trophies.

By 1911, influential friends were working at getting through the House of Representatives a bill recognizing then Captain Peary's attainment of the North Pole by retiring him as a rear admiral effective April 6, 1909. A similar bill had sailed through the Senate, but in the House a vociferous minority of a subcommittee of the Naval Affairs Committee opposed the bill. Some of the committee members favored Cook, some were cynical about either explorer's claims, and some shared the resentment of certain Naval officers of the line against a civil engineering officer who had never commanded a ship being promoted to the Navy's highest rank. Also, working behind the scenes, was General Adolphus Greely, whom Peary had been so tactless as to publicly criticize for his abandonment of Fort Conger, where he himself had found that game was plentiful, for the frozen swamps of Cape Sabine where so many of his men starved.

Peary did not lack friends on the committee, and some members who questioned him extensively, like Congressman Roberts, seemed genuinely anxious to establish a comprehensive record. On the other hand, Congressman R. B. Macon of Arkansas, in particular, subjected him to blatantly hostile interrogation. For three full days, the 7th, 10th and 11th of January, 1911, Peary patiently answered all questions about his journey and his records, including inquiries about his navigation, ice conditions on the Arctic Ocean, the speeds and distances he had attained on the spurt to the Pole and back, and why he had not taken a "credible" witness with him. He also submitted for inspection copies of his celestial observations (along with the detailed analysis of Mitchell and Duvall), his report to the Coast and Geodetic Survey on his soundings, his many photographs, and his polar diary. But Peary became testy and scarcely concealed his annoyance when the questions became ludicrous,[8] detracting from the favorable impression he might otherwise have made not only on the congressmen but on later day readers who turn to the record for information. In the end the committee recommended approval; the bill passed the House by a large majority and was signed by President Taft. Peary received the "Thanks of Congress" and retirement pay as a rear admiral of $6,500 annually retroactive to April 6, 1909.

But the bitter Congressional hearings had left their mark upon the man. Jo would write later: "No one will ever know how the attack on my husband's veracity affected him, who had never had his word doubted in *any* thing at *any* time in his life ... [T]he personal grilling which he was obliged to undergo at the hands of Congress, while his scientific observations were examined and worked out, although it resulted in his complete vindication, hurt him more than all the hardships he endured in his sixteen years in the Arctic regions and did more toward breaking down his iron constitution than anything experienced in his explorations." (Weems, p. 325)

For the next few years, despite the outbreak of the war in Europe in 1914, Peary enjoyed a relatively contented life with his family, spending long hours getting to know his children and helping them with their studies. But in 1916, he faced a new battle with the Congress when a bill was introduced by Congressman Henry Helgesen of North Dakota to repeal the earlier act bestowing on him the rank of rear admiral. Behind the move was the re-emergence of Doctor Cook, who had by then written a

---

[8] The following excerpts will indicate the tenor of the questioning at times:

Mr. Macon: Explorers and a certain class of scientists tell us that conditions are such in the Arctic Zone that ... an ordinary hare would be the size of a good-sized animal and that an object that might appear small here would be about the size of a mountain ... if that condition does exist, that animal is so magnified or an object is so magnified, how do you explain to the committee that you took a correct observation?
Mr. Dawson: It would not affect the instrument?
Captain Peary: It would not affect the instrument.
Mr. Englebright: And it would not affect the eye?
Captain Peary: I do not see how the eye would be affected.
Mr. Macon: The same eye that looked through the instrument would look at the animal.

Also, with regard to Peary's compasses:

Mr. Macon: Did the needle answer to the primary or the secondary magnetic pole?
Captain Peary: The direction of the compass was fairly constant there.
Mr. Butler: (to Mr. Macon) Will you tell me please what that means?
Mr. Macon: I asked him whether the needle answered to the primary or the secondary magnetic pole.
Mr. Butler: What are they?
Mr. Macon: Oh, they are known in science ...
Mr. Englebright: Did you ever hear of a primary or secondary magnetic pole?
Mr. Macon: Yes, I have.
Mr. Englebright: Where—in Arkansas?
Mr. Macon: Where I have heard of everything else—not in Washington. And I want to say to the gentleman from California if he intends it as a slur in regard to Arkansas, it is unworthy of him.

book, *My Attainment Of The Pole*, and had taken to the lecture circuit to denounce Peary as the morally corrupt "Sultan of the North" — a scoundrel who took monies from innocent school children and used them to support a harem of Eskimo concubines.[9] Also very much in the picture was Peary's old foe General Greely. The charges Helegesen brought forth were based upon the allegedly fictitious reports of the "Peary Channel" and "Crocker Land." Peary was tormented by private anger, but did not publicly respond. The bill came to naught when Helgesen died in 1917 and the bill died with him.

Ironically in the same year, Peary was diagnosed as suffering from then incurable pernicious anemia. He retreated during his last years to Eagle Island where he chronicled his illness as dispassionately as he had, for the most part, chronicled his arctic journeys. He died on February 20, 1920, at the age of sixty four, and was buried in Arlington Cemetery at a service attended by many notables. On April 6, 1988, Matt Hensen, who died in March, 1955, at the age of eighty eight, was removed from an obscure grave in New York City and reburied beside him.

---

[9] The members of the audience were provided with postcards to be sent to their congressmen demanding that Peary's honors be rescinded on moral grounds, and thousands of the cards had poured in by this time. We came across some in the Archives.

Josephine Peary

Matthew Henson

Ross Marvin

Captain Bob Bartlett and Donald MacMillan

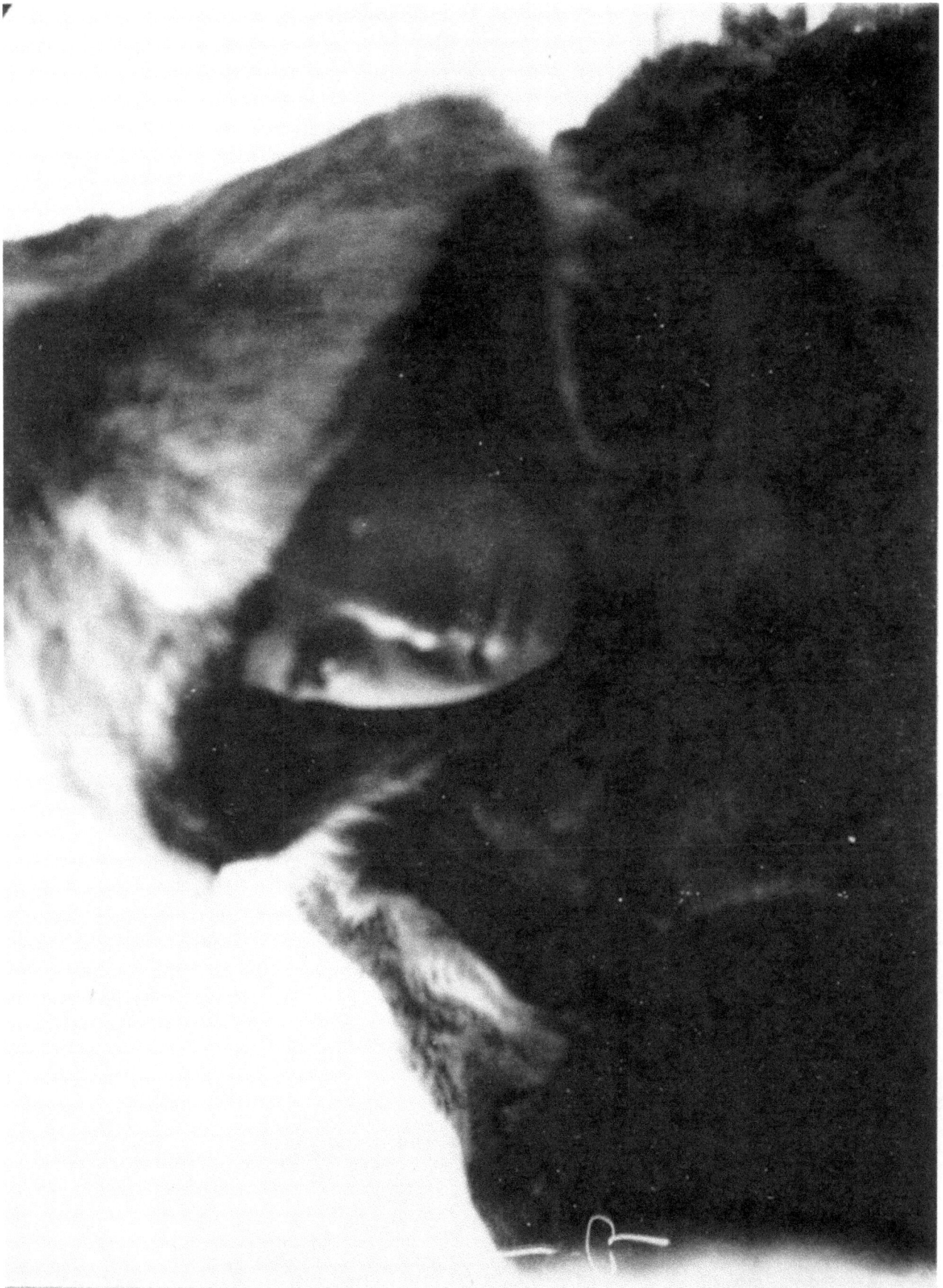

Josephine Peary

Part Two

PEARY'S NAVIGATION

One of the major questions that the critics have raised about the 1909 polar expedition is "How did Peary stay on the meridian?" He has been described by one critic, Dennis Rawlins in *Peary at the Pole: Fact or Fiction?* (hereafter *Fiction*, pp.135-137;141) as claiming to have made a "beeline" to the Pole with an aiming accuracy of 0.6 degrees — a "straw man" figure that is based on the assumption that Peary had no information which would have permitted a mid-course correction to his aiming at any point in the entire 413 mile trip from Cape Columbia to the Pole. The incredibility of this supposed feat leads the layman to assume that Peary ignored sound navigation procedures and therefore his claimed performance was impossible.

Wally Herbert, in his recent *The Noose of Laurels* (hereafter *Noose*), advances the theory that Peary's navigational methods could not reasonably be expected to have led him to the Pole, particularly in view of the fact that the ice across which he was traveling was drifting in an uncertain manner due to winds and currents in the Arctic Ocean.

Herbert readily acknowledges that in 1909, Peary's greatest single strength was "the sum total of his polar experience, and in particular his experience in 1906." "On this final expedition," Herbert states, Peary "had his first real chance to succeed and he knew it." Yet Herbert assumes, without any evidence to support his assumption, that Peary navigated like a rank amateur in the conduct of the 1909 expedition, making errors that "can only be described as astonishing." (*Noose* p. 259)

Herbert recognizes that Peary was well aware of the effect of wind on the movement of the ice as a result of his 1906 journey, but states that Peary "appears, in

1909, to have completely ignored the possibility that he might have been blown off course by the easterly and north-easterly gales[1] he experienced during the early stages and the mid-point of his outward journey." (*Noose* pp. 259-260)[2] He then asks "Why would a polar traveller of this man's undoubted calibre have risked the entire success of his journey, and his last opportunity of reaching the Pole, by simply assuming he knew which way the pack ice was drifting from the movement he could see locally? ... What ... gave him the crazy idea that he could strike out across the drifting pack ice, and without any observations for longitude or any checks on the variation of the compass, could aim for and hit the Pole?" (*Noose* at 260) Why indeed, we ask? The simple answer is that Peary did not have any such "crazy idea." Herbert's premises are flawed, and, like Rawlins, he sets up a straw man that he can then proceed to knock down.[3]

Herbert's and other of Peary's critics' main premises are (a) that Peary did not periodically check the variation of his compass; (b) that Peary could not determine the direction to the Pole without taking observations for longitude; and (c) that Peary's only inkling of the motion of the ice was based on the movement he could observe locally. We will examine each of these assertions in the light of all of the available facts. However, first let Peary describe his navigation.

A. Peary on the Record

Peary's earliest and most direct discussion of his navigation was that in his *Hampton's Magazine* article of 1910 (p. 784), a number of lines of which are quoted below (with emphasis added):

> The distance which we traveled day by day was at first determined by dead reckoning, to be verified later by observations for latitude. Dead reckoning was simply the compass course for direction, and for distance the mean estimate of Bartlett, Marvin and myself as to the length of the day's march ...

---

[1] Herbert criticizes Peary for his occasional use of the term "gale," which, he says "according to the 1805 Beaufort Wind Scale is a wind average of between thirty and forty knots." He observes: "During our sixteen month crossing of the Arctic Ocean in 1968-9, we recorded no wind speed over forty knots, and from weather observations at various locations on the Arctic Ocean over the past forty years we now know that true "gales" are unheard of ..." (*Noose*, p. 264) Thus Herbert apparently uses the imprecise term "gales" here for dramatic effect.

We add that the Beaufort Wind Scale in use in 1909, familiar to all mariners, had four classifications of the word "gale": Moderate Gale, winds of 40 statute miles per hour; Fresh Gale, 48 mph; Strong Gale, 56 mph; and Whole Gale 65 mph.

[2] We should note that the key word is "appears." In a discussion of Peary's navigation written for the National Geographic Society in connection with his article in the *National Geographic* magazine (September, 1988), Herbert acknowledged that "... we cannot be certain that Peary's course was deflected to the west by wind simply because he himself makes no mention of having countered it by setting his course to the east of north."

[3] Herbert goes so far as to make the outlandish claim that Peary "set out on that crowning achievement of his polar career with apparently *nothing more than the certain direction of his destiny* to guide him across the drifting pack ice to his goal!" (*Noose*, p. 272) How can one say this of the most experienced polar traveller of his time, or for that matter, of any time?

Dead reckoning alone, unchecked by astronomical
observations, should not be depended upon for too great
a number of marches, but during the earlier stages of
our journey there was no sun by which to take observations,
and later when we were making good progress day by day,
*I did not choose to waste any of the energy of Marvin,
Bartlett, or myself in taking unnecessary observations*. We
took the observations often enough to check our dead
reckonings *and no oftener*.

Then, from the first Congressional Hearings (1911):

"Q. In using a compass in the northern regions you use it with calculated
variation?
A. You use it *checking by observations* wherever you can.
Q. Then if you took no observations (sights) would your compass lead you
directly, over a broken course of 133 miles to the north pole when it tended
to point toward the magnetic pole?
A. *In connection with other means, yes*; it would assist me in doing so".

In a letter of April 12, 1912, in response to a question by a Miss Rosenthal:

The compass is of use in showing the direction to take
towards either pole, *when it is corrected* by means of
observations of either the sun or the stars.

In the Peary papers of 1909 is a slip with the following words in his handwriting:

The sun setting due E. & W. Mar. 21 & 22 *gave accurate
checks on compasses*, also just touching northern horizon
Mar. 26 & 27.

In summary, Peary described his navigation as dead reckoning with estimated
distances checked by latitude observations. He steered by the magnetic compass, also
corrected by observations. A further elaboration might have been in order, but he did
not deem it essential. Furthermore, a number of associates had advised him to
minimize such discussions because of Dr. Cook.[4]

The foregoing seems to be a simple explanation of Peary's technique and yet there
is one aspect of it, obvious to him but left unstated, which needs elaboration because
it has been overlooked by his numerous critics. The essence of his navigation is
"homing".

Homing refers to the technique of first finding a reasonably accurate direction
toward a target point (a compass heading), then "keeping it" and following that

---

[4] Peary's associates recommended that he minimize any detailed public discussions of his methods because
whatever information he revealed might be used by Cook to support his own claim or serve as a basis for attacks
on Peary that, even if-meritless, might seem plausible to the public. This seems to have been good short term
advice in view of the fact that Cook's claim ultimately foundered on his inability to demonstrate any competence
as a navigator. Peary might justifiably have assumed that his own ability as a navigator, on the other hand, was
clearly established by his training as a surveyor, his survey work in Nicaragua, and his prior experiences in the
Arctic. Unfortunately, that experience has not weighed heavily with his later day critics.

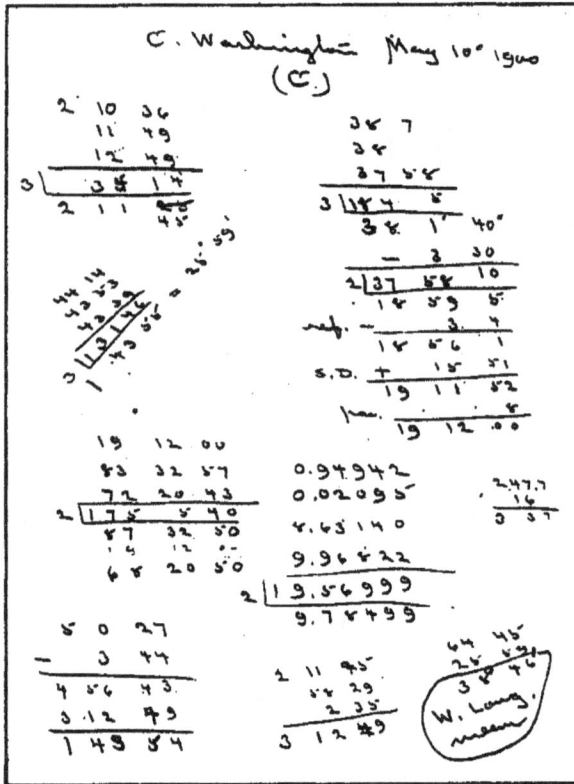

Figure II-1

direction (compass heading) until another direction-finding opportunity arises. This is in sharp contrast with the technique insisted upon by Peary's numerous critics, which requires using latitude and longitude for determining location and precise time for getting direction from the sun. The navigator simply "homes" on the Pole, using previously calibrated dead reckoning distances to decide when he has arrived there.

Note that homing does not mean staying on a meridian, taking longitude sights to determine one's meridian or trying to "return" to a meridian after some divergence. It further does not require a correct time for any particular meridian. It is a technique that is familiar to airmen. An aircraft homes on an electronic beacon and never really gets a precise position until it passes over the beacon. Peary's beacon was the Pole.

There is a difference between this form of navigation and that of an explorer (viz. Sverdrup) who is mapping a coastline. In that case correct knowledge of longitude is essential to chart the location of a land feature, and this requires celestial determination of longitude as well as latitude sights. Figure II-1 is a sample of one of several surviving determinations of longitude (1900) by the "method of transport of chronometers", which required the taking of "time sights" by Peary. This sight is used for determining longitude when correct time is available, and demonstrates that he was quite capable of taking such sights when necessary. Homing was generally used for expeditions whose goal was attaining the Pole or achieving a new "farthest north," in contrast to mapping unexplored territory.[5]

B. The Compass and its Variation

In polar surface navigation, homing requires determining, as often as possible, "which way is north", or "which way is the Pole", since north is the direction to the Pole from any point. Once the direction is determined, the primary instrument for "keeping" this direction is the magnetic compass. Critics have alternatively asserted that (a) the compass was unusable in the regions where Peary was operating; or (b) that Peary used the compass improperly by failing to consider changes in "variation," i.e., the angle between true north and the direction that the compass pointed. As discussed below, both criticisms are unfounded.

The first assertion is based on the fact that as one gets close to the north magnetic pole of the earth (now and in Peary's time located near King William Land in northern Canada), the earth's magnetic field becomes very nearly vertical. Thus the horizontal

---

[5] See Section E on "The Longitude Sight."

```
Model Used:  BGS1910                              Model Used:  BGS1910

Input                    Output                   Input                    Output
-----                    ------                   -----                    ------
Latitude:  87 deg  0' 0" N   TI = 56672.99 nT     Latitude:  83 deg  0' 0" N   TI = 56962.16 nT
Longitude: 70 deg  0' 0" W   HI =  4000.41 nT     Longitude: 70 deg  0' 0" W   HI =  3999.77 nT
Altitude:          5 FT      X  = -2260.18 nT     Altitude:          5 FT      X  = -1621.10 nT
Date:      1/ 1/1909         Y  = ......... nT    Date:      1/ 1/1909         Y  = -3656.53 nT
                             Z  = 56531.62 nT                                  Z  = 56821.55 nT
                             DIP =   85.95 deg N                               DIP =   85.97 deg
                             DEC =  124.40 deg W                               DEC =  113.91 deg


Model Used:  BGS1910                              Model Used:  BGS1910

Input                    Output                   Input                    Output
-----                    ------                   -----                    ------
Latitude:  88 deg  0' 0" N   TI = 56631.60 nT     Latitude:  84 deg  0' 0" N   TI = 56871.94 nT
Longitude: 70 deg  0' 0" W   HI =  4014.00 nT     Longitude: 70 deg  0' 0" W   HI =  3993.22 nT
Altitude:          5 FT      X  = -2415.08 nT     Altitude:          5 FT      X  = -1786.46 nT
Date:      1/ 1/1909         Y  = -3206.17 nT     Date:      1/ 1/1909         Y  = -3571.32 nT
                             Z  = 56489.17 nT                                  Z  = 56731.58 nT
                             DIP =   85.94 deg N                               DIP =   85.97 deg
                             DEC =  126.99 deg W                               DEC =  116.58 deg


Model Used:  BGS1910                              Model Used:  BGS1910

Input                    Output                   Input                    Output
-----                    ------                   -----                    ------
Latitude:  89 deg  0' 0" N   TI = 56602.94 nT     Latitude:  85 deg  0' 0" N   TI = 56793.42 nT
Longitude: 70 deg  0' 0" W   HI =  4034.75 nT     Longitude: 70 deg  0' 0" W   HI =  3990.79 nT
Altitude:          5 FT      X  = -2570.74 nT     Altitude:          5 FT      X  = -1947.21 nT
Date:      1/ 1/1909         Y  = -3109.75 nT     Date:      1/ 1/1909         Y  = -3483.50 nT
                             Z  = 56458.96 nT                                  Z  = 56653.03 nT
                             DIP =   85.91 deg N                               DIP =   85.97 deg
                             DEC =  129.58 deg W                               DEC =  119.20 deg


Model Used:  BGS1910                              Model Used:  BGS1910

Input                    Output                   Input                    Output
-----                    ------                   -----                    ------
Latitude:  90 deg  0' 0" N   TI = 56587.01 nT     Latitude:  86 deg  0' 0" N   TI = 56726.99 nT
Longitude: 70 deg  0' 0" W   HI =  4063.85 nT     Longitude: 70 deg  0' 0" W   HI =  3992.96 nT
Altitude:          5 FT      X  = -2728.50 nT     Altitude:          5 FT      X  = -2104.68 nT
Date:      1/ 1/1909         Y  = -3011.67 nT     Date:      1/ 1/1909         Y  = -3393.24 nT
                             Z  = 56440.89 nT                                  Z  = 56586.29 nT
                             DIP =   85.88 deg N                               DIP =   85.96 deg
                             DEC =  132.18 deg W                               DEC =  121.81 deg
```

Figure II-2

component of the earth's magnetic field might not be strong enough to bring the needle to point toward any consistent direction.

To examine the validity of this theory, we have compared the magnetic field strength at various points along Peary's track with the field strength required for reliable operation of the magnetic compass. Since the earth's magnetic field and the location of the north magnetic pole change over time, modern measurements of the magnetic field strength along Peary's route are not necessarily accurate for 1909.[6] Fortunately such a field strength existed for the area at the time of Peary's trip.

Bowditch establishes that the compass is useable if the horizontal component of the Earth's magnetic field is at least .03 oersted. The U.S. Naval Oceanographic Command ("NAVOCEANO") at Bay St. Louis, Louisiana, maintains a computer model that gives the historical values of the magnetic field strength of the earth at any location for various dates. NAVOCEANO has kindly provided data from that model for various locations along Peary's track for the year 1909, which data are presented in Figure II-2. These data show that in 1909 the strength of the horizontal component of the magnetic field along Peary's route varied from .039 to .040 oersted, plainly adequate for Peary's use.

---

[6] Modern measurements show values at or slightly below .03 oersteds, for which the magnetic compass (on shipboard) is characterized as "useless."

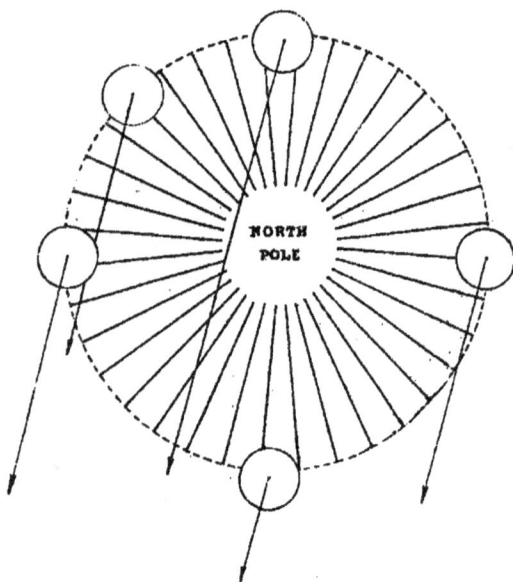

Insert Figure II-3

As for problems posed by "variation," it is technically correct to say that variation changes dramatically near the Pole. Yet the rate of change in the direction the compass needle points is no more of a problem there than in many other locations. What changes dramatically near the Pole is not the direction that the compass points, but the direction of the meridians of longitude. Only because variation is measured with respect to the observer's meridian of longitude, does it change rapidly.

Figure II-3 shows a polar chart with the direction that the compass points shown for various locations. If a person walks around a small circle centered at the Pole, the point on a far away horizon to which the compass needle points will not vary measurably. However, the person at some point on the circle is on each of the 360 meridians of longitude, and the direction of the observer's meridian (the compass bearing to the Pole) will change through the full 360º of the circle. Meanwhile the compass needle remains almost stationary, pointing to the direction of the magnetic pole. The compass has no sense of the numerical value of variation on the artificial grid of latitude and longitude but merely seeks the magnetic field.

Measuring compass variation from the direction of the meridian of longitude is convenient for navigation in normal latitudes, where longitude is used to define position. However, as one gets close to the Pole, longitude is not useful in defining one's position. This is because small errors in position can equate to large errors in longitude, due to the fact that the lines of longitude (meridians) come so close together and ultimately converge at a single point. (See Figure II-3)

Charts for conventional navigation and compass variation are difficult to use in the polar areas because of this rapid convergence of the meridians, as Wally Herbert found in his trek across the Pole in 1968. According to his book, *Across The Top Of The World* (pp. 260 on), when he used conventional navigation to determine his position at about 7 miles from the Pole, he cited it in terms of latitude *and longitude*. He then tried without success to use his longitude as the direction to the Pole. Since he found himself still 7 miles away after traveling 7 miles, one can only conclude that he was considerably off in longitude — a not surprising error and one which demonstrates the correctness of Peary's statement before the Congressional committee:

> [I]n the neighborhood of the pole it is generally recognized that longitude observations are not practicable with any degree of accuracy.

Shortly after World War II, aircraft navigators began flying over the Pole routinely and encountered the longitude and directional problems generated by the rapid convergence of the meridians. Their solution was the development of "Grid Navigation." In this system true direction is measured from a rectangular grid instead of from

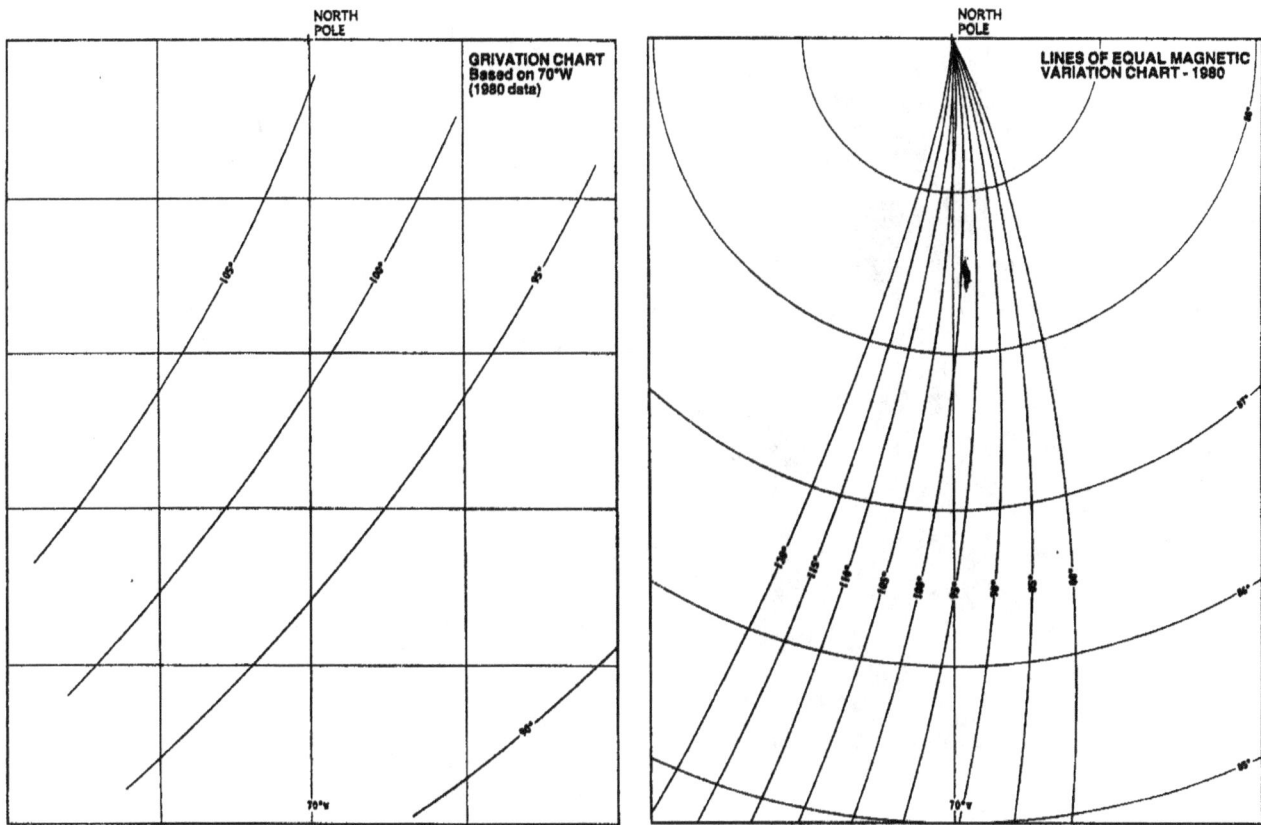

Figure II-4

the normal latitude/longitude grid. While normal variation is the angle between the direction of the compass needle (corrected for deviation) and the *meridian,* the grid equivalent is called "Grivation" and is the angle between the compass needle and the appropriate *grid line.* Grivation maps give a useable picture of the action of the compass near the Pole.

Figure II-4 shows a Grivation Map and a Variation Map using the normal latitude-longitude grid. Comparison of the 5 degree variation lines with the 5 degree "griva-tion" lines shows why the grid system was developed. The Grivation Map shows that the real change in direction of the compass needle from 88 N to 90 N (the latitudes between the Bartlett camp and the Pole) is only about 5 degrees. What this means is that a compass course determined by a bearing on the sun actually changes very little while one is travelling north and will be useful for several days. Further, taking another bearing at the same time a day later enables one to correct any change that may exist. It should be noted that *correct* local time is not required for doing this. The time being kept by the chronometers need only be consistent over a period of use.

In preparation for his expeditions, documents found in the archives show that Peary bought twelve hand held compasses and a number of "boat compasses" and railroad pocket compasses. One of his compasses is to be found today in the Civil Engineer Corps Museum of the Navy, at Port Hueneme, California, and another is owned by Peary's grandson, Commander Edward Peary Stafford. Peary had practiced steering by compass over the ice for many thousands of miles of sledging in the northern polar areas since his earliest Greenland expeditions, and over the years had made many measurements of compass variation along the Greenland coast. He surely was capable of handling compass variation on the trip to the Pole.

In *A Negro Explorer at the North Pole*, Matt Henson records (p.88) that Peary and Bartlett performed a check on a compass known in marine navigation as "swinging ship." Swinging ship is a standard procedure at sea for correcting for the effect on the compass of magnetic disturbances caused by the steel on the vessel. In this case it was the steel runners of the sledge which could possibly have produced a significant deviation of the compass. Bartlett apparently wished to keep a compass mounted to a sledge for continuous use, in the manner that a compass is used on a ship, and took the necessary precautions to assure that such use would be accurate.

For short distances the compass was used to sight ahead periodically and pick a "landmark," usually an ice hummock, which would be established as the aiming point for the next leg. The trailbreaker generally would be responsible for choosing the landmarks and the course, but Peary or another member of a following group could also check the course and advise the trailbreaker of any need for a course correction.[7]

Figure II-5

The trailbreaker would not have to keep track of individual deviations in course along the route to the chosen landmark, provided that he eventually reached the landmark or kept a mental note of how far he passed to one side or the other of it. In 1909 Bartlett was used as the trailbreaker until he turned back. The captain's ability to use the compass may be presumed, but it is also attested by a letter of his written to Dr. Grosvenor, of the National Geographic Society, on January 23rd 1916. The relevant portion is quoted below:

> He (Representative Helgesen) speaks about compasses used
> and the variations. The last thing I did was to cheque [sic]
> up the courses from headland to headland around Cape
> Columbia and Cape Aldrich and from Cape Hecla to Cape
> Columbia in and out bays all along the coast: and tried
> out the compasses on many courses. We went out on the
> meridian true north from Columbia and saw the sun rise and set.

---

[7] Figure II-5 is a 1906 note from Peary to Henson, who was then the trailbreaker, indicating the need for a course correction. A transcription follows: "It looks now as if you could get a very early start in the morning. We are likely to have another spell of fine weather after the storm & I expect you to lay out some dandy marches which will keep the rest of us hurtling to make good. Look very carefully after your course. You are improving but are still side stepping to the west more than you should. Have your shadow square on your left at 7 o'clock in the morning, exactly *in front* of you at 1 o'clock & square on your right at 7 o'clock in the afternoon. It is not necessary for ..."

C. Determining the Direction to the Pole

Peary had several sources of direction to use to set his compass direction, as is indicated in his diary. None of these required "correct" time, knowledge of longitude or keeping on a meridian. For example, the first rising of the sun on March 5th "for a few minutes" provided the way to go. The sun's setting and rising on March 21st and 22nd gave an east and a west that was easily converted to a useable compass heading to the Pole from his locations at the time. Subsequently the sun touching the horizon on March 26th and 27th provided a true north and therefore a true direction to the Pole from his position on those dates. None of these phenomena are affected by the "equation of time" since they are not based on knowledge of mean time.

An important source of accurate direction to the Pole that has gone unmentioned by the Peary critics is the meridian transit sight, as carried out by Marvin and Bartlett until each turned back, and then by Peary himself. By means of the sextant and *artificial horizon*, when the sun was visible, these three experienced navigators took meridian transit sights for latitude. At the same time each was necessarily determining "local apparent noon," noting the time from his watch type chronometer, and also noting the direction his compass pointed relative to the sun's direction at "culmination." Culmination is the point at which the sun reaches its maximum altitude, and therefore is essentially on the local meridian.

When a ship is at sea celestial navigation depends upon the accurate measurement of the angle of the sun between some fixed celestial body, such as the sun or a star, and the visible horizon of the earth. Combining this angle with the exact time of the observation the navigator can, with mathematical tables, calculate a line of position, and with two such sights, a complete position. For centuries, this angle has been measured with the sextant, a device that has been the trademark of the mariner.

Because of ship's motion, the meridian transit sight taken with an artificial horizon (a pan of mercury) is not used by mariners. However, it is frequently used on land by *surveyors,* who have the advantage of a stable base, and who frequently have no natural horizon. Its use results in increased accuracy because it halves the error of the measurement by doubling the angle being measured. Thus the equipment and technique used by Peary and his assistants made possible the determination of the time and consequently the direction of the sun at "local apparent noon" with useable accuracy. Figure II-6 is a diagram showing the operation of the sextant with the artificial horizon as Peary and his colleagues used it for all their sights.[8] The plan view (top) shows that the observer, his sextant and the artificial horizon are all in a line pointing true south, at the time of the sun's culmination.

Since, as mentioned above, the artificial horizon is not useable at sea due to the rolling and pitching of the ship, Captain Bartlett was not altogether familiar with it, while the surveyors, Marvin and Peary, were at home with it. When the device is used to measure the meridian transit of the sun, the time of transit is the time at which the direction of the sun is the reciprocal of the true direction to the Pole *from that location.* It is taken at the moment when the sun stops rising and reverses its direction. To detect this may take a number of minutes of waiting, but the error in direction is small.

---

[8] Peary described his use of the artificial horizon in *The North Pole* at pages 288-289.

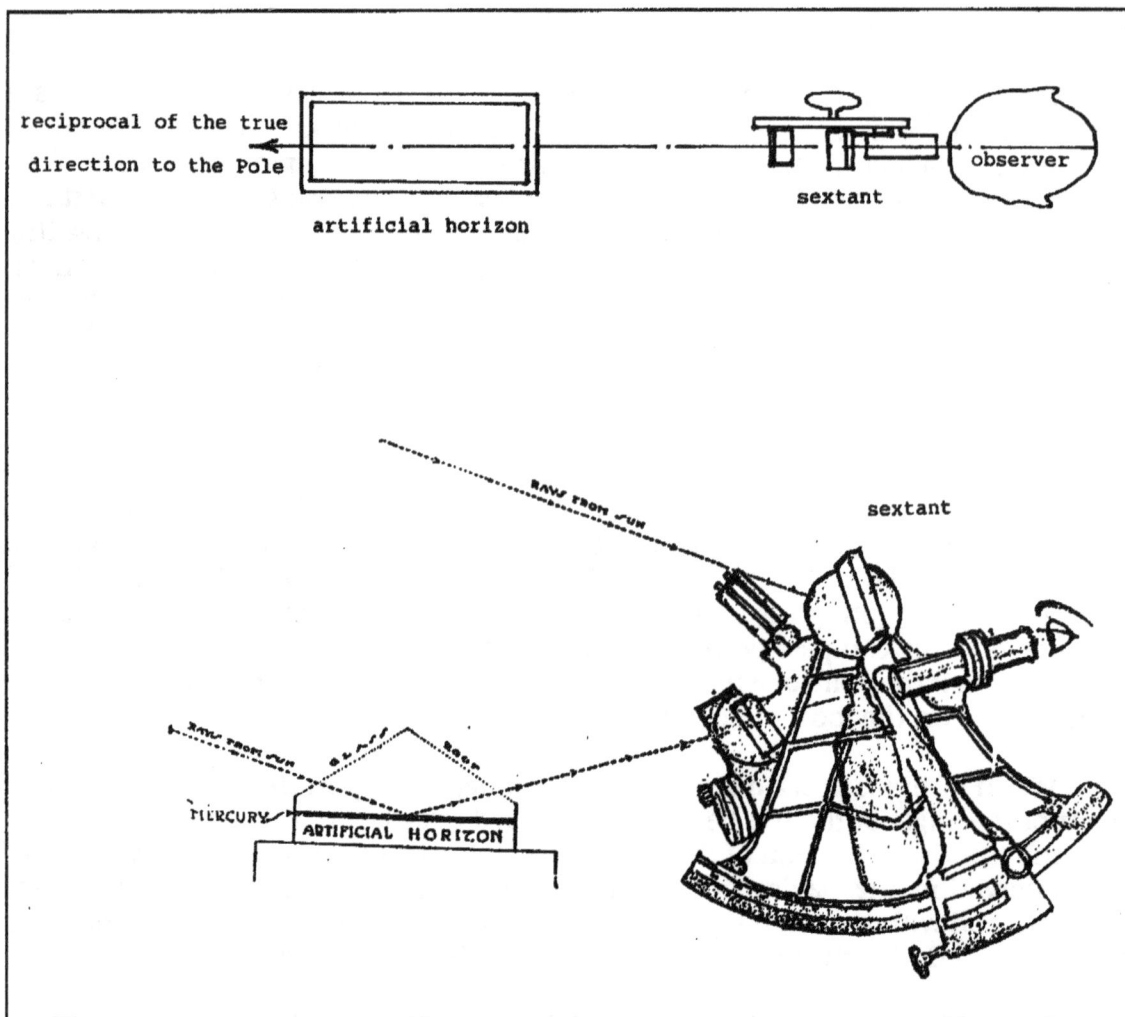

reciprocal of the true
direction to the Pole

artificial horizon

sextant

observer

sextant

RAYS FROM SUN

RAYS FROM SUN

MERCURY

ARTIFICIAL HORIZON

Figure II-6

This culmination of the sun is the basis of the meridian altitude, and therefore the latitude, as well. The *direction* derived by this method is unaffected by the uncertainties of arctic atmospheric refraction. There is but a small error (about one degree) from declination rate, which Peary was quite capable of correcting if he felt it was worthwhile.

A probability analysis (See Appendix B) of the recorded data of Ross Marvin's two sets of sights shows that they match the path of the sun at meridian transit (culmination). They therefore were indisputably meridian transit sights which gave direction to the Pole. Bartlett did not take a series of sights as Marvin did; thus his data cannot be analyzed by the same technique to determine whether the altitude value represents culmination. However, in a letter to Peary, dated October 25th, 1909, Bartlett explains that his sight was taken at culmination. He writes:

> I did not take a series of sights and work them down, but
> just as I do at sea doing it mentally *till the sun has ceased to rise.*

Bartlett's technique, sometimes used by mariners, was to set the sextant very close to an anticipated altitude and watch the two images (the direct image and that produced by the artificial horizon) of a limb of the sun until there was no relative movement. The separation or overlap at the time of culmination was corrected by a final adjustment of the sextant. At polar latitudes the observer may extend the time of waiting for culmination to fifteen minutes or more, but after the culmination is clear, a time correction back to a mid-point may be made. Clearly the observations at 85-48 N, 86-38 N and at 87-45 were all culminations that provided direction to the Pole as well as latitude.[9]

A letter from Bartlett to Dr. Grosvenor dated January 23, 1916 (when the "Helgesen" hearings were in progress) describes the expedition's use of the direction from the meridian transit sights in the following typically salty words:

> We used the dead reckoning, judging it by marking from hour to hour. And then the *latitudes taken by Marvin could tell whether we were making too much departure* on our difference of latitude. [Note: "Departure" is a maritime navigator's word of that era and is defined as east-west miles measured along a parallel of latitude].

The accuracy and utility of the direction obtained from the meridian transit even at very high latitudes can be shown by computing the track onward to the Pole using such a direction. Table II-1, below, shows the probable angular error and "miss distance" at the Pole from these directions alone, tabulated for several high latitudes which include those of the Marvin and Bartlett sights. It assumes that a direction so determined at each of these latitudes could be followed from that point to the Pole (since this is the real objective), and calculates the maximum left-right distance that the worst case direction would bring one.

The accuracy with which the observer can identify the time of culmination determines the accuracy of the direction obtained. He does this by noting the altitude of the sun with his instruments; therefore the table shows values for the observer's precision of 10", 20" and 30" for such observations. These are reasonable values for Marvin, Bartlett or Peary and their equipment. The accuracy of the unaided human eye is usually taken as about 1 minute of arc by optical designers. The use of the artificial horizon doubles the angle being measured which has the effect of halving the error to about 30" of arc. Also, Peary's sextant which we have examined at the National Archives, used a 3 power telescope. The telescope effectiveness in reducing error is fully realized in land based observations, unlike those at sea. It therefore had the effect of reducing the error to one third, or 10" of arc. To provide a spread of possible precisions which might be expected under the conditions which existed, Table II-1 shows value of 10", 20" and 30".

---

[9] Dennis Rawlins is therefore mistaken when he asserts in *Fact Or Fiction?* (p. 131) that "the expedition's steering north was determined exclusively by compass, and throughout the trip Peary never determined the variation of the compass from north."

Table II-1

Probable Angular Error +or-/ Miss-distance at the Pole (n.m.)

Sight Latitude		84 *t /mi	85 t /mi	86 t /mi	87 t /mi	88 t /mi
Precision of	10"	1.7/11	1.9/10	2.1/9	2.5/8	3.0/6
Sight	20"	2.5/15	2.7/14	3.0/13	3.5/11	4.3/9
	30"	3.0/19	3.3/17	3.7/15	4.3/13	5.2/11

* t is the angular error in degrees at each latitude.

The equation used to calculate the change of meridian angle t which produces a change in altitude of the stated precision is:

$$\cos t = (\sin h1 - (\sin L)(\sin d))/(\cos L)(\cos d)$$

$$\text{where } h1 = 90 - L + d - .002778 \text{ (for 10")}$$

Thereafter:

$$(\tan t)(60)(90 - L) = \text{miss distance in miles}$$

Where t = meridian angle at the time that the alt. of Sun = alt. at transit - sight precision (10, 20 or 30 arc seconds).

L = latitude
d = declination of sun (1.75 degrees, the value at the time of Marvin's sights)

Note that while the probable angular error increases at higher latitudes, the miss-distance resulting actually decreases. The use of the homing technique continually diminishes the error at the Pole as it is approached, so the larger miss-distances at the lower latitudes are still quite useable. The probable error can also be represented as time in minutes during which the sun changes altitude by an amount equal to the observer's precision. The time to take a culmination would therefore be about this long. Table II-2 shows the data in that form but computed for the specific latitudes of Marvin's and Bartlett's sights to indicate the length of time involved in determining the culmination. In the case of Marvin these times and precisions compare favorably which the details of his sights shown in Figures II-11 and II-12.

Table II-2

Minutes of Time

Sight Latitude		85-48	86-38	87-45
Precision of	10"	8.3	9.3	11.5
Sight	20"	11.8	13.2	16.3
	30"	14.4	16.1	19.9

Note that the above tables apply only to Marvin and Bartlett. Peary's sights at the Pole were not culminations, since the sun did not culminate daily there.

Peary, in his diary, says that he sometimes used the moon for direction. Critics have scoffed at this, labeling it but another example of his allegedly faulty navigation, but it can easily be accomplished. On any day, using the compass and watch, one can determine when the moon is on the local meridian. From the Nautical Almanac (which Peary had with him), one can then determine difference, in minutes of time, when the moon will have the same angle on the following or any succeeding day. This determines the time when the moon will again be on the meridian. It is true, of course, that the moon's rapid rate of declination change (about 14 times that of the sun) would distort the direction at rising, setting and touching the horizon. However at Peary's latitude the moon rose on March 24 and after the next day did not set until April 4. During the interim it simply circled at increasing and then decreasing altitudes above the horizon, the angle between it and the sun changing slowly.

D. Applying the Homing Method

In the overall navigation of the 1909 expedition, it is clear that Peary "homed" to the Pole using the initial known compass variation at Cape Columbia (which he and others had earlier determined) to start steering, and thereafter had a number of opportunities to get the direction to the Pole quite independent of knowledge of his longitude or the "correct" time. His statements make clear that he used such opportunities to correct his compass, and the geometry of the situation is such that he automatically headed in the right direction regardless of drift or the vagaries of the ice travel. Table II-3 shows the dates and locations where the directional updates were available.

Table II-3

Availability of Direction to the Pole

Date	Latitude	Difference in compass course since last update
March 1	83-07	0
5	84-00	2
21	85-33	5
22	85-48	0
25	86-38	2
26	86-38	0
27	87-00	1
April 1*	87-45	4
6-7	89-57	5 **

* The Moon was above the horizon from March 24 to April 4
** The above computations are based on 1909 variation information.

The small compass corrections shown in the table would mean to Peary that he was roughly on course. Should one of the indicated corrections come in quite large, say 10-15 degrees, he would have concluded that he had experienced substantial drift. His action, in any event, would have been the same, i.e. to steer north. However, because he told the Congressional committee "we were able to keep our course," and advised the U.S. Coast and Geodetic Survey that his soundings could be plotted as taken along the 70th meridian, we are persuaded that course changes were no greater than we have calculated them to be.

From the above table, it is clear that Peary had so many opportunities to correct his direction to the Pole before reaching Camp Bartlett at 87-45 N, that he must have arrived there on a course very close to that he intended. Modern data indicates a slow course change totalling 5 degrees from there to the Pole. Data from 1909 computer model of the Earth's field at the Naval Oceanographic Office supports the 5 degree change. Even if we assume that Peary made *no* adjustments after getting his last accurate direction from Bartlett's meridian transit, his course would have brought him within about 9 miles (left) of the Pole in the absence of ice movement or other divergence.[10]

Peary's method of deciding when he had neared the Pole was to add the estimated mileages made good until they totalled the 135 miles (he thought it was 133) he had to go. His diary indicates that he took a quick sight on April 5 at 89-25 although the details of the sight were apparently not recorded. This gave him a good idea of when to stop for his final sights, taken on April 6-7. His final probes conducted on April 7, ensured that he passed as close to the Pole as the accuracy of his navigation would permit.

E. The Longitude Sight

Peary's method of determining direction was recognized and accepted as reasonable by Henry Gannett, one of three members of the committee appointed by the National Geographic Society in 1909 to consider the validity of Peary's claim. Gannett, a Harvard-educated engineer who held the title of Geographer, U.S. Geological Survey, testified before the House Committee on Naval Affairs on March 4, 1910, as follows:

> Q: ... You do not mention how he kept his longitude?
> A: I saw no longitude observations, and my understanding
> is he didn't make any; I do not see why he should. He kept
> his direction by the compass and the direction of the sun
> at noontime, and his purpose was to go north.

Peary's first priority was to find the answer to the question "Which way is north?"[11] He testified at the hearings:

> Mr. Macon: You said, I believe, you took no longitude
> observations at all?
>
> Captain Peary: I took no observations for longitude on the trip.
>
> Mr. Macon: I am advised by astronomers and geographers and
> explorers and scientists that it is impossible for anyone

---

[10] It is unfortunate for the controversy, though not surprising, that Peary kept no record of his compass variations as he had on other trips. His mission this time was simply to get to his destination and back alive. Moreover, any record of his course changes would have been useless to a later traveller without impossibly precise positions. And as for using the record as a later "proof" of his attainment of the Pole, the problem introduced by the convergence of the meridians would have applied.

[11] In Section I we discuss timekeeping of the 1909 expedition.

in a broad field as you were going over on your explorations of the North Pole to tell exactly the direction they were traveling unless they took longitude observations. What do you say about that? ...

Captain Peary: My opinion is that we were able to keep our course. My opinion also is that at the time of the year and under the conditions existing there, any attempt at taking longitude observations would have been a waste of time.

Mr. Macon: Why so?

Captain Peary: In the middle part of the journey the sun was so low that presumably any longitude observations would have been unnecessary, and in the neighborhood of the pole it is not generally recognized that longitude observations are not practicable with any degree of accuracy.

Peary declined to elucidate, or to get into a general discussion, though urged by Mr. Macon to do so: "I do not think I care to go into a discussion of general principles." We will, however, go into a discussion of general principles here.

First, a longitude sight (Peary would have taken it with a "time sight") was unnecessary and would have been time consuming. Such a sight requires an accurate time and latitude, and would have necessitated far more observations (at hours apart) than those Peary took. Peary could well dispense with longitude sights because from any position in which he found himself as a result of ice drift or other vagaries of polar travel, the meridian transit sights (culminations) he was taking permitted him to head straight for the Pole. The longitude sights would merely have been duplicative, because from the culminations he already had his direction to the Pole. That direction, expressed as a compass course to the Pole, gave him everything he would have derived from the determination of longitude; direction is the end use of longitude after all.

Secondly, a longitude sight would have been impractical. At the latitude and date of Marvin's sights the altitude of the sun when on the "prime vertical" for a longitude sight would have been about 1.75 degrees. Observing such a low altitude would have been physically difficult with the artificial horizon, and eyestrain was always a factor to be considered. Moreover, Arctic refraction variability is such at low altitudes that the sight would have been virtually worthless.

It is interesting to compare Peary's navigational method and his independence of longitude sights with that of other polar explorers, such as Roald Amundsen. The fact that Amundsen had attained the South Pole in December of 1911 was attested by Captain Robert Scott's diary and an artifact from Amundsen's cairn found in Scott's possession at his last camp.[12] Consequently there was no interest in reviewing Amundsen's navigational data afterward, as in the case of Peary. However, Volume 19 of the "Polar Record" (1978-1979), the publication of the Scott Polar Research Institute,

---

[12] On reaching the South Pole and finding Amundsen's flags flying and his nearby black tents, Scott wrote the poignant words: "Great God! This is an awful place and terrible enough for us to have labored to it without the reward of priority." Scott and the last members of his polar party died on the return trip just eleven miles from a supply depot.

contains an article by D. J. Drewry and R. Huntford, "Amundsen's Route to the South Pole," which offers the first real analysis of the Norwegian explorer's navigation. They write:

> He took no longitude sights during the whole polar journey....he trusted to latitude observations alone, combined with dead reckoning based on compass courses and distances run. The compasses were checked by frequent azimuth observations, the logical method at high latitudes. Amundsen's navigation was specifically designed for simplicity and time-saving on the march, based on the comparatively easy meridian observation. In contrast, Scott used conventional marine navigation as employed at lower latitudes. His navigator, Henry Bowers, made ex-meridian observations and longitude sights, spending considerable time and effort on calculations for a few kilometers, sometimes a few hundred meters, of meaningless accuracy.

It appears that Italian Navy Commander Umberto Cagni, the leader of the expedition of the Duke of the Abruzzi (1899-1900), similarly did not take longitude observations en route to establishing a new "farthest north" record. In *On the Polar Star in the Arctic Sea* (Vol.II, pp. 455, 462, 481 and 488), we find him recording the taking of "meridian altitudes" for latitude with no mention of longitude sights. That he was getting *direction* from these culminations is clear where, on page 488, he not only records latitude from his meridian altitude, but *compass variation* which could only be available from direction to the Pole. At latitude 86-34 N., where the party decided to turn back south toward Prince Rupert Island, the first longitude sight was taken (p. 490). This makes sense because the use of meridian altitudes alone would have taken him south, in the direction away from the Pole, but probably not to his specific destination.

Navigation back to land always requires a knowledge of longitude if the land target is small and the return trail is not visible or has been displaced by ice movement. In Peary's case the homeward trail was visible and continuous because on their return south Bob Bartlett and his Eskimos had "knit" it together for him. Thus a longitude sight was not required on the return trip either. Judging from the equipment and data Peary carried with him, he could have taken a "longitude" sight at any time if the trail-and- compass technique failed.

In summary Peary's navigation, like Cagni's before him and Amundsen's after him, was designed for simplicity and time-saving on the march. Peary proposed to waste no time and effort on unnecessary and useless sights, and he did not do so. Those who have subsequently insisted that he should have taken longitude sights to ensure that he stayed on the 70th meridian, and who have presumed that he was dependent on maintaining accurate time for months away from civilization in order to do so (See Section I, below) appear to have missed some of the practical aspects of elementary polar navigation.

F. Ice Movement

Many of Peary's critics maintain that Peary's navigation was inadequate to deal with movement of the polar ice, and that his understanding of the effects of wind on ice was marginal. Their criticisms have tended to be extremely conclusory; only Wally Herbert has made any substantial attempt to quantify the effect of ice movement on Peary's journey to the Pole. For that reason, we will deal with the effect of ice movement on the 1909 expedition primarily in the light of Herbert's 1988 *National Geographic* article and his recently published book, *The Noose Of Laurels*.

1. Movement Due to Currents

At the outset let us note that Herbert implicitly acknowledges that along Peary's route there would have been little or no long-term movement of the ice. That is, the ice could have shifted back and forth due to local winds, but was not to any significant extent being moved as a mass by currents. This fact is demonstrated by Figure II-7 which is a plot of data showing measurements of long term ice movement. Each arrow represents one year's movement of a manned ice station or ship. The pattern of this long term drift reflects the ocean currents as they are now known.

Of particular interest is the "Beaufort Gyre," a large vortex generated by the operation of Coriolis effect on the transpolar drift stream from the Bering Strait toward Greenland. The effect of this gyre is to produce an area of stagnation with essentially no long term ice movement directly off Cape Columbia (where Peary started). For example, from November of 1971 to November of 1974 the position of ice island T-3 changed from latitude 84°36', longitude 84°48' to latitude 84°32', longitude 85°48', with a few meanderings in between. This amounts to a net drift of about 6 nautical miles in three years.

Further evidence of the stagnation in the area north of Cape Columbia is visible in Figure II-8 which is a plot of several years' movement of drifting buoys in that area. In fact, one buoy became trapped in that area for several years and finally was deactivated for lack of any substantial movement.

As Peary approached the Pole a long term drift in a southerly direction (parallel to Peary's track) at about 1 n.m. per day would be expected. This can be seen in the tracks la-

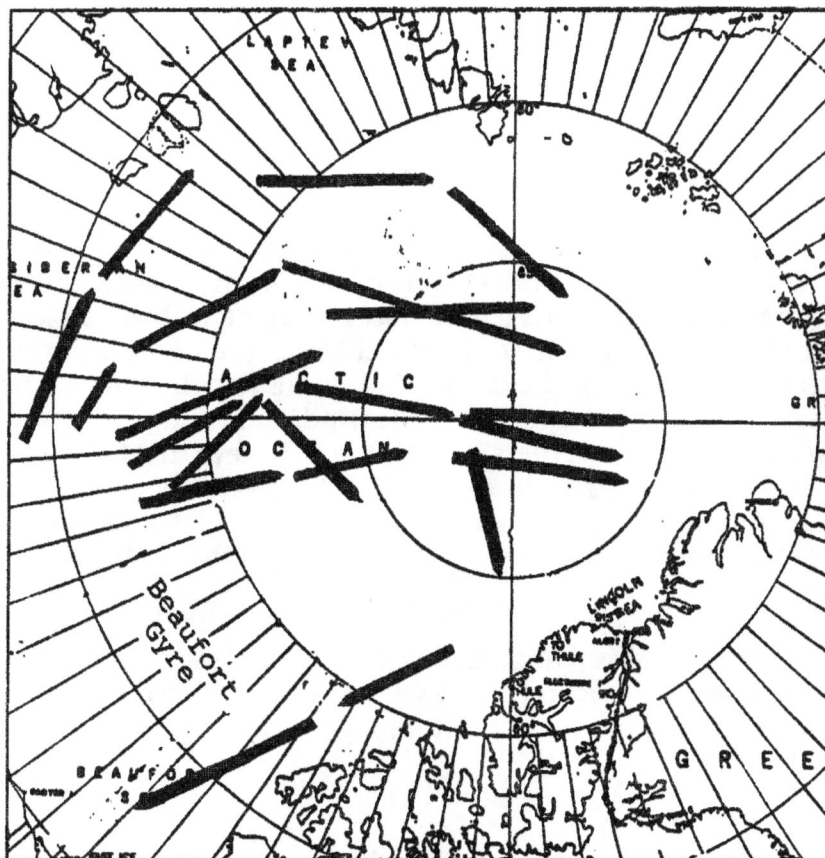

Figure II-7

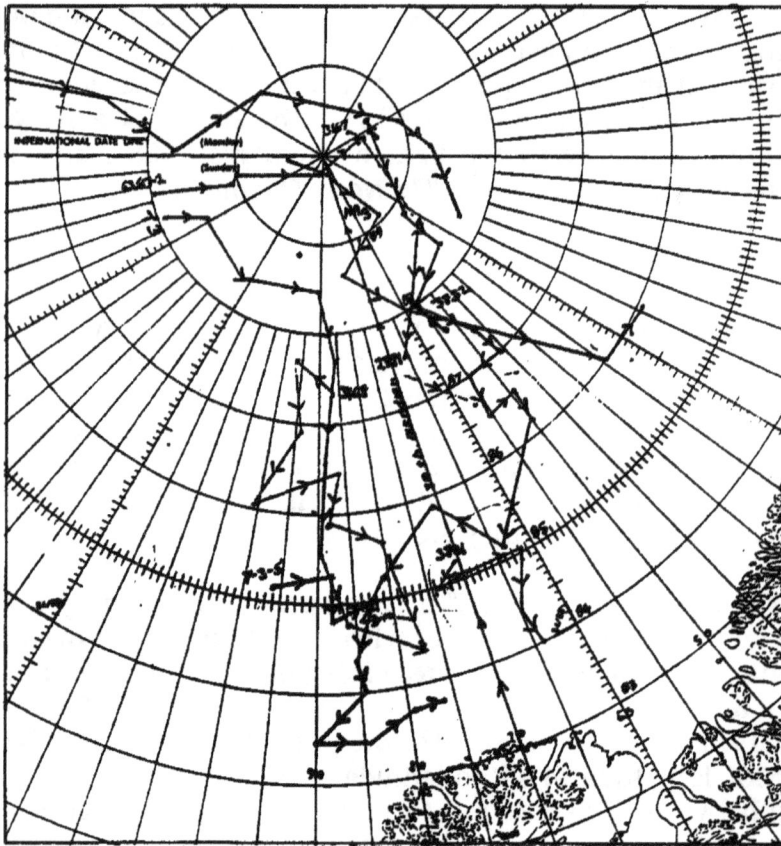

Figure II-8

beled NP-3 and 2891 in Figure II-8. Approaching latitude 88º N. Peary mentions a southerly movement of the ice in his diary, but he (probably correctly) attributed this drift to northerly winds. Only very close to the Pole was the trans-polar current oriented across his path. In the region north of latitude 89º north, Peary would be likely to drift about 1 n.m. per day to the right due to this current, as shown by the tracks in Figure II-7 and Figure II-8.[13]

In summary, modern data shows that the long term drift (due to current) was probably very slow (less than 1 n.m. per day), non-existent at the beginning of the trip, southerly and parallel to Peary's track in the middle part of the trip, and across Peary's track only at the very end. Considering only the long term effects of drift, one would expect any significant lateral (east-west) drift only for the last five days, in the amount of about 5 n.m. to the east.

2. Movement Due to Winds

Short term movement of the ice due to wind is more difficult to estimate, even if the wind speed and direction is known. Such movement depends on, among other things, the extent to which ice floes are separated by open leads that can close up, or newly frozen leads in which the thin ice can easily be crushed. Peary provided a reasonable amount of data on wind speeds and directions, and occasionally refers to leads opening or closing due to the wind, and young ice crushing in leads, in his book and diary. However, there is no reason to believe that these sources reflect the totality of his observations in either regard, and any attempt to reconstruct the ice motion due to wind starts with this disadvantage. Nevertheless, an analysis of wind directions and speeds is useful to gain some understanding of the potential effect of ice drift on Peary's track.

First, however, let us examine Peary's expressed understanding of ice movement to estimate his reaction to the winds he experienced. In a letter of April 18, 1912, in answer to a John Hall of Creston, Iowa, Peary writes:

---

[13] See track 63517-2 and NP-3 in Figure II-8.

Replying to your inquiry, the general movement of the ice in the Arctic Ocean, north of the northern coasts of Grant Land and Greenland, is to the eastward.

This movement is neither regular nor continuous. There are periods of weeks when there is essentially no movement of the ice. This movement is the result of the effect of the prevailing winds rather than of an ocean current.

In a letter of May 15, 1914, commenting upon a paper by a Lieutenant Solely on Polar currents he writes:

There is no question in my mind but what this movement of the ice is the resultant of the average wind movement of the year, which under normal conditions is from the cold ice-covered areas lying between the pole and Bering Strait, towards the open water and warmer temperatures of the North Atlantic between Greenland and Norway.

When asked whether he attributed his 1909 success to luck or better equipment he replied:

It was a combination of both. The absence of strong, continued winds at right angles to my line of march helped me greatly. That was what always bothered me in former expeditions. Headwinds or winds from the south don't bother me a bit. Of course the wind in your face makes bad sledging, but the cross winds cause the ice to drift east or west and throw you out of your calculation. This time we had the wind dead ahead. That pressed the ice against the land which we had left and made good footing.

Before the Congressional committee Peary testified:

Captain Peary: In the Arctic Ocean the movement of the ice is more dependent on the winds than on the current.

Mr. Macon: How thick is the ice?

Captain Peary: Anywhere from a few inches — newly formed ice — to 20 or 25 feet thick.

Mr. Macon: You do not mean to tell the committee that the wind could move that ice?

Captain Peary: The pressure of the wind would move that ice if there was any space to move it in ... If the ice is up against the land, it cannot move; but if it is ice between the sea and the land ... with comparatively thin ice

interspersed between it, that ice will twist and endeavor
to slide, and the result will be that in some places the
young ice will crush up ...

Mr. Macon: This ice being 25 feet thick when it would pack,
what would cause it to produce the leads you speak of so
often in your book?

Captain Peary: The wind would be the most important factor
in producing pronounced changes in the ice ... Also, what
has been determined by my last two expeditions and which,
as far as I know, was not recognized before, is the fact
... that the strong tides of every month, the tidal waves
crossing the polar basin, result in a movement of the ice
that will form leads, and the tidal wave passing under
the ice will buckle the ice and cause the lead to form,
and then with the ebb tide that lead will slowly open
without any pronounced and, perhaps, any perceptible
current of the water.

These views are consistent with the best of modern knowledge of ice movement
in the polar sea. Consequently we must believe that Peary's reaction to observed wind
was rational and intelligent, and that his comprehensive knowledge of ice movement
reflected his long experience in the Arctic.

3. Critical Analysis of Ice Drift

Although ice drift was raised as an issue by Captain Hall in 1917, as noted above,
Herbert is the only critic who provides a more-or-less quantitative analysis. He begins
his discussion of ice drift by noting that "In recent years a great deal of data has been
collected on the effect of wind on the drift of pack ice." (*Noose* p. 264) Ironically,
however, he then analyzes Peary's probable drift in terms of "Nansen's Law," which
is based on empirical data, of which Peary was well aware, obtained by Nansen circa
1893. Nansen's Law is that the ice tends to drift at 1/50th of the wind speed and at an
angle about 30 to the right of directly downwind.[14] Although we have not found any
document in which Peary described the effect of wind in precisely these terms, as
shown above, Peary was entirely aware of the effect of wind on ice drift. Moreover, we
know that he was he was capable of estimating drift because he did it on his 1906
expedition when ice conditions due to winds and open leads caused him to give up his
assault on the Pole.

Herbert states (*Noose*, p. 260): "It is simply not acceptable to assume that Peary
set his course to counter the drift of ice, for there is no way of knowing which way the
ice is drifting, or at what speed, without frequent position checks by solar observations." The statement is correct in that it is impossible to *set* one's course to counter
ice drift by the application of Nansen's law or otherwise. But as we have shown, Peary
took solar observations that enabled him to *adjust* his course to counter ice drifts or
other hindrances to Arctic travel at many points enroute to the Pole. One cannot
assume that he kept a record of all his observations, anymore than Herbert kept a record

---

[14] The rightward drift is the result of Coriolis force. The accuracy is such that, as Herbert admits, taking drift into
account in deciding which way to head is not feasible. (*Noose* p.260)

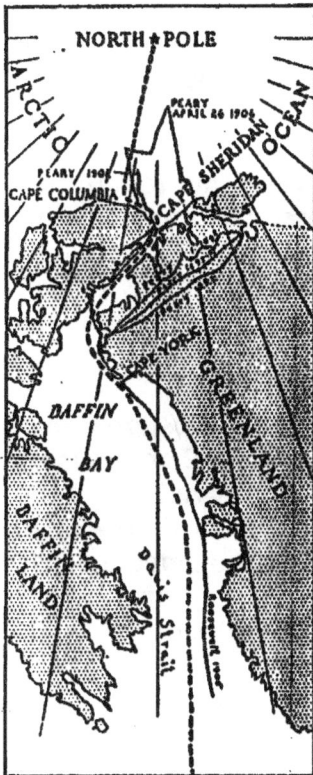

PEARY'S OWN MAP OF THE ROUTE
FOLLOWED ON THE JOURNEY
TO THE POLE.

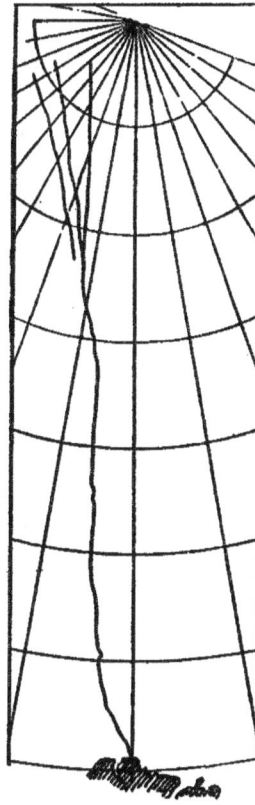

Herbert's reconstruction
of Peary's track

Figure II-9

of his observations on his trip "across the top of the world."[15] But we do not find it acceptable to assume that so seasoned an explorer would not have taken the necessary corrective action when winds blew him off course.

Nansen's Law offers no magic formula. It is an empirical law which merely correlates the available data on ice drift better than any other rule that considers only wind speed and direction. Whether the ice moves to the extent predicted by the law depends on various factors including, most importantly, the degree of freedom of individual ice floes to move (which depends on the amount of open water or relatively thin ice that can be crushed between floes), and whether the entire mass of the ice is moving in unison as a result of winds of long duration and constant direction over a large area of the ice.

Figure II-9 shows the tracks of the 1909 expedition as laid out by a) Peary and b) Herbert. The first column of Table II-4 shows our compilation of wind speeds and directions from Peary's diary and the resultant ice drift obtained by applying Nansen's Law. This shows a net westward drift of 20 n.m. by the time Peary reached the Pole, in contrast to Herbert's calculated 50 n.m. (*Noose*, chart at p. 265). In reaching this result, we assume that Peary had already drifted a net 12 n.m. west by the time of his fifth march (first march north of the "big lead" about 84°-08' N.). Beyond that point, we estimate that the additional drift amounted to only 8 n.m.

In estimating the 50 n.m. westerly drift due to winds, Herbert fails to consider that during the early going two of Peary's parties returned to land for additional supplies and rejoined the main party just north of the big lead. The experience of these parties (led by Borup and Marvin) clearly demonstrates that the ice was initially driven to the west by easterly winds, but that countervailing westerly winds subsequently drove the ice farther back to the east than would be predicted by Nansen's empirical law. Borup had been in the trailbreaking party and returned to Cape Columbia from the third

---

[15] Herbert laments that Peary did not bring back a complete record of his trip — "a mass of acceptable proof that he and his five courageous companions had finally succeeded in reaching the Pole." He disparages the observations Peary brought back with the comment: "He had merely offered as proof of his claim the sort of simple observations which my companions and I, at local noon on a travelling day during our crossing of the Arctic Ocean, used to work out ... by scratching the numbers with the point of a ski stick on a smooth patch of wind packed snow." (*Noose*, p.20) At the same time, he declines to give Peary credit for taking any observations whatsoever unless they have been preserved.

camp on March 3. After crossing a lead he had to divert 5 n.m. to the east to pick up the trail and then reached the shore ice 12 n.m. further west than he expected to be. (*A Tenderfoot with Peary* p. 155). Thus, the ice had indeed drifted about 17 n.m. west as would be predicted by Nansen's empirical law.

Marvin returned to land on March 4. He followed the same trail to land that Borup had followed, but reached the shore ice some 5 n.m. east of Borup's landing. Thus, by March 5, the ice had drifted about 5 n.m. east, or about 1 n.m. less than the prediction based on Nansen's law. It is not surprising that the drift was initially somewhat less than would be predicted, since the wind had to overcome the westward momentum of the ice.

Borup and Marvin then sought to return to the main party. They started out a "few miles" west of where the trail had initially started (*Tenderfoot* p. 162 on) and were held up by open water a few miles from land. At this camp, they observed that the ice continued to move rapidly to the east, even after the westerly winds died down. This in all probability meant that the westerly movement of the ice had opened up space between ice floes that closed up when the wind reversed direction. Peary himself made note of the tendency of the ice to "rebound" when a strong wind dies down.

Since the Borup/Marvin party was within sight of land, and since various members of the party made frequent return trips to Cape Columbia during the period of delay, we are confident that Borup was correct in observing that the sea ice was moving east (rather than the shore ice moving west).

When the Borup/Marvin party finally crossed the lead, they were surprised to find that the main trail was only about a mile to the west. They picked it up easily and overhauled Peary within a few days. Thus it is clear that, as of March 12, when Borup and Marvin rejoined the main party, the trail was only a few n.m. west of its initial position. More important, when they reached Peary, they had just covered the trail in a few days of calm winds starting from a known point near land. Thus they were in a position to give Peary the precise details on how far the trail had moved, and Peary could take any corrective action that he thought was justified.

We have presented a computation of the ice drift in Table II-4 that reflects the eastward drift of the ice observed by Borup and Marvin. The "best estimate" column shows that the ice drift would have carried Peary about 4 n.m. west as of March 12, and a net 9 n.m. west as of the arrival at Bartlett's Camp.

The "best estimate" column in Table II-4 contains one other adjustment that Herbert fails to make, which is to account for the transpolar drift stream in the region north of Bartlett's last camp. In discussing Peary's distances, Herbert states that the transpolar drift stream caused a "general ice drift on calm days in the vicinity of the Pole ... between two and three nautical miles a day in the direction of longitude 30ºW." (*Noose*, p.270) Herbert applies this drift to reduce Peary's distance by 12 n.m. from Bartlett's Camp to the Pole camp (which reflects a 2.5 n.m. per day drift at 40º from the left of Peary's heading), but takes no account of the nearly identical eastward set (about 10 n.m.) that this drift speed and direction would produce.

We believe that Herbert's typical drift speed is overstated, based on the data shown in Table II-4. Further, Peary encountered winds on April 5 and 6 that would have produced about 2 n.m. of eastward drift. Allowing 5 n.m. of westward set for the transpolar drift stream would result in a net westward drift from Bartlett's camp onward of 3 n.m., or a total net eastward drift for the entire journey of about 6 n.m.

The final column in Table II-4 shows Herbert's estimate of ice drift as accurately as we are able to reconstruct it from the track shown in his recent book (*Noose* p. 265). Herbert shows greater drift than even the uncorrected Nansen's law calculations reflect because he appears to have ignored several significant westerly winds. His estimate is that the ice had drifted west by 32 n.m. as of Bartlett's camp, and did not drift any further thereafter.[16]

G. Peary's Track As Reconstructed By Herbert

Herbert's reconstruction of Peary's track in his *National Geographic* article (See Figure II-9) derives three final positions based on the assumption that Peary did not make any correction for: (a) ice drift (as estimated by Herbert and shown in the last column of Table II-4); (b) a possible 2.5° heading error based on an assumed chronometer error of 10 min.[17]; and (c) possible errors due to compass variation. Herbert's most favorable (to Peary) estimated position assumes that Peary's track was influenced by ice drift, but that his heading was always determined by local noon on the Columbia meridian (i.e., always parallel to the 70th meridian). As noted above, based on Herbert's estimate of ice drift, the most favorable position is about 30 n.m. west (and a little short) of the Pole.

Herbert's second position for Peary is displaced 18 n.m. further to the west to reflect an assumed 10 min. chronometer error in determining local noon on the Columbia meridian (i.e., a course 2.5° west of a line parallel to the 70th meridian). Herbert's third position is displaced further to the west based on an assumed difficulty with changes in compass variation.

All of Herbert's estimated tracks are based on his overstated estimate of ice drift and ignore the data provided both by depth soundings and by local apparent noon sights taken along the route to the Pole. Our analysis of Peary's depth soundings (in Part IV) shows that the sounding by Marvin at 85°-23' (310 fathoms) had to have been taken at a point 5 n.m. east to 5 n.m. west of the 70th meridian, whereas Herbert's most favorable track reconstruction has him 24 n.m. west of the 70th meridian.

Herbert's second and third tracks, which include 18 n.m. of error as a result of chronometer error, would place Peary 30 n.m. west of the 70th meridian. At these points 24 and 30 n.m. west of the 70th meridian, we will show in Part IV that the water depth would have been at least 650 to 700 fathoms, instead of Peary's 310 fathoms.

We also demonstrate that the most likely position for the sounding by Bartlett at 87°-15' is 3 to 8 n.m. west of the 70th meridian. Herbert's most favorable track is, we repeat, about 24 miles west of the 70th meridian at that latitude, and Herbert's second and third tracks would be 33 and 35 n.m. west of the 70th meridian at that point.

---

[16] Herbert incorrectly adds various westerly mileages to Peary's last leg to reflect assumed navigational errors that really would have affected the entire track.

[17] See "Timekeeping", Section I, below

Table II-4

Date Wind		Description		Ice Movement/Cumulative					
	Peary's Diary	Beaufort Scale		Speed (kt)	Nansen Law		Best Est.		Herbert
3/1 E	violent wd.	fresh brz		19	8	8	8	8	7 7
3/2 E	wind	mod.brz		14	3	11	3	11	6 13
3/3 E	fresh w.	fresh brz		19	8	19	6	17	4 17
3/4 W	wind	mod.brz		14	-6	13	-5	12	1 18
3/5 W	light brz	light brz.		5	-2	11	-3	9	-2 16
3/6 E	light air	light air		2	0	11	-3	6	-2 14
3/7	calm				0	11	-3	3	0 14
3/8	calm				0	11	0	3	0 14
3/9 E	tendency	light air		2	1	12	1	4	2 16
3/10	calm				0	12	0	4	2 18
3/11	calm				0	12	0	4	0 18
3/12	calm				0	12	0	4	0 22
3/13	n.a.				0	12	0	4	0 22
3/14	n.a.				0	12	0	4	0 22
3/15 E	light air	light air		2	1	13	1	5	2 24
3/16	n.a.				0	13	0	5	0 24
3/17	n.a.				0	13	0	5	0 24
3/18	n.a.				0	13	0	5	0 24
3/19	n.a.				0	13	0	5	0 24
3/20	n.a.				0	13	0	5	0 24
3/21 E	faint air	light air		1	0	13	0	5	0 24
3/22 E	light air	light air		2	1	14	1	6	0 24
3/23	n.a.					1	14	1	6 0
3/24 W	light air	light air		2	-1	13	-1	5	0 24
3/25 W	light air	light air		2	-1	12	-1	4	0 24
3/26 —	variable air			0	0	12	0	4	0 24
3/27 NE	light air	light air		2	1	13	1	5	0 24
3/28 NE	light air	light air		2	1	14	1	6	1 25
3/29	n.a.				0	14	0	6	0 25
3/30 NW	breeze	gentle brz		9	-1	13	-1	5	1 26
3/31 N	wind	mod. brz		14	2	15	2	7	2 28
4/1 NNE	wind	mod. brz		14	3	18	2	9	2 30
4/2	calm				0	18	-1	8	2 32
4/3	calm				0	18	-1	7	0 32
4/4	calm				0	18	-1	6	0 32
4/5 S	light air	light air		2	0	18	0	6	0 32
E	freshening	light brz		5	1	19	0	6	0 32
4/6 E				5	1	20	0	6	0 32
E				2	0	20	0	6	0 50

Herbert's positioning of Peary's track also ignores Marvin's two celestial observations at 85-48 and 86-38, respectively. As demonstrated in Section H, below, these sights were taken at or very near to the time of the sun's culmination upon passing the local meridian and provided directional course corrections.

Herbert's most favorable reconstruction of Peary's track purports to give Peary the benefit of the doubt by assuming that Peary obtained an accurate compass correction on March 22 that would correct any prior errors *due to magnetic compass variation.* However, if indeed Peary got an accurate compass check on March 22, it would have corrected for any errors *from any source* prior to that date by giving him the new correct direction to the Pole. Thus, for example, the 24 n.m. of ice drift that Herbert assumes occurred in the early part of the trip would cease to be relevant. Even by Herbert's overstated analysis, the subsequent ice drift would be expected to amount to a total of only about 8 n.m. By our analysis, there was no net east-west ice drift after March 22.

In sum, Peary's intended track to the Pole, roughly up the 70th meridian, was not significantly offset by ice movement, by faulty navigation, by changes in magnetic compass variation, nor by any of the other factors that Herbert conjures up.

H. The 1909 Celestial Sights

1. Faking Sights

All critics of Peary's 1909 expedition have asserted that celestial sights such as those taken at the Pole and those taken enroute by Marvin and Bartlett, *could* have been readily fabricated by a reasonably competent navigator. Peary admitted as much in the Congressional hearings (no doubt anticipating fakery by Dr. Cook), and even such supporters as Donald MacMillan have said the same. In *How Peary Reached the Pole* (pp. 282-283), MacMillan went so far as to manufacture two artificial sights, supposedly taken at the Pole, to dramatize his point. Members of the National Geographic committee that passed on Peary's "proofs," Mr. Gannett and Mr. Tittmann, when questioned at the hearings, expressed their opinion that it would take a great expert to fake observations so that the fakery was undetectable — that there would be a high likelihood of a mistake which would be caught by careful analysis of any substantial number of sights. The Coast and Geodetic Survey's expert computer, Hugh Mitchell, opined: "I believe it is altogether a matter of experience that any dishonesty in observations or computations will show up in the reduction of those observations or computations ... At some point of the work it will come out."

These experts were right. Careful analysis will very likely detect certain types of anomalies or even "over-perfection" in sights which could be the result of counterfeiting, although this result cannot be guaranteed.

The extensive recomputation of Peary's sights made by Mitchell and his Coast and Geodetic Survey colleague, Charles Duvall, after careful analysis, adequately covers latitude and location of Camp Jesup, which they placed within 5 miles of the Pole (Appendix B). That being the case, it is our intention to analyze Peary's polar observations from the standpoint of *genuineness* only. Even Peary's severest critics concede that Peary's polar observations, if genuine, place him in the immediate vicinity of the Pole.

In conducting such a critique, it is desirable to scrutinize individual observations within a set of sights rather than dealing solely with averages, as was done by Mitchell and Duvall who were not really concerned with "fakery." Fortunately for our analysis all of the 1909 sights except Bartlett's and the first of Peary's are multiple and can be analyzed in this way.

To digress for a moment, Donald MacMillan's sample "faked" sight was actually only a single limb of the sun, with the result that analysis was limited; it was the sort of sight that a shrewd faker would produce. In the one identifiable case of *actual* sight-faking, the alleged observations of Dr. Cook (published in his 1911 book, *My Attainment of the Pole*), later ascribed to a maritime navigator, Captain August Loose, two limbs of the sun were shown. Consequently these sights *were* susceptible to critical analysis, and played an important role in Cook's downfall.

Certain specific questions pertaining to Cook's navigation were raised by Peary's assistant, Hudson Bridge Hastings, a Bowdoin College mathematics instructor, in a 1909 letter to Herbert Bridgeman; others were raised by computational expert, Hugh Mitchell, mentioned above. Both expressed skepticism as to Cook's unrealistic recording of longitudes to arc-seconds while 29 miles from the Pole. And Mitchell also pointed out grossly erroneous sextant readings (diameter of the sun wrong by a factor of two). Neither of these criticisms involved a mere mistake in the reduction of calculations — i.e. computational errors — so the dubious sights could not be explained away as resulting from innocent arithmetical errors.

There is an interesting aspect to one of Captain Loose's errors. The merchant captain produced an observation that reflected the common practice of taking a sight on an upper and a lower limb —and averaging them for the altitude — without the need to apply the semi-diameter of the sun. However, this gave two sights which indicated the sun's diameter. Like most seamen, Loose was not familiar enough with the use of the artificial horizon to realize that when so measured the sun's diameter should give a difference in sextant readings of about 64 minutes instead of 32, since the angles are doubled by the artificial horizon. His alleged sextant readings showed a difference of only 32', an obvious error that could only be the result of a fabrication.

Such a mistake is representative of the sort one would expect to find with seamen navigating (or in Loose's case pretending to navigate) on ice. Robert Bartlett was also not accustomed to using the artificial horizon and made a mistake in reducing his sight of 1 April 1909. A fundamental difference was that he erred in the sight reduction calculations, not in the taking of sextant readings. Bartlett mistakenly applied the refraction correction and the correction for the semi-diameter of the sun, *before* dividing the double-altitude by 2. Consequently his mistake does not imply forgery (i.e. the creating of sextant readings) but only unfamiliarity with the reduction method. These mistakes resulted only in a small (2 miles) difference in his latitude reading. The error was detected and corrected by Mitchell and Duvall in the calculations they did in preparation for Peary's congressional hearing. Though it was not mentioned in the hearings, it has been mentioned by later analysts.[18] In general small *computational* errors reinforce the credibility of the observer rather than the opposite, since a careful forger would be more likely to turn out "perfect" sights.

---

[18] We have taken the error into consideration in this report by correcting the latitude Bartlett certified to Peary from 87-47N to 87-45N. And, to reflect the correction, we have placed Peary at the time Bartlett turned back at 135 miles from the Pole in lieu of the generally accepted 133 miles.

2. Scatter and Differential Refraction.

There are two interrelated characteristics of the several sets of sights from the 1909 expedition that will serve to indicate their *genuineness*. A necessary correction when making the calculations of a sight is that for refraction of the atmosphere. In the case of sights of the upper and lower limb of the sun, the correction is usually applied only once to an averaged altitude. However actual sights of the sun's upper limb and lower limb have different corrections for refraction, which, at very low altitudes, may be clearly identified, although usually inconsequential for navigational purposes.[19] This is called differential refraction. Figure II-10 is a picture taken recently out on the Arctic ice (courtesy of Dr. Robert Francois of the Applied Physics Laboratory of the University of Washington) that demonstrates the effect of differential refraction on the sun at low altitude, causing it to appear elliptical. Peary noted this same phenomenon in a report to the Peary Arctic Club in which he wrote: "At noon of March 5 the sun, red and shaped like a football by excessive refraction, just raised itself above the horizon for a few minutes and then disappeared again."

Figure II-10

---

[19] We hasten to point out that atmospheric refraction has no effect on the determination of *direction* from observations.

If a set of sights is manufactured, only a very sophisticated faker could be expected to take account of differential refraction, so the existence of it can be taken as a reasonably good indication of the genuineness of the sights. We will examine each set for evidence of differential refraction by comparing the sun's diameter as measured by the sights, with twice the value of the semi-diameter given in the *Nautical Almanac*. Any difference is evidence of the reality of the sights. Of course this difference in refraction will become smaller rapidly as the altitude of the sun increases.

For a set of several sights by one observer, one can expect some variation between the values of each of the sights. This phenomenon is called *scatter*, and is the second characteristic of the 1909 sights that we will take as evidence of genuineness. A plot of the sights should show that not all of the values are the same, and they should scatter randomly. The magnitude of the scatter is to some degree a characteristic of the individual observer and his experience. However in order to examine the true scatter of a set of sights we must first determine differential refraction and literally take it out of the sights.

Differential refraction has been calculated by comparing the average difference between sights of the upper and lower limbs, with twice the Almanac value for the sun's semi-diameter. In the tables that follow the value so determined has been indicated at the bottom of each. The two sets of Marvin's sights (which are clearly in his handwriting) show values of 37" and 64". Since they are on different days and at different temperatures, they are reasonable values for the sun's altitude at that time; a little over 5 degrees. Peary's sights, taken at a higher altitude (about six and one half degrees), show a value of 10". These are consistent with Marvin's sights as well as some 1900 sights of Peary's (at about nine and one half degrees) which we have analyzed for scatter comparisons. From this evidence we conclude that all of the sights show credible amounts of differential refraction.

In the tables below the refraction has been removed by splitting the differential refraction between the upper and lower limb sights, using the value from the refraction tables as the mid-point. This produces a set of values in which the upper limb sights and the lower limb sights should be equal, if it were not for scatter. Therefore a plot of the final values (H) should show whatever scatter is there.

Table II-5

Marvin I

St#	1 U	2 U	7 U	8 U	3 L	4 L	5 L	6 L
H	5-13-23	5-13-13	5-13-13	5-13-08	4-41-38	4-41-53	4-41-33	4-41-28
Rf	-9-31	-9-31	-9-31	-9-31	-10-08	-10-08	-10-08	-10-08
S	5-03-52	5-03-42	5-03-42	5-03-37	4-31-30	4-31-45	4-31-25	4-31-20
SD	-16-05	-16-05	-16-05	-16-05	+16-05	+16-05	+16-05	+16-05
H	4-47-47	4-47-37	4-47-37	4-47-32	4-47-35	4-47-50	4-47-30	4-47-25

(S = Sum)   Differential R = 37"

Table II-6

Marvin II

St#	1 U	2 U	7 U	8 U	3 L	4 L	5 L	6 L
H	5-33-27	5-33-37	5-33-32	5-33-47	5-02-22	5-02-27	5-02-37	5-02-32
Rf	-9-03	-9-03	-9-03	-9-03	-10-07	-10-07	-10-07	-10-07
S	5-24-24	5-24-34	5-24-29	5-24-44	4-52-15	4-52-20	4-52-30	4-52-25
SD	-16-05	-16-05	-16-05	-16-05	+16-05	+16-05	+16-05	+16-05
H	5-08-19	5-08-29	5-08-24	5-08-39	5-08-20	5-08-25	5-08-35	5-08-30

(S = Sum)   Differential R = 64"

Note: These sights are grouped by upper limbs and lower limbs for ease of refraction correction. The number above each column indicates the actual sequence in time and whether an upper (U) or lower (L) limb sight.

With the differential refraction corrected these sights can now be examined for scatter, which would otherwise be masked. Figure II-11 is a plot of these values and shows that the scatter of Marvin's sights is a credible 20", as would be expected of this careful observer under the arctic ambient. The scatter probably would not be there if they were worked backward (faked). They clearly are not "perfect" sights such as might be expected to be manufactured by a counterfeiter.

Figure II-12 is a plot of the Marvin II sights and shows a consistent pattern with those of Marvin I. The latitudes computed by averaging these sights will be essentially the same as those computed by Mitchell and Duvall in their report,[20] which is in Appendix B.

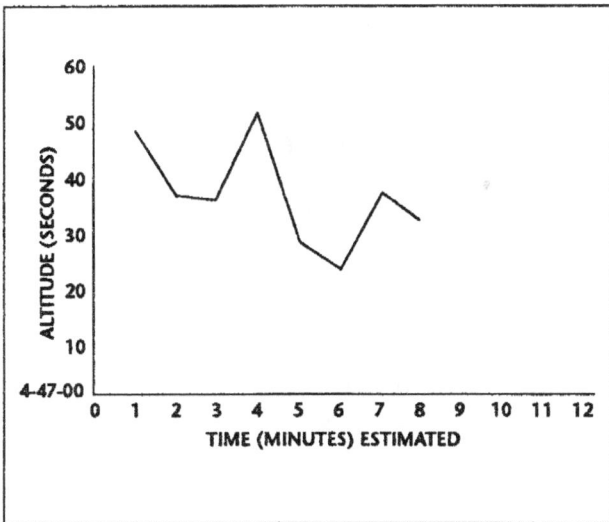

Figure II-11

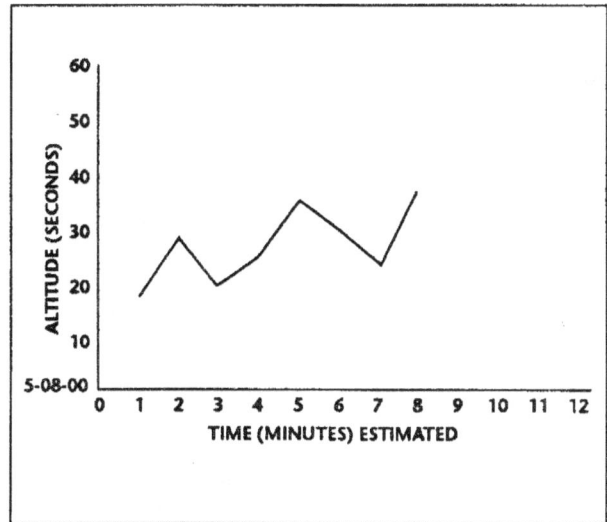

Figure II-12

---

[20] Since Bartlett records only the value at culmination, a similar analysis cannot be made for his sights.

The sights taken by Peary in the near vicinity of the Pole consist of a single sight taken at 1700 GMT April 6th, and three sets taken about 0500 GMT April 7th, 1100 GMT April 7th, and 1700 GMT, 1909. Each of the sets consists of two upper limbs and two lower limbs which were averaged to eliminate the sun's diameter, by Peary when doing the original reduction, and also by Mitchell and Duvall in their recomputation for the Congressional committee. For our purposes these are treated as 12 separate sights, correcting for differential refraction as explained above. A sight taken at 89-25 (noted in the 1909 Diary) was apparently not recorded so it cannot be analyzed nor can the above technique be applied to the single sight.

Differential refraction is evident in each set of sights in the amount of 10" of arc, as shown at the bottom line of the following tables. This number is about what would be expected at the value of altitude shown (6-37 to 6-48). In the tables differential refraction is eliminated as was done with Marvin's sights. Thus the corrected altitudes should show the scatter.

Table II-7 (set 2)

	1 (lower)	3 (lower)	2 (upper)	4 (upper)
H	6-37-30	6-37-40	7-09-40	7-09-30
Rf	-7-25	-7-25	-7-15	-7-15
Sum	6-30-05	6-30-15	7-02-25	7-02-15
SD	+16	+16	-16	-16
H	6-46-05	6-46-15	6-46-25	6-46-15

Differential R = 10"

Table II-8 (set 3)

	1 (lower)	3 (lower)	2 (upper)	4 (upper)
H	6-28-45	6-29-00	7-00-30	7-00-40
Rf	-7-34	-7-34	-7-24	-7-24
Sum	6-21-11	6-21-26	6-53-06	6-53-16
SD	+16	+16	-16	-16
H	6-37-11	6-37-26	6-37-06	6-37-16

Differential R = 10"

Table II-9 (set 4)

	1 (lower)	3 (lower)	2 (upper)	4 (upper)
H	6-40-10	6-40-00	7-11-45	7-11-55
Rf	-7-23	-7-23	-7-13	-7-13
Sum	6-32-47	6-32-37	7-04-32	7-04-42
SD	+16	+16	-16	-16
H	6-48-47	6-48-37	6-48-32	6-48-42

Differential R = 10"

Note: These sights are grouped by upper limb and lower limb for ease of refraction correction, as in the other tables.

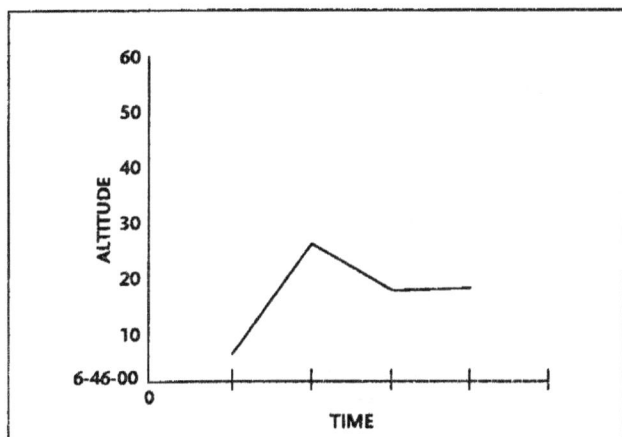

Figure II-13

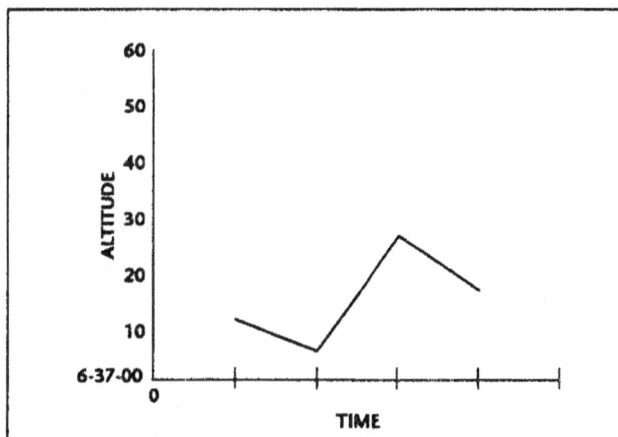

Figure II-14

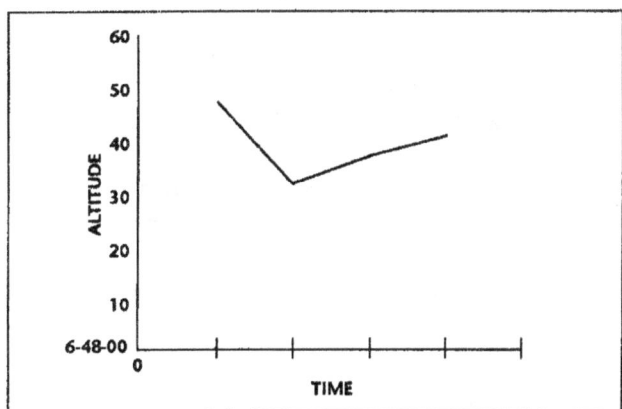

Figure II-15

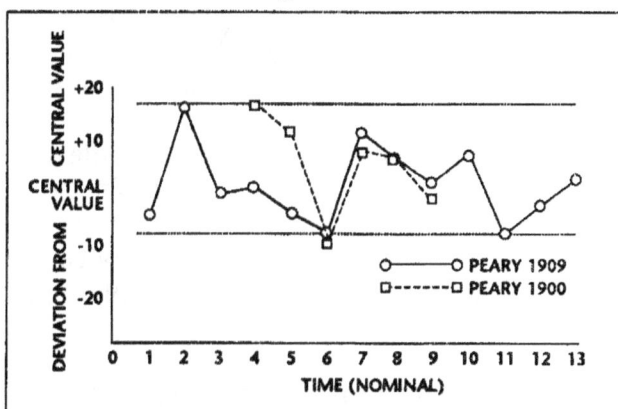

Figure II-16

Examination of Figures II-13, II-14 and II-15 shows that these scatters are representative of the land-based sextant/artificial horizon in the hands of an experienced user such as Peary. The very small sample size of the individual sets makes any suggestion of *randomness* hard to identify. Thus Figure II-16 was prepared, showing all three sets in sequence (with average values lined up so that location and declination differences can not generate false scatter) to suggest one longer set. Here "randomness" begins to show. In any event the measure of scatter for the aggregated set is about 21", a reasonable value for an experienced and careful surveyor-navigator like Peary.

For comparison with the scatter of the 12 polar sights Figure II-16 also includes a plot of 6 sights taken by Peary in 1900 while determining the longitude of Cape Washington. These sights are of a descending sun so the plot is actually of the *difference* of each sight from the "least squares" line through the set. They are of upper and lower limbs and there is a slight differential refraction correction (very small, about 2", since the altitude is over 9 degrees). The resulting measure of scatter is clearly consistent with Peary's sights at the Pole. Other available samples of his work are consistent.

These sights show the scatter that should be expected from the equipment employed and the experience of the observer. Mitchell and Duvall in their contemporaneous recomputation have shown that the sights are consistent with the change in declination of the sun and with location. In summary the Pole sights show realistic differential refraction and realistic scatter, two characteristics that might well be overlooked by any but the most sophisticated faker. Our analysis gives no basis for questioning their authenticity. Therefore our conclusion is that they are genuine.

I. Timekeeping on the 1909 Expedition

Considerations of some consequence are (a) what time was kept by the 1909 expedition, and (b) what were the sources of this time and how they were dealt with. There is entered in the record of the Congressional hearing of 1910 a letter from the John Bliss & Co of New York (who was the purveyor of Peary's two chronometers) which gives the calibrations of both before leaving New York in 1908, and upon returning in 1909. Although there were two chronometers, Mitchell and Duvall seem to have assumed that one (#2998) was the only one used. Based on this assumption, they showed a watch correction at the date of Peary's watch comparisons (departure from the *Roosevelt*) of 10 minutes fast when calculating the sun's declination from the Nautical Almanac. Of course this 10 minutes made only a trivial difference in the result of their sight reductions, and so has never been corrected.

Two modern critics of Peary, Herbert and Rawlins, have used this 10 minute chronometer error as the partial basis of a conclusion that he drifted off course and missed the Pole. The implicit assumption is, as ridiculous as it sounds, that Peary did not have enough experience with timepieces to know that their rates drifted unpredictably, and further that he was incapable of a correction by time sight before leaving his last land base. "Correct time" was of major importance to these critics because they tacitly assumed Peary would have adopted a navigation method which was dependent upon it. Since in our view of Peary's navigation technique, "correct time" was immaterial, it becomes of less importance. Nonetheless, we consider all aspects of Peary's timekeeping herein.

From the records of Peary's earliest polar expeditions, we found ample indications of his careful attention to his time and timepieces. There are innumerable "time-sights" used both to establish the longitude of locations that he was mapping (by the method of transport of chronometers as described in Chauvenet), and to "calibrate" or determine the correction for his chronometers and watches. In 1891 he purchased three watch-type chronometers which he had the manufacturer, the Howard Company of Boston, mount in a single aluminum casing. He carried them on all of his expeditions thereafter, and after each return, he sent them to the maker for cleaning, resetting and rating.

There are 1909 records of detailed "watch comparisons" on 6 separate days, from 15 to 21 February, prior to leaving the ship. These show there were 10 watches compared, set, and in some cases, adjusted. Besides the 3 Howard chronometer-watches, Peary had a Waltham, an Elgin and a special temperature-compensated Howard which the company had asked him to use on this trip. No record of a 1909 time sight has been located, so it seems that the ship's chronometers were the standard for these calibrations.

The *Roosevelt* had the rather unusual arrangement of having only two chronometers. Normally a ship carries three, with one treated as a master for comparison with the other two, so that if any one chronometer develops an unprecedented rate drift it can be easily determined which one it is. In the case of only two, as in the *Roosevelt*, the navigator can only average them when they drift apart, not knowing which is wrong. In our search of the National Archives we were not able to find the 1908-09 log of the *Roosevelt* but we do have the 1905-06 log (from the Ross Marvin collection at the Chemung County Historical Society, Elmyra, NY) The sample page of the log at Figure

II-17 clearly shows a daily comparison of the two chronometers showing that neither was considered a master; thus to set watches an average would have to be used.

Before the *Roosevelt* departed for the north on July 3, 1908, Bliss & Co. calibrated the two chronometers and reported as follows:

#2998 fast 25.8 sec. losing .2 sec/day

#3013 slow 1.6 sec. gaining .4 sec/day

Upon the return, on October 7, 1909, the following values were reported (461 days later):

#2998 fast 17min 12.9 sec, for 461 days gaining 2.2 sec/day.

#3013 slow 5 min 58.1 sec, for 461 days losing .8 sec/day.

Unfortunately Bliss & Co. did not establish the rate of each upon the return, but merely divided the total gain by the total time (461 days) and reported that as the rate. Yet it is obvious that #2998 could not always have been gaining 2.2 sec/day because on the first day their record shows it was losing .2 sec/day. So we have the start points and rates, but only the finish points, not the finish rates. In any event, chronometer drift is a common experience for navigators and that experience suggests that the rate of drift will be a curve, not the abrupt change of rate assumed by Bliss nor that implied by the straight line assumption of Mitchell.

The curves of Figure II-18 show the most probable drift of the chronometers. If Peary actually used these chronometers rather than a time sight as the basis for the calibration of his time pieces then at the mid-point of his calibrations, February 18, 1909, the two time pieces would probably be reading about 2m 30s fast (2998) and 1m 30s slow (3013) and the observer could only

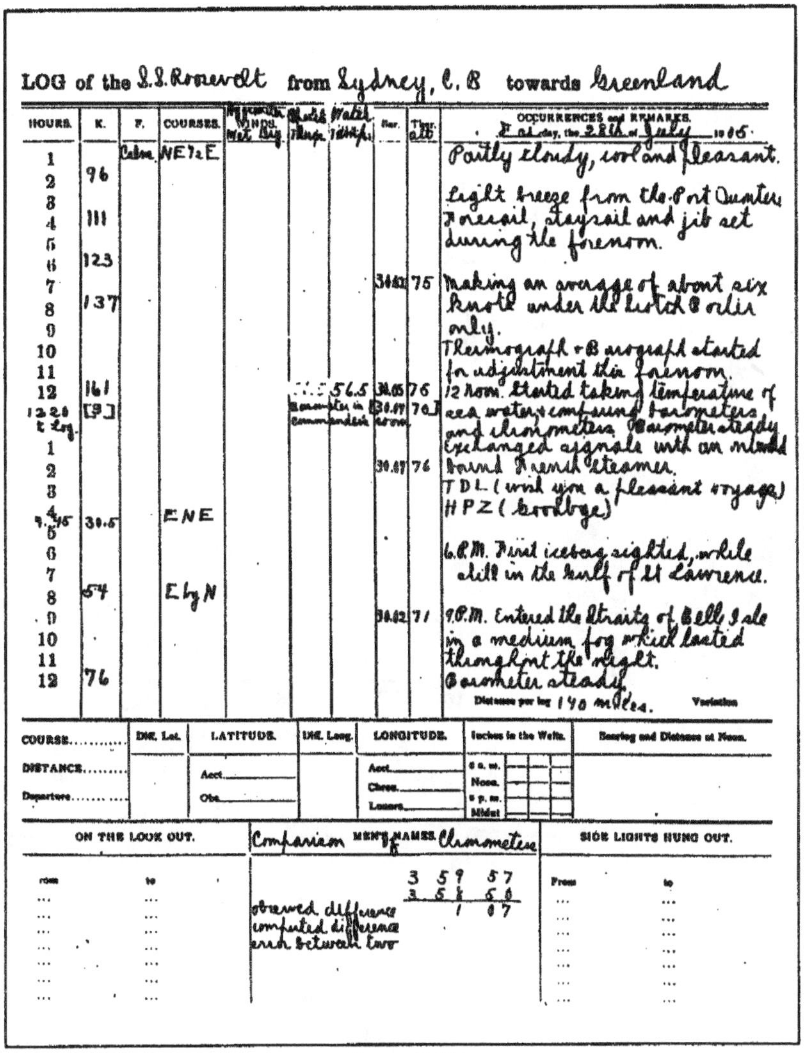
LOG of the S.S. Roosevelt from Sydney, C.B towards Greenland

OCCURRENCES and REMARKS. Friday, the 28th of July 1908

Partly cloudy, cool and pleasant.
Light breeze from the Port Quarter. Foresail, staysail and jib set during the forenoon.
Making an average of about six knots under the Scotch boiler only.
Thermograph & Barograph started for adjustment this forenoon.
12 Noon. Started taking temperature of sea water & comparing barometers and chronometers. Barometer steady.
Exchanged signals with an inward bound French steamer.
TDL (wish you a pleasant voyage)
HPZ (Goodbye)
6 P.M. First iceberg sighted, while still in the Gulf of St Lawrence.
9 P.M. Entered the Straits of Belle Isle in a medium fog which lasted throughout the night.
Barometer steady.
Distance per log 140 miles.

Comparison Chronometers

3 59 57
3 58 50
1 07

observed difference
computed difference
each between two

Figure II-17

average them for a value very close to the correct time. The use of the 1908 rates (the only rates Peary had) would have led to a value quite different from what appeared on the faces of the two instruments. This is illustrated in the table below.

At 12-00-00, 18 February 1909

Chronometer	By using 1908 rates	Most Probable
#2998	11-59-40	12-02-30
#3013	12-01-30	11-58-30
#3013 minus #2998	(+) 1m-50	(-) 4m-00

If the two timepieces showed the probable values, it was obvious to any user that their rates had drifted substantially from those determined before departure from New York in 1908. The predicted difference was (+) 1 m - 56 s while the actual probably was (-) 4m - 00 s, more than 5 minutes difference. Clearly the user would know that the drifts had deviated, and that with only two chronometers it was impossible to tell which was off: The two values would therefore be averaged, giving a time of 12-00-30, only about 30 seconds fast. It does not appear that this time *was* used for steering, but *if* it was used, it would have produced an error of about one eighth of a degree.

In summary it is clear that Peary had a good practical understanding of the importance of time for both surveying and navigation, that he used his chronometers properly (he kept the three-piece set in a special pocket in his arctic underwear where it would be near body temperature) and that he was completely capable of getting time by celestial observations when needed. The ship's chronometers, as we have shown, were probably only about 30 seconds off when Peary set his watches. This slight error could not have had any significant effect on his steering on the trek to the Pole. In Section C, we established that his steering was independent of correct time. Thus we can say that whatever small error there was in the *Roosevelt* chronometers did not affect Peary's ability to maintain his course for the Pole.

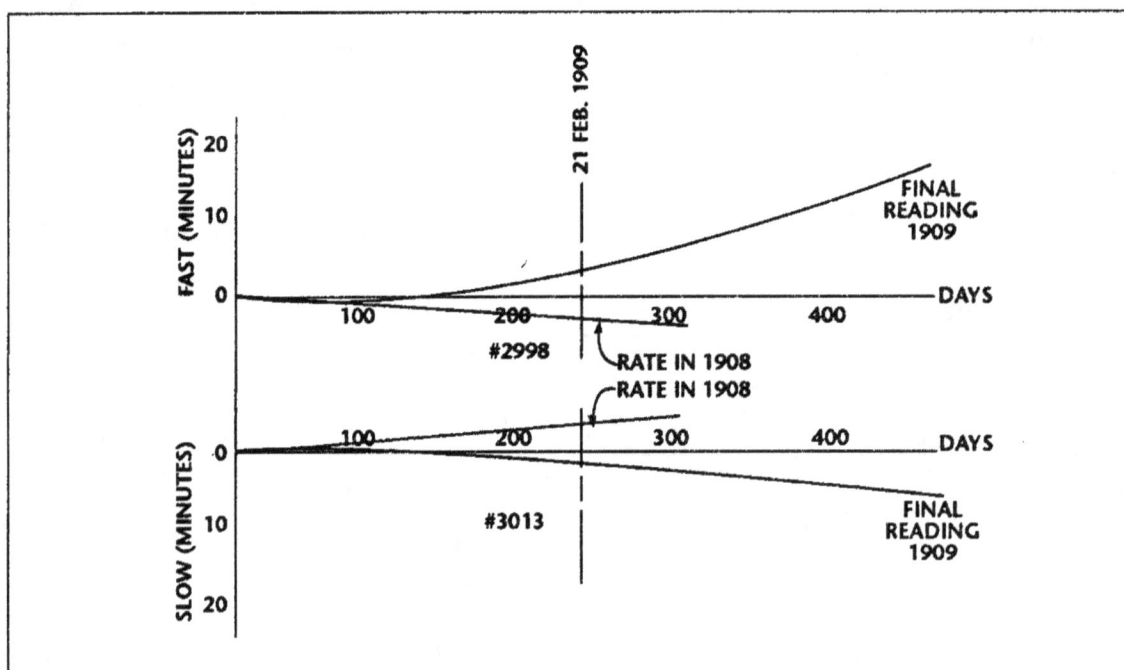

Fig. 11-18

Part Three

PEARY'S SLEDGING SPEED AND DISTANCES

The second of the two major arguments relied on by Peary's critics is that the distances he claims to have travelled on each march from Camp Bartlett at 87-45 North and back are unbelievably high, both in absolute terms and in relation to the daily distances that the expedition had logged prior to April 1st. In terms of "nautical miles made good," the stripped down polar expedition covered the 135 mile distance from Camp Bartlett to the Pole in five marches averaging about 27 miles per march, at an average speed of about 2.5 nautical miles per hour. On the return trip, the same distance was covered in three forced marches, with only brief stops for food and rest, averaging about 45 miles per march at an average speed of about 2.8 nautical miles per hour.

Peary defended his claimed distances before the subcommittee of the House Naval Affairs Committee in the 1911 Congressional Hearings that passed upon his claim of attaining the Pole, promoted him, and accorded him the "Thanks of Congress."[1] We consider below the explanations he offered that were ultimately accepted by a majority of the committee. First, however, let us point out that some important witnesses were missing from those hearings.

Unfortunately, Henson, who with his years of sledging experience was as good a judge of miles made good as anyone, was not called before the committee because he was a Negro. But Henson, in *Dark Companion* and *A Negro Explorer At The North Pole*, and in innumerable interviews he gave over the remainder of his eighty-eight year life span, consistently maintained that he and Peary went *all the way* to the Pole together.[2]

---

[1] The matter of Peary's distances was brought up again in the House debates in 1916 upon Congressman Helgesen's bill that would have rescinded these honors. We will confine our discussion to the 1911 hearings, however, since Peary did not publicly respond to Congressman Helgesen's charges.

[2] Many of Peary's critics, who use Henson's minor inconsistencies in his telling and retelling of the polar venture, are prone to overlook this fundamental truth.

It was he, Henson claimed, who decided when the party had covered the distance from Camp Bartlett to the Pole and commenced the construction of the northernmost camp, Camp Jesup, forty five minutes before Peary arrived there.

Terris Moore, mountaineer, navigator, explorer and erstwhile Lieutenant Governor of Alaska, who knew Henson over a period of twenty years, tells us that Henson was a credible witness to the distances Peary claimed. In "Charge of Hoax Against Robert E. Peary Examined" (*Alpine Journal*,1983), Moore criticizes and responds to "hoax" advocate David Roberts in *Great Exploration Hoaxes* (Published by the Sierra Club, 1982). He offers the following observations in response to Robert's charge that "Matt Henson and Eskimos were not credible witnesses for Peary after Bartlett's turnaround from 87-47:"

> In *Great Exploration Hoaxes*, Roberts introduces Matthew Henson, refers to him as "Peary's oldest accomplice, a former manservant ...neither the Eskimos nor Henson knew how to take observations of latitude and longitude ...was Matthew Henson privy to the fraud? Rawlins thinks not." The book condescends: "Like the Eskimos, Henson had no independent way of knowing whether he was at the Pole or not." It then asserts: "He never actually confirmed the astounding sledging distances claimed by Peary."

> Sorry to have to differ again,[3] but Matt Henson *did* know how to determine latitude and longitude, and *did* confirm Peary's sledging distances ...

> Matt did know how to determine latitude and longitude from solar sights at the noon and midnight meridian passages. Professor Ross Marvin of Cornell's College of Engineering taught him this during the winter of 1908-9 aboard the *Roosevelt*.

Moore believes that Henson was in on the last sextant reading at the Pole, quoting from Bradley Robinson's *Dark Companion*:

> "Matt lay in the snow beside Peary writing down his readings as Peary called them off. At last Peary snapped shut the vernier, rested his eyes a moment, picked up the pad with Matt's figures, and finished his calculations."

> The Eskimos had been astonished and quite let down ...that nothing tangible or even different was to be seen. "We have found what we hunt," Matt said to Ootah. Bewildered, Ootah

---

[3] Moore had already responded to Roberts' allegation that "Peary did not make longitude determinations necessary to steering the sledges true north," explaining how "Peary's method was actually the same simplified navigational method employed by Amundsen and his navigators in their attainment of the South Pole in 1911." Moore had also rebutted Robert's assertion that Peary's dog-sledging speeds and "impossible distances" are "proof enough that Peary failed to reach the Pole." In particular he took exception to the remark, "Certainly no one since has been able to approach Peary's apparent sledging times." Moore pointed out that the Iditarod drivers, in the 1,047 mile race from Anchorage to Nome, Alaska, "have consistently done over 75 miles per day carrying sleeping gear, tent, and the necessary food provisions."

stared. Finally he shrugged: "There is nothing here. Just
ice, just ice."

Returning to Peary, Matt found him lying on his, Matt's
sledge, "utter exhaustion engraved on the man's face.
Now that his goal had been reached, the energy with which
he had driven himself ... had suddenly abandoned him.
Touching Peary's shoulder lightly, Matt held out his
hand. "Let me be the first to congratulate you, sir."
Peary shook Matt's hand weakly and lay back on the
sledge ... "Let us go home, Matt, let us go home."
This is what Hensen remembers.

Variations of these incidents and these words abound in the ghostwritten stories
of Henson's life. Which versions are more authentic than others is immaterial here.
What is significant is that Henson *did* affirm Peary's distances by affirming that he and
the Eskimos had reached the goal that Peary was seeking, as the words excerpted above
indicate.[4]

The four Eskimos, Ootah, Ooqueah, Seegloo and Egingwah also were credible
witnesses, for they knew which way was north from observing the sun, and were keen
judges of distances because of their nomadic existence in their arctic homeland. On
April 2, Peary noted in his diary: "Have no doubt we have covered 30 miles but will be
conservative and call it 25. My Eskimos say they have come as far [as] from the *Roosevelt*
to Porter Bay. This, by our winter route, scales 35 miles on the chart." Obviously,
estimating distances to them was a matter of comparing distances between known
points, but at the end of each march, they had a keen sense of the party's progress north
based on the ice conditions encountered along the way.

In November, 1934, several years after the Reverend James Gordon Hayes'
vitriolic *Robert Edwin Peary* (1929) was published, Danish author and explorer Peter
Freuchen wrote a long letter to his friend, Vilhjalmur Stefansson, telling of his talks
with Ootah (the then only living survivor of Peary's Eskimos) and other of Peary's
Eskimos within their lifetimes. Freuchen stated:

[As] to the foolish accusal against Peary done by Gordon
Hayes, I find it kind of funny that anybody cares what
he says.

I know from the stories of the natives that Peary reached
the point he told them was the Pole in excellent condition.
He was favored by many things: Good going, good dogs, the
very best natives and exceptional good weather. Furthermore
he had during his many years developed such a technique
as a traveler that is far beyond the understanding of Hayes.
He had his system of travelling completed from many un-
successful expeditions. The natives say he had his men

---

[4] David Roberts' answer to Terris Moore, whom he describes as a friend and "one of my mountain climbing heroes" was: "I wonder then whether Moore's unstinting loyalty to Matthew Henson —who was *his* hero and friend —has not helped persuade Terris that Peary's critics have a thin case." He admits to knowing less about navigation than his friend and suggests that "the interested student should read Rawlins."

trained from childhood ... they all wanted to do what he wished; it was not only employer and his men, they were *friends.*

Only one of them is left now; the oldest, Odark [Ootah]. The others are dead; Iggianguark, Ukujark, Sigdlu (as we spell them in Greenland.) They have told me time after time about it...

They could have travelled much longer, they always liked to tell (emphasis supplied), but they were at the very spot Peary displayed his happiness so evident that everyone could understand he was where he wanted to be during the many years.

Now, let us turn to Peary's own account of the trip to the Pole as he gave it to the Congressional committee:

A. Peary on the Record

From his diary entry of April 1, 1909, Peary read aloud to the committee:

After about 4 hour's sleep everyone turned out at 5 a.m. [I] announced which 2 Eskimos ... are to go back from here with the captain, culled the best dogs from their teams to replace poorer ones in the other teams, repaired sledges thoroughly with the material from one broken up, and rearranged loads, compacting everything. Captain went north some 5 miles in forenoon, returning took latitude observation (87 46 49) ... Then left with his 2 men, 1 sledge and 18 dogs.

We are ready now for the final lap of the journey, sledges thoroughly overhauled and strengthened, dogs the pick of 133, and dogs and men in training. It is the time for which I have reserved all my energies, and I feel tonight as if I was in trim and equal to the demands upon me of the next few days.

Assuming the captain's figures to be correct, we are 133 miles from the pole. Eight marches same average as our last will do the trick.[5]

Weather clear, north wind continuous, temperature in -30's Today the sky, the light drifting snow, the hazy horizon, the biting character of the wind at not excessive low temperatures, *everything except the surface of the ice* are the replica of ice-cap weather.

---

[5] Critics have distorted these words to mean that it was impossible for Peary with his stripped down party and lighter loads, given breaks in the weather and ice conditions, to cover the approximate 133 mile distance to the Pole in five long marches instead of eight. We frankly do not see how the words can be construed in this way.

I do not regret the wind, though it has stolen some of our miles, for it will close up everything behind us for the captain and others still out on the ice.

Continuing, Peary read from his entry of April 2:

Eight hours' sound, warm refreshing sleep. Left camp 5 a.m., leaving others to break camp and follow. A fine morning; clear; temperature -25. Wind of last day subsided. *Going the best and most equable of any day yet.*

Large old floes, hard and level, with patches of sapphire blue ice (the pools of last summer), and surrounded by pressure ridges, *some of which almost stupendous yet easily negotiable* either through some convenient gap or up the slope of some huge drift ...

Came on at a good clip for about 4 hours, when the sledges overtook me ... Kept the pace for 10 hours. Have no doubt we covered 30 miles, but will be conservative and call it 25. My Eskimos say we have come as far from the *Roosevelt* to Porter Bay. This, by our winter route, scales 35 miles on the chart.

Whatever the distance is, we are likely, now that the wind has ceased, to retain what we have made. It is possible that with release from wind pressure the ice may rebound some and return us some of the hard-earned miles it stole from us yesterday and the day before. In any event we are beyond the 88th parallel, and *I am a tired and satisfied man.*

While building igloos a long lead forms south and southeast of us some miles distant as shown by water clouds. *Dogs show effect of yesterday's rest.*

On April 3, Peary continued reading from his diary:

Got on the trail 3 hours earlier this morning after a small sleep ... Weather fine, clear and calm. Ice as yesterday, except at beginning of march it was rougher, requiring use of pickaxes. This and a brief delay at a narrow lead cut our distances some. Ten hours (20 miles) half way to 89 degrees. Dogs frequently on trot.

Some gigantic rafters, but not in our path. Ice grinding audibly in various directions, but no visible motion. Either twisting into equilibrium after the wind, or else the spring tides. (Full moon about tomorrow)

Yesterday's lead to E. & S.E. closed up or crusted over. A similar one visible W. & N.W. during early part of march.

Then, quoting from his April 4 entry:

> Hit the trail again before midnight after a short sleep.
> If weather holds good, should be able to get in the extra
> march. The day a duplicate of day before yesterday as to
> weather and going. The latter even better. *The surface is*
> as even (except for the pressure ridges) as the glacial
> *fringe from Hecla to Columbia, & harder.* Something over
> ten hours on a direct course, dogs often on the trot,
> occasionally on the run. 25 miles.
>
> Near end of march, crossed a hundred yard lead on thin
> young ice. As I ran ahead to guide the dogs obliged to
> slide my feet and travel wide, bear style... The men let
> sledges and dogs come on by themselves & came gliding
> across where they could. The last two came in on all fours.
>
> *Am tired but satisfied with my progress.* We are in sight
> of 89. Give me three more days of this weather.
>
> Temperature at beginning of march -40; put all poorest dogs
> in one team tonight and began expending them.

Peary's next entry, on April 5, shows his increasing expectations of a victory on this last try for the Pole:

> Over the 89th!! Started early last evening. The march a
> duplicate of the previous one as to weather and going.
> Temperature at startling -88. Sledges appeared to haul
> a little easier, dogs on trot much of the time. *Last*
> *two hours on young ice on a north-south lead* they were
> often galloping. 10 hours, 25 miles or *more. Great.*
>
> A 50-yd. lead open when I reached it, moved enough by
> the time the sledges came up to let us cross. Still
> biting cold ...the natives complain of it. Light air
> from S. during first part of march, veering to E. and
> freshening as we camp. Another dog expended here.
>
> Tomorrow if ice & weather permit, I shall make a long
> march, "boil the kettle" midway, and try to make up for
> the 5 miles lost on the 3rd.
>
> We have been very fortunate with the leads so far, but I
> am in constant & increasing dread of encountering an
> uncrossable one. Six weeks today since I left the
> *Roosevelt.*

On April 6, Peary recorded:

On the trail before midnight,[6] though I gave the party more
sleep at this camp than at the previous ones, as we were
all needing it; but I wanted to make the next camp in time
for a noon sight if the sun was visible ... Weather thick
like the last march before Marvin turned back. A dense
lifeless pall of grey overhead, almost black at the
horizon, & ice ghastly chalky white with no relief. Like
the ice cap and just the thing an artist would paint for
a polar ice-scape.

The going better than ever, hardly any snow on the hard
granular, last summer's surface of the old floes, the
blue lakes larger. The rise in temperature to -15 has
reduced the friction of the sledges 25% & gives the dogs
appearance of having caught the spirit of the party.
The more spritely ones as they trot along with tightly
curved tails, repeatedly toss their heads with short
barks and yelps.

12 hours on a direct course (30) miles. Can I wait to cover
those other 5? ... The thick weather gives me less concern
than it might had I not been forehanded yesterday
and fearing a cloud bank in the south took a latitude sight
(89 25)[7] This is 2 miles ahead of my dead reckoning &
indicates that I have been conservative in my estimates
as I intended, or that the ice has slackened back, or both.
The wind, which was from the east when we started,
gradually veered to the south and died away. While we were
in camp it blew fresh from the east for some hours.
Temperature when we arrived at the camp (10 a.m.) -11.

Peary interrupted his reading here, stating with some hesitancy: "I have this
entry, after we had built our igloos and entered them:"

The pole at last!!! The prize of 3 centuries, my dream and
ambition for 23 years.

Here he stopped: "I do not care to read this... It sounds a bit foolish to be reading
it oneself." Mr. Roberts insisted, however, that the words be put in the record to make
a continuous narrative inasmuch as they had already appeared in *The North Pole*. Accordingly, Peary continued:

Mine at last. I cannot bring myself to realize it. It all
seems so simple and commonplace ...

---

[6] Since on arctic expeditions intervals of time are recorded in terms of "marches" rather than days, the dates
and corresponding marches become a little confusing from here on. Note that this last march before reaching
the Pole began "before midnight" (i.e.on April 5) and the party arrived at Camp Jesup at 10 A.M. the following
morning (April 6).

[7] This sight has been the subject of controversy because it is not mentioned in *The North Pole* and the reductions do not appear in the "proofs" Peary submitted for expert evaluation. Henson told Bradley Robinson that
the observation was taken. *Dark Companion*, p. 223.

Peary resumed, continuing to read from the same entry:

> Light breeze from the west after our arrival. Just caught
> the sun through the clouds at 12:45 (89°- 57'); again ahead
> of reckoning. Sun disappeared again until about 8 p.m.,
> then cleared away brilliantly, the west wind still
> continuing. Eskimos rebuilding sledges. Drove on 10 miles
> with double team dogs, two Eskimos. Observation at 1 a.m.
> (89°- 50' on other side) ... took some photos and then back
> to camp.

He then read from his entry for April 7:

> Spent day with light sledge, double team, going east and
> west. Noon observation and looking for a crack where a
> sounding would be possible. Leave 4 p.m., 30 hours.
> Minimum temperature, -32; maximum, -11; at starting, -25.
> Impossible to find place to sound; 5 miles south from
> camp 1500 fathoms, no bottom, lose lead and wire.

This concluded the diary entries Peary had made before starting back to Cape Columbia on April 7. He had made no entry for April 8, he informed the committee. From his entry on April 9, he read:

> A wild day, strong NNE (true) wind, increasing to a gale.
> Temperature -18 to -22. All upward leads greatly widened
> and new ones forward, one north of 88th at least a mile
> wide. *All covered with practicable young ice.* Last half
> of march ice raftering under and all about us under
> pressure of the gale. Dogs scudding before it, most of
> the time on a gallop. Would have been impossible to travel
> except before the gale and following a trail.
>
> Ice going south with us. There has been no lateral movement
> yet.
>
> From here to the pole and back has been one glorious sprint
> with a savage finish. Its results due to hard work, little
> sleep, much experience, first-class equipment, and good
> fortune as regards weather and open water.[8]

The committee took a break for lunch, then commenced questioning Peary.

> Mr. Englebright: What was your best day's travel in your
> Arctic trip either coming or going?
>
> Captain Peary: The best day's travel was on the second march on
> the return from the pole.

---

[8] Peary's three forced marches back to Camp Bartlett took place between 4 p.m. April 7 and 12:30 a.m. on April 10.

Mr. Englebright: How far did you go?
Captain Peary: Fifty geographical miles, estimated.

Mr. Englebright: In one march?

Captain Peary: In one march. The second best marches were the one after that and the last two marches from Cape Columbia to the ship.

Peary volunteered:

> The weather was not bad. The character of the ice was as
> we had experienced it going up ... The men were in good
> condition. The dogs were in good condition. They had
> double rations at the pole twice. We had lightened our
> load in every possible way. We threw away some items of
> clothing and had gotten rid of the sounding apparatus.
> We had the trail to follow and the igloos.[9]

Peary acknowledged that he could not say exactly how many hours were required for that longest (50) mile march since he had made no diary entry. He recalled: "We travelled until we reached the [second] igloo, and went into it and made tea." At the first igloo, he said, they had stopped only for a short time for tea and lunch.

Here a statement by the Assistant Postmaster General regarding the speeds of dogsled teams on Alaskan mail routes of 500 miles or more was entered into the record, prompting the congressmen to ask how Peary how his dogs compared to Alaskan Eskimo dogs. Peary responded:

> I cannot say that they [the Alaskan dogs] are precisely the
> same kind of dogs, because the dog of the Whale Sound region
> is not as much interbred as the dog of any other place,
> either South Greenland, or Alaska, or Labrador, and
> consequently they are nearer to the type of the Arctic wolf.

When asked whether his dogs knew they were on the route home, Peary replied:

> I think every dog did. An Eskimo dog certainly knows when he
> is following a trail. We have an idea that an Eskimo dog
> knows when he is pointed home. He knows enough to know when
> he is pointed back the way he has come.

Peary volunteered that all returning members of his expedition had made remarkably fast trips on homeward bound journey as compared to the outbound journey, when the main party was travelling together:

---

[9] Bartlett's diary indicates that he had been able to follow the old trail to within 45 miles of Cape Columbia. From there he had made a new trial, which Peary testified that he was able to follow when he came along. He thus had an unbroken trail for the entire return trip.

Borup returned [for supplies] in 1 march over 3 outward marches. MacMillan returned in 4 marches over 7 outward marches. Borup returned in 7 marches over 12 outward marches. Bartlett returned in 13 marches over 22 outward marches. Peary returned in 16 marches over 27 outward marches.

While on the subject of distances, Peary was queried about his normal sledge weights and loads on the expedition as follows:

Mr. Roberts: What is the weight of the sledge itself?

Captain Peary: My impression is that it was eighty-odd pounds. Each sledge would vary some.

Mr. Roberts: What weight did you carry on these sledges on this trip?

Captain Peary: Of course none were weighed — we had no facilities — but from Cape Columbia in no instance did the weight of a single sledge exceed about 500 pounds. The standard load ... as the unit for heavy work of a man and a team of 8 dogs, would be a sledge weighing less than 100 pounds and a total gross load on the sledge not to exceed 500 pounds at the start.

At one point Mr. Roberts asked the question that was uppermost in many of the members' minds: "I am going to take the liberty of asking you why, when you went to the pole on your final dash, you did not take with you some of the members of your party in order that there might be credible corroborative evidence if the question was ever raised as to your attaining the pole?"

Peary answered frankly: *First*: "I have always made my final spurt work up there, with the one exception when Lee was with me across the Greenland ice cap, with one man and the Eskimos...the man I took with me was more effective for the combined demands of extended work than any white man I have ever had with me."

Second: "The pole was something to which I had devoted my life; it was a thing on which I had concentrated everything, on which I had expended myself, for which I had gone through such hell and suffering as I hope no man in this room may ever experience, and in which I had put money, time and everything else. I did not feel that under those circumstances I was called upon to divide with a man who, no matter how able and deserving he might be, was a young man and had only put in a few years of that kind of work and who had, frankly as I believed, not the right that I had to it."

What had been left unsaid was that in addition to being a young man, Robert Bartlett was a Newfoundlander — in those days an Englishman — and that Peary also believed that the honor of being the first at the Pole should go to an American. He knew also that this was what his sponsors, the members of the Peary Arctic Club, had hoped for in backing him financially.

Mr. Macon made it plain that he was not satisfied with Peary's explanation:

> Mr. Macon. Now Captain, at the risk of incurring the displeasure of some of the members of the committee, I want to ask you again why it was that when you concluded to find the pole that you rid yourself of every white man who had any knowledge, any astronomical knowledge and experience in the northern regions, and sent them back and only took one Negro and four Eskimos with you to testify to your work?
>
> Captain Peary. I think I answered that.
>
> Mr. Macon. So I will ask you this question: You know that Columbus discovered the West India Islands and that he had quite a party that accompanied him and that none of them shared the glory of the discovery with him...[and so on, naming Americus Vespucius [sic], Magellan and Desoto ... I want to ask why you feared that Captain Bartlett would share the discovery of the pole with you when you were the leader of the Peary Arctic expedition?
>
> Captain Peary. I do not recall that I considered while north those particular examples that you give, but I thought of the sharing that would be inevitable under those conditions.

Here Peary plainly was thinking of the international race for the Pole that had gone on for decades, and the emphasis that was placed on "priority" Macon's example were not analgous. But Peary did not elucidate. He simply repeated, "It would have been inevitable under the circumstances."

Mr. Macon went on to make the point that Henson and the Eskimos were not only ignorant of navigation, but were pliant to Peary's will:

> Mr. Macon. I believe you said, Captain, that the Eskimos that you selected to go with you to the pole would walk through hell with you if you said so...
>
> Captain Peary. I think those men would go with me out on the ice as far as I went, even if they felt pretty satisfied in their own minds that their ever coming back to land was a doubtful question. That is my opinion.
>
> Chairman Butler. [To Mr. Macon] Of course that statement presupposes that there is a hell.
>
> Mr. Macon. And it presupposes they would say whatever the Captain told them to say and abide by it.

Before leaving the subject of the Congressional hearings, it should be noted that Dr. Gilbert Grosvenor, of the National Geographic Society, submitted a statement which provided helpful comparisons between Peary's distances travelled on his polar trip and distances travelled on his previous expeditions which demonstrated that the former were not remarkable for him. Said Dr. Grosvenor, for the record: "Anyone who cares to take the time and trouble can verify these figures and will find the following results"

Peary's average distance from Cape Columbia to where Bartlett turned back was 12.8 miles. Had it not been for the north wind two days setting them back, this average would have been thirteen and two thirds miles. Between two observations taken by Marvin the average of three marches was sixteen and two thirds miles. Several of the marches were 20 miles.

His average, from the time Bartlett left him, to the pole was 26 miles. His average on his return was 25.6 miles.

For comparison with the above figures, as showing that these averages were not at all excessive, the following facts can be taken from the narrative of the last expedition and the previous ones.

Peary's last two marches on the return, from Cape Columbia to the *Roosevelt* were 45 miles each. On this and previous expeditions the journey from Cape Hecla to the *Roosevelt*, a distance of 45 to 50 miles was made in one march ... The march from the *Roosevelt* to Porter Bay, a distance of 35 miles, was repeatedly made in 8, 10 and 12 hours. MacMillan and Borup returning from Cape Morris Jesup to the *Roosevelt* made the distance of 250 miles or more in 8 marches, an average of over 31 miles a march.

Peary, in one of his earlier expeditions, made the distance from Cape Wilkes to Cape D'Urville, a distance of 65 to 70 miles in one march. He repeatedly made the march from Cape D'Urville to Cape Fraser, a distance of 40 miles, in one march, and in the winter of 1899-1900 traveled from Etah to a point in Robertson Bay, 60 miles distant, in less than 12 hours.

On his return from Independence Bay to Bowdoin Bay, Peary averaged 20 miles a day for 25 successive marches, 210 miles in 7 successive marches (an average of 30 miles a day), making the last march of 40 miles, all these with dogs not driven with Eskimo drivers.

On more than one occasion in the fall of 1900, Peary's parties went from Lake Hazen to Fort Conger, distances of 50 miles ... overland in one march. This after the sun had set for the winter.

In February, 1899, before the sun returned, Peary (with both feet frozen six weeks before, sledged from Conger to Cape D'Urville, a distance of over 200 miles in 11 marches, in an average temperature of 53 1/2 below zero, an average of

about 20 miles. In March of 1902 he went from Cape Sabine to
Fort Conger, a distance of 250 to 300 miles as traveled, in
12 marches, and average of 21 to 25 miles, and later covered
the same distance again in 11 marches, an average of 22 to
27 miles.

Dr. Grosvenor added for good measure:

In the history of polar explorations no one has had so much
and such long continued training in ice work as Peary; his
speed is the result of long years of practice, resulting in
great physical endurance and skill in the use of the sledge.

B. Peary's Speeds and Distances Analyzed

In the years since the Congressional hearings, beginning with Captain Hall's vituperative *Has the North Pole Been Discovered?*, published in 1917, and continuing through Wally Herbert's *Noose Of Laurels* in 1989, Peary's critics have continued to maintain that the distances he claimed were impossible, or at least highly unlikely. But with the exception of Herbert (who as a rival for Peary's laurels cannot be considered entirely objective), none of them appears to have had any sledging experience. Nor have any of the critics produced any in-depth study of the speeds and distances recorded by Peary on previous expeditions or by other arctic explorers, such as we attempt here.

In Table III-1 we have compiled from Peary's 1909 diary, his daily distances per march on the entire trek from Cape Columbia and back. In Table III-2, we have collected from Peary's books, *Northward Over The "Great Ice"* and *Nearest The Pole*, the distances recorded on his earlier expeditions. In Table III-3, we have compared Peary's distances with those achieved by other sledgers. Since distances that can be covered by dogsledge in a day are highly variable, depending upon the skill of the driver, the condition of the dogs, the total weight of the sledge, weather and ice conditions and the number of hours marched, insofar as possible, we have considered all these factors in our comparative analyses.

All mileages are expressed as nautical miles "made good" as was customary with Peary and most of the other polar explorers. No amounts are added to reflect detours[10] around leads or hummocks. Though we realize, of course, that such detours are unavoidable, they are variable and cannot be calculated with any degree of precision.

As noted above, there are two separate issues with respect to Peary's sledging distances over the Arctic Ocean ice: *First*, critics have attempted to impeach his speed on the "final dash" to the Pole by reference to the lesser speeds recorded during the earlier portion of the expedition. Like certain minority members of the committee, they attribute his claimed increases after April 1 to the fact that he had sent back all

---

[10] As Wally Herbert acknowledges in *The Noose of Laurels* (p. 269), there is "an element of uncertainty in the question of detours."

Table III-1

Basic Statistics from Peary's Diary

Date	March	Distance	Hours	Speed	Cumulative Distance
Mar. 1	1	4			
	2	2			15-20
3	3				
4	4				40
5	-				
6	-				
7	-				
8	-				
9	-				
10	-				
11	5	16			57
12	6	12			
13	7	12			
14	-				
15	8				
16	9				
17	10				
18	11	15	12	1.3	
19	12	12			136
20	-				
21	13		7		
22	14	15	10	1.5	161
23	15	15	9	1.7	
24	16	15			
25	17	20	7.5	2.7	211
26	18	15			
27	19	12	6	2.0	
28	20	12	6	2.0	
29	-				
30	21	20			
31	22	23			
Apr. 1	-				278
2	23	25+	10	2.5	
3	24	20	10	2.0	
4	25	25	10	2.5	
4-5	26	25	10	2.5	
5-6	27	30	12	2.5	132

Return (travel at the pole omitted)

Date	March	Distance	Hours	Speed	Cumulative Distance
Apr. 7	1				
8	2				
9-10	3	15			132
10	4	23	(captains last)		
11	5	15	(lunch at lead igloo)		
12-13	6	18			200
13-14	7	30	(Camp Nansen)		230
14-15	8				
15-16	9				
16-17	10				
17-18	11				
18-19	12				
19-20	13	24	13		303
20-21	14	10			
21-22	15	12			
22-23	16				410

Table III-2

Record of Peary's Sledging Distances per March

Trip/Distance	Dates	Marches (or days)	Avg. Dist (per march)
1898 - 99			
C. Hawkes to C. Lawrence	12/20 12/28		
C. Lawrence to Ft. Conger (220 mi.)	12/29 1/6	9	24.4
Ft. Conger to C. Hawkes (220 mi.) (Dark, Peary crippled, dogs in poor condition)	2/18 2/29	11	20.0
C. Hawkes to Ft. Conger (220 mi.) (Peary still crippled)	4/18 4/29	11	20.0
Ft. Conger to C. Hawkes (220 mi.) (Light loads)	5/23 5/29	6	36.7
1899 - 1900			
Etah to Whale Sound area and Return — 210 n.m. (50 to 60 mi. on first and last marches)	Dec. '99	6	35
Etah to Ft. Conger by way of C. Sabine (300 mi.)	3/4 3/28	19	15.8
Ft. Conger to Lockwood I. (260 mi.)	4/11 5/18	27 d.	9.6/d
Lockwood I. to C. Jesup (40 mi.)		4	10.0
C. Jesup to C. Bridgman (39 mi.)		1	39.0
North to 83-50 (12 mi.)		4	3.0
Return from 83-53 (15 mi.)		1	12.0
C. Washington to C. North		4	
C. North to C. Bryant		1 (25 hr.)	

Trip/Distance	Dates	Marches (or days)	Avg. Dist (per march)
(fog)			
C. Bryant to Blackhorn Cliffs		3	
Blackhorn Cliffs to Ft. Conger		4	
total 260 mi.		12	21.7

1900 - 1901

Trip/Distance	Dates	Marches (or days)	Avg. Dist (per march)
Ft. Conger to Lincoln Bay and return (150 mi.)	4/5 4/13	8	18.7
Ft. Conger to Payer H. (260 mi.)	4/17 5/6	19	13.7

1901 - 1902

Trip/Distance	Dates	Marches (or days)	Avg. Dist (per march)
Payer H. to Ft. Conger (260 mi.)	3/6 3/20	12	21.7
Ft. Conger to Crozier I.	3/24 4/1	7	
Crozier I. to 84-17' (87 mi.)	4/6 4/21	14	6.2
Return from 84-17' to Crozier I. (87 mi.)	4/21 4/29	7	12.4
Crozier I. to Ft. Conger	4/30 5/3	4	
Ft. Conger to Payer H. (260 mi.)	5/6 5/17	11	23.6

1906

Trip/Distance	Dates	Marches (or days)	Avg. Dist (per march)
Sheridan to markham (60 mi.)	10/3-5 10/7-8	4	15
Sheridan to C. Hecla (50 mi.)	2/23-26	3	16.7

Note: The distances are from the following books:

1. Nearest the Pole
2. Northward Over "the Great Ice"

his "credible" witnesses.[11] *Second*, again reverting back to the minority committee members, these same critics find "incredible" in absolute terms the speed and distances that Peary claimed to have attained on the trip to the Pole, the return to Camp Bartlett, and from there to the *Roosevelt.*

We believe we have demonstrated that Henson and the Eskimos were credible witnesses and that the stories they have told fully support Peary's own account of how he reached the Pole. Thus we will not belabor the point.

Table III-1 and Table III-2 , when compared, demonstrate that Peary's speeds and distances on the final spurt to the Pole were not exceptional for him, as Dr. Grosvenor informed the committee. Table III-2 shows that Peary was routinely able to average 20 or more nautical miles per march, occasionally achieved 30 to 40 nautical miles per march, and on two occasions covered 50 to 60 nautical miles per march. Ironically, Herbert credits him with being able to achieve even greater distances. Recounting Marie Peary's story of how her father learned from the Eskimo's that his family was aboard the *Windward* at Payer Harbor and took off "without pausing for a moment," Herbert begs to differ. He accuses Peary of dawdling, stating: "Such eagerness to cover *the last seventy five miles* should have taken him to the ship *in one long day's march across good sea ice*—two at the most." (*Noose* pp135-136). As we point out below, and as Peary told the committee, he found surfaces as smooth as "good sea ice" on the sprint to the Pole and back to Camp Bartlett.

Table III-3, drawn from diverse sources, compares the maximum recorded nautical miles per single march attained by Peary before the 1909 expedition and *other sledgers* on various ice surfaces.

Table III-3

Traveler	Miles per March	Location
Peary	39	ice foot
	50-60	ice cap
Sverdrup/Isachsen	70	sea ice
Macmillan	25	(56 day avg.)
Borup	40	sea ice
Borup	35	ice foot
Amundsen	60	land
Lord Shackleton	70	ice foot
Postal Carriers	63	land
Iditarod Racers	100	land (10 day avg.)
Herbert	38	land
Herbert	20	sea ice
Nansen	20	sea ice
Abruzzi (Cagni)	20	sea ice

---

[11] For example, Dennis Rawlins writes (*Fact Or Fiction*, p. 127): "Peary's 1909 expedition included a group of five educated men, anyone of whom would have been a competent witness to the Pole. Instead, beyond 88 N. Peary took four Eskimos and Matthew Henson, none of whom knew navigational mathematics."

Also, (p.107), "When pondering our latest 1909 coincidence, that Peary turned back exactly as many supporting parties as he had educated witnesses, one realizes the obvious ... The heavy reliance on illiterate savages in itself places the 1906 and 1909 claims of Peary (and Cook's 1908) one) in a uniquely peculiar category."

And (p.108): "[On] April 1, the mysteries were just commencing. Bartlett was now out of sight. As Peary critic Captain Thomas Hall put it: 'All Fool's day, 1909, marked the beginning of an epoch in arctic history.'"

These figures demonstrate that Peary's distances of 27 n.m. per march or even 45 n.m. per march are well within distances that have been attained by other sledgers on numerous occasions.

Critics have sometimes focused upon the sledging speeds of Nansen, Abruzzi and Herbert in their efforts to show that Peary's speeds are unrealistic by comparison. But, as we point out below, those explorers' expeditions differed so materially from Peary's 1909 expedition that there is really no sound basis for drawing comparisons.

Nansen

Nansen led the expedition in which his vessel, the *Fram* was beset in the ice north of Siberia with the hope of drifting over the Pole. When it became clear that the *Fram* would not pass closer than about 240 miles from the Pole, Nansen and his meteorologist Johansen, set out for the Pole with three dogsledges on March 14, 1895 (after two false starts) from latitude 84°-4'. They reached latitude 86°-14' on April 8, 1895. Thus the expedition made good 130 miles to the north in 25 days, an average of only 5.2 miles per day. Nansen's account in his two volume *Farthest North* (1897), does not make clear whether he was able to march every day; he does state that he tried to march 8 to 10 hours each day.

Nansen was disappointed in his abysmally slow progress, which he attributed to three factors: *First*, he found that overall ice conditions were far worse than he had expected based on his two years of drifting in the *Fram) Second*, he concluded that the ice had drifted considerably southward during his trek.[12] *Third*, he was convinced that his Siberian dogs did not perform as well as Greenland dogs.

Another factor could well have been his inexperience in dog sledging. On his heroic expedition across the Greenland ice cap, sledges had been manhauled. Further, for much of the trek, he and Johansen were handling three sledges between the two of them. This meant that they had insufficient manpower for hoisting the sledges over the many ridges they encountered.

When Nansen turned back at 86°-14', he did not attempt to return to the *Fram*, which he had left in the care of her captain, Sverdrup, but instead set out for Franz Josef Land. His average speed over that portion of the trip (to the edge of the ice) was only about 2.1 nautical miles per day, primarily because he was frequently held up by open water.

Nansen's best distances over the polar ice, nonetheless, were in the surprising range of 20 miles. On the northward journey, he estimated his distance for March 22 at 21 miles. The number of hours for this march is not recorded, but there is no indication that he deviated from his plan of marching 8 to 10 hours per day. On March 23, he estimated that he had covered 14 miles in 6 hours.

On April 12, on the southward journey, he estimated his distance at 15 miles, noting that it was the best yet.[13] Thereafter, he reckoned that he had covered 20 miles

---

[12] Nansen's route put him directly against the south polar drift stream that runs about 1 nautical mile per day near the Pole and much faster as it approaches the East Greenland Sea. See section II F, above, on ice drift.

[13] This suggests either (a) that he had revised his estimate of 21 miles on March 22 to reflect his later observations that he had drifted southward, or (b) that he was speaking here only in terms of the southbound journey.

per day on each of April 13, 21, 22 and 28, and that for the four days prior to and including April 22 he had averaged 17.25 miles. He subsequently reports that on May 26 he made 20 miles with only 4 dogs per team for his two remaining sledges.

Nansen's sledge loads were somewhat lighter than Peary's (initially about 440 lbs. compared to 540 lbs.), but Nansen appears to have carried more nonconsumable items (for example, two kayaks weighing 41 lbs. each) than did Peary.[14] Further, Nansen reduced the number of sledges from 3 to 2 after May 14th, thereby increasing the weight of the two that were hauled from then on. Though Nansen started out with the same number of dogs per sledge as Peary (8 to 9), as noted above, he was reduced to four dogs per sledge by May 26. Thus it is not clear that Nansen's loads, in comparison to the size of his dog teams, were any lighter than Peary's on any of the dates mentioned above, and it is likely that they were much higher on May 26.

In sum, Nansen's distances cannot reasonably be compared with Peary's because of his inexperience in dogsledging, the inferiority of his dogs as compared to Peary's Whale Sound dogs, his shortage of manpower for lifting loaded sleds over ridges (for which Peary used Henson and his four Eskimos), and a seeming lack of Peary's good fortune in the overall prevailing ice conditions.

Abruzzi

The 1899-1900 expedition of the Duke of the Abruzzi, led by Commander Umberto Cagni, started for the Pole from Rudolf Island in Franz Josef Land, using a system of supporting parties similar to the system used by Peary in 1909. The lead party reached latitude 86°-34' on April 25, 1900, after 45 days. This works out to be 6.2 miles per day. Cagni's return trip took 60 days, due primarily to delays caused by the open water that he, like Nansen, encountered in May and June. He was not able to follow his own upward trail. Like Nansen also, Cagni and his men had no prior experience with sledging in the Arctic; they were for the most part mountain climbers like the Duke himself.

We submit that there is no sound basis for comparing Cagni's speeds and distances with Peary's, since he and his sledge drivers were inexperienced, he did not reach the latitudes above the 88th parallel where Peary found that his going improved due to favorable ice conditions, he and his men were inexperienced sledgers and he did not have the benefit of a ready-broken trail on the return journey.

Herbert

On February 21, 1968, British explorer and author Wally Herbert commenced his multi-year trek "across the top of the world," that is, across the Polar Sea from Alaska to Spitzbergen. While Herbert approached the Pole from a different direction than

---

[14] Peary explained to the Congressional committee that he carried on each sledge, in addition to food and fuel, a very light pickax, a pair of snowshoes, an ice lance, a little hatchet for chopping pemmican, and some spare clothing. He did not carry sleeping bags, he said, because he had discovered on his first Greenland expedition that they became exceedingly heavy when wet. He and his men made the fur costume worn during the day the sleeping bag at night. Of course igloos, constructed by the Eskimos, served in the place of tents. Each team, in a division of four sledges, carried a camp cooker, an ice saw with blades for building igloos, and navigational instruments. In addition, one party carried a sounding device, and two carried reels of specially made piano wire to be used with it. The wires were lost and the apparatus was discarded on the return from the Pole. Peary's aim always was to keep the nonconsumables to a minimum.

Peary, several comparisons may be drawn with regard to their speeds over the ice. Although Herbert's party of four had the advantage of periodic air drops of supplies, their four sledges transported loads considerably exceeding those of Peary's sledges. Each sledge started out weighing as much as 1300 pounds, in contrast to Peary's 540 pounds. Further, the four men (including one with an injured back) were not as physically qualified as the six men in Peary's party (four of whom were young and sturdy Eskimos) to wield pickaxes and heft heavily loaded sledges over ice hummocks. The inevitable result was slower going and more detours.

Nonetheless Herbert reports (*Across the Top of the World* p. 261) that on April 2nd the party covered 24 "route miles" (no time is given), including a substantial delay incident to the dunking of some dogs because of a break-through of the ice.[15] Considering that the sledges were almost three times the weight of Peary's sledges and pulled by the same number of dogs (8 to 9 per sledge), it would appear that this mileage is comparable to Peary's better mileages.

As an example of Herbert's sledging with lighter loads, we note (*Across the Top of the World*, pp.65-72) that during his training period he made 38 miles in just under 8 hours, a speed of 3.8 nautical miles per hour. That speed is remarkably high, even though the travel was on land, when one considers that it was achieved at a point in Herbert's career at which he reports that the Eskimos (who did not accompany him) regarded him as a clumsy amateur. Moreover, it appears that the trip included an ascent as well as a descent over treacherous icy slopes during which the sledges took a terrific hammering.

In sum, Herbert's mileages are not so far from Peary's when the relevant facts are taken into consideration that he is justified in stating, as he does, "that Peary's distances seem truly incredible." (*Noose*, p. 269)

C. Ice Surfaces above 88° North

The critics, in particular Herbert, maintain that the Arctic Ocean ice is far rougher than land ice, the ice foot, or sea ice outside of the Arctic Ocean, and that therefore no distances achieved by explorers over ice other than "ocean ice" are relevant. These critics overlook the fact that the long history of arctic exploration has proved that the surface of the Arctic Ocean ice is extremely variable — not only from place to place, but from year to year; it can be navigable, frozen smooth or chaotic. Will Steger writes: "A person climbing a mountain knows what geological features he will run into. But the ice of the polar sea gets rearranged every year and we have no idea what we will encounter." (*North To The Pole*, p.284)

Peary asserted again and again in his diary that ice conditions north of about 88°N. were exceptionally favorable. In our intensive research, we have found nothing whatsoever to cast doubt upon the following observations and much to support them:

---

[15] Herbert tells us that he usually calculated his mileage in terms of nautical miles and applied a 75% factor for detours. We take it that here, however, "route miles" refers to "statute miles made good" on the day in question; otherwise the event would scarcely have been worth mentioning.

April 1. "Today, the sky, the light drifting snow, the lazy horizon, the biting character of the wind ... everything except the surface of the ice, are the replica of ice cap weather."[16]

April 2. "Going the best and most equable of any day yet ...Large old floes, hard and level...and surrounded by pressure ridges...easily negotiable either through some convenient gap or up the slope of some large drift."

April 3. "Ice as yesterday, except at beginning of march it was rougher, requiring use of pickaxes...Some gigantic rafters but not in our path."

April 4. "The day a duplicate of day before yesterday as to weather and going. The latter even better. The surface is as even (except for the pressure ridges) as the glacial fringe from Hecla to Columbia, & harder."

April 5. "The march a duplicate of the previous one as to weather and going...Last two hours on young ice on a north-south lead. A 50 yd. lead open when I reached it moved enough by time sledges came up to let us cross."

April 6. The going even better than ever, hardly any snow on the hard granular last summer's surface of the old floes."

April 9. [Back at Camp Bartlett] "A wild day, strong NNE (true) wind, increasing to a gale...all upward leads greatly widened and new ones formed...All covered with practicable young ice"

"From here to the pole and back has been one glorious sprint with a savage finish. Its result due to hard work, little sleep, much experience, first class equipment, and *good fortune as regards weather and open water.*"

Many modern day polar explorers have found Peary's speeds and distances on his spurt to the Pole and back entirely credible. In a letter to the editor of the *London Times* published on May 17, 1989, Lord Shackleton (son of Sir Ernest Shackleton, a famous explorer of Antarctica) and Dr. Geoffrey Hattersley-Smith, an internationally known glaciologist and geologist, both of whom travelled extensively in Greenland and on Ellesmere Island by dog sledge in the 1930s, 1950s and 1960s wrote:

It was clear from our conversations with the Greenlander, Odaq [Ootah], the last survivor of the polar party, that Peary found very good travel conditions on the last stretch

---

[16] We take this to mean that the ice surfaces were a vast improvement over the ice surfaces on the ice cap, because never did Peary encounter rougher going than on his journeys across "the great ice." See, generally, *Northward Over "The Great Ice."*

to the North Pole. We ourselves have travelled up to 70
statute miles [61 nautical miles] 'between sleeps',
admittedly on very good surfaces, so Peary's distances,
allowing for deviations of route, were by no means
extraordinary."

Like Peary, other travellers on the ocean ice have experienced improved ice surfaces north of 88°N. These include Will Steger, Colonel Gerry Pitzl, navigator of the successful polar snowmobile expedition lead by Ralph Plaisted in 1968, and even Wally Herbert himself.

Writing in *Arctic* magazine (1970) Pitzl describes the ice surface above 87° North as being made up of floes which were "mostly very old and large... Most were 4 or 5 miles in diameter and 1 was measured 8 miles long and estimated 3 miles wide. Their surfaces were quite flat with hard packed snow. Old pressure ridges outnumbered the new and were generally smaller than in Zone II (below 87° North)."

Again, in *Navigation*, the journal of the Institute of Navigation, Pitzl describes the traveling during the last two weeks before attaining the pole as "practically unrestricted." "We were virtually moving at will," he writes. "We had entered a region of the pack which had two major characteristics 1) Extensive old weathered flows which were several miles in width and separated by worn and decimated pressure ridges which presented no obstacle, and 2) Many extremely large and newly frozen leads. In many cases the lead direction was north, affording us the luxury of effortless travel."

Wally Herbert in *Across the Top of the World* (p. 256), observes that at latitude 88°40' N: "[T]he surface was improving too; we were finding for the first time during the journey that we were constantly travelling across hard wind-packed snow and seeing 'sastrugi' from time to time. Sastrugi is caused by the wind which packs down the snow, polishes it, then starts chiseling it into sharp-edged waves. The sastrugi, while not quite as regular as a plowed field, nevertheless was a perfect surface across which to sledge —in fact sledges hardly left a track at all."

Will Steger, writing in *North To The Pole* (p.303), the story of his 1986 sledging expedition that set out to retrace Peary's route to the Pole, observes: "*As did we and all other polar expeditions of this century*, Peary found steadily improving ice conditions during the last few hundred miles, which nearly eliminated the need for detours."[17]

D. Detours

An argument frequently made by critics is that Peary's claimed distances, expressed in terms of nautical miles made good, are incredible because a substantial factor must be added to account for detours. Herbert points out that he and Plaisted made detours in the neighborhood of 75% Then, ostensibly giving Peary the "benefit of the doubt," he arbitrarily adds 25% to Peary's distances in an effort to show that Peary's figures are inflated. However, if ice conditions were as good as Peary reported them to be above 88° North, it is unlikely that detours would have increased the miles traveled by anything close to 25%. As Steger noted above, the improving ice conditions

---

[17] Steger also comments on the sastrugi patterns of which Herbert speaks. He suggests sastrugi patterns are also helpful in steering, and that knowledge of the patterns "must have been part of the 'sixth sense' Peary and Hensen had developed through their vast experience."

his party enjoyed during the "last few hundred miles...nearly eliminated the need for detours" (*North To The Pole*, p.283) Plainly, one cannot take detours into account by adding an across-the-board percentage factor for an entire trip.

We have found one slip of paper in the National Archives which indicates that Peary did, after his return, estimate his detours at approximately 25 % for the first part of the trip. His relatively low mileages for that part of his journey, however, are not in dispute. That the detours were substantially less north of 87°-17'N. than before must be assumed from Peary's description of the ice conditions that permitted him to travel, for the most part, on level floes.

Steger's mileages "made good" for the region above 88° N reflect the improved ice conditions that he reported experiencing. Herbert's blanket claim that Steger estimated detours of 50 % (*Noose*, p. 269) is misleading. The 50% figure Steger used in his table of distances recorded in his daily log (*North To The Pole*, pp. 326-327) is an average allowed for his entire trip, including a substantial portion of the trip during which the expedition was moving supplies forward by shuttling back and forth between caches, covering many miles of the trail *three times*. See our Table III-4. The same factor cannot logically be applied to the latter portion of the journey.

The 75% figure attributed to Plaisted by Herbert, even if accurate, would not be applicable to Peary because their two expeditions are not comparable. Since Plaisted was using snowmobiles, he would have found it far easier to drive around obstacles, such as hummocks, than to lift his snowmobiles and the heavy sledges they towed over them. Moreover, it would have been impossible for the snowmobiles to have crossed the thinly frozen leads that Peary and his party sometimes crept across on snow shoes or on all fours. Plaisted's must truly have been a zig-zag course to the Pole considering the nature of his equipment.

Herbert all but concedes that Peary could have made the sledging mileages he claimed from Bartlett's camp to the Pole and back "in 7.8 days — an average of 37.9 nautical miles a day" (even allowing 25% for detours) if he were traveling on smooth ice. "Across flat sea ice," Herbert states, "this is not unreasonable; but across polar pack ice this sort of average is nothing short of phenomenal." (*Noose*, p.261) Herbert's real difficulty, it seems, is his refusal to accept Peary's description of the prevailing ice conditions.

It should be noted here that Herbert's route to the Pole (and therefore his experience) was completely different than Peary's. Herbert's plan was to use the transpolar drift for transport across the Arctic Basin that made his approach to the Pole about 90 degrees to that of Peary. Therefore, his experience does not include any observation of ice conditions in the area that Peary and Steger traveled through.

E. The Dash To The Pole And Back

The increase in speeds and distances on what is frequently referred to as Peary's "dash" to the Pole,[18] resulted primarily from the significant improvement in ice conditions above latitude 88°N. that we have noted. Yet it was also attributable to the smaller size of the party, and the consequent reduction in delays. Peary wrote in *The North Pole* (p.285-286):

---

[18] Peary himself preferred to use the term "drive" or "spurt." A final "spurt" was what he had planned from the start; the word "dash" more aptly describes his frantic effort to establish a new "farthest north" on his beleaguered 1906 expedition.

Table III-4

Statistics from the 1986 Steger Expedition

Trip Day	Date	Miles Made Good	Remarks
1	3/8	1.5	Sledge wt. 1350 pounds
2	3/9	1	Relaying
3	3/10	2.5	"
4	3/11	0	advance outpost only
5	3/12	2	Relaying
6	3/13	7	"
7	3/14	0	
8	3/15	7	"
9	3/16	6	"
10	3/17	7	4 mi. on N-S frozen lead
11	3/18	8	Relaying
12	3/19	3	"
13	3/20	0	"
14	3/21	7	"
15	3/22	8	"
16	3/23	3	Sledge Wt. 650 pounds
17	3/24	0	
18	3/25	5	Try to stop relaying
19	3/26	9	No Relay
20	3/27	7	Back to Relaying
21	3/28	6	Relaying
22	3/29	8	"
23	3/30	6	"
24	3/31	8	"
25	4/1	0	"
26	4/2	8	1st dog flyout, end relay
27	4/3	14	no relay
28	4/4	16	"
29	4/5	0	Dogs worn down, day of rest
30	4/6	14	no more relays
31	4/7	0	Storm & dog rest
32	4/8	10	Lat. 85, ice cond. improved
33	4/9	4	
34	4/10	0	Dog rest
35	4/11	3	"corn ice" bad snow
36	4/12	0	Airlift, 600 lb loads 3 sledges
37	4/13	16	
38	4/14	8	
39	4/15	24	Followed NW frozen lead
40	4/16	12	Lat. 86 N, improvm. continues
41	4/17	16	Followed N frozen lead
42	4/18	18	Followed N frozen lead (2)
43	4/19	15	Latitude about 87 N
44	4/20	18	
45	4/21	16	
46	4/22	18	Latitude 87-48 (128 m. to go).
47	4/23	0	Rest day
48	4/24	23	12 hrs. march
49	4/25	26	
50	4/26	32	12 hrs. march
51	4/27	24	
52	4/28	23	
53	4/29	0	All day repairing sextant
54	4/30	0	90 degrees off course
55	5/1	0	
56	5/2		At the Pole,

Note: Marches after 87-48 based on satellite navigation data.

Many laymen have wondered why we were able to travel faster
after the sending back of each of the support parties,
especially after the last one. To any man experienced in
the handling of troops, this will need no explanation...

Take a regiment, for instance. The regiment could not make
as good an average daily march for a number of forced
marches as could a picked company of that regiment. The
picked company could not make as good an average...as
could a picked file of men from that particular company;
And this file could not make the same average...that the
fastest traveler in the whole regiment could make.

Will Steger likewise had the advantage of a manageable party of six (eight persons started but two turned back). His and Peary's expeditions shared many experiences in common, but there was one all-important difference—Steger's trip to the Pole was one way only, with a projected air lift out. His party was spared the anxiety of knowing that every delay on its journey north diminished the prospects of a safe return. Thus speed was not of the essence for Steger as it was for Peary.

A less dramatic difference is that Peary used a logistic system, involving supporting parties that turned back from various points along the way, which was very different from the relay system used by Steger.

When the two expeditions are compared, as we have attempted to compare them below, we think it plain that if Steger reached the Pole (as we know he did because what better proof could an explorer have than an airlift out?), Peary could have done so. For our purpose here, we consider separately Peary's upward and outward journeys.

1. The Outward Journey

Table III-5 summarizes the daily distances (nautical miles[19] made good) in the direction of the Pole by the Steger and Peary expeditions over four segments of the journey along an identical route. The distances [intervals between latitudes] are expressed in terms of miles per marching day; rest days and days during which either expedition was held up by leads or for other reasons are excluded. However the total days (marching/resting) are shown for comparison of the number of days in which the two expeditions were in the field.

---

[19] In *North To The Pole* Steger gives all mileages in statute miles, which must be multiplied by 0.88 to convert them to nautical miles.

Table III-5

Latitude Range,	Mi. per March		Total - Marching- Resting Days					
	Steger	Peary	Steger			Peary		
83.0-84.5	4.4	11.4	30	24	6	22	14	8
84.5-85.8	11.0		9					
85.8-87.8	16.0	14.6	9	8	1	9	8	1
87.8-90.0	25.6*	26.2	8	6**	2	6	5	1

   *   Based on Satellite navigation positions.

   **   Includes one short day marching at right angles to intended course and not included in calculation of average distance per march. The detour turned out to be a blessing in disguise because it permitted the expedition, inadvertently, to avoid a substantial area of open leads that could have slowed it down or even brought it to a halt.

These data show that Steger and Peary covered comparable distances per marching day in each latitude range, except that during the early going, Steger was much slower. His discouraging progress was the result of the relay system that he was forced to use, advancing the sledge loads one half at a time to avoid impossibly heavy sledge loads.[20]

In particular, Table III-5 shows that Steger, like Peary, was able to increase his speed dramatically north of 87°-8' latitude, and achieved almost exactly the same number of miles per marching day as did Peary in that zone.

The dramatic increase in speed reported by both Steger and Peary was at least in part attributable to improving ice conditions encountered as their parties got further from land. Peary reported that above 87-47 his party traveled on large floes of summers past, and in gaps between towering pressure ridges, on an almost direct course for the Pole. And the Steger party likewise found themselves on an increasingly smooth course "during the last few hundred miles, which nearly eliminated the need for detours." (*North To The Pole*, p.303)

There are two respects in which the speeds attained by Steger and Peary over the last 130 miles on the way to the Pole are not directly comparable, but they operate in different directions and tend to offset each other. First, Peary probably was carrying heavier sledge loads over the last 130 miles, since he had supplies for the return trip. Steger's expedition during the last nine days consumed virtually all their food and fuel supplies, lightening their loads considerably. On the other hand, Peary and his men and dogs were probably better rested than were the men and dogs of the Steger expedition.

---

[20] Steger elected, for most of the first 30 days, to use a relay system, whereby all five sledges went forward with partial loads to establish a new camp, from which two or three sledges would be sent back to pick up the balance of the loads while one other sledge team went forward to scout the next day's trail. This system resulted in each mile being covered three times. The effect was not to reduce the speed of advance by a factor of three, since the second traverse of the trail was done with empty sledges and both the second and third traverses of the trail had the benefit of the trail breaking and scouting done for the first traverse. In addition, the time spent in backhauls provided time for scouting. Nevertheless, the numbers suggest that the relay system caused at least a 50% reduction in speed.

Steger's team, when it began the final dash, had already been on the ice for 54 days, including 43 marching days. By contrast, Peary and his party had been on the ice only 31 days when they began the final spurt for the Pole. More importantly, Peary's party had, with few exceptions, not been breaking the trail; on many days Peary covered the day's march following behind the pioneer party in only about 6 or 8 hours. But all members of Steger's party had shared in the pioneering and the pickaxing it entailed.

Steger writes (*North To The Pole*, p.275) :

> Peary's strategy ensured that his final dash team ...
> was relatively well rested and well fed when it left
> 88 degrees. At this point our crew, I'm sure, was
> less vigorous than his had been.

He adds (p.303):

> Our dogs had started this journey pulling payloads that
> weighed nearly three times those on Peary's ...sleds.
> Surely, by the time we reached 88 degrees, our dogs were
> far more exhausted than Peary's were when he started on
> his final dash from nearly the same point. Yet the average
> mileage for our last five marches — just under thirty
> four miles — was virtually the same as what he clocked
> on his final dash.

Ultimately Steger concluded (p.303):

> Thus, while the jury is still out on (Peary's) navigation
> claims, *I find his mileage claims to be plausible.* (emphasis
> added)

Based on our analysis of the two expeditions, Steger's conclusion is warranted. In fact, in view of the close parallels between the expeditions, whoever challenges Peary's outbound distances bears a heavy burden of showing why Peary could not have accomplished what Steger accomplished.

2. The Return Journey

Peary's return journey has been considered even more suspect than the outward journey because he increased his miles per march.

As we noted above, in terms of "nautical miles made good," the polar party covered the 135 mile distance from Camp Bartlett to the Pole in five marches, averaging 27 miles per march at a speed of about 2.5 miles per hour. On the return trip the same distance was covered in three forced marches, averaging 45 miles per march, at a speed of about 2.8 miles per hour.

The first return march started at about 4:00 p.m. (ship's time) on April 7, and the third march ended about 0:30 a.m. on April 10. Thus, the three marches spanned an elapsed time of about 57 hours, with about 9 hours allowed for "sleeps."

His speed, which works out to be 2.8 miles per hour, is only slightly more than the 2.5 miles per hour he achieved on the way to the Pole. Plainly, therefore, the number of marches was reduced by the long marching hours.

In addition to reflecting the lengthened marches, the distances achieved represent, first and foremost, gains from following a broken trail and occupying previously-constructed igloos along the route. As Peary demonstrated to the Congressional committee, each of the members of his party on his return trip very nearly halfed the time of his outward bound marches. Peary was not alone in returning south with his party much faster than he had journeyed north.

Will Steger writes (*North To The Pole*, p.303):

> Critics have had a field day scoffing at his reports
> of returning to 88 degrees in three marches, averaging
> forty-five miles a day. But I hasten to point out that
> he was following a well-marked trail, camping at the
> same igloos he had used on the way up, though skipping
> every other one. Only seasoned dogsledders know how
> motivated dogs become when they suddenly have scent
> marks to follow, when they know they are headed home
> to food and rest. Mushers, too, find a reservoir of
> energy they didn't know they had when a long journey
> nears its end. In Peary's case, he and his crew had
> an added shot of adrenaline, knowing they were
> virtually running for their lives with spring advancing
> rapidly upon them.

It is true that Peary was motivated on the return trip by a fear of encountering open leads on the way home, as had happened on his "farthest north" expedition. He wrote in *Hampton's Magazine* of his awareness that —

> Success in the attainment of 90 degrees North would
> not inevitably carry with it the safe return. We had
> learned *that* in recrossing the "big lead" in 1906.

To us it is entirely logical that every member of the polar party would have pushed himself to the bounds of his endurance to reach land while weather and ice conditions remained favorable. The Eskimos, who would not even have ventured upon the open ocean ice except under the command of Peary, knew as well as anyone that there was no time to lose.

Why the relatively unexceptional returning speeds should be suspect under such dire circumstances is hard for us to conceive.

In short, from our review of the experiences of both Peary's contemporaries and present day explorers, it seems clear that Peary's speeds and distances are not phenomenal, either en route to the Pole or back. They are well within the capabilities one might expect of Peary, who was, after all, the most seasoned Arctic explorer of them all, of Matt Henson, his most stalwart assistant, and of his carefully selected Smith Sound Eskimos.[21]

F. The Fallacy Of The "Hoax" Theory

The twin cornerstones of the "hoax" theory of Peary's "discovery" of the Pole, which is given more credence today than at the time the Reverend Hayes was writing, are the concepts (1) that Peary's navigation did not take him to the Pole because of his failure to take longitude sights, and (2) that his claimed distances are incredible. We hope that we have now put both of these notions to rest.

Yet we do not wish to put these topics behind us without pointing out the fallacy of the critics' allegations on a third ground — a simple matter of logic.

It is generally conceded that on April 6 and April 7, Peary took observations in the vicinity of Camp Jesup that revealed to him the true location of that northernmost camp. If he had then found himself short of the Pole, or to the left or right of it, as his critics contend, one must ask, why would he not push on? Why would he have turned back and forfeited his chance to fulfill his lifelong dream when he was within a stone's throw of the Pole in favor of faking a claim?

Most expeditions turn back because they are in dire straits, but Peary and his men were hard, lean and in good spirits on April 6. They had dogs a plenty, and on their five sledges, they had provisions enough to last them for another forty days.

As Mr. Gannett observed during the Congressional hearings:

> It is hardly believable that a man would sit down within
> 130 miles of the Pole and [fake his claim] after he had
> undertaken the uncertainties, the dangers, and the risks
> to life, leaving aside the question of Peary's personality.

And as Peter Freuchen observed of Peary, replying to the Reverend Hayes' accusations of fraud:

> Such a man never comes back and fakes results from such
> an expedition. If that had been in his mind, he could
> have done it years ago; but he never was afraid of
> anything in the world. He would not have been afraid
> of telling about a defeat either. (Letter to Stefansson)

It is true that Peary was not afraid to admit defeat. He had done so when he gave up on reaching the Pole on his 1906 expedition. But he was no defeatist. On this 1909 expedition he had taken every precaution to assure success — precautions that would

---

[21] Peary stressed before the committee: "There is one point, Mr. Chairman, that I would like to note, and that is, as far as I know, no other expeditions than my own have utilized Eskimo drivers and the full-blooded Eskimo dogs in their entirety and perfection."

Peter Freuchen writes in his letter to Stefansson: "[I]t seems to me like an insult that I shall sit here and defend Admiral Peary against Mr. Gordon Hayes. If this gentleman only has the speed of dogs to hang his hat on, it is because he never saw how Greenland Eskimos can travel. And if he sees Greenland Eskimos travel, he may not understand how they would do it when they have a leader [such] as Robert Peary to do the command."

have overcome any steering errors or miscalculated distances once he got within the vicinity of the Pole. Indeed, at 135 miles away, he was close to the Pole when he started!

Upon Bartlett's departure at the 88th parallel, Peary was left with two divisions, his and Henson's, fully readied and raring to go. He, and to a lesser extent, Henson, had reserved themselves for the final drive by leaving the pioneering to Bartlett's division on the entire trek until then. Their dogs were the pick of 133 that had started on the journey, and their sledges had been overhauled and put in good shape. Peary writes (*The North Pole*, p.273):

> As to the dogs, most of them were powerful males,
> as hard as iron, in good condition, but without an
> ounce of superfluous fat...My food supplies were
> ample for forty days, and by gradual utilization of
> the dogs themselves for reserve food, might be made
> to last for fifty days if it came to a pinch.

Also, he was taking no chances on arriving at the northern coasts of Greenland or Ellesmere Island on the return and being dependent on the local game supply as had happened in 1906. He had instructed members of his support parties to cache food supplies along both routes.

Though Peary had hopes of reaching the Pole in five marches after Bartlett turned back, he was conservatively counting on eight — "eight marches like the three from 85-48 to 86-38...would do the trick."

He also had two contingency plans should his distances come up short. "One was to double up the last march — that is to make a good march, have tea and a hearty lunch, rest the dogs a little and then go on without sleep." The other was "at the conclusion of my fifth march [not necessarily the fifth day] to push on with one light sledge, a double team of dogs, and one or two of the party leaving the rest in camp." (*The North Pole*, pp. 269-270)

Then why in heaven's name would Peary have turned back short of the Pole at the end of five marches, as his critics claim, when he was mentally prepared for eight, and had sufficient provisions for another six weeks on the trail? If his observations at Camp Jesup showed him to be still some distance from the Pole, why would he not have put one or the other of his contingency plans into effect?

Today's leading proponents of the hoax theory, Rawlins and Herbert, to our mind, have failed to come up with satisfactory answers to these questions.

Rawlins, in *Fact Or Fiction*, suggests that Peary simply became terror stricken at the prospect of the homeward journey, suddenly recalling his harrowing episode of being pinned down at the lead he dubbed "the Styx" on his return from his "farthest north" in 1906. (pp. 117-118) He hypothesizes that Peary asked himself, "What better way to gain days [on the return journey] than to start homeward early?" (p.117)

Thereafter Rawlins quotes selectively from Peary's diary to bolster this shaky proposition which runs contrary to everything in Peary's career. Rawlins notes that in his entry of April 5, Peary expressed his "constant and increasing dread of wide leads stopping his progress north" (p. 119) But he fails to note that on April 5 Peary also wrote: "Tomorrow if ice conditions permit, I shall make a long march, 'boil the kettle' midway, and try to make up the 5 miles lost on the third." Does this sound like a man contemplating defeat?

Rawlins also speculates that the sudden rise in temperature on April 6 from about -25F to -11F worried Peary "as he took such behavior in the thermometer to indicate open water nearby." (p. 119) But this is not what Peary says in reporting the temperature rise. Peary displayed pleasure when he also wrote on April 6: "The rise in temperature to -15 has reduced friction of the sledges 25%, and gives the dogs the appearance of having caught the spirit of the party." He notes without comment a later rise to -11F —a mere four degree increase.

Finally Rawlins reveals his "key to the temptation for turning back short of the goal." He explains: "To prevent the risk of again finding himself adrift in a lethally lead-filled ice field, Peary had to get back in about three weeks. The moon was due in early May, about the time of the near disaster of 1906." (p.120)

This makes no sense whatsoever. Peary was fully aware of the cycle of the moon and its effect on tides and ice conditions; he notes in his diary of April 3, "Full moon about tomorrow." However he expresses no concern either about its occurring then, or recurring in a month. Since the May full moon was about four weeks away, it is unlikely that it would have figured one way or another in any determination to turn back on April 6 or 7 when the observations at Camp Jesup were taken.

Finally, Rawlins makes the unsubstantiated assumption that at the time Peary turned back, reaching the Pole would have "require[d] another week." When one looks for an explanation, one encounters the following arcane paragraph (pp 116-117):

> Henson records times [when Peary took his April 7 observations] that seem to place the first transverse observation as the one taken out of sight beyond the camp. Whenever it was taken, it probably indicated to Peary that he was at least a week away from the Pole, which would have to be approached now at a sharp angle (see Fig.   ) [sic] with respect to the previous trail, and the return would either be equally circuitous or partly over an unbroken route.

Henson's allegedly "recorded" times amount to no more than his speculation as to observations taken on Peary's sidetrips around the Pole while he, Henson, was left behind. Henson is a therefore an unreliable witness in regard to those particular observations. Rawlin's reliance upon Henson's account as evincing that Peary was "at least a week away from the Pole," and that the Pole would "have to be approached ...at a sharp angle," is nothing less than irresponsible.

But assuming *arguendo* that Peary *was* a week away from the Pole and not in a direct line for it, why would he not have put one of his contingency plans in effect? Surely he had time enough to do so before warming weather or ocean tides cast him adrift in "a lethally lead-filled ice field."

Sorry, we do not buy the sudden panic theory, and Rawlins offers nothing else.

Leads were a nightmare to every explorer, but in 1906, Peary pushed on with a small hand-picked party through a veritable mesh of leads to establish a new farthest north record before turning back to cross those same dangerous leads again. If leads did not deter him in 1906, they would not have deterred him in 1909 when he was within reach of a goal that was much nearer to his heart.

Wally Herbert attempts to explain why Peary would have turned back after only five marches when, by Herbert's calculations, he found himself about 55 miles from the Pole due to navigational errors and the "treadmilling misery of going against the ice" (*Noose*, p. 270), as follows:

> He had enough food on his sledges to make [the necessary] correction and, at the rate they had been travelling over the past five days, they could reach the Pole in two days — or three at most. But the pull to return to safety was now a strong one and, as he says in his book, "All plans for the expedition were formulated quite as much with an eye toward a safe return from the Pole as toward the risk of reaching it."

> That plan was also based on the principle that the return would be faster than the outward journey because they would be sledging along a blazed trail and using igloos already built. If they were to correct their course and head directly to the Pole, they would have to return along their tracks or risk missing that trail which had been kept open by the returning parties, and *that two or three days' extra travelling to reach the Pole would therefore be doubled to a round trip of some five or six days north of their Camp Jesup.* (Emphasis added)

To this we can only say, why would a round trip of "five or six days" deter an avid explorer from proceeding on to the goal that he had been pursuing for twenty three years? As for the safe return of the expedition, this was, of course, a factor in Peary's planning, but a five or six day delay would have created no undue risk.

Next Herbert moves on to psychoanalysis:

> But there was another factor in that dilemma. To reach the Pole now he would have to admit to his five bone-weary companions who had reached their lives to get him to that point, and later to his supporters and public, that "the greatest Arctic explorer of the Age" (as Jo had proudly called her husband) had made an error of navigation that would certainly stain his reputation.

As one might guess from the title of his book, *The Noose Of Laurels*, Herbert presumes that rather than confess to "an error of navigation" that would "stain" his reputation, Peary chose to put his achievements of a lifetime in jeopardy by faking a claim of attaining the Pole, a decision for which he paid dearly.[22] Does this make sense? Of course not, though it makes for good soap opera. It is the stuff of "docudramas."

In sum, the "hoax" theory of Peary's "discovery" of the Pole fails on three grounds that we have covered thus far: (1) Peary's navigation by dead reckoning corrected by observation was designed to take him directly to the Pole and it served him well; (2) Peary's distances on the dash to the Pole and back were not even extraordinary for him, much less incredible; and (3) simple logic tells us that if Peary found himself short of the Pole when he took his observations at Camp Jesup, he would have taken corrective action and proceeded on to his goal with the courage and determination that characterized all his previous explorations.

In the next two parts of this report, which deal with Peary's soundings and his photographs, we offer hard evidence of Peary's attainment of the Pole that has been studiously overlooked by his critics.

---

[22] Herbert professes empathy for Peary, however. He closes his book with the suggestion (p.329): Surely it is only fair to see the man for what he was and not what he failed to be. Those doubts that have for eighty years hung round his controversial claim, distorting every image of the man and his achievements, would surely then be understood, and Peary's striving wounded spirit finally find peace.

Part Four

PEARY'S SOUNDINGS

In a letter of July 3, 1908, to the Secretary of Commerce and Labor, President Theodore Roosevelt refers to Peary's recently having been assigned to the U. S. Coast and Geodetic Survey and requests that he be directed to make tidal observations along the Grant Land and Greenland shores of the Polar Sea during his projected 1909 expedition. The President goes on to say:

> It is believed that such observations will throw light upon
> the Coast Survey theory of the existence of a considerable
> land mass in the unknown area of the Arctic Ocean.

This theory was based on a conviction that there was a substantial restriction to the flow of water across the polar sea, based on estimates of tides and velocities at each end of its path. In 1948 the discovery of a large submarine ridge by a Soviet polar expedition showed that there was indeed an obstruction to the flow of water across the Arctic Ocean. The obstructing ridge was named for the eighteenth century Russian scientist M. V. Lomonosov.

When Peary's 1908-09 trip was firmed up, the Coast and Geodetic Survey, following the President's instructions, directed that he take the proposed series of tidal measurements and soundings. The tidal measurements that were ultimately taken by Marvin and MacMillan, assisted by Borup and members of the *Roosevelt's* crew, consisted of 26 volumes of data. They represented an attempt to analyze the tidal effects along the coasts of Greenland and Grant Land which might illuminate the land mass theory.

During the 1909 trip from Cape Columbia to the Pole and back, Peary and the members of his party took ten soundings, generally along the 70th meridian. Two of these, made close to shore, are not significant. The other eight are shown below in Table IV-1.

Table IV-1.

Name	Date	Latitude	Fathoms	meters
MacMillan	March 2	83-25 N	96	175
Bartlett	March 4	83-53 N	110	201
Marvin	March 14	84-29 N	825	1509
Marvin	March 15	84-39 N	580	1060
Marvin	March 20	85-23 N	310	567
Marvin	March 21	85-33 N no bottom at	700	1280
Bartlett	March 29	87-15 N no bottom at	1260	2304
Peary	April 7	89-55 N no bottom at	1500	2743

Note: Although Peary's report uses fathoms, these soundings are also expressed in meters to facilitate comparison with the contours of the chart of Figure IV-2.

These soundings were reported, along with the tidal observations, to the Coast & Geodetic Survey. Most of Peary's critics, however, have denigrated these data as being of no real scientific interest because of lack of precision (the "no bottom" soundings). Rawlins incorrectly asserts that they do not show that Peary crossed the Lomonosov Ridge, a major bottom feature (*Fact Or Fiction*, p.130) He also suggests that Peary may have faked the "no bottom at 1500" sounding, reasoning that he could safely assume that the depth at the Pole would be much deeper than 1500 fathoms because of Nansen's depth information from the *Fram* voyage of 1893 (p.156). What he neglects to point out is that the *Fram* was about two hundred fifty miles from the Pole. Finally Rawlins surmises that some of Peary's soundings, which were more than likely taken far from the indicated meridian, are distorting contours on modern charts of dangerous waters.[1]

Wally Herbert's only statement addressing the soundings in *The Noose of Laurels* is that "... Peary's line of nine soundings was not taken on the meridian of Cape Columbia, as he believed, and to date the only line of soundings that has been made on that meridian was recorded by *HMS Sovereign* in October 1976, and these do not match up with the 1909 data." (*Noose*, Appendix II, p. 343)

The discussion below will show that charts quite adequate for comparing Peary's soundings existed at the time Herbert was writing in 1989. Furthermore, as we will show, Peary's soundings *do* match up with current data indicating depths along the 70th meridian.[2] We are forced to conclude, from his and Rawlins truncated treatment of the subject, that research of Arctic Ocean bathymetry by Peary critics to date has been negligible.

---

[1] Rawlins states: "Indeed Peary's southernmost 1909 soundings are still used on most official maps of Arctic Ocean bathymetry. If actually taken far from the indicated meridian, as is highly likely, they are thus distorting contours on modern charts of dangerous waters."(*Fact Or Fiction*, p.11) The notion that the soundings are still on the charts is patently absurd in view of the vast of amount of bottom data available at the time Rawlins was writing (1973)

[2] The Defense Mapping Agency has advised us that the soundings taken by *HMS Sovereign* were made available to it and were included in the data supplied for this report

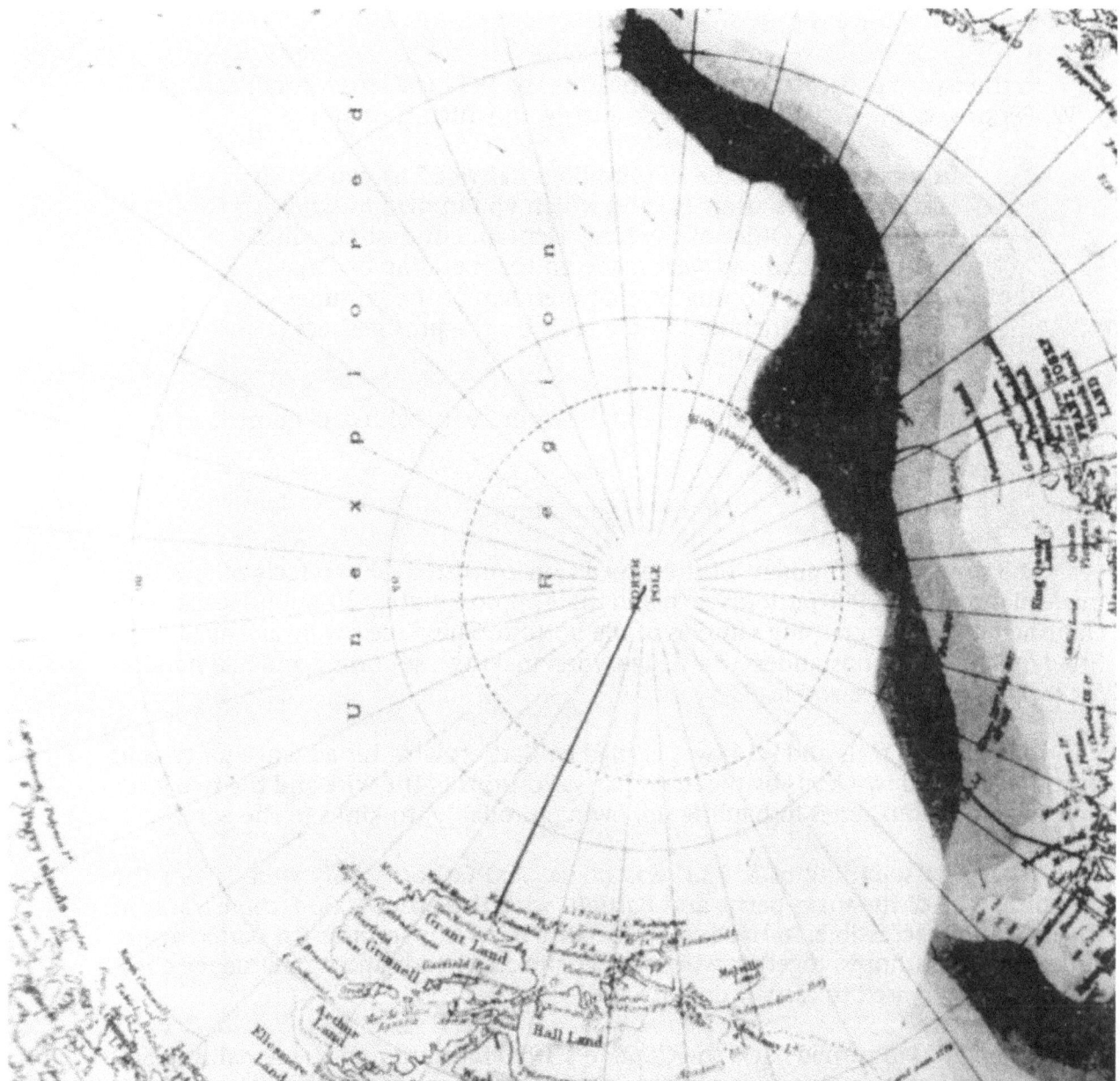

PHYSICAL CHART OF
NORTH POLAR REGIONS
1897
BY J. G. BARTHOLOMEW, F.R.S.E.

COMPILED FROM LATEST SOURCES, INCLUDING Dr NANSEN'S DATA

Scale of Latitude 1 : 16000000

Nautical Miles

NOTE		SEA COLOURING		NOTE	
Ocean Soundings in Fathoms		SEA LEVEL		Arctic Region of Snow & Ice	
Soundings, no bottom reached		100 Fathoms			
Extreme Limit of Floating Ice		200		Tundra & Barren Lands	
Limits of Pack Ice		1000		Region of Forest & Grass Land	
Points reached by Explorers & dates		2000		The Northern Limits of Principal	
Ocean Currents are shown by arrows		Below 2000		Trees are shown separately	
				Glaciers	

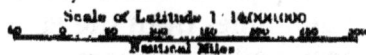 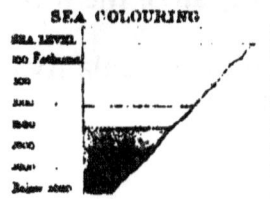

Track of the 'Fram' in Open Water .... The 'Fram's' Drift in the Polar Ice _____ Nansen's & Johansen's Sledge Journey ....

FIG. IV-1

A. Peary's Testimony on his Soundings

In the record of the Congressional hearings of 1911 is a letter from Peary to Mr. F. W. Perkins, of the Coast and Geodetic Survey, in which he states:

> In regard to the profile of soundings delivered to you by Mr. Nichols [Peary's attorney] and which you inform me the Hydrographic Office of the Navy Department desires, will say that these soundings were made on the meridian of Cape Columbia, and plotting on that meridian at the latitudes which I think are noted in the table on the profile sheet will give their position.

Following this letter is a memorandum from Peary which is quoted, in part, below.

Notes on Soundings

The sounding equipment of the expedition consisted of two reels of specially made piano wire of 1000 fathoms each and three approximately 20-pound leads, with clamshell device for grasping samples of the bottom. These reels were arranged to be fitted quickly to the upstanders of a sledge when making a sounding and had handles for reeling in the wire and lead.

One of these reels and leads was carried by Bartlett with his advance party, and the other reel and two leads by the main party. Portions of the wire and the two leads were lost at various times in hauling up, owing, probably, to kinks in the wire.

When the sounding of 85°-33' was made, 700 fathoms only were left of the sounding wire of the main party, and Bartlett, with the other 1000 fathoms, was in advance and inaccessible. In hauling up the wire from this sounding it parted again, and some 200 fathoms, together with the two pickaxe heads and a steel sledge shoe, which had been used to carry it down, were lost.

When Marvin turned back, the Captain's 1000 fathoms and the remaining 500 fathoms of the other reel were combined. When Bartlett made the sounding at 85-15, I gave him explicit instructions to use the utmost caution in regard to the wire, in order to not lose any more of it, as I wanted it all for a sounding at the pole, should I succeed in getting there.

Acting upon these instructions, Bartlett ran out 1260 fathoms and then stopped on account of a small kink in the wire, which he feared would part when the wire was hauled up. When I made my sounding about 5 miles from the Pole, the wire parted, as had been feared, and the last lead and nearly all of the wire were lost.

> The above facts are noted to explain the irregularity of these soundings, which did not get bottom.

B. Arctic Bathymetry

Figure IV-1 is a map showing the knowledge of the ocean bottom in 1897, which would not have changed significantly by 1909. It was issued to show the bottom data

FIG. IV-2

obtained by Nansen and Sverdrup during the three years drift of the *Fram* in the polar ice from a point on the northwest coast of Siberia to Spitzbergen. It is clear from this chart that depths in the vicinity of the *Fram* track are remote from the area along the 70th meridian that Peary was measuring. It is also clear that it would have been impossible for anyone to guess the contours of the bottom in 1909 and come up with anything resembling the accuracy of Peary's data when the set of soundings is considered as a whole. There were no extant data as to depths anywhere near the track Peary was following, as can be seen from the blank areas of the chart.

The first depth data collected after Peary's data was that collected by the Soviet expedition of 1937 led by Papanin. This expedition camped on an ice island (actually a giant ancient floe) in the general area of the Pole and drifted from there to the Greenland Sea. Thereafter, in 1948, another Soviet expedition, this one led by Professor Gakkel', made observations at more than 200 sites and collected enough data to define at least the northern end of the Lomonosov Ridge.

By 1952 the United States and other nations were devoting substantial resources to determination of the bathymetry of the region, and by 1954, the Soviets had published a bathymetry chart on which the Lomonosov Ridge is so well defined that the soundings of Peary could have been shown to be either compatible or incompatible with its contours. The particular area that was traversed by Peary had been fully covered by this time, largely by the depth measuring equipment on the United States' ice island T-3, known as Fletcher's Island. (For a plot of the island's gross movement see Part II, Figure II-8). The submarine ridge was crossed and recrossed numerous times by T-3, and the track of the island was well monitored. As a result the bathymetry of the area critical to the analysis of Peary's soundings was, even in 1954, quite well defined.

Figure IV-2 is a section of a bathymetric chart issued by the Naval Research Laboratory in 1985, based on information supplied principally by United States, Canadian, Swedish, Norwegian and German efforts. The sources of depth information used in making the bathymetric interpretations shown on the chart include 6 U.S. Ice Stations (commencing in 1952); 4 U.S. submarines (commencing in 1957); 800 U.S. Air-Lifted Gravity/Bathymetry Stations (commencing in 1960); Canadian ice stations set out by 3 Canadian polar expeditions (commencing in 1966); more than 7300 Canadian Bathymetric and Gravity stations (commencing in 1966); and about 64 cruises made by ice breakers and research ships from 1962. Of course these sources were spread over the entire Arctic basin, but a substantial number covered the area of Peary's soundings. We can therefore say that the bathymetry of that area has been adequately measured and charted to the extent that verification of Peary's soundings has been possible for many years, though to our knowledge it has never been undertaken.

To ensure that we utilized the most modern data, the 1985 Naval Research Laboratory chart was checked against recent unclassified submarine-reported depths in the vicinity of the 70th meridian. More than 20 of these made available by the Defense Mapping Agency proved to be generally in agreement with the Naval Research Laboratory map. Three submarine depths were in slight disagreement (5 to 10 miles off) with the detailed contours, and the chart was updated on the basis of these. (The slight changes made to reflect the submarine data do not affect the conclusions we have drawn with regard to Peary's soundings).

This bottom data was used to produce two three-dimensional computer generated maps of the bottom, from two different perspectives. They are reproduced as

Figures IV-3 and IV-4. On the maps is the line of the 70th meridian, "draped" over the contours of the bottom. This represents Peary's approximate (we know that he was slightly to the west of this) track to the Pole. Bottom contours at each of the eight soundings in Table IV-1, have been indicated along that line by the dark areas. To allow for inaccuracies in measurement as well as normal variations of the bottom surface, an uncertainty factor of + or - 50 meters (+ or - 25 fathoms) was applied to each depth as measured. Using this tolerance, the bottom traces are darkened in areas where the depth is equal to (or more than, in the case of "no bottom" soundings) the depth that Peary reported. The extent of the darkened areas was arbitrarily limited to circles of 15 miles radius around the reported positions at which the soundings were taken, since the contours continue indefinitely. The area at the Pole, where the depth is at least as great as Peary's sounding (no bottom at 1500 fathoms), is extended to 30 miles radius to show the limiting contour of that sounding.

The first view (Fig. IV-3) is plotted looking over the Pole back toward Cape Columbia. Because some of the earlier soundings are not visible behind the far dog-leg of the Lomonosov Ridge in this view, a second view (Fig. IV-4) was plotted looking in the opposite direction. In this view the earlier soundings are clearly visible.

The important fact shown by these plots is that a track close to the 70th meridian would cross every marked area at approximately the point at which Peary said the soundings were taken. Further, it is clear that Peary's reported soundings do change from deep to shallow when passing over the dog-leg of the Lomonosov Ridge nearest Cape Columbia. With absolutely no knowledge of the nature of the bottom along this route to the Pole it is beyond belief that Peary could have fabricated a *series* of depths which coincide with the now-known bottom contours as closely as these do.

It is also noteworthy that the soundings do not support the track conjectured by Herbert in his National Geographic article, and shown on Figure II-9. This is particularly true since the contour in the vicinity of the March 20th (85-23 N.) sounding curves back to the east and limits Peary's track to about 10 miles west of the 70th meridian, while Herbert places him 24 to 30 miles to the west of the meridian at this point. This limit makes the possibility of Peary's being far to the west in the northern reaches of the track extremely unlikely. In *Noose of Laurels* Herbert designates the center of the three tracks shown in his article in the National Geographic Magazine (Fig. II-9) as his ultimate track for Peary. This track places Peary about 55 miles to the west of the Pole where his sounding would have hit bottom well before 1500 fathoms. Thus the track is clearly inconsistent with Peary's soundings at significant points. We will, in the Part VII of this report, develop Peary's most likely track based in part on these soundings.

C. Peary and the Lomonosov Ridge

In the above mentioned report to the Coast and Geodetic Survey, Peary continues as follows:

> The sounding of 310 fathoms at 85°-23' naturally impressed me at once as surprising, and when Marvin reported the result to me, immediately after taking the sounding, I at once asked him if he was sure that he had the bottom, and he replied that he was, as the fact of this pronounced shoaling from 825 fathoms to 310, impressed him at once, and he made sure that his depth was correct.

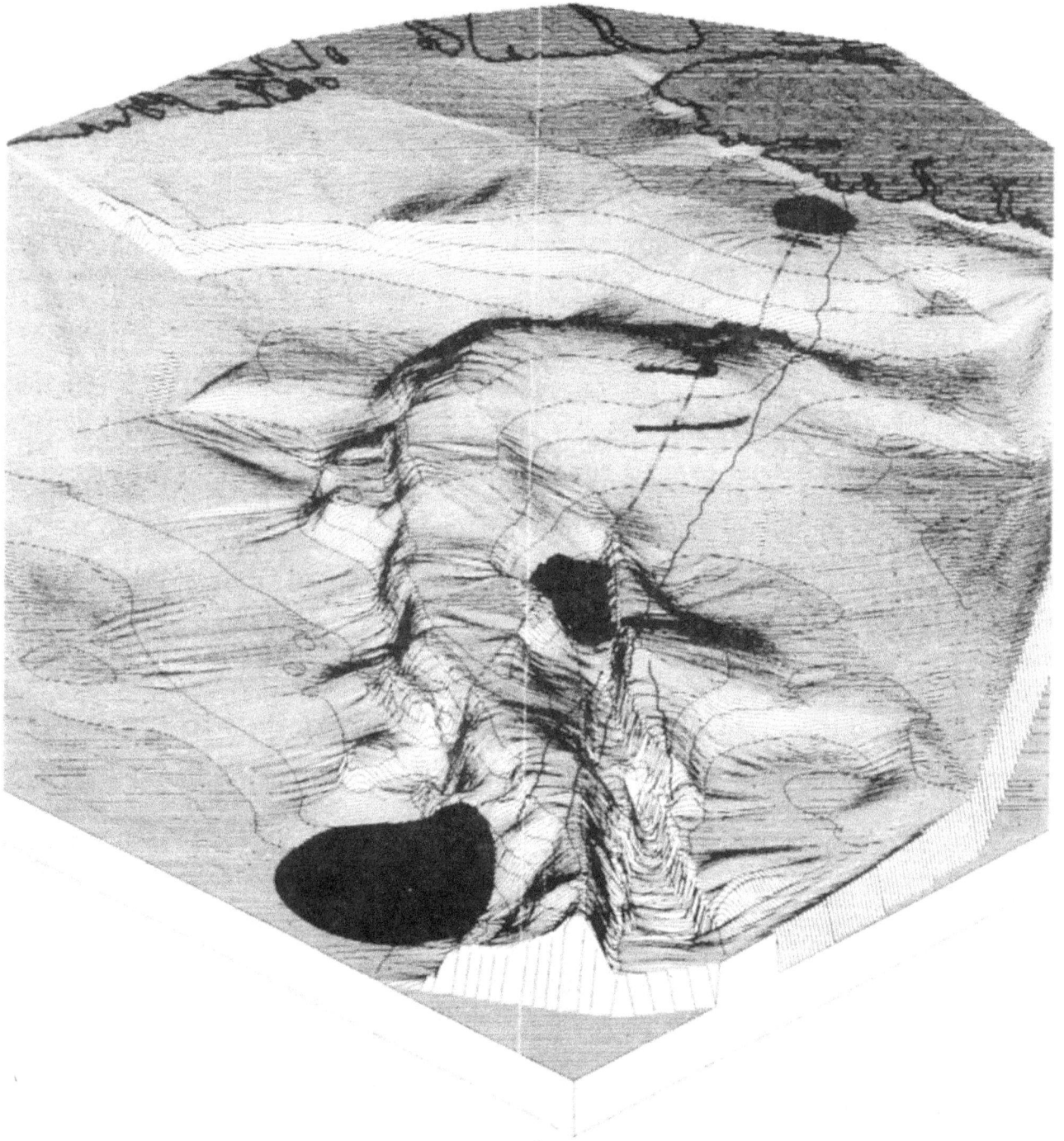

FIG. IV-3

138 — Robert E. Peary at the North Pole

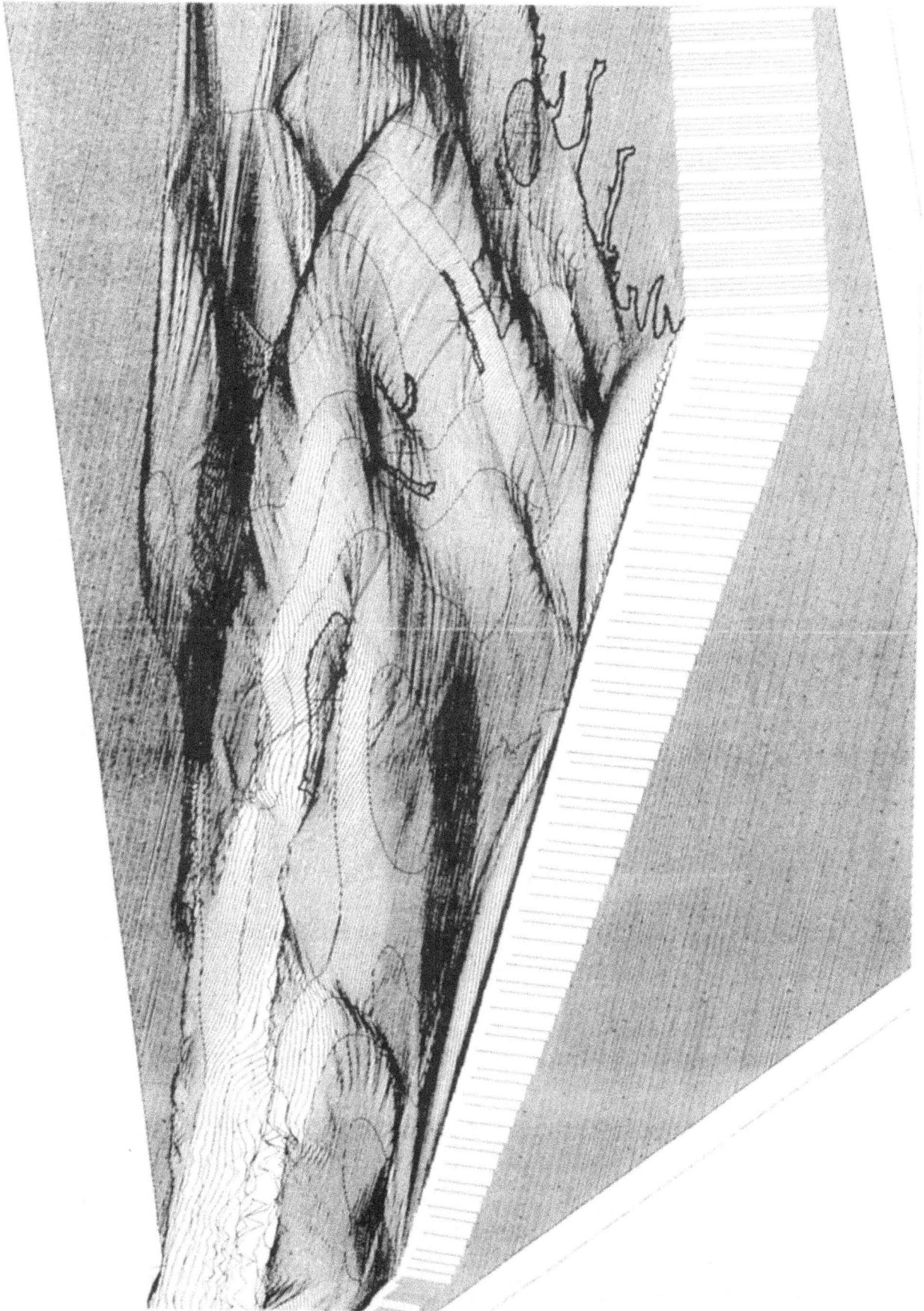

FIG. IV-4

Again when the sounding of 700 fathoms and no bottom was made about ten miles farther north, we both spoke of the peculiar fact of this outlying ridge with deeper channel intervening between it and the continental shelf, and Marvin again said that he was sure of his 310 fathoms reading.

Had it not been for the loss of the last lead and practically all the wire, while making the sounding at the pole I should, on the return, have interpolated other soundings.

The profile indicates that a line of 5 mile interval soundings from Cape Columbia to the 86th parallel might develop a particularly interesting profile of the bottom of the Arctic Ocean.

In view of Marvin's sounding, and Peary's suggestion that a line of soundings 5 miles apart from Cape Columbia to the 86th parallel might develop "a particularly interesting profile of the bottom of the Arctic Ocean," it is reasonable to assert that Peary was the real discoverer of the southern leg of the bottom feature that is now known as the Lomonosov Ridge.[3]

Bartlett's sounding at 87°-15' N. can best be observed on Figure IV-2. Although it is a "no bottom" sounding it clearly falls within the limits of the "trench" alongside the ridge and places Peary no more than 10 miles to the west or 20 miles to the east of the 70th meridian. The bottom contours there would also agree with Bartlett's sounding had he been more than 30 miles to the west, but that is improbable in view of Marvin's earlier soundings.

It is somewhat unfortunate that Peary's sounding at the Pole was, due to previous wire failure, a "no bottom" sounding. However the nature of the abyssal plane (very little change in depth) which underlies the Pole and extends a long distance toward Spitzbergen, is such that a more complete sounding would not have served to give us his location with much more accuracy. Nonetheless the contours of the near slope of the Lomonosov Ridge do serve to limit his position to about 30 to 40 miles from the Pole in the direction of Melville Sound.[4]

The "no bottom at 1500" sounding was not a complete waste insofar as attempting to verify Peary's position at the Pole is concerned.

---

[3] Ironically, A. P. Crary and Norman Goldstein of the Air Force Cambridge Research Center proposed naming one of their discoveries which they took to be a ridge at about 87 to 88 N. for Ross Marvin, wishing to honor the young explorer who had died on Peary's expedition. Later bathymetric measurements caused the "ridge" to be downgraded to a "spur." Thus we have on today's charts, "Marvin Spur."

[4] It is also true that the sounding would match the contours if Peary had been about 70 miles from the Pole in the same direction. While this does seem to present an ambiguity, the earlier soundings taken along the way, and other data we consider elsewhere in this report, rule this location out.

As he explained to the Congressional committee:

> If a line of soundings were carried to the pole and every
> one touched bottom, that would be an absolute identification
> and verification right straight through. If a line of
> soundings were taken and they reported 1,500 [fathoms] bottom
> and somebody else should go there and get only 100 fathoms,
> that would not look well, but if someone else should go
> there and should get 2,000 fathoms or 2,500 fathoms,
> I would say that it would not show anything.

To reverse the analogy, had Peary come back with a sounding that showed shoaling (a shallow depth) at the Pole, that would not look good in the light of current data. At the North Pole the depth of the ocean bed is now known to be 2,346 fathoms. Peary's "no bottom sounding at 1500" fathoms is therefore plausible.

From our comparison of Peary's data with our charts, we concluded that Peary's soundings are credible and reasonably accurate as they indicate bottom contours consistent with the bottom as it is known today. Moreover, in the light of the knowledge of the bottom in 1909, there is no chance that this set of soundings could have been produced by guesswork or fraud.

Part Five

SHADOWS ON THE NORTH POLE PHOTOGRAPHS

In a letter dated April 4, 1910, to the *New York Times*, Admiral Colby Chester, who was a member of the original three-man board evaluating Peary's data for the National Geographic Society, said that he had examined a number of Peary's photographs taken enroute to the Pole and found that the length of the shadows agreed with Peary's recorded latitude in every case. Since the details of Admiral Chester's study of Peary's photographs have not survived we don't know how sophisticated his analysis was. Rawlins has questioned Admiral Chester's evaluation on the grounds that the pictures were not conclusive inasmuch as shadows of any length could be obtained by selecting an appropriate local time. Rawlins also maintains that the Pole pictures are fuzzy with no useful shadows. Finally he suggests that the pictures Henson took at the Pole have been suppressed.

In 1917 the idea of using shadows to determine the elevation or altitude of the sun as recorded in the Peary photographs was again advanced by Captain Thomas Hall in *Has the North Pole Been Discovered?* Captain Hall, a merchant captain, was one of several early critics publishing books or articles elaborating on criticisms of Peary developed in the 1911-1912 Congressional hearings. On page 150 of his book he describes the value of analyzing the photographs in the following words:

> "Shadows are nature's witnesses. They never lie
> and they testify on other subjects besides that of altitudes."

We will demonstrate the significance of these words in this part of this report.

Hall, who had access only to the photographs as reproduced in Peary's book, *The North Pole*, asserted that the shadows in certain Camp Jesup pictures showed that the sun was at an elevation of 30 degrees above the horizon. Hall maintained that other pictures had been deliberately tampered with so that shadows were not visible. He took this as proof that Peary was not at the Pole when the pictures were taken. Subsequently these assertions were repeated by several Peary critics, none of whom claimed to have actually analyzed the pictures. Of course if Hall's allegations had been correct the shadows would have indeed been "proof" that Peary was *not* at the Pole, because on April 6th and 7th, the sun was actually only about 7 degrees elevation ("altitude" in navigation parlance), and the altitude made only a slight change during the entire time he was there.

A large number of negatives of Peary's Camp Jesup pictures, including most of those in the various editions of Peary's book, are available in the picture files of the National Geographic Society. These negatives are actually contact copy negatives made from the original nitrate negatives (around 1960) because of the possible fire hazard the old negatives presented. Some of the negatives had been "improved" (either by Peary or his publisher) for optimum appearance in his book. This consisted of cropping and opaquing the sky for maximum contrast with the figures in the picture. As one might expect, the printing exposure in all the pictures was set for best viewing of the *people* and thus the snow was washed out and shows very few shadows. To overcome this we have had a set of prints made with the shadows brought out at the expense of losing detail for the people.

In analyzing the shadows certain information about the photo is essential. First the horizon must be identifiable to determine the tilt of the camera (up or down and left or right). In addition the focal length of the lens and the actual size of the negative must be known in order to calculate the various angles that are to be measured. Details of how this is done are given below. Finally the optical center of the picture must be located (at least approximately), which can only be done with a complete, uncropped negative. The center can be located from the negative or from a contact print from it in which the frame of the negative is visible.

Not all of the pictures are suitable for quantitative analysis, but a number are satisfactory, with horizons showing and shadows brought out by over-printing. We have applied modern techniques of "rectification" to the shadows on these photographs, to correct for the effects of perspective, and then actually measured the Sun's altitude from them. The Sun's diameter (about one half degree) blurs the shadows very slightly and we have applied the standard correction of deducting 8 minutes of arc to reflect the fact that the perceived edge of the shadow is offset from the mid-point of the "blur" toward the dark part of the shadow.[1] Of course the focus and quality of the photograph also affects the accuracy of the result. The best accuracy obtainable has been stated to be plus or minus 5 minutes of arc (see footnote 1); however in view of the quality of the pictures we have used plus or minus 15 minutes as a practical limit on accuracy.

Without the negatives (or contact prints) available to him and without knowing the camera used and its focal length, Hall could not have used this technique, and therefore it is not possible for him to have precisely measured the altitude of the Sun from the shadows. In his book he makes no pretense of rectifying the shadows, and in fact it is likely that he had no knowledge of the principles involved. His attempt to determine the Sun's altitude from the angle of a shadow in the plane of the photograph simply does not work unless the shadows are oriented 90 degrees to the axis of the camera.

---

[1] *Simple Photogrammetry*, J.C.C. Williams, 1969, p. 80.

Identification of Peary's camera was essential for determining the focal length to be used in the calculations used in the rectification method employed.

Peary stated that he used Kodak cameras, and a review of *Kodak: The First Hundred Years* (by Brian Coe) showed that relatively few models were available in the 1906 - 1909 period. With the help of Mr. Philip Condax of the Eastman House Museum of Photography, in Rochester , N.Y., we were able to identify the type of cameras Peary used in 1906 and 1909. This was accomplished through matching the picture frame of the camera type with the format of the negatives. The camera used by Peary in 1906 was identified as a #4 Kodak in the Peary Exhibit in Explorers Hall at the National Geographic Society. The 1909 camera was identified as a #4 Folding Pocket Kodak by matching its frame to the negative format. A sample of this model was provided by the Eastman House Museum in Rochester, New York. Both cameras — and most other Kodaks of that time — used the same Rapid Rectilinear lens. One additional camera was identified as #1A Folding Brownie. This type of camera was used for several photographs of Eskimos and scenes around Camp Jesup which we could not use. It may have been Henson's camera.

A. Methodology

The analysis of the photographs is based on the principle of perspective. To illustrate the method a perspective drawing of a simple cube is shown in Figure V-1.

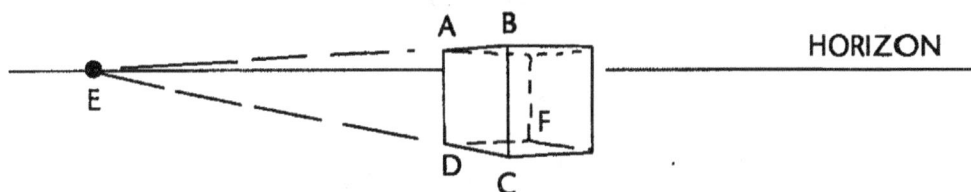

Figure V-1.

The two edges AB and CD have been extended to point E which is called the "vanishing point." If the cube has these sides parallel to a horizontal ground plane, the vanishing point will lie on the horizon. The other two visible edges will also have a vanishing point on the horizon if extended sufficiently. The exception to this occurs when the edges are parallel to the plane of the picture in which case they do not converge and never intersect.

Now if the cube is tilted a small amount about the edge DF as in Figure V-2, the vanishing point is below the horizon by the distance HE, vertically below the original vanishing point.

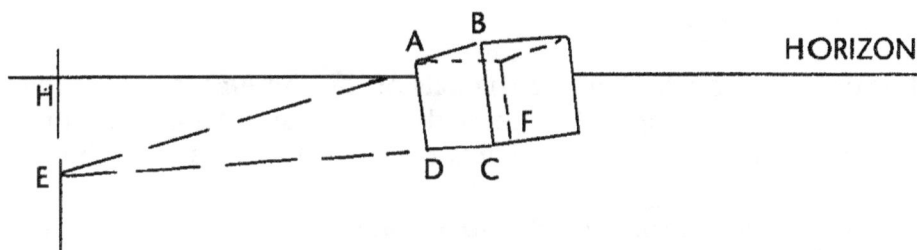

Figure V-2.

In our case we can say that the edges AB and CD represent the line between the initial point and the terminus of two shadows. Each of these lines is defined by a ray of light from the Sun, and all rays from the Sun are parallel. The vanishing point will be below the horizon by an amount which represents the elevation of the sun. This angle can be quite accurately computed if the focal length of the camera lens which produced the image is known. It is also necessary to see the horizon in the picture since the angle measured in this manner is first determined relative to the optical axis of the camera and must then be related to the horizon.

The application of this method to rectify the shadows requires great care to ensure that both the initial point and the end point of each selected shadow are clearly visible and that one or the other is not obscured by a mound of snow intervening, or by the surface on which the shadow is projected being too short to register the entire shadow. Consequently many shadows are not useable. Those that are used should produce lines which converge at one vanishing point. The fact that a number do so converge is a check that the method is being correctly applied. Since many of the useable shadows are small and detailed, altering a picture to be used in this way is next to impossible.

The geometry for measurement is shown in Figures V-3 and V-4 below. Figure V-3 depicts the plane of the picture, on which is shown the horizon line and a line through the optical center of the picture, C, parallel to the horizon. E represents the vanishing point determined as discussed above. The horizontal coordinate of E is X, and the vertical is Y. These are measured along and perpendicular to the horizontal line through the optical center of the picture (determined from the contact print). Thus they are relative to the optical axis and a horizontal through it.

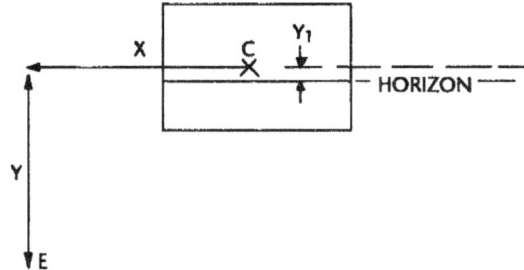

Figure V-3

The first step of the measurement is done by dividing X by the focal length, F^2, of the camera. This quotient is the tangent of the angle Z, the angle that the vertical plane of the sun's rays make with the axis of the camera. If the local apparent time is known the direction that the camera was pointed can be determined. The vertical angle of the sun *relative to the horizontal plane through the camera's axis* is determined by dividing Y by D, where D is the focal length divided by the cosine of Z. The result is the tangent of the angle A.

The vertical tilt angle T (along the axis of the camera) is determined from the distance (Y1) between the optical center of the picture and the horizon line. The effect of the tilt angle on the angle of the Sun's rays above the plane of the camera's axis

---

[2] The value to be used must be corrected slightly to reflect the specific distance at which the camera is focussed. The focal length (F) at any distance (d) is given by the equation:

$$1/F = 1/F' - 1/d, \quad \text{where F' is the focal length at infinity.}$$

(measured in the vertical plane of the Sun's rays) is determined using spherical trigonometry to give the sun's angle S with the *horizontal plane*. Figure V-4 shows the geometry of this operation.

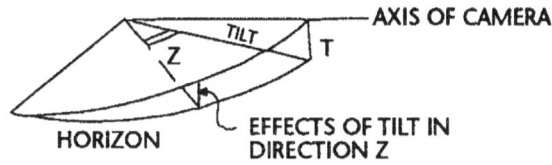

Figure V-4.

A summary of the calculations is given below:

1) Z = arc tangent (X / Focal Length)

2) D = Focal Length / cosine Z

3) A = arc tangent (Y / D)

4) T = arc tangent (Y1 / Focal Length)

5) S = A - arc tangent ((cosine Z) tangent T)

The focal lengths of Peary's cameras were determined by focussing the camera on objects of known size at a known distance and measuring the images at the plane of the film. The relative size of the image at the plane of the film, the true object size, and the distance to the object was used to determine the focal length as shown in Table V-1.

Table V-1

Camera Focal Lengths

Record of measurements made with several cameras to determine focal length: Cameras I and II are both #4 Cartridge Folding Kodaks as was used in the 1906 expedition. Camera III is a #4 Folding Pocket Kodak as used in the 1909 expedition. Camera V is that used for the picture of Will Steger's expedition, as a check of the methodology.

Camera	Year	A	B	C	f	F	mm	Frame Size
I	1906	381	106.0	1.96	6.92	6.80	172.7	3.72 x 4.66
II	1906	381	106.0	1.95	6.88	6.76	171.7	3.72 x 4.66
III	1909	381	107.5	1.97	6.86	6.74	171.2	4.0 x 5.0
IV	1909	367.5	106.3	1.45	4.95	4.88	124.0	2.48 x 4.25
V	1986	371	106.0	.314	1.096	1.092	27.76	24 x 36 mm

Computed using the equation: $1/f = 1/F - 1/(A-f-x)$

Where:
- A = Distance from film to object
- B = Object dimension
- C = Image dimension
- f = Focal length at distance A
- F = Focal length at infinity
- x = distance between principle points of lens

(estimated from measurements of lens).

As a test and demonstration of the technique we applied it to a modern picture taken at a known time, date and location, see Figure V-5. It was taken at the North Pole on May 3rd 1986 at 1530 GMT by Kent Kobersteen of the National Geographic Society. The occasion was the arrival at the Pole by Will Steger and his party, hence the celebration.

The picture was taken with a 35 mm auto focus camera, with a nominal 28 mm lens. We measured this lens as 27.76 mm (at infinity) and used this in our calculations. The Nautical Almanac for 1986 shows the sun's declination, and therefore its altitude at the Pole, to be 15 degrees 43 minutes. The shadow lines were drawn through the several points that can be identified as complete shadows and their intersections can be readily seen, overlying the shadow of the photographer's head. In this picture the existence of the photographer's shadow gives a clear indication of the general location of the vanishing point[3], but the shadows are still required for exact location.

Several methods of estimating the focus distance were used, one based on the height of one of the participants and another based on the distance of the photographer's shadow measured by the angle of depression. These indicated that the most probable distance was 15 feet. At this distance the effective focal length is 27.93 mm. The scale factor is 6.924 so the effective focal length of the enlargement is 193.4 mm. Our measured coordinates of the vanishing point, on the enlargement, are X = 62.3 mm, Y = 63.6 mm and Y1 = 6.0 mm. However we also had 3 independent observers plot their vanishing point and the mean of all of the coordinates give a value of 15 degrees 47 minutes for the altitude of the sun. At this altitude there is a refraction correction of 3 minutes (subtracted).

From the resulting value of 15 degrees 44 minutes we corrected for the effect of the sun's diameter by subtracting 8 minutes[4], because the photographs do not record all of the "penumbra" which fades into the non-shadow area beyond the shadow's end. Thus the final value of the sun's altitude by this technique is 15 degrees 36 minutes, which compares favorably with the Almanac value of 15 degrees 43 minutes. We estimate the accuracy to be plus or minus 15 minutes of arc for this high quality photograph. In Appendix C is the report of William G. Hyzer, a photogrammetrist certificated by the American Society of Photogrammetry and Remote Sensing, who reviewed and confirmed the correctness of our methodology. A second photogrammetrist, D. R. Graff, also tested the method on the Steger picture. His report is also included in Appendix C.

B. Application to the Peary Pole Photographs

We have examined all of Peary's photographs taken at or near the North Pole and have ascertained that not a single photograph shows shadows that would contradict Peary's claim that he was at the Pole. In virtually all of the photographs, it is possible to determine that the sun is very low, as it would have been at the Pole, but for many photographs it is not possible to measure the angle of the sun with any degree of precision, either because there are not enough clearly identifiable shadows or because the horizon cannot be precisely located. However, the 13 photographs listed in Table V-2 warrant careful analysis. As discussed below, although not all of these photographs are susceptible of precise quantitative analysis, taken together they provide a great deal of information about the location of Camp Jesup and Peary's activities in and around Camp Jesup. In particular we will show that the pictures were taken at several different times which will allow us to get a single area in which Peary must have been when the pictures were taken.

---

[3] The vanishing point is the point at which the shadow of the camera's lens would appear.

[4] This method is recommended by Williams in *Simple Photogrammetry*.

Table V-2

Figure	Peary's #	Our Title	Sun's Alt.	Bearing
V-11	B15	Camp Jesup (Overcast)	-	-
V-12	D1	Stars & Stripes on the North Pole	7-02	-121.2
V-13	E1	Looking towards Cape Columbia	6-33	143.5
V-14	E2	Looking towards Bering Strait	7-04	50.0
V-15	E3	Looking towards Cape Chelyuskin	6-44	-39.6
V-16	E4	Looking towards Spitzbergen	6-50	-130.4
V-17	E5	Two men in front of Pinnacle	6-45	-149.7
V-18	F7	Man on Pinnacle with Flag		-100.
V-19	G3*	Five men in front of Pinnacle	7-06	335.
V-20	G4	Five men with flags at Pinnacle	7-08	140.7
V-21	G5	Men marching with Flags (side)	6-34	-155.2
V-22	G6	Men marching with Flags (rear)	7-04	147.5
V-23	G8	Sounding	6-55	174.7

* Peary's number is not visible, but our study shows it was taken at the same time as G4.

The numbering of the photographs in Table V-2 reflects numbers that appear to be in Peary's handwriting on the edge of the negatives. We believe that these numbers show the time sequence of the photographs.

1. Analyzing Sun's Bearing and Direction

Five of these photographs (D1, E5, F7, G3, and G4) show what, on close inspection, is clearly the same ice pinnacle viewed from different directions. Figure V-6 is a "top view" of the pinnacle with the approximate viewing direction of each of the 5 pinnacle pictures indicated. Estimates of the Sun's relative bearing in these pictures can be used to determine the approximate time difference (within an hour or two) between the pictures. As shown below in Table V-3 the bearing of the sun relative to the camera axis, Z, in each of these 5 pictures is measured, using the methodology discussed above. These equations give an angle Z between 0 and 90 degrees, measured either left or right of the camera viewing direction or the reverse of the camera direction as appropriate. These angles are converted into an angle between -180 and 180 degrees, using the convention that an angle of 0 degrees means the Sun is directly ahead of the photographer and positive angles are measured clockwise (viewed from above). The estimated viewing direction is taken from Figure V-6 and added to Z to give the direction of the Sun for each photograph relative to the viewing direction of E-5.

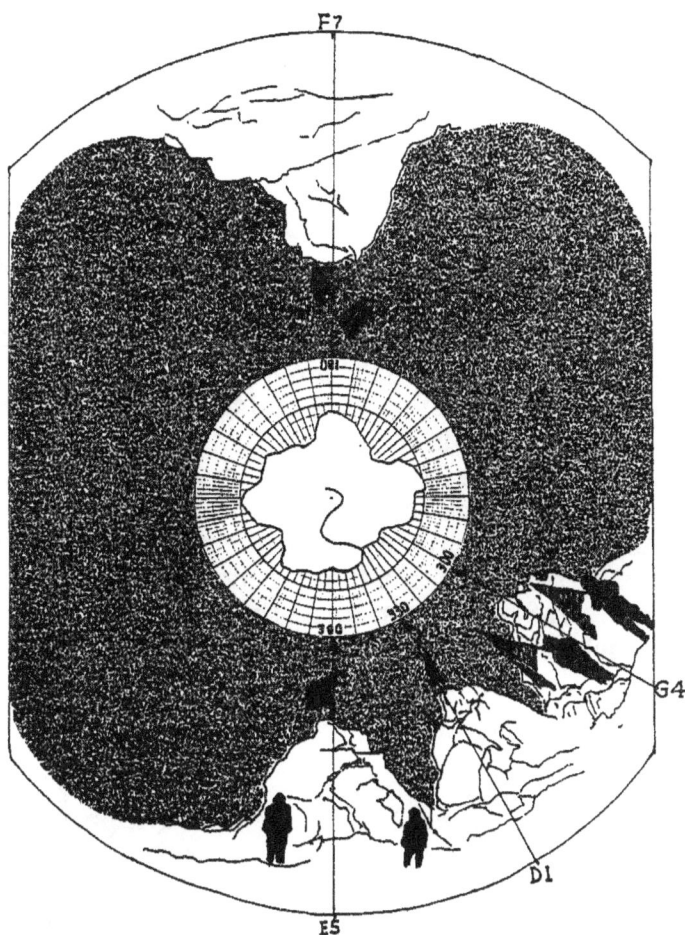

Fig. V-6

Table V-3

Photo #	Relative Viewing Direction	Sun Relative to Camera Axis (Z)	Relative Sun Direction
D1	330	-120	210
E5	360	-150	210
F7	180	-100	80
G3	300	140	80*
G4	300	140	80

* 440 - 360

Since the Sun's relative bearing at the Pole changes by 15 degrees per hour, it is clear that photographs D1 and E5 were taken at about the same time (within a span of about an hour or two), and that photographs F7, G3, and G4 were taken about 15 to 16 hours after D1 and E5[5]. Based on Peary's description in *The North Pole* of his activities at Camp Jesup, the "flag ceremony" shown in G3 and G4 took place on April 7th some time after Peary's 12:40 p.m. sights and before his 4:00 p.m. departure on the homeward journey. Allowing a reasonable time for Peary to work out his sights and get organized for the flag ceremony, and considering that the party attempted to sleep after the flag ceremony, before deciding to start the return march, the flag ceremony most likely took place at about 2:00 p.m. on April 7th. Thus the earlier pinnacle shots (D1 and E5) taken about 15 to 16 hours earlier, as shown in table V-3, were taken at about 10:00 p.m. on April 6th.

2. Time from the Directional Shots

The directional shots (E1 through E4) are particularly useful in determining the *time* of the photographs because we know the directions that Peary said that he was facing when he took them[6]. Thus we can determine the Sun's direction for each of the photographs relative to the camera axis and determine the sun's true bearing which can be related to time. The four shots were said to have been taken at approximately 90 degree bearing intervals: one in the direction of Cape Columbia (70 W), one in the direction of Spitzbergen (20 E or 340 W), one in the direction of Cape Chelyuskin (105 E or 255 W), and one in the direction of the Bering Strait (170 W). It is not clear whether Peary meant to take these shots in the precise direction of the geographical references given; more likely, he simply meant that he took the shots in four approximately orthogonal directions. Table V-3 summarizes the results of the quantitative analysis of these four photographs.

Table V-4

Shot #	Viewing Direction (Approx.)	Sun Bearing (Approx.)	Sun's Meridian (GHA)
E-1	070 W	145	215
E-2	170 W	50	220
E-3	255 W	-40	215
E-4	340 W	-130	210

We were able to determine the sun's bearing for E1 reasonably precisely. Our measurements for E2 and E3 are within about 3 or 4 degrees and our measurement for E4 is less precise since the shadows are very small. Considering that Peary probably was pointing by "seaman's eye" the results are remarkably consistent. The first point to note about these results is that, based on Peary's stated directions, each of the photographs shows the sun's direction (meridian) to be about 210-220 degrees. Thus, assuming that the four shots were taken at the same time, they were directed at roughly the 90 degree intervals that Peary stated. The Greenwich Hour Angle of the sun of 210-220 W means that the four photographs were all taken at about 10:00 p.m. Cape Sheridan Time, about the same time determined above for shot E5 at the pinnacle. It is reasonable to conclude that the first pinnacle shot and the directional shots were taken at approximately the same time since they are numbered sequentially. In addition they appear to have been taken at the same place. This can be observed by noting that the directional shot facing Spitzbergen shows in the extreme left fore-

---

[5] It is clear that Photograph E5 was taken earlier than photographs G3 and G4, since there are far fewer footprints in E5. The two mounds on which the Eskimo men are standing in G3 and G4 can be seen in the center and left foreground of E5, showing that the photographer's vantage point changed by about 60 degrees counterclockwise (viewed from above) between the earlier and the later shot, as shown in Figure V-6.

[6] The reader will note that a piece of tape has been placed over the horizon on E3. This apparently was done to provide a pure white sky for the narrow strip of the photograph printed in the U.S. edition of Peary's book *The North Pole*. The full photograph was printed in the British edition of *The North Pole*, using an unretouched negative. This print shows that the tape does not obscure significant information.

ground what appears to be the upper right corner of the pinnacle. In addition, in the center foreground is an indistinct shadow that appears to be the shadow of the flag flying from the pinnacle.

The analysis of the Sun's bearing in the North Pole photographs does not by itself say anything about Peary's location. That is the subject of the analysis of the Sun's elevation presented below. However the analysis of the timing of the photographs on the basis of the Sun's bearing agrees well with Peary's reports of his activities in and around Camp Jesup, thus supporting the credibility of his story and confirming that the photographs are genuine.

For example, the fact that Peary took two photographs of the U.S. flag on an ice pinnacle (suggesting that he had reached his goal) at about 10:00 p.m. on April 6, supports his statement that he wrote his note starting with "The Pole at last..." shortly after waking[7] from his first sleep at Camp Jesup. The photographs also support Peary's testimony before the House Committee on page 126 of the record, about when he took his North Pole photographs:

Mr. Roberts. Just one moment. You recall now that I am speaking of the four that were pointed out in the book (North Pole, opp. p. 299); those are the particular ones I am talking about. I wanted to identify those particular ones.

Capt. Peary. Yes. I can not say exactly when they were taken, but they were taken after 8 o'clock on the 6th; I can say that. I do not know that I can recall the precise time, other than to say that they were taken after 8 o'clock, because they were taken in sunlight.

Mr. Roberts. They were taken after 8 o'clock of the 6th?

Capt. Peary. They were taken after 8 o'clock of the 6th.

Mr. Roberts. In the morning?

Capt. Peary. They were taken some time between 8 p.m. of the 6th and 4 p.m. of the 7th.

Thus Peary made it clear that he took his first photographs at the Pole sometime after 8:00 p.m. on April 6th. Prior to that time, he indicated, the sky was overcast. Photograph B1, showing Camp Jesup, and apparently taken well before D1, shows an overcast sky, since there are no distinct shadows. This provides support for Peary's claim that conditions were not clear enough for a 6:40 p.m. sight.

The time span covered by the photographs supports Peary's claim with respect to the amount of time he spent at the Pole. The timing of G3 and G4 supports his statement that, after a noon sight on April 7, he conducted some "more or less informal ceremonies" and then headed south at about 4:00 p.m.

---

[7] Presumably a little before 6 p.m., since he went to sleep for a few hours after his noon sight on April 6 and got up to attempt a 6:40 p.m. sight .

Finally, the analysis of the directional shots shows that they were very probably taken in the direction that Peary said they were. One of the two prongs of Hall's criticism of the Peary photographs is based on his assumption, without any justification whatsoever, that the directional shots were taken shortly before 4:00 p.m. on April 7. On that assumption, the Sun's bearings in the photographs would be wrong. However we have shown that there is good reason to believe that the directional shots were taken at 10:00 p.m. on April 6, and on that assumption the bearings are precisely correct.

As significant as these findings are, the greatest value in knowing the approximate times of the North Pole photographs is the ability to use those times, in conjunction with measurements of the Sun's elevation, to obtain an approximate "fix" of Peary's position. That analysis follows.

3. Analysis of Sun's Elevation

The Sun's elevation (altitude) at the North Pole should be equal to its declination, which, at the season we are considering, varies only slowly (about 23' per day). Table V-5 shows the Sun's declination taken from the *Nautical Almanac* for the times of Peary's various photographs. If the altitude in a photograph is greater than the declination it would place Peary along a line perpendicular to the bearing of the Sun, and offset from the Pole in the direction of the Sun's bearing by one n.m. for each arc-minute of altitude that the measured altitude exceeds the declination (subject to inherent accuracy limitations). Thus knowing the bearing of the Sun allows the development of a "line of position" based on the Sun's altitude. Altitudes corresponding to several different bearings of the Sun (i.e. different times), permit the development of several different lines of position that intersect at the photographer's approximate position.

Table V-5

Corrections to Sun's Declination (Almanac) for Time and Refraction:

Picture(s)	Date +4	Time GMT	Mean Noon Dec.	Corr.	Refr.	Altitude
E1-E5	06 2200	070200	6-41-34	-9	+9	6°-42'
G3, G4	07 1400	071800	6-41-34	+6	+9	6°-57'
G8	07 1800	072200	6-41-34	+9	+9	7°-00'

The 10:00 p.m. Photographs. As shown above photographs D1 and E1-E5 were taken at about 10:00 p.m. on April 6. Two of these, E1 and E5, permit quite precise determination of the Sun's altitude within about 20' standard deviation.[8] In these photographs, the vanishing point and horizon can be located with a great degree of precision. Two other photographs, D1 and E3, permit a determination of the Sun's altitude with less precision, since there are not enough clear long shadows to permit an accurate determination of the vanishing point. Photograph E2 permits only a rough determination of the Sun's altitude, but at least provides some further confirmation of the results.

Table V-6 summarizes the altitudes determined from D1 and E1-E5, showing the standard deviation estimated for each altitude. These standard deviations are estimated by determining the reasonable maximum variations from the best estimate of the locations of the vanishing point and the horizon line.

At 10:00 p.m. the Sun's declination (and therefore its true altitude at the Pole) would have been 6-33. Adding a refraction correction of 9 minutes of arc means that the Sun's apparent altitude, to an observer at the Pole, was about 6-42.

The average of the altitude in Table V-6 is about 6-50, which means that the best estimate of Peary's *line of position* is located about 8 n.m. (6-50 minus 6-42) from the Pole, as shown in Figure V-7. A band of probable locations is shown based on the 13' (13 n.m.) standard deviation for the results.

Table V-6

Summary of Sun's Altitudes
10:00 p.m., April 6, Photographs.

Photo #.	Est. Altitude	Std. Deviation (min.)
D1	7-02	25
E1	6-33	20
E2	7-04	45
E3	6-44	25
E4	6-50	40
E5	6-45	20
Average	6-50	13*

* 1/6 of square root of sum of the squares of individual values.

Our best estimate of Peary's claimed location at 10;00 p.m. on April 6th is also shown in Figure V-7. This estimate is based on the location of Camp Jesup determined from Peary's observations and the fact that the pinnacle was fairly close to Camp Jesup (since the entire polar party went to the pinnacle from Camp Jesup for the final "flag ceremony"). Figure V-7 shows that our estimate of Peary's claimed position is within about 5 n.m. of the line of position determined from the 10:00 p.m. photographs and falls well within the band of probable error. These results do not by themselves rule out other positions far from the Pole along the line of position; that must be done by examining the photographs taken at other times.

The 2:00 p.m. Photographs. As shown above, photographs G3 - G6 were taken at about 2:00 p.m. on April 7th, shortly before Peary left the Pole. Table V-7 summarizes the Sun's altitude measured in these shots.

---

[8] That is the actual measured altitude will be within one standard deviation of the measured altitude with a confidence of just under 70%, and will be within two standard deviations (plus or minus 40') with near certainty.

Table V-7

Summary of Sun's Altitudes
2:00 p.m., April 7, photographs

Photo #	Est. Altitude	Std. Deviation
G3	7-06	30
G4	7-08	30
G5	6-34	30
G6	7-04	30
Average	6-58	15

These results are not as precise as the best of the 10:00 p.m. photographs for a variety of reasons. In G3 and G4, the horizon cannot be located precisely, and a "worst case" estimate is used. G5 and G6 are fuzzy and contain relatively few clear shadows. The average altitude determined from these four photographs is probably accurate to within about 15' (one standard deviation).

As shown in Table V-5, the Sun's declination at 2:00 p.m. on April 7 was about 6-48. Adding 9' for refraction gives an apparent altitude of 6-57. The average altitude from Table V-7 is 6-58, the line of position determined from these shots passes about 1 n.m. south of the Pole, as shown in Figure V-8. The fact that this line of position passes exactly through the estimated position of the pinnacle should not be accorded too much significance in view of the band of probable error. The important point is that, again, Peary's claimed position falls well within the band of probable positions determined from the photographs.

The 6:00 p.m. photograph. The final photograph to be analyzed in detail is the photograph G8, of the sounding that Peary said he took about 5 miles south of Camp Jesup on the return trip. This is a particularly useful photograph since the time and place at which Peary says he took it are reasonably well defined. Peary left Camp Jesup at 4:00 p.m. on April 7, and he would have arrived at the point 5 miles south of Camp Jesup at about 7:00 p.m. The Sun was essentially due west at that time so the sun's elevation in this photograph provides an excellent check on Peary's position to the left or right of his intended track. Unfortunately, this photograph does not show the horizon; however, it is possible to establish the maximum altitude for the sun by determining the highest possible location of the horizon in the photograph and to determine a best estimate of the horizon. When this is done, the sun's maximum elevation is 7-11. For an estimated reasonable location of the horizon, the sun's altitude is 6-55. The sun's elevation as measured in the photograph at 7:00 p.m. on April 7 should have been 7-00 if Peary had been precisely on the Columbia meridian. These values indicate that Peary was probably no more than 11 miles west, nor more than 19 miles east, of the Columbia meridian. The band of probable positions is plotted in Figure V-9. Again, Peary's claimed position falls well within the band of probable positions. All 3 bands of probable location are shown on Figure V-10. The conclusion the Peary was not very far west of the Cape Columbia meridian is also supported by his sounding, with which he did not reach bottom with 1500 fathoms of wire. The curved line on Figure V-10 is the boundary line to the west of which Peary would have reached bottom with that amount of wire.

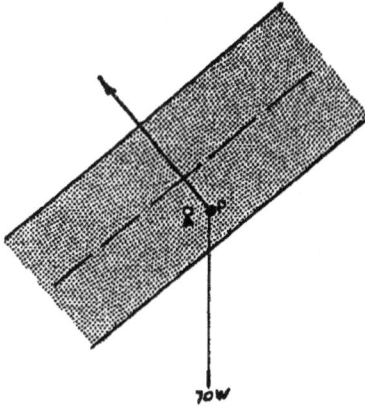

Figure V-7 Band of Positions,
10:00 p.m., April 6.

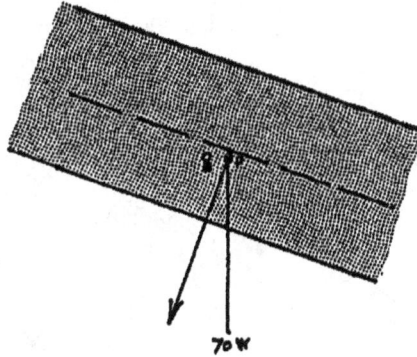

Figure V-8 Band of Positions, 2:00
p.m., April 7.

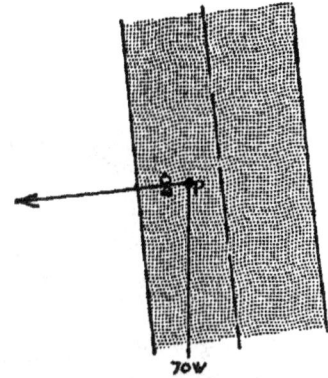

Figure V-9 Band of Positions,
6:00 p.m., April 7.

The intersection area (shaded) in Figure V-10 is the probable area from which *all* of the photographs must have been taken. The impressive internal consistency of the photographs, the magnitude of detail analyzed, which makes "faking" essentially impossible, and the excellent "match" with Peary's published story, all lead us to the conclusion that such was the case.

The shaded area includes Peary's claimed position for Camp Jesup, some 2 miles short of the Pole and 4 miles to the "left". It also includes positions to the left and slightly short of the Pole, at total distances up to 20 miles from the pole. If one had nothing but the photographs to go on, one could conceivably argue that Peary *might* have missed the Pole by up to 20 miles.[9] However, if the sights that Peary took at the Pole showed that he was 20 miles away, it is difficult to imagine that he lacked the courage or the will to cover the last 20 miles. Since our analysis of the sights gave us no reason to doubt their authenticity we conclude that Camp Jesup was located where the sights showed it to be — within the limits of the precision of Peary's instruments and the arctic ambient — about 5 miles from the North Pole.

---

[9] Even in that case, the 8 mile run that he made to the east on the morning of April 7th would have brought him within about 12 miles of the Pole.

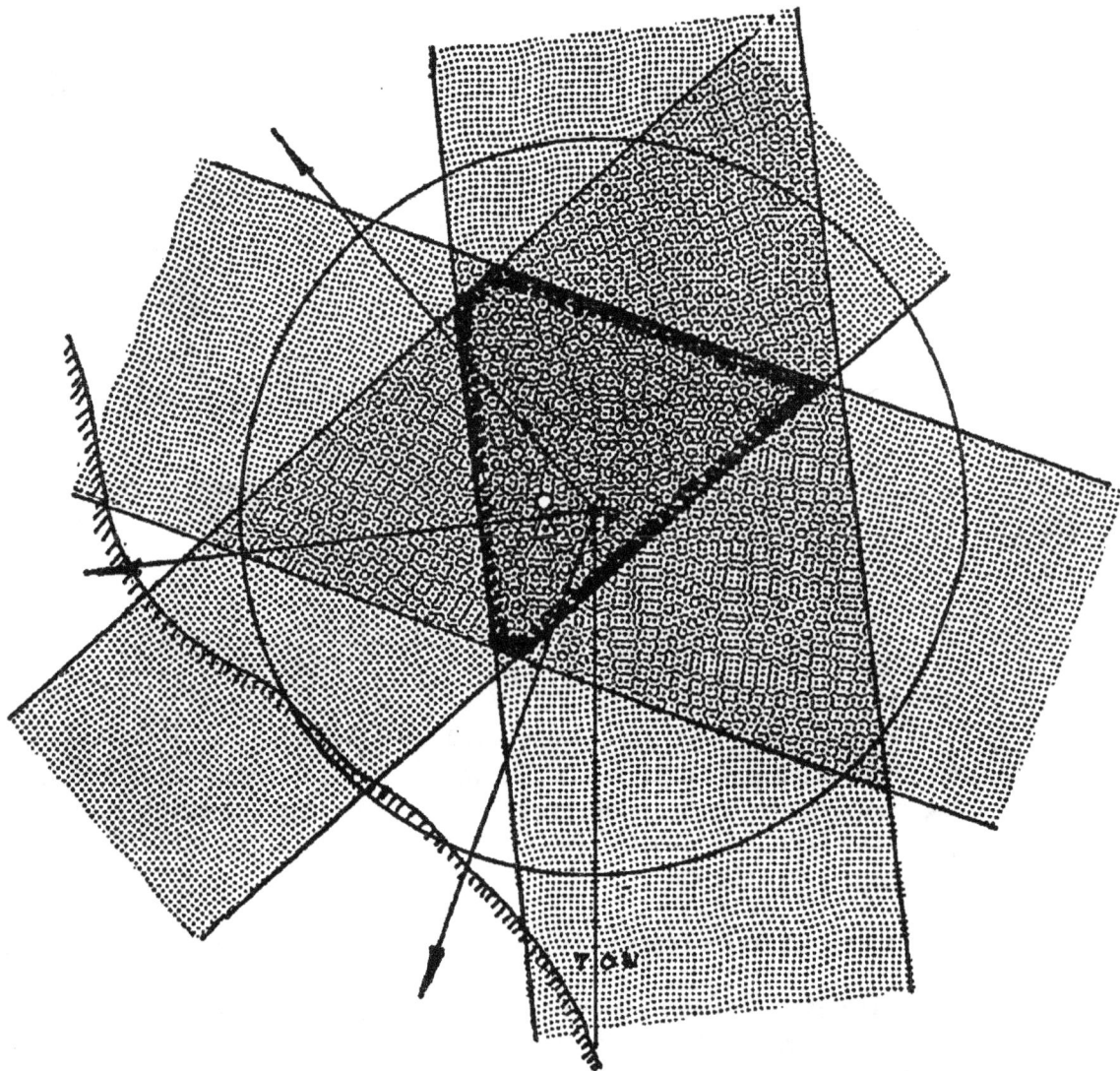

Figure V-10

The Common intersection area of all three bands.
The circle is 30 miles radius. Camp
Jesup is represented by the triangle, the
Pinnacle is estimated to be about 1 mile
north of that position. The bearing of the
Sun at each time is shown by the arrows.
The common polygon is the most probable
area from which the pictures were taken.

Figure V-11 CAMP JESUP Peary's #B15

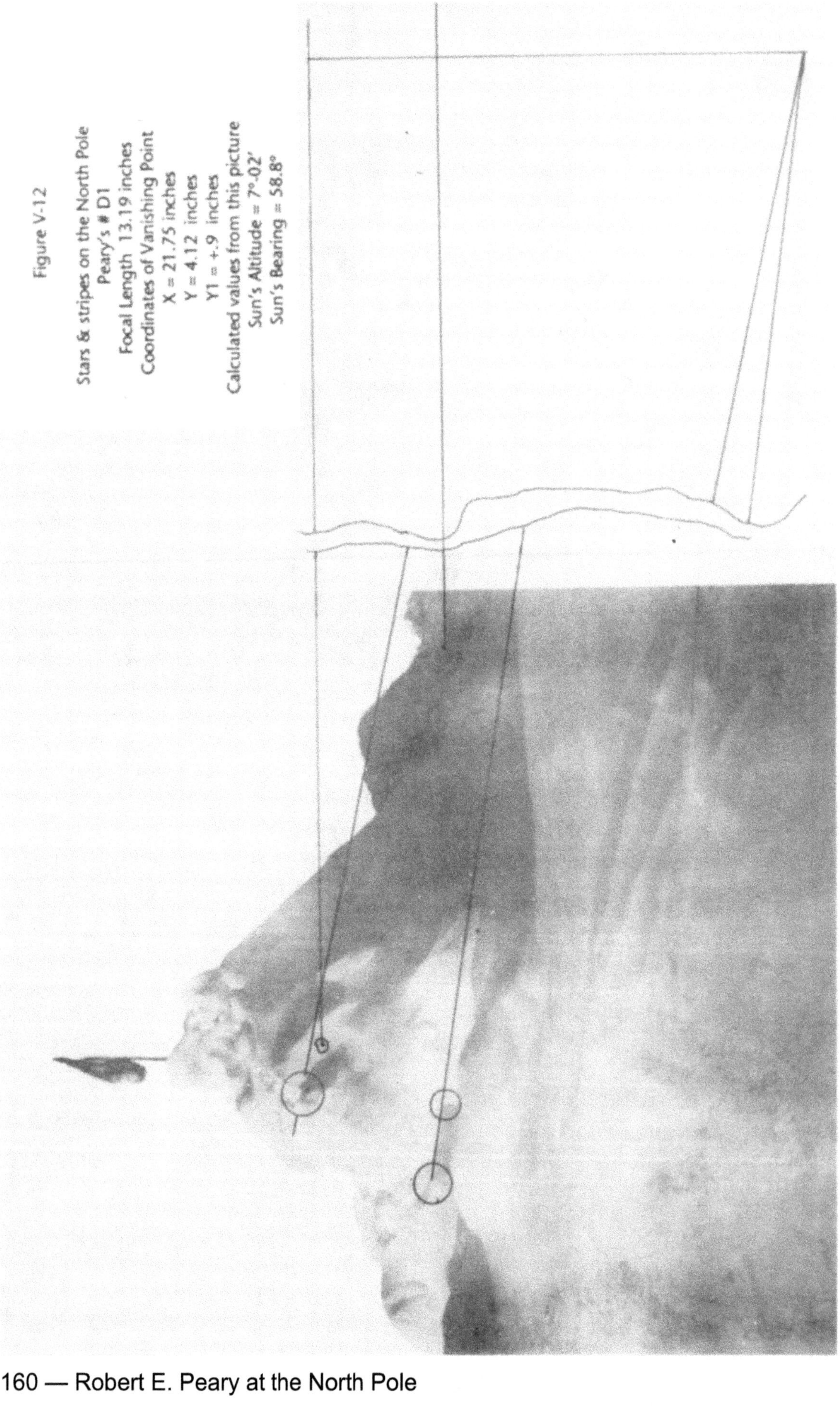

Figure V-12

Stars & stripes on the North Pole
Peary's # D1
Focal Length 13.19 inches
Coordinates of Vanishing Point
X = 21.75 inches
Y = 4.12 inches
Y1 = +.9 inches
Calculated values from this picture
Sun's Altitude = 7°-02'
Sun's Bearing = 58.8°

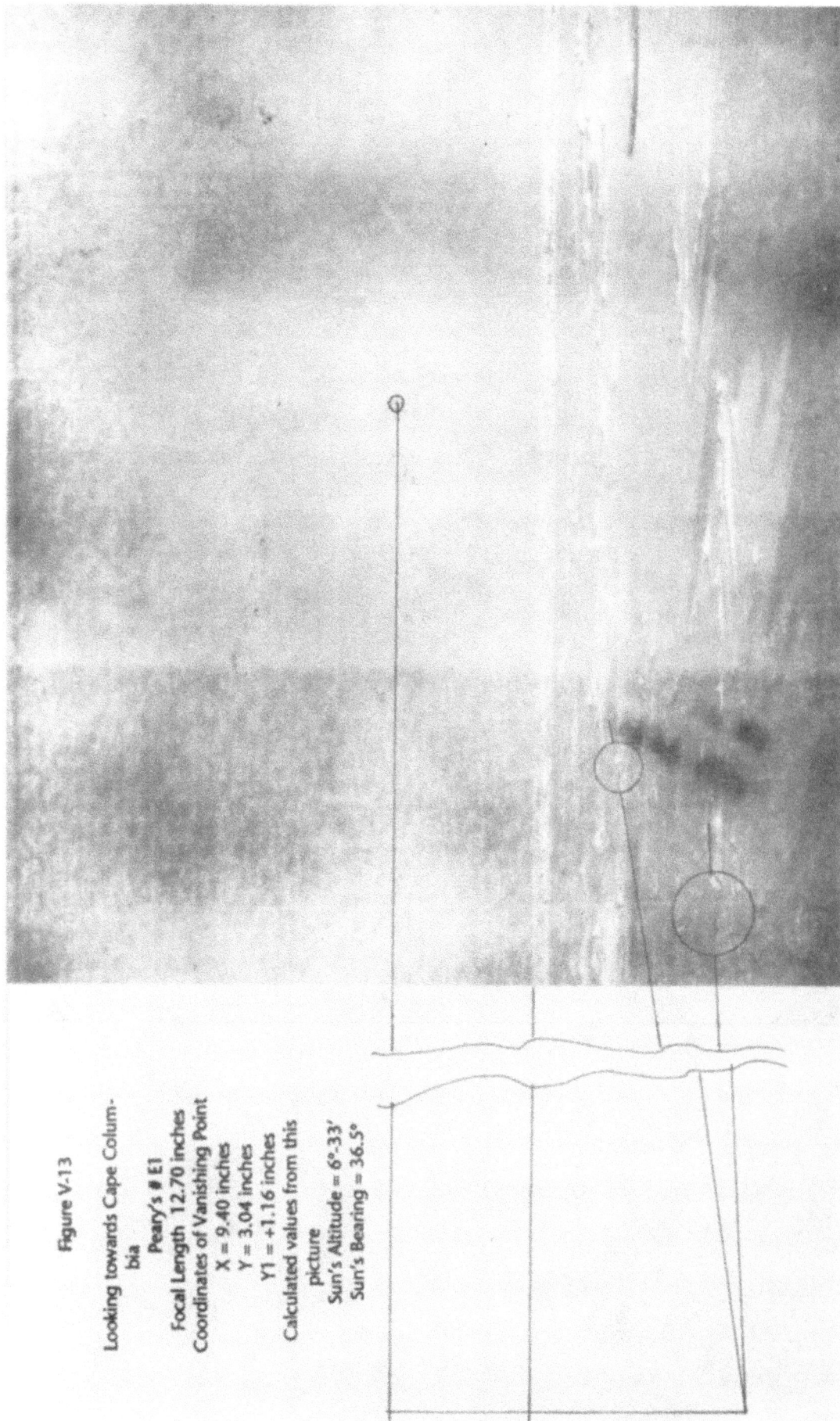

Figure V-13

Looking towards Cape Columbia

Peary's # E1

Focal Length 12.70 inches

Coordinates of Vanishing Point

X = 9.40 inches

Y = 3.04 inches

Y1 = +1.16 inches

Calculated values from this
picture

Sun's Altitude = 6°-33'

Sun's Bearing = 36.5°

Figure V-14

Looking towards Bering Strait
Peary's # E2
Focal Length = 12.60 inches
Coordinates of Vanishing Point
X = 15.00 inches
Y = 1.80 inches
Y1 = -.67 inches
Calculated values from this picture
Sun's Altitude = 7°-04'
Sun's Bearing = 50.0°

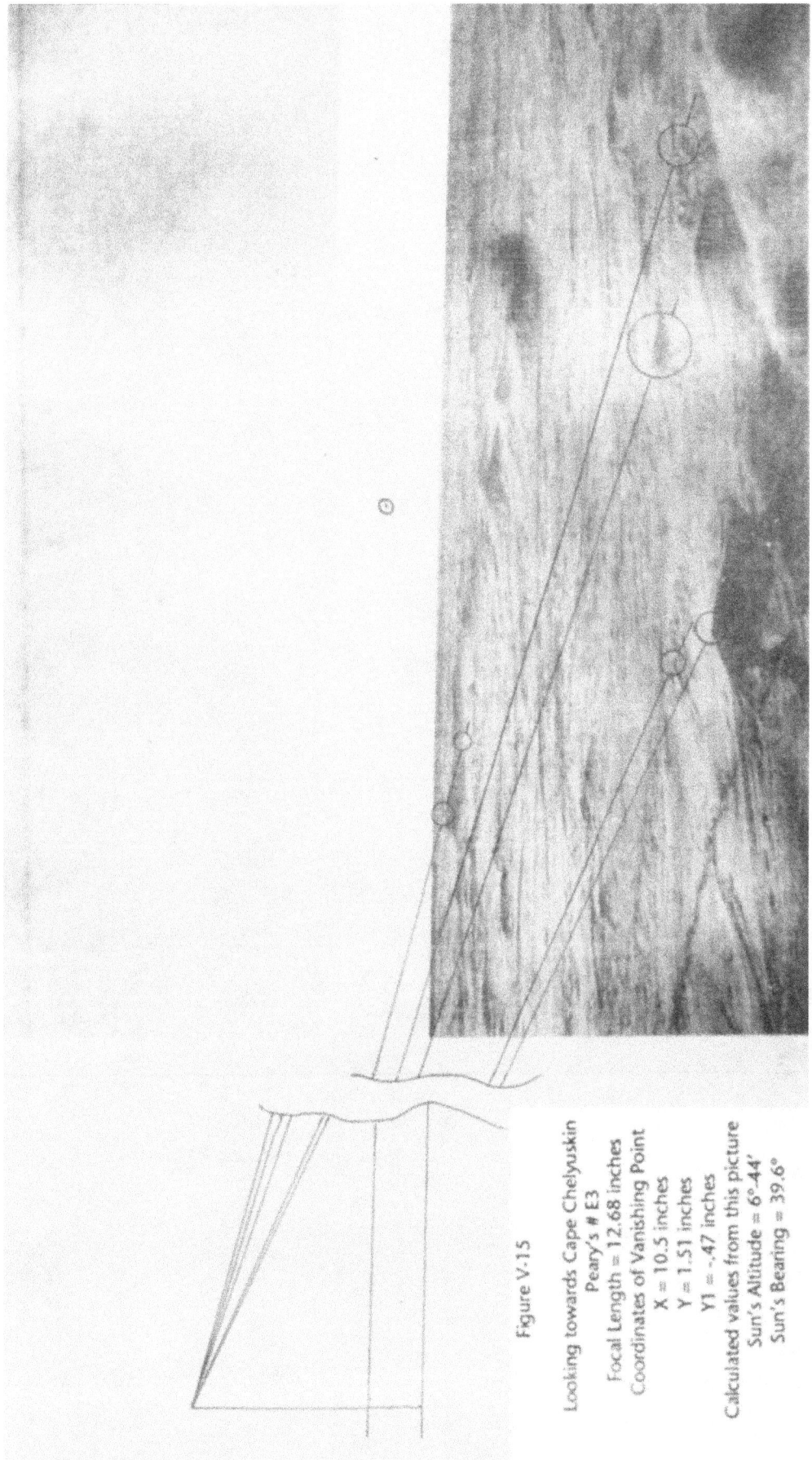

Figure V-15

Looking towards Cape Chelyuskin
Peary's # E3
Focal Length = 12.68 inches
Coordinates of Vanishing Point
X = 10.5 inches
Y = 1.51 inches
Y1 = -.47 inches
Calculated values from this picture
Sun's Altitude = 6°-44'
Sun's Bearing = 39.6°

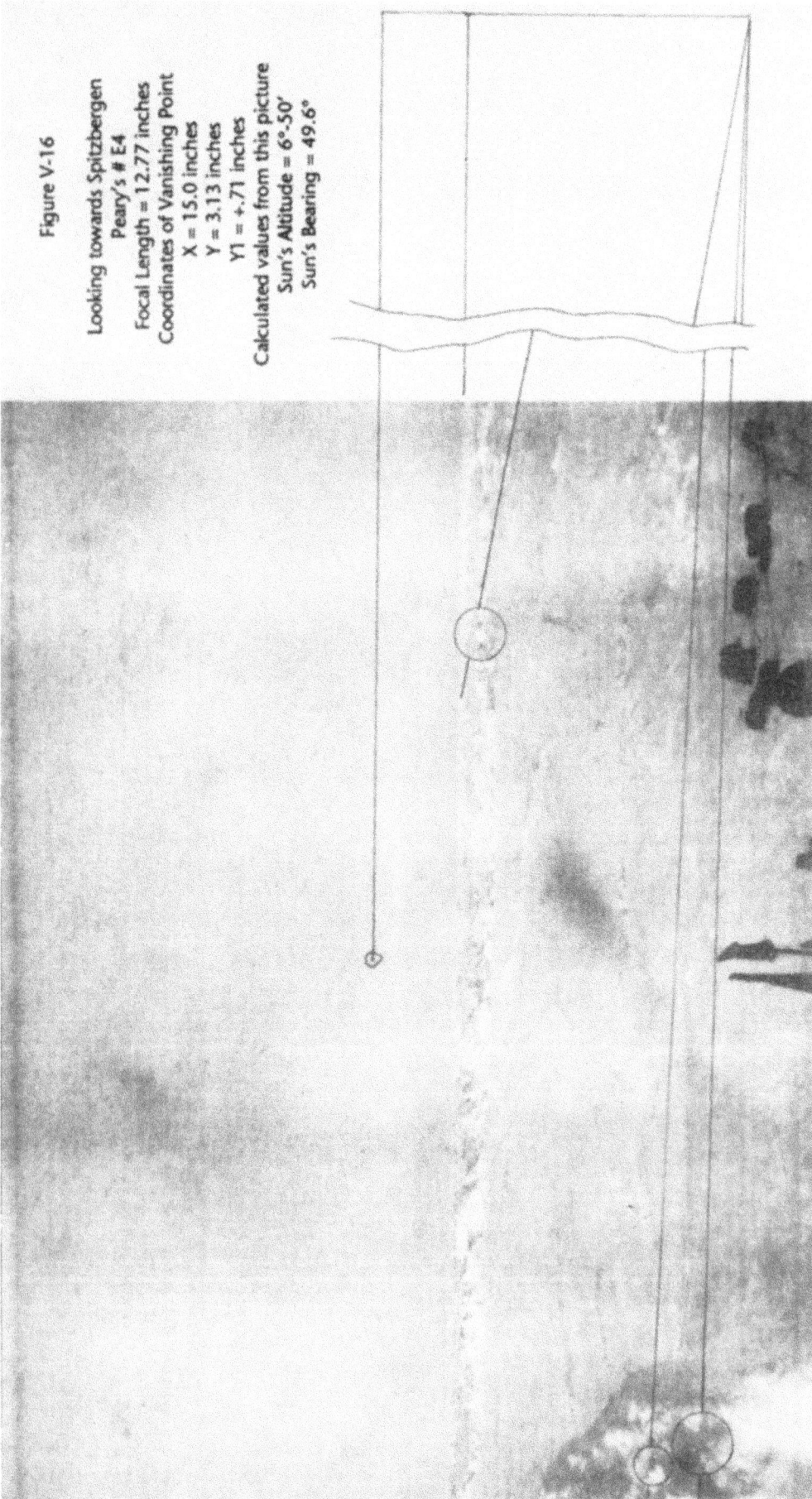

Figure V-16

Looking towards Spitzbergen
Peary's # E4
Focal Length = 12.77 inches
Coordinates of Vanishing Point
X = 15.0 inches
Y = 3.13 inches
Y1 = +.71 inches
Calculated values from this picture
Sun's Altitude = 6°-50'
Sun's Bearing = 49.6°

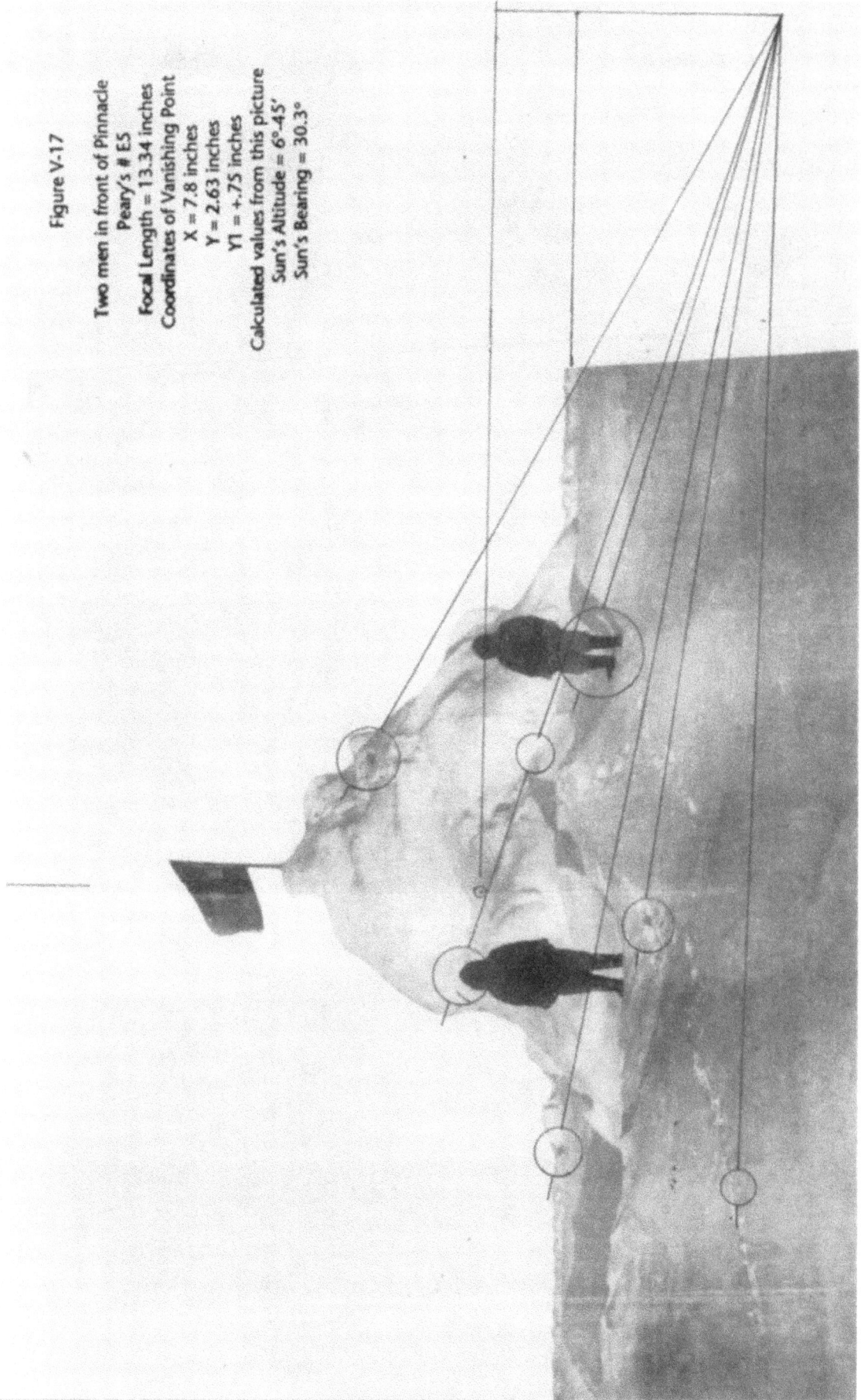

Figure V-17

Two men in front of Pinnacle
Peary's # E5
Focal Length = 13.34 inches
Coordinates of Vanishing Point
X = 7.8 inches
Y = 2.63 inches
Y1 = +.75 inches
Calculated values from this picture
Sun's Altitude = 6°-45'
Sun's Bearing = 30.3°

Figure V-18

Man on Pinnacle with Flag
Peary's # F7

Used for orientation only

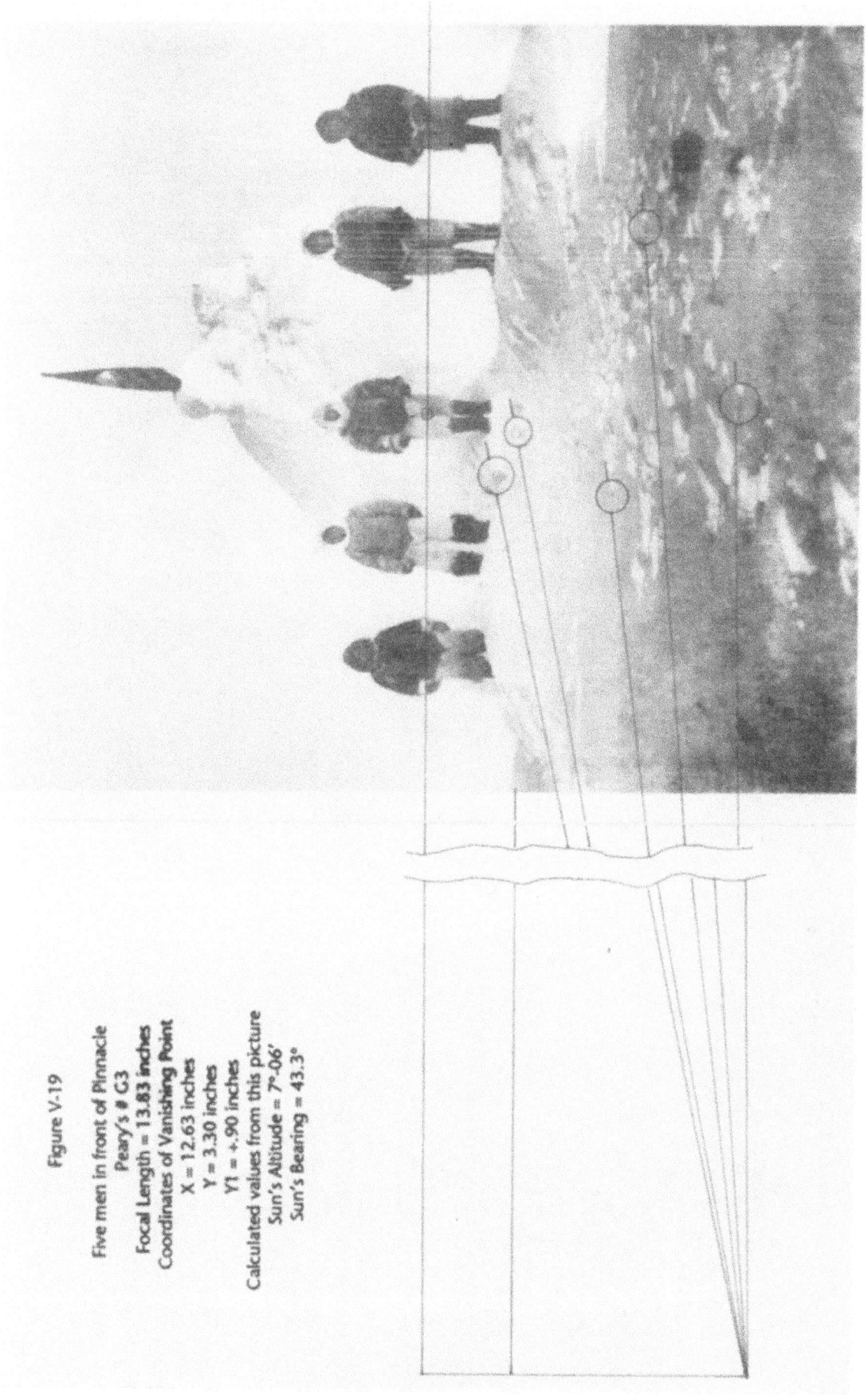

Figure V-19

Five men in front of Pinnacle
Peary's #G3
Focal Length = 13.63 inches
Coordinates of Vanishing Point
X = 12.63 inches
Y = 3.30 inches
Y1 = +.90 inches
Calculated values from this picture
Sun's Altitude = 7°-06'
Sun's Bearing = 43.3°

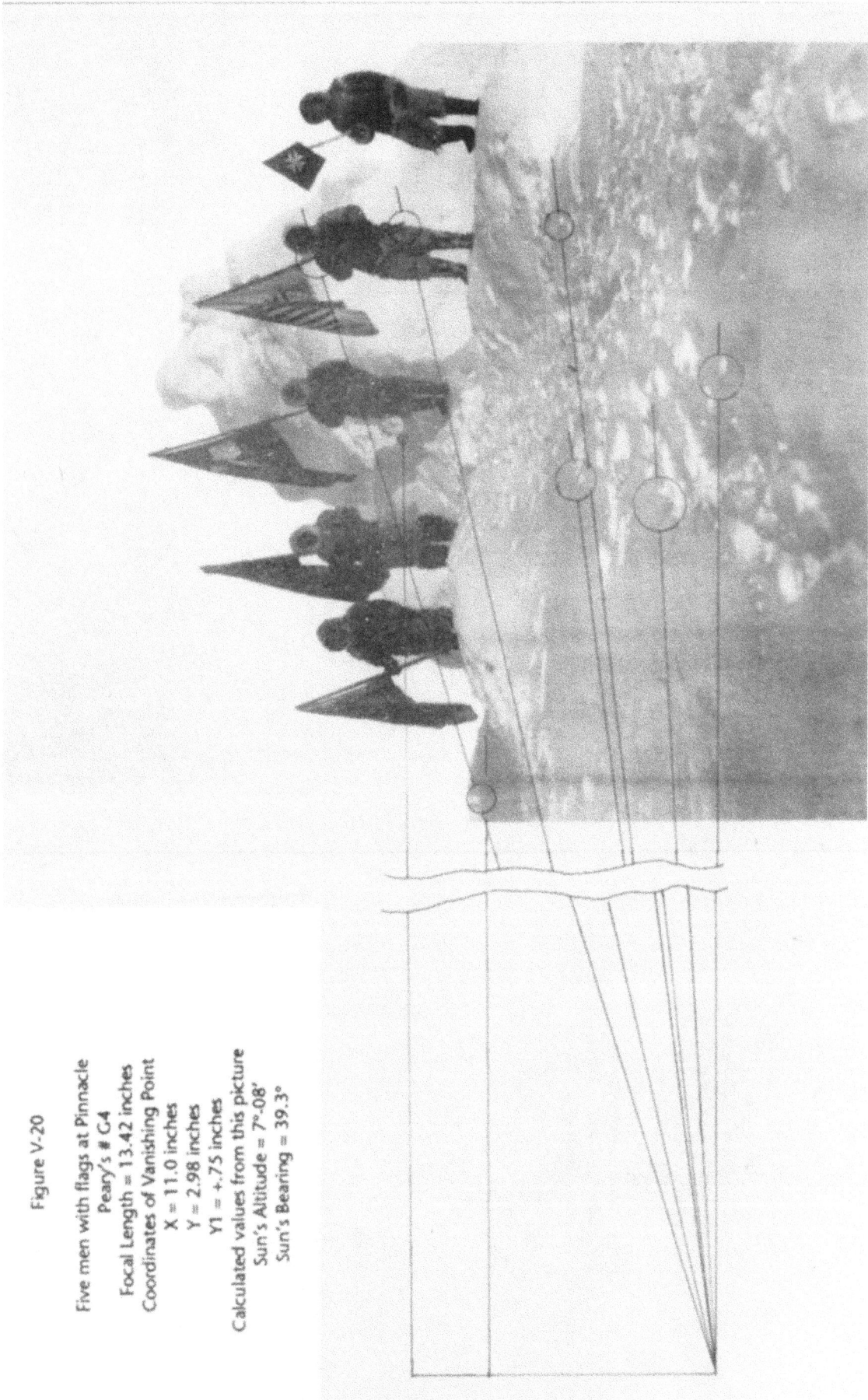

Figure V-20

Five men with flags at Pinnacle
Peary's # G4
Focal Length = 13.42 inches
Coordinates of Vanishing Point
X = 11.0 inches
Y = 2.98 inches
Y1 = +.75 inches
Calculated values from this picture
Sun's Altitude = 7°-08'
Sun's Bearing = 39.3°

Figure V-21

Men marching with Flags (side)
Peary's # G5
Focal Length = 12.86 inches
Coordinates of Vanishing Point
X = 5.93 inches
Y = 1.37 inches
Y1 = -.29
Calculated values from this picture
Sun's Altitude = 6°-34'
Sun's Bearing = 24.8°

Figure V-22

Men marching with Flags (rear)
Peary's # G6
Focal Length = 12.96 inches
Coordinates of Vanishing Point
X = 8.26 inches
Y = 1.94 inches
Y1 = 0 inches
Calculated values from this picture
Sun's Altitude = 7°-04'
Sun's Bearing = 32.5°

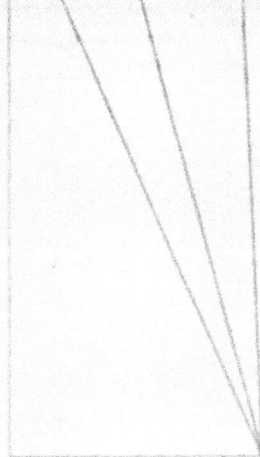

Figure V-23

Sounding
Peary's # G8
Focal Length = 13.34 inches
Coordinates of Vanishing Point
    X = 1.23 inches
    Y = 1.12 inches
    Y1 = -.53 inches
Calculated values from this picture
    Sun's Altitude = 6-55
    Sun's Bearing = 5.3

Part Six

ANCILLARY MATTERS

Over the years Peary's critics have bolstered their hoax theories by seeking evidence of a proclivity to deceive with regard his past explorations, in certain discrepancies in his 1909 diary, and in various stories told by Henson which indicate a strained relationship between Peary and himself. Peary's friends and fellow explorers, on the other hand, contended that Peary was incapable of deceit — that he was his own sternest critic and could not have lived with himself had he faked his attainment of the Pole. Roald Amundsen wrote: "I know Admiral Peary reached the Pole. The reason that I know is that I know Peary." (*My Life As An Explorer*, p. 225)

We address here the oft-repeated allegations (1) that Peary's 1906 "farthest north" record is dubious; (2) that his "discovery" of Crocker Land in 1906 was a ploy to curry favor from a financial backer; (3) that his 1909 diary entries are suspiciously incomplete or irregular; and (4) that he deceived Henson as to the location of Camp Jesup, keeping from him the secret that the party was nowhere near the Pole, and avoided him later aboard the ship while suffering pangs of conscience.

We show below that there is no merit to any of these allegations and that some are downright irresponsible.

We begin with the most serious of them advanced by Wally Herbert in *The Noose Of Laurels* — that Peary deceived even his wife, Jo, by claiming to have surpassed Umberto Cagni's northernmost latitude record by reaching latitude 87°-06′.

A. The Farthest North Record

In July, 1905, Peary sailed for the North on the *Roosevelt* with high hopes of attaining the North Pole at last, for he was now equipped with a ship that could penetrate farther up the ice clogged channel between the coast of Greenland and

Ellesmere Island than had been possible for the fragile *Windward*, and thus shorten his land journey for the final assault on the Pole. He took with him the largest expedition he had yet assembled, sufficient men for a number of teams that would relay supplies from the ship to Cape Hecla, and afterward from station to station on a trail that would be forged by pioneer parties and kept open almost to the Pole itself.

Captain Bartlett, sailing for his first time as the skipper of the *Roosevelt*, worked the ship as far north as Cape Sheridan, and in March, 1906, the first parties began leaving from Cape Moss, about twenty miles from Cape Hecla. Peary brought up in the rear on March 6. The weather was clear and the going good at first, except that as early as March 7, Peary noticed pronounced ice movement. On the following day, Bartlett's support party returned and the Captain reported the ice in motion everywhere; then on the next day, Peary observed that his party was "steadily drifting eastward." On March 21-22, the wind "came on fresh from the west blowing with distinct fierceness all night... and causing pronounced changes in the ice." And on March 26, Peary came across three parties backed up "by a broad open lead extending east and west across [the] course." The next day he sent all but Henson's party back for more supplies, reasoning that he could not afford to feed so many teams for what might be a several day wait. April 1 found the remaining teams still at the "big lead," which they had begun to call the "Hudson River."

Finally, on April 2, the lead was crossed after what had proved a ten day delay for Henson's party, and a seven day delay for Peary's. Peary moaned that without the delay, "we should have been beyond Abruzzi's highest now." More misfortune was to come. On April 6, the two parties were stalled by a snowstorm; interminable gales blew for six days. When calm returned, Peary was able to get meridian transit observations which gave a latitude of 85°-12', and a longitude "slightly west of the ship at Sheridan." On April 14, a good march was made, but after midnight two men arriving from the south reported that they had lost the trail and "been stopped by open water and completely shattered ice, extending as far as they could see from the highest pinnacles." Peary realized that his relay plan was doomed and the time had come to put a contingency plan in effect: He wrote, *Nearest The Pole*, p.130):

> It was evident I could no longer count in the slightest
> degree upon my supporting parties, and that whatever was
> to be done now, must be done with the party, the equipment,
> the supplies I had with me. Unfortunately the party was
> larger than it need be (eight of us in all), and the
> supplies much smaller than I could have wished.

He gave his men a few hours sleep, removed everything from the sledges that was not absolutely needed, and the next morning set out to march as far north as he could reach within the limitations of his supplies.

Some slight good had come of the storm (p.130):

> Such snow as the wind had not torn from the face of the
> floes was beaten and banked hard, and the snow which had
> fallen had been hammered into the areas of rough ice and
> the shattered edges of the big floe, so that they gave us
> little trouble. North of the Storm Camp we had no occasion
> for snowshoes or pickaxes.

Since the marches from here on are a matter of dispute, and rather vaguely recorded in the book, let us pick up the day by day accounts from the typed transcript of Peary's diary:

April 15: "Travelled ten hours, then camped in very thick weather. Traversed several large level old floes which my eskimos remarked at once looked as if they did not even move in summer. Have ___ at a good pace again today and feel that we must have covered twenty five miles. I hope it is more.

April 16: When starting at 8 A.M. clear and bright with light wind and drift. At noon a dark bank came over from the west and wind increased. At 3:15 came to an open lead some 50 feet wide...and I give word to camp. Hope we have come at rate of 2 miles an hour at least.

April 17: No Entry

April 18: What contrasts this country affords. Yesterday hell, today comparative heaven, yet not such heaven as one would voluntarily choose... Started at 6:45. No trouble in crossing lead as I had suspected. First entirely calm day since leaving big lead...Travelled till 5 P.M., 10 1/4 hours.

This is thirty six hours in all from storm camp, and if our rate has been two and one half miles per hour, we are close to Abruzzi's highest. Two miles per hour puts us above 86.

April 19: Another contrast, this time reverting to the reverting side. We were underway at 6:45. At 9:30 found ____ in a network of leads between two large ones and the ice in motion. Backed out of this as quickly as possible, in two places barely getting sledges over leads, in time to escape being caught on detached floes.

I then stopped to get an observation before an advancing bank of cloud from the north should obscure the sun. Set up transit and got one uncertain ante meridian sight before sun disappeared.

We then followed the ____ by big lead south for a mile or two to see if we could cross, but found it slowly widening and so camped. Thick bank of fog and slight snow began at same time.

Friday, April 20. Turned out early and sent two men in opposite directions along the lead to see if any possible change during the night had made it possible for us to cross. Sipsu found a place and at 9 A.M. we got under way. At this time sun visible through drifting fog or frost smoke. An occasional glimpse of blue sky and cirrus clouds overhead ... made me hope that by noon I might have clear sight.

Stopped at 11, until 12:15, but impossible to get a satisfactory sight, the same limb being sharply defined. (The one obtained is on previous page). Went on crossing three narrow leads, and at 1 P.M. brought up against a lead some two hundred yards wide, trending N.E. & S.W. (true) and crossing around to the east into the one we crossed this morning.

Had the men build the igloos and eat, then sent them out in each direction to see if there is any chance to get across. I do not care to tax the strength of the dogs by making them do useless travelling, and to go into ___ apparently another "cul de sac" would be useless.

The April 20 entry continues:

Have reached [sic] yesterday's and to-day's sights and they give very similar results, the mean of which is 86-30 (the places are in the same lat. only yesterday's position was east of to-day's) but I fear that both altitudes are a little low, one before the meridian, the other after it.

We are in a perfect mesh of leads the understream from which keeps the sun obscured and doubtless has much to do with this incessant wind.

The next page of the diary is missing (as unfortunately are many other pages of the 1906 journal), so here we must return to Peary's book. In *Nearest To The Pole* (pp. 133-134), Peary writes that after a few hours sleep, hurrying on between the leads, a forced march was made. The party pushed on "till a little before noon of the 21st."[1]

Then (p.134):

When my observations were taken and rapidly figured, they showed that we had reached 87-6 north latitude, and had at last beaten the record, for which I thanked God with as good a grace as possible, though I felt that the mere beating of the record was but an empty bauble compared with the splendid jewel on which I had set my heart for so many years, and for which, on this expedition, I had almost literally been straining my life out.

---

[1] Peary adds: "In this last spurt we crossed fourteen cracks and narrow leads, which almost without exception, were in motion."

In other words, picking up at precisely where the diary entry of the day before left off, Peary is saying that the party found its way out of the "perfect mesh of leads," by crossing one narrow lead at a time.

Peary adds (p.134):

> I was more than anxious to keep on, but as I looked at the
> drawn faces of my comrades, at the skeletal figures of my few
> remaining dogs, at my nearly empty sledges, and remembered
> the drifting ice over which we had come and the unknown
> quantity of the "big lead" between us and the nearest land, I
> felt that I had cut my margin as narrow as could reasonably be
> expected.

Accordingly (p.135):

> My flags were flung out from the summit of the highest
> pinnacle near us, and a hundred feet or so beyond this I
> left a bottle containing a brief record and a piece of the
> silk flag which six years before I had carried around the
> northern end of Greenland.
>
> *Then we started to return to our last igloo, making no camp
> there.* (Emphasis added)

Wally Herbert, who does a more extensive analysis of the 1906 expedition than any other of Peary's critics, concedes that Peary went north after leaving the "Storm Camp," but questions that he reached 87°-06'. "Of course he went north!" Herbert exclaims, "No other conclusion carries any credence, for what other explorer in Peary's position would have done otherwise?"[2] He adds: "How far north he went is another issue entirely."

As is customary for him, Herbert gives no credence to Peary's speeds and distances, or to his navigation. He also considers the missing page of the diary transcript for April 21 suspicious,[3] and focuses on the April 20 entry which left Peary in a "perfect mesh of leads,"[4] and somewhat concerned that his altitudes derived from his observations of that day and the preceding day (April 19) were "a little low." To Herbert, all of these factors suggest that latitude 87°-06' was never reached (*Noose*, pp.182-185) Herbert then complains that tracing the details of the homeward journey to northern Greenland, which was a nightmare for Peary all the way, is impossible because of insufficient data in his published account (p 186). He points out: "Some of Peary's critics maintain that his vagueness about the events of his return journey are

---

[2] One may ask why Herbert discarded such a sensible approach by assuming that in 1909, at a time when Peary had everything going for him, he decided to give up his quest of the Pole within 50 miles of it (according to Herbert's estimate), rather than admit to an "error of navigation" that would have constituted a "stain" on his reputation. See Part III-F above. Was Peary no longer an explorer "worth his salt?"

[3] Herbert notes, incidentally, that Peary's original handwritten diary for the journey is missing, and that he came upon the typed version "by chance amongst Peary's galley proofs and draft manuscripts at the National Archives." (*Noose*, p. 177) Would not this suggest to any fair-minded person that the critical page might have simply been mislaid by the printers?

[4] Either distrusting or disregarding the account in *Nearest The Pole*, Herbert reasons that "this hardly sounds like the sort of area from which he is about to extricate himself and make a final dash of [by Herbert's reckoning, not Peary's] between thirty-eight and forty three nautical miles..." (*Noose*, pp 183-184) But as his diary shows, Peary had been extricating himself from leads ever since the dash to the north began, often making very good mileage despite them.

not the result of his exhausted state, but had a deliberate purpose, namely to suppress or to 'remove every scrap of evidence that could be used to check, and thereby prove or disprove, the authenticity of latitude 87°-06'N.'"[5] (*Noose*, p 186)

Though Herbert thus far has limited himself to asking rhetorical questions about the "dash" to latitude 87°-6' North, he comes out squarely in favor of a hoax by the end of his chapter entitled, "Farthest North, 1906?" Musing sympathetically over how difficult Peary's obsession with the Pole was for Jo to bear — "as hard as her husband's love of another woman" — he states (*Noose*, p. 201):

> This was her burden. His was his need to reach the North Pole, *made heavier now by a deception which Peary could not even share with the woman who understood him.*

So after a good deal of hemming and hawing, Herbert concludes that the 1906 "farthest north" claim was a hoax after all.

Fortunately, we are spared the task of responding to his arcane arguments for we have resolved the matter of Peary's claim to have surpassed Cagni's record by reaching latitude 87°-06' by resort to the photogrammetric techniques explained in Part V above. In short, by forensic photography.

In the files of the National Geographic Society, we found contact copies of Peary's photographs from the 1906 expedition. One picture, identifiable by both notations on the edges and the unique format of the film as having been taken by Peary's 1906 Kodak camera (preserved in the Society's Explorers Hall) corresponds to the events of April 21 as Peary describes them. He tells us (*Nearest The Pole*, p.135) that after noon observations had been taken, "My flags were flung out from the summit of the highest pinnacle near us, and a hundred feet or so beyond this I left a bottle containing a brief record and a piece of the silk flag which six years before I had carried around the northern end of Greenland. He adds: "Then we started to return to our last igloo, *making no camp here.*" (emphasis added).

The photograph in question, Figure VI-1, which shows the expedition with its sledges in the foreground and in the background a flag flying from a pinnacle, is ideally suited for photogrammetric analysis because it contains shadows that provide an excellent vanishing point. The fact that the shadow of the photographer's (Peary's) head and shoulders appears within the picture provides greater accuracy of the result than might otherwise be the case.

The photograph gave us an excellent altitude of the sun, but some assumptions had to be made to calculate the latitude that would match the angle of elevation. We had to assume a time in order to determine whether the latitude was approximately 87°-06', as Peary had determined by his observations. We approached the problem on the basis of our knowledge that the noon sight had to have been taken at local apparent noon, when the sun was due south. We then allowed a reasonable time thereafter for a quick noontime repast, the hoisting of flags, and the taking of pictures, recognizing that the time would be minimized because of the urgency of returning south as soon as possible. As Peary indicates, the plan was not to make camp there but to return to the last igloo.

---

[5] Here Herbert is quoting J. Gordon Hayes, *Robert Edwin Peary.*

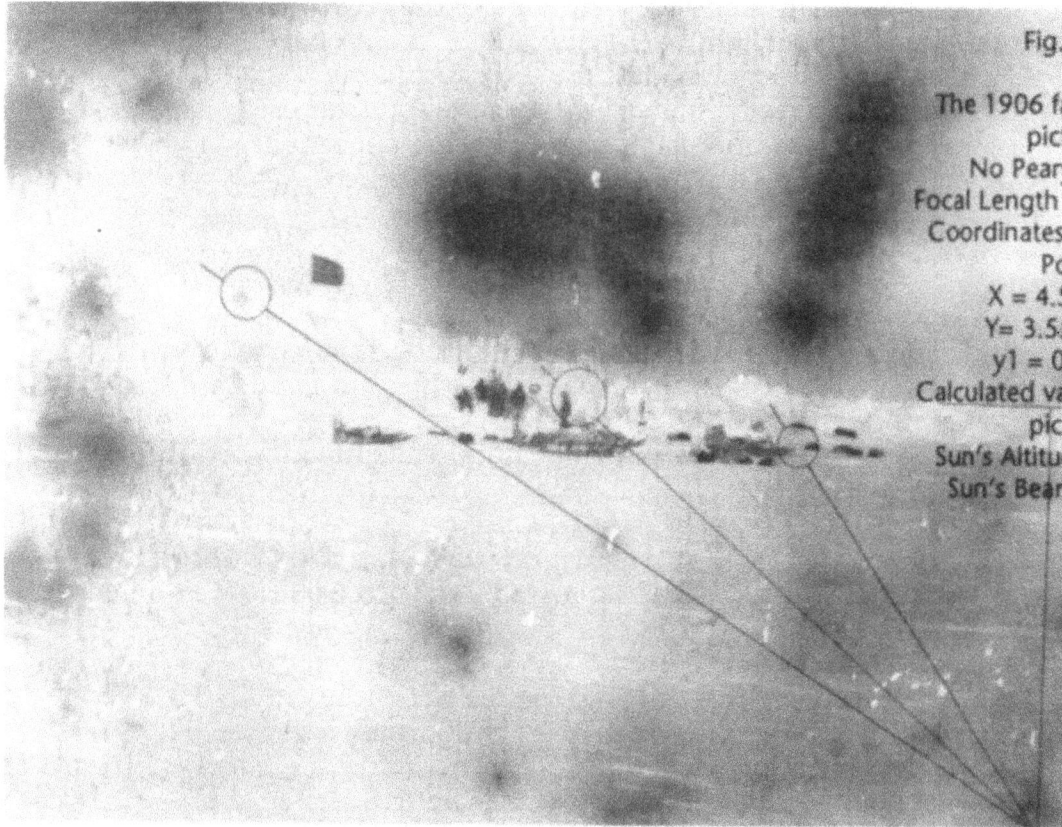

Fig. VI-1

The 1906 farthest north picture.
No Peary number
Focal Length =13.37 inches
Coordinates of Vanishing Point
X = 4.5 inches
Y= 3.55 inches
y1 = 0 inches
Calculated values from this picture
Sun's Altitude = 14°-04'
Sun's Bearing = 19.6°

Table VI-1 shows the measured sun angle (+ or - 15') and the calculations leading to the calculated angle, tabulated for a range of (apparent) times.

Table VI-1

Declination of the sun, noon 21 April, 1906   11-41
Altitude from the photograph (incl. refraction) 14-04

Local Time	Dec.	Alt.at 87-06*	Measured Altitude
1300	11-42	14-30	14-04
1400	11-43	14-14	14-04
1500	11-44	13-46	14-04

* These computed altitudes are taken from the Nautical Almanac.

From this table it can be deduced that at about 1430 (2:30 P.M.), Peary's latitude would have been 87°-06' as his observations showed. Since the sight at noon was taken facing south, departure times earlier than 1430 (2:30 P.M.) would place Peary somewhat *north* of 87°-06'.

In any event, we have concluded that Peary exceeded the Cagni record of 86°-34' by a comfortable margin. Accordingly, he deserved the hard won laurels for a new "farthest north" record that the world accorded him. The achievement of the record was not, however, of any real consolation to him. He writes (*Farthest North*, p. 134):

[M]y feelings at this time were anything but the feeling of
exultation which it might be supposed that I should have.
As a matter of fact they were just the reverse, and my
bitter disappointment combined with a certain degree of
physical exhaustion from our killing pace on scant rations,
gave me the deepest fit of the blues that I experienced
during the entire expedition.

B. Crocker Land

A bone-weary Peary returned to the *Roosevelt* from latitude 87°-06' in the waning
days of May. After a short rest aboard ship, in June he led an expedition westward across
the ice to explore the northern coast of Axel Heiberg Land as far as a point on its
northernmost tip he would name Cape Thomas Hubbard, after a supporter of the Peary
Arctic Club.[6]

In *Nearest The Pole* (p.202), Peary relates that on June 24, on the way to Cape
Thomas Hubbard, he ascended a peak at Cape Colgate and from its 2,000 foot summit,
laid eyes on a new land. He wrote:

North stretched the well-known ragged surface of the
polar pack, and northwest it was with a thrill that my glasses
revealed the faint white summits of a distant land which my
Eskimos claimed to have seen as we came along from the last
camp.

Upon reaching Cape Thomas Hubbard, where he laid a cairn, he again reported
sighting this new land (*Nearest The Pole*, p. 207):

On the summit we built a cairn similar to that on the summit
of Cape Columbia, in which I deposited a brief record and a
piece of my silk flag as usual.

The clear day greatly favored my work in taking a round of
angles, and with the glasses I could make out apparently a
little more distinctly, the snow-clad summits of the distant
land in the northwest, above the ice horizon.

My heart leaped the intervening miles of ice as I looked long-
ingly at this land and in fancy I trod its shores and climbed its
summits, even though I knew that the pleasure could only be
for another in another season.

At the conclusion of *Nearest The Pole* (p.280), published a year later, Peary lists this
discovery of "new land" as the second most important achievement of his 1906
expedition. He enumerates:

---

[6] Peary called Axel Heiberg Land, Jesup Land, after another member of the Peary Arctic Club. However, the name
given it by Otto Sverdrup, who had explored the vast island extensively, was shown on most charts of that time.
The northern region of Axel Heiberg Land was then known as "Grant Land."

First.—The attainment of the "highest North," leaving a distance of but 174 nautical miles yet to be conquered this side of the Pole ...

Second.—The determination of the existence of a new land northwest of the northwestern part of Grant Land probably an island in the westerly extension of the North American archipelago.

The difficulty is that this land, which Peary does not name in his book, has never been found. When Donald B. MacMillan went in search of it in 1914, he reluctantly came to the conclusion that it did not exist.

Peary first gave his "island" a name sometime after his return from his 1906 expedition. He named it "Crocker Land" after George Crocker, West Coast railroad magnate and a silent sponsor of the expedition. Crocker had contributed the munificent sum of $50,000, keeping the donation quiet for unique personal reasons. In sending his donation to Morris Jesup, the then president of the Peary Arctic Club, he had written on January 27, 1905:

> In making this subscription I am prompted to add that notwithstanding my belief in the utility of the knowledge acquired by explorations of this character, and my desire that the United States shall reap the credit which will attach to the accomplishment of Commander Peary's plans, I should hesitate to send men upon a voyage so hazardous, if the starting of the expedition depended upon my contribution. But as the exploration is an assured fact, and as no responsibility for suggesting it rests on my shoulders, I am glad to render it such assistance as I may, in evidence of my high appreciation of the courage, pertinacity and intelligence of Commander Peary, and in the hope that it may result in the acquisition of valuable knowledge.

On April 14, 1907, Peary wrote Crocker:

> I regret that the land to which I have attached your name in the north, is not a continent instead of an island. Only a continent would be proper recognition of your magnificent action in connection with the last expedition.

On April 17, Crocker wrote Peary to advise him that he would not be assisting in financing the 1908-1909 expedition because of the San Franciso earthquake of 1906:

> Replying to yours of April 16th, I am sorry that I can do nothing for you in your next trip to the North Pole, as the destruction in San Franciso which occurred just a year ago has greatly crippled my income.
>
> My interests there are in a stock company and the Directors have decided to rebuild the buildings, hence it is necessary for me to provide my portion of the expense.

In dealing with the subject of Crocker Land, one must admit at the outset that Peary wished to honor George Crocker and was at the same time seeking from him a contribution for his next polar venture. One must remember, however, that American discovery expeditions were entirely privately financed; there was no available government funding, as in the case of today's space program. Peary's fund raising efforts were essential if he was ever to get to the North Pole, though fund raising was not something he enjoyed. We might add that in this case, it does not appear that George Crocker was the sort of man who would be swayed by the naming of an island for him, nor were Peary's other benefactors, Morris Jesup and Thomas Hubbard in the business of sponsoring explorers in return for such favors. These men saw the fostering of Arctic explorations as civic undertakings in the perceived public interest of the United States.

Thus in naming "Crocker Land," Peary was merely following a time honored tradition for explorers — American, British, Norwegians and so forth — who name their discoveries after their patrons. We must therefore start with the premise that there was nothing reprehensible in his naming the island he reported seeing "northwest of the northwestern part of Grant Land" for George Crocker if indeed he believed in its existence.

Many critics, including Rawlins and Herbert, believe that Peary invented Crocker Land, placing a great deal of store in the fact that there are no references to its discovery in his diary entries (called "field notes" by Rawlins). We do not find this absence of references indicative of deceit, however, especially when one considers that the handwritten diary is fragmentary and frequently illegible. Some entries break off in the middle of sentences, and others have been washed away or obscured by stains. On many days there are no entries at all.

There is an entry for June 24, the date Peary climbed the 2,000 feet peak of Cape Colgate and claimed to have seen "the faint white summits of a distant land." It breaks off, however, in the middle of a sentence in the middle of a page. On the next day, June 25, Peary writes: "No entry, very tired and sleepy and eyes entirely out of commission from using transit." This suggests that he might have fallen asleep in the midst of writing his entry for the day before without saying everything he wanted to say. He was not in the habit of going back and filling in entries later.

For the dates "June 27 & June 28," Peary makes a single long rambling entry. On June 28, while a cairn was being constructed on a high point at Cape Thomas Hubbard, it will be recalled, he claims to have seen "a little more distinctly, the snowclad summits of the distant land in the northwest." In his diary he reports a deer hunt carried out by the Eskimos, and notes that while the hunt went on he was carrying his binoculars over his shoulders and using them to view the coast. At the conclusion he reports that winds are blowing and clouds forming indicating an end to a spell of good weather, but adds, "I have no reason to complain, it has lasted *long enough for me to get to see what I wanted.*" Perhaps one of the things he had wanted to do was to get a second look at the "distant land" he believed he had seen earlier.

We know, at least, that Peary did not keep his discovery to himself, even though he seems to have made no written note of it. Dr. Louis Wolf, a surgeon who accompanied Peary on his "farthest north" journey, recorded in *his* diary that Peary spoke of it upon his return from the Grant Land expedition.

It is interesting to note that J. Gordon Hayes, one of Peary's harshest critics, believes that "Crocker Land" was something Peary *really saw, whatever or wherever it may have been." (Robert E. Peary*, p.78, emphasis supplied.)

Most people today believe that "Crocker Land" was a mirage, since the frequency of mirages in the Arctic has been remarked on by a great many arctic explorers and scientists. The extreme temperature gradients in the region are responsible for these optical illusions, as well as for the sometime extreme refraction effects on celestial sights. Fig. VI-2 is an example of an arctic mirage phenomenon appropriately called "The Great Wall of China Effect."

Fig. VI-2

Under date of August 21, 1914, from Etah, North Greenland, Donald MacMillan wrote a long personal letter to Admiral Peary telling of his futile search for Crocker Land:

> At the end of the fifth march all clouds and mist rolled away and we began to have beautiful weather. By dead reckoning our distance was 75 miles off shore. The top of Cape Colgate could just be seen low down on the horizon and ahead of us as plain as day was a tremendous land extending through 120 degrees. Hills and valleys and snow capped peaks were so easily seen that we even picked out a prominent point toward which to head. Our enthusiasm was dampened a little bit when Pee-ah-wah-to said it was nothing but "poo-jok [mist]."

For three successive days we saw this same appearance of land but we noticed that its shape and extension were continually changing and never appeared nearer than the first day.

On the ninth day sights for longitude and latitude gave us 108°-22'-30" west and 82°-30' north. We were on the brown spot and not a thing in sight, not even our old friend the mirage.

In another letter from Etah, November 16, 1916, MacMillan wrote a letter to Mr. Charles Wellington Furlong, of Boston, which includes this statement:

> From the summit of Cape Thomas Hubbard, sixteen hundred feet above sea level, standing in the very spot where Peary had stood eight years before, we saw the same thing. Had I never left the land at all, I would have reported this new land in good faith.

An alternative theory is that "Crocker Land" is an ice island drifting in the Arctic Ocean. This possibility was first advanced by then Lieutenant Colonel Joseph O. Fletcher, United States Air Force, who in 1952 landed on the large ice island (T-3) that bears his name — "Fletcher's Island." In an article in *National Geographic Magazine*,[7] Colonel Fletcher describes the ice islands, which were discovered by airmen in B-29s flying over them. He himself was the first commander of America's northernmost outpost and, for a quarter of a year, lived 150 miles and less from the very top of the world.

Fletcher writes:

> Gentle parallel swells, or waves of ice, from a few inches to 15 feet high and from 800 to 1,000 feet apart, crossed the islands' relatively flat ice surfaces. Imperviousness to the battering of the pack suggested frozen fresh water, harder and stronger than salt ice. Thicknesses of 200 feet or more, 20 times that of sea ice, were deduced from their height above sea level.

> Lt. Pelham Aldrich, member of the British Arctic expedition headed by Sir George Nares in 1875-6, and Rear Adm. Robert E. Peary 30 years later, had seen a unique ice foot or shelf, fast to Ellesmere Island's north shore and extending far seaward. This was apparently a glacial remnant, part of the prehistoric ice that once covered Ellesmere and the surrounding sea as the icecap now covers the interior of Greenland.

> A puzzled Peary wrote a description of the shelf that perfectly fits today's ice islands. Later we were to land on Ellesmere ourselves, and, by comparing corings, match islands to the glacial shelf still extending 10 miles to sea in places.

---

[7] "Three Months on an Arctic Ice Island," April, 1953.

It is thus still true that there are no icebergs in the Arctic Ocean; bergs as we know them in the Atlantic break from "live," moving glaciers when they reach the sea. Arctic ice islands, much older and larger, have split off from the dead Ellesmere shelf. The process must have been rapid since the turn of the century, for Peary described a far more extensive ice foot than now exists—further evidence of a steady warming in the Arctic.

From a geographer's point of view, the most interesting result of recent ice island studies is a possible solution to mysteries of "new lands" never seen again after "discovery." Crocker Land, sighted by Peary in 1906 and marked on Arctic maps until Comdr. Donald B. MacMillan in 1914 disproved its existence, may well have been an ice island.

In the matter of Crocker Land we can accept either possibility: (1) the statements of MacMillan confirming definite mirages in the area; or (2) the descriptions of drifting ice islands reported by Fletcher and well known today. But we cannot accept that Peary invented Crocker Land so as to be able to name a geographical feature for a financial backer. The absence of a diary entry — given the poor condition of the diary and Peary's haphazard approach to record-keeping — is not significant since Dr. Wolf mentioned the discovery in *his* diary.

C. "Discrepancies" in the 1909 Diary

Peary made his journal of his 1909 expedition available for examination by the congressional committee in 1911. He would not, however, consent to leaving it with the committee. "I do not care to let it our of my possession," he asserted, "it never has been." [8] He explained that the journal contained not only a record of his journey, but personal notes, to which Mr. Roberts responded: "I would like to look at simply what you might call your log of the trip."

Upon examining the diary, the committee pointed out that the cover page read "No.1. *Roosevelt* to _____ and return, February 22 to April 27, R. E. Peary, United States Navy." Later, as Peary read aloud from his entries between April 1, the day Bartlett turned back, and April 9, when Camp Bartlett was reached on the return journey, he explained that there was no entry for April 8. He acknowledged that he did not make an entry on every day: "Sometimes we were so busy I did not make entries ... I left them for later, but I did not get around to it."

Scanning the journal, Mr. Roberts noticed that on April 6, the date of the arrival at Camp Jesup, the diary entry was followed by "two loose pages." He observed, "Without careful reading I cannot say whether or not they are part of that day's record."

On one loose page, though the congressman was not specific here, the "The Pole at last!!!" entry had been written and inserted at the date, April 6. He then went on,

---

[8] Herbert claims in *The Noose Of Laurels*, to have been the "first man in seventy-five years to be granted access to the famous 'Peary Diary.'" (Jacket Cover) This is incorrect. John Edward Weems was granted access to the diary by the Peary family for use in his biography, *Peary: The Explorer And The Man*, published in 1967.

noting the pages that were left empty on the homeward journey — April 7 (but he was mistaken there), April 8, and so forth —and the days on which entries were limited to a few lines.

Mr. Robert's primary concern, however, was to establish for the record the whether the journal entries were actually written from day to day:

Mr.Roberts: You have told us, I think, the conditions under which the record was kept. The record for that day was all written that day, or at least the whole entry of that day was written at one time?

Captain Peary: Probably. I might, perhaps, have filled in something in connection with it at the next camp, but within those limits, yes.

Mr. Roberts: You never filled anything in any later than the next camp?

Capt. Peary: No, sir; I do not think so.

Mr. Roberts: Are you certain?

Capt. Peary: I feel quite sure.

Mr. Roberts: Everything written was written the day it purports to have been written here or on the following day?

Capt. Peary: Very soon afterward. As I say, I left some pages open to fill in if I had the time afterward.

Mr. Roberts was impressed with the condition of the book. "It shows no finger marks or rough usage," he remarked, "a very cleanly kept book."

Peary explained in a later session how he had carried the journal during his trip:

> As a result of my experience in previous expeditions in the case of notebooks, this bag [indicating] was made of surgeon's waterproofing, with waterproofing inside, and my notebook was carried in it. Here is a drawstring and my notebook was carried in here [indicating]. This during the day was carried also in a canvas pocket on my sledge...When I went in the igloo at night this [indicating the waterproof bag] was carried into the igloo and laid down beside me. The notebook was taken out to make notes and immediately returned to it, and tied up again to protect the notebook from the moisture in the igloo, the dropping of snow which was the condensation from our breaths.

Ever since the hearings Peary's critics have pointed to these alleged discrepancies in the Peary Diary — the incomplete wording on the cover, the loose pages and the missing pages — as evincing that he did not attain the Pole. Two alternative theories are (1) that in view of its immaculate condition, the entire diary was written back in his cabin on the *Roosevelt* or (2) that at least the separate "The Pole at last!" entry was written after he was back aboard the ship.

Dennis Rawlins remarks with regard to the cover entry:

How strange that Peary had not filled in the blank with the words "North Pole." He had noted the dates of his departure from the ship and his return to it; why omit any mention of the Pole? Evidently, three weeks after the discovery, Peary still wasn't certain that he had made it. There were symptoms of at least temporary uncertainty at extremely critical points *inside* the diary too. (*Fact Or Fiction*, pp. 229 -230)

At least we can say, as a result of our forays into the Archives, that the skepticism engendered by the incomplete cover entry is unfounded. The omission is explainable by the laxity with which Peary maintained his journals in general, and filled in (or failed to fill in) his cover entries in particular. The covers of other notebooks for various segments of the overall 1909 expedition are marked as follows:

#1 Journal from Sydney out		No end position or date
#2 Etah to		This time he entered the starting point, not the ending point, but gave
Aug. 18th - Oct. 1		both starting and ending dates
1908		
#3 No title on cover		
#4 No title on cover		
#6 No 2		Here he gave no positions but a starting date which was corrected by
27		a day and never filled
Apr. 28 1909		in a finishing date
to		
#7		On this log he had the
9 09		year wrong and
July ~~10~~ 19~~10~~		corrected it. The entries show months
to		
		but not the year, so the cover was probably erroneously dated later and corrected.
09		
Aug. 26 1910		Also on this log under the ink dates pencil dates are scratched with a dull pencil
July 8 1909 to		No closing date.

As for the content of the logs, Peary recorded personal comments along with trip data, often scrawling the former across the top of the page, along the margins, or on the reverse side of the page. He often left blank pages and did not complete one notebook before starting the next. Undated celestial observations were jotted down in any blank space that was handy. In sum, he had little concern for proper journal keeping, which is somewhat surprising for a person of his engineering background.

The important point is that the journals were never intended to be Navigation Logs, such as ships maintain, but day to day accounts not just of his expeditions but of his random thoughts. Their primary purpose was to provide material for his books and articles, and he intended to keep them strictly private.

Wally Herbert agrees:

> The diary ... was not written by Peary with publication in mind, as was the diary of Robert Scott. It was written as a private log of his journey, a log he had intended simply as a reminder of the events which he would later expand and polish for publication, and as a convenient notebook for ideas and memos, thoughts which it is truly astonishing that Peary should have taken the risk of committing to paper, let alone to his diary. (*Noose Of Laurels*, p. 13).

Plainly Peary could identify his book by its cover without the words "North Pole" written on it, and that was all that mattered to him.

The several blank (but dated) pages, and minimal entries for the portion of the expedition covering the return from the Pole give us no trouble either. As Peary explained to the congressional committee, he was sometimes "too busy" to write in his diary. This would be especially true of the return marches which Peary described in his entry of April 9 as "a savage finish" to a "glorious sprint" to the Pole and back. At the time he was exhausted from his upward forced marches and his almost constant activity in the vicinity of Camp Jesup. His efforts were being devoted to getting his party and himself back to safety before the favorable ice conditions they had enjoyed changed for the worse. The niceties of a fully completed diary seem trivial when one is focussing upon staying alive.[9]

Finally there is the matter of the loose sheet of paper on which Peary wrote "The Pole at last!!!" We studied this sheet carefully, hoping to determine whether it came from the diary. The paper is identical to the paper of the diary notebook; however it was not torn out of that notebook where the date, April 6, occurs. We surmise that it came from a similar pocket sized notebook that Peary kept handy and used for sending notes to his expedition members. There is in the Archives a note that Peary left for Marvin (when he gave up waiting for him to return from a trip back to the base at Cape Columbia) written on paper that also looks as though it had been torn from the diary. Yet the diary itself is seemingly intact.

While it is possible that both slips were torn from the diary notebook together (one from one side and one from the other, leaving no telltale extra leaf), it is equally

---

[9] Robert Scott kept a meticulous diary that was found with his body when he perished on his return from the South Pole just eleven miles from a supply depot that might have meant salvation.

probable that Peary had a second notebook from which he removed leaves to send messages to members of the expedition. In that case he may have used that notebook to write his "The Pole at last !!!" entry — which he said he wrote in the afternoon of April 6 — simply because it was at hand when his diary was not. During the day, Peary said, he kept his diary in a special canvass bag lashed to the upright of his sledge, removing it only at night.

It is also possible that Peary wrote his carefully composed dramatic announcement on a separate sheet of paper because this, unlike the rest of his diary entries, was drafted for public consumption. Such a statement falls in the same category as Astronaut Neil Armstrong's famous "That's one small step for a man, one giant leap for mankind." Neither are the pedestrian words normally recorded in a working diary or log. In each case the pronouncements were composed for posterity. Thus Peary may have deliberately chosen to write his statement on a piece of notepaper that could later be photographically reproduced for publication (as it ultimately was), and meanwhile inserted it in his diary in its proper place for safekeeping.[10]

In any event, it seems to us that none of the questions the diary has engendered would have been raised had Peary sat down in his cabin and written his entries there as his critics maintain. A reasonably intelligent faker would have ensured that there were no loose pages, no unwritten pages, and that the cover was properly labelled.

D. The Henson Stories

Henson gave several accounts of his journey to the Pole with Peary that critics have since attempted to use against Peary. One was given in an early interview with a *Boston American* reporter in which he told how Peary had slipped away with his Eskimos and taken observations a few miles from Camp Jesup —observations which the Eskimos said, "told him that he had overstepped and gone past the Pole which we had reached the night before." Then:

> "Well, Mr. Peary, I spoke up cheerfully enough, "we are now at the Pole, are we not?

> "I do not suppose we can swear that we are exactly at the Pole," was his evasive answer.

> "Well, I have kept track of the distance and we have made exceptional time," I replied, "and I have a feeling we have now just about covered the 132 miles since Captain Bartlett turned back. If we have traveled in the right direction we are now at the Pole. If we have not traveled in the right direction then it is your fault." (Quoted in *Noose Of Laurels*, p. 249)

Another early account is given in Henson's ghost-written *A Negro Explorer At The North Pole*, published in 1912, with a foreword by Peary.

---

[10] The page was so inserted when the Peary Diary was placed in the National Archives.

When we halted on April 6, 1909, and started to build the igloos, the dogs and sledges having been secured, I noticed Commander Peary at work unloading his sledge. He pulled out from his *kooletah* (thick, fur outer-garment) a small folded package and unfolded it. I recognized his old silk flag, and realized that this was to be a camp of importance ...I asked what the name of this camp was to be — "Camp Peary"? "This, my boy, is to be Camp Morris K. Jesup, the last and most northerly camp on earth." (p.132)

Then:

It was about ten or ten-thirty A.M. on the 7th of April, 1909 [actually the 6th], that the Commander gave the order to build a snow-shield to protect him from the flying drift of the surface snow. I knew he was about to take an observation, and while we worked I was nervously apprehensive, for I felt that the end of our journey had come ... Lying flat on his stomach he took the elevation and made notes on a piece of tissue paper at his head. With sun-blinded eyes, he snapped shut the vernier ... and with the resolute squaring of his jaws, I was sure that he was satisfied, and I was confident that the journey had ended. Feeling that the time had come, I ungloved my right hand and went forward to congratulate him on the success of our eighteen years of effort, but a gust of wind blew something into his eye, or else the burning pain caused by his prolonged look at the reflection of the limb of the sun forced him to turn aside; and with both hands covering his eyes, he gave us orders to not let him sleep for more than four hours ...(pp.134-135)

In his *Noose Of Laurels,* Herbert deduces from these journalistic renderings Henson's words that Peary attempted to deceive Henson as to their true position, which he determined from his observations was nowhere near the Pole. He exclaims:

How much sharper now seems that remark which Henson had made "cheerfully enough" in his innocence of their true position: that if they had not travelled in the right direction, it was *Peary's* fault! How much more poignant too now seems that moment when Henson had ungloved his right hand and gone forward to congratulate the man whom he served on the success of their eighteen years of effort, and Peary, "with both hands covering his eyes," had turned and walked away.

Could it be that the heart-broken Peary could not bear that Henson might read the misery in his eyes and suddenly know the cruel truth that they had come the right distance — but in the wrong direction?

Could it be that Peary had left Henson behind at Camp Jesup because he needed time to think, time perhaps to adjust himself to that heartless mocking truth? (p.251)

Suffice it to say that Herbert goes on to conclude that Peary's mental anguish is reflected in the missing pages of his diary, for which he substituted a phony "The Pole at last!!!" entry written back in his cabin aboard the *Roosevelt*. And meanwhile, back aboard the *Roosevelt*,[11] Herbert surmises, his guilty conscience led him to avoid Henson. He bases this upon a seeming coolness between Peary and Henson that is also recounted in *A Negro Explorer:*

> From the time of my arrival at the *Roosevelt*, for nearly three weeks, my days were spent in complete idleness. I would catch a fleeting glimpse of Commander Peary, but not once in all that time did he speak a word to me. Then he spoke to me in the most ordinary, matter of fact way, and ordered me to get to work. Not a word about the North Pole or anything connected with it; simply, "There is enough wood left, and I would like to have you make a couple of sledges and mend the broken ones. I hope you are feeling all right." (p.153)

Herbert announces in the Prologue of *The Noose Of Laurels* that he will "read behind the lines" of Peary's story as told in his diary, and perhaps "stumble upon a story that appears to be more human and *therefore more likely than the one the record shows.*" (*Noose*, p. 14) In our opinion, however, in reading behind the lines of Peary's documented story in this instance, he has come up with a story that is much more *unlikely* than the record shows.

Rawlins too makes use of Henson's stories to support his hoax theory. Speaking of Peary's excursions in the vicinity of the Pole with his Eskimos, he writes:

> Henson, after learning of the intended secret jaunt, was convinced Peary was trying to beat him to the Pole. This naturally made Henson prone to hope and convince himself — certainly his weary bones told him he had gone at least 130 miles! — Camp Jesup was smack at the Pole. This conviction Peary opportunistically exploited via subsequent flag-raising ceremonies right at the camp. (*Fact or Fiction*, p. 153)

The author goes on to hypothesize that, having duped Henson, Peary decided that he would take no further observations and risk having them come out wrong. He would play it safe and settle "for just the genuine Marvin and Bartlett observations en route, *plus a few manufactured North Pole observations.*" (p.154, emphasis added) Rawlins concludes:

---

[11] Herbert conjectures that even upon reaching the *Roosevelt* Peary had not quite decided whether to go through with his fraudulent plans. "But what evidence is there to suggest that Peary, having reached the ship, had still not decided to go through with his claim?" (*Noose*, p.257) He then sights a slip of paper he had come across in the Archives which reads:

> Goodsell returned to ship from 84-29 in 12 days. MacMillan in 11 days including establishment of depot at Ward Hunt Island. Borup returned from 85-23 in 23 days including establishment of depot at C. Fanshaw Martin. Marvin's men came in from 86-38 in 23 days. Captain came in from 87-47 in 24 days. Self came in from—in 20 days (18 marches).

This, like the cover entry on the polar journal, is but another example of the laxity of Peary's record-keeping. It may indicate that he had not yet worked out to his satisfaction how close he came to the Pole in his side trips with the Eskimos. In any event, it falls far short of indicating any mental anguish as to whether or not to go through with a fraudulent scheme.

...Peary reached the *Roosevelt*, perhaps still unsure not only of what story eventually to put in writing, but of whether or not to go through *with this final exploring hoax*, the greatest not only of his career, but in all the history of science. (emphasis added)

Bartlett, who had returned to the ship only three days before, greeted him and, before Peary had uttered a word, shook his head and said, *"I congratulate you, sir, on the discovery of the Pole!*

Well, if it was going to be *this* easy...! (p.160, emphasis in original)

Both authors absolve Henson of conspiring in Peary's "final exploring hoax." But we find it distressing that both should use the innocuous journalistic prose attributed to Henson against the man Henson so loyally served for so many years. The effort must fail, in any event, for Matt Henson was too experienced in navigation,[12] in steering by the magnetic compass and in estimating distances covered by dogsledge, to have been so easily duped as they assume.

Henson knew even before Peary took his observations that the party had reached the Pole, if we would believe another of his ghost-writers, Bradley Robinson. In *Dark Companion* (1947), Robinson writes:

On April 5, Peary took an observation. Their position was 89 degrees 25 minutes. The Pole was 35 miles away!

They tried to rest but there was no sleep for Matt or Peary that night. Only the Eskimos slept, and theirs was the sleep of innocent children... (p.223)

On the next march Matt and Ootah crossed a narrow thinly frozen lead which Henson crashed through, to be rescued by the Eskimo. They then marched on to a point where Matt reasoned that "he, the humble Negro, born in a mud-chinked hovel in Charles County, Maryland, *was standing at the apex of the earth.*" Then:

Calmly Matt and Ootah set to work to build an igloo. *Forty-five minutes later, Peary arrived* .

"I think this is it," Matt said, as he hurried to meet him. Without a word, Peary began unpacking his observation equipment.

When he had finished taking an observation of their position, Peary got slowly to his feet. He nodded to Matt. "Eighty-nine degrees fifty-seven minutes," he said, and his voice quivered with emotion. He sank down wearily on his sledge. His tired, drawn face glowed with joy and elation.

---

[12] He had been taught celestial navigation by the merchant captain of a ship on which he had sailed in his youth, and by Ross Marvin during idle days on the *Roosevelt* during the 1906 and 1909 expeditions. Though he could not do complex mathematical reductions, he understood the fundamentals.

"The Pole at last!" he whispered softly. "Mine at last. Mine!"
Then he rose, went into the igloo and fell into an exhausted
slumber. (p.225)

If one is willing to believe "Henson" stories, why not believe this one?

As for the coolness between Peary and Henson after the return to the *Roosevelt* (assuming that it was not a figment of Henson's imagination and that Peary's reluctance to speak about the Pole was not merely due to his natural reticence) a later author offers a possible explanation.

In *American History Ilustrated* (May, 1966) Robert Fowler wrote:

> *Henson was 88 when he told me this story. It was the only time his manner became in the least agitated in our conversations but once he began talking he seemed unable to stop until he had told it all.*
>
> I had my igloo built when Peary came in. I said, "I think I've overrun my mark two miles. I think I'm the first man to sit at the top of the world."
> "What?" he said. Then "We'll see tomorrow."
>
> *Was Peary angry because Henson had not stopped and waited for him?*
>
> Oh, he got hopping mad. No, he didn't say anything, but I could tell. I didn't know what he would do. I took all the cartridges out of my rifle before I went to sleep. Took them out and buried them in the snow. I had the only rifle in the party...
>
> *Did Peary remain angry because Henson had disobeyed him and failed to halt just short of the Pole?*
>
> He didn't speak to me if he could help it. When we got to Cape Columbia he told me, "Now give me the best dogs and Egingwah will drive me back to the ship. You wait a couple of days before you follow." *He wanted to be the first to take the news back.* I didn't care.

Here we have an account (neither more nor less reliable than the others) that counters Rawlins' and Herbert's theory that Peary evaded Henson because he had deceived his Negro assistant as to their reaching the Pole. It suggests instead that he was still "hopping mad" because Henson had disregarded his instructions and marched on to the Pole before him. And here he observed that Peary was anxious, not reticent to talk about the Pole.

The critics assert that upon his return to the ship Peary isolated himself in his cabin and told no one other than Bob Bartlett of his "discovery" of the Pole. In fact, Rawlins' maintains that Bartlett merely deduced it for himself ("I congratulate you sir, on the discovery of the Pole"). However, such is not the case.

Peary went immediately to his cabin, to be sure, to bathe, change his clothes and to rest from his harrowing journey. He also wanted time to reflect on the death of Ross Marvin — his trusted first assistant and closest confidant — who had drowned in a lead on his trip home.[13]

His next move, however, was to despatch two Eskimos to MacMillan and Borup, who were on an expedition along the Greenland coast laying supply depots against the contingency that parties should be drifted to the west, to tell them of his success.[14] The two were told to take soundings instead, and the Eskimos carried the necessary equipment to them.

Then came a celebration for the Eskimos aboard the ship, including those who had accompanied him to the Pole. He observes in *The North Pole* (p. 323):

> One of the first things done after reaching the ship and bringing our sleep up to date was to reward the Eskimos who had served us so faithfully. They were all fitted out with rifles, shotguns, cartridges, shells, reloading tools, hatchets, knives and so on, and they behaved like so many children who had just received a boundless supply of toys. Among the things I have given them at various times, none are more important than the telescopes, which enable them to distinguish game in the distance. The four who stood with me at the Pole were to receive whale-boats, tents, and other treasures when I dropped them at their home settlements along the Greenland coast on the southward journey of the *Roosevelt*.

This does not sound like a man who was sulking in this cabin keeping quiet about his success while he determined how to perpetrate the "greatest exploring hoax ...in all the history of science." (Rawlins, *Fact Or Fiction*, p.160.

We firmly believe that Peary, Matt Henson, and the four Eskimos reached the North Pole just as they said they did on April 6, 1909, in the absence of any evidence, scientific or otherwise, to the contrary.

---

[13] Peary writes in *The North Pole* (pp. 317-318):

As we approached the ship I saw Bartlett going over the rail. He came along the ice foot to meet me, and something in his face told me he had bad news even before he spoke.

"Have you heard about poor Marvin?" he asked.

"No, I answered."

Then he told me that Marvin had been drowned at the "Big Lead," coming back to Cape Columbia. The news staggered me, killing all the joy I had felt at the sight of the ship and her captain. It was indeed a bitter flavor in the cup of our success.

[14] Previously, Borup had deposited a cache at Cape Fanshaw Martin on the Grant Land coast, Some eighty miles west from Cape Columbia, thus providing for a drift in either direction.

Part Seven

PEARY'S TRACK

As the final step in this report we assembled all the information gathered herein and used it to construct Peary's probable track from Cape Columbia to the Pole.

The track shown in Figure VII-1 has been plotted on a chart of the Arctic Ocean. It combines the evidence we developed as to Arctic navigation, ice movement, bathymetric soundings, and photogrammetric rectification as they affect Peary's long disputed claim.

The track shows that the movement of the ice that carried Peary and his party west between Cape Columbia and the "Big Lead" reversed itself as Ross Marvin and George Borup returned to the base for supplies, and brought them back closer to the 70th meridian. Thereafter the net effect of the wind-driven ice movement was compensated for by the heading corrections made possible by Peary's method of navigation, which was fundamentally "dead reckoning" corrected by noontime observations.

The locations of the soundings shown on the track correspond to the estimates of latitudes reached by the expedition as determined by Marvin's and Bob Bartlett's "local apparent noon" sights on the northward journey. It is assumed that compass corrections were made and the party steered due north after each sun sight was taken.

The early going was slow, particularly after the main party was delayed by open water at the "Big Lead Camp" from the 5th of March to the 11th of March. Then after passing over the Lomonosov Ridge, where Marvin's sounding shoaled at 567 meters, the going improved.

At latitude 86°-38' Marvin, who would drown while crossing a lead on his homeward journey, took his final sunsight and turned back.

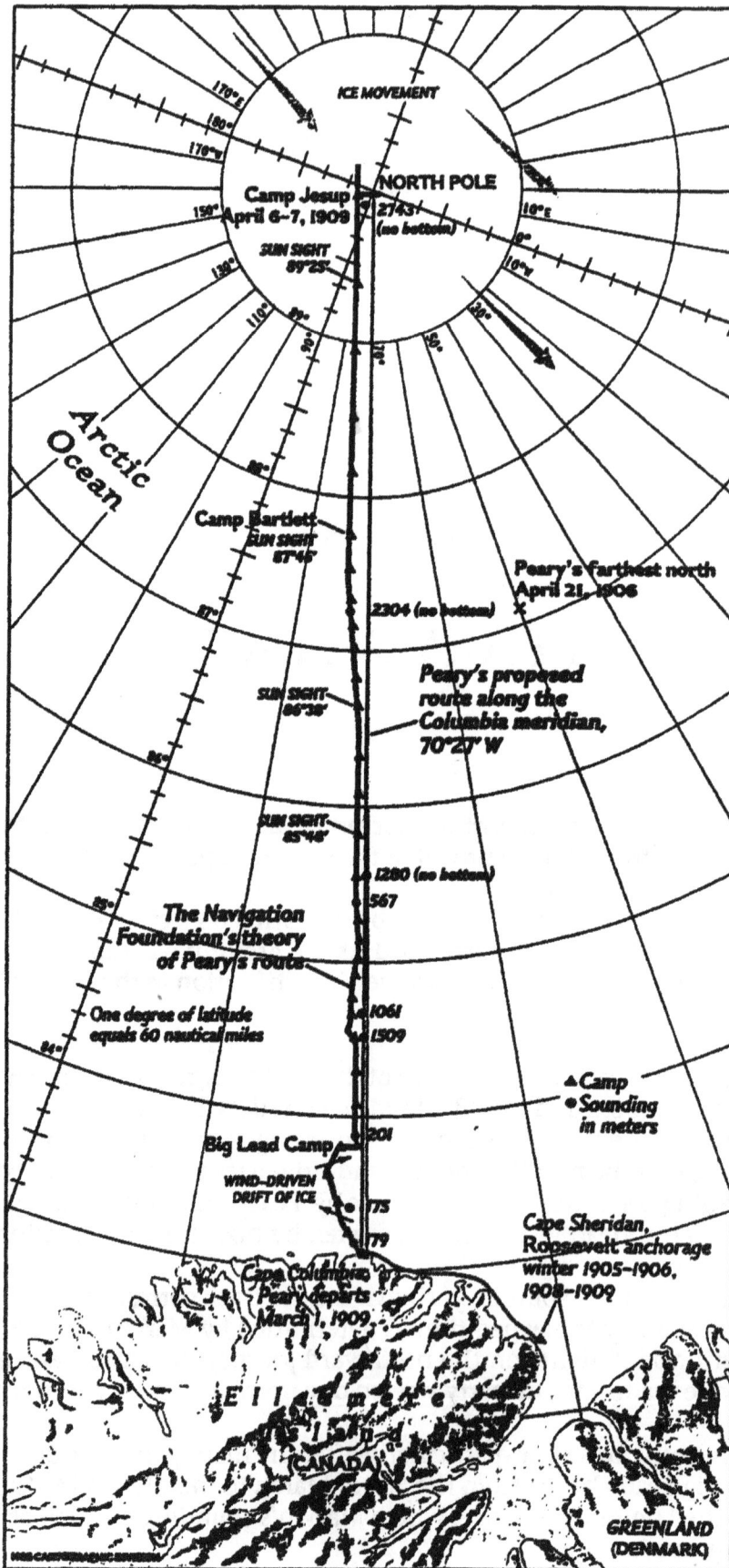

Fig. VII-1

The final "dash" for the Pole began from Camp Bartlett, where "Captain Bob" turned back after taking a sunshot which showed that latitude 87-45 had been reached.

North of latitude 88 North, the ice surface permitted higher speeds as modern polar expeditions have confirmed. The stripped down polar party, consisting of Peary, Matt Henson and four Eskimos, doubled the length of their marches and bent every effort toward reaching the Pole while favorable weather prevailed. Camp Jesup, their northernmost camp, was reached after five marches on April 6, 1909.

Our track places Camp Jesup within five miles of the Pole, exactly where several sets of observations taken by Peary on April 6-7 showed it to be. After a detailed analysis of these observations we determined that they were genuine, not faked as Peary's critics claim.

In sum, the track reflects the Navigation Foundation's unanimous conclusion that within the probable error of their navigation instruments (about five miles), the polar party reached the North Pole on April 6, 1909, as Peary, Henson, and the Eskimos Ootah, Egingwah, Seegloo and Ooqueah maintained for the rest of their lives.

Appendix A

Foundation for the Promotion of the Art of Navigation
"THE NAVIGATION FOUNDATION"
A NON-PROFIT CORPORATION OF MARYLAND
P.O. Box 1126, Rockville, MD 20850 (Tel. 301-622-6448)

(301) 299-7713

January 13, 1989

Mr. Gilbert M. Grosvenor
President and Chairman
The National Geographic
    Society
Washington, D.C. 20036

Re: Interim Report on the Peary Project

Dear Mr. Grosvenor:

The National Geographic Society has asked The
Navigation Foundation to conduct a thorough review of all
available navigational evidence to determine what light can be
shed on the controversy surrounding Rear Admiral Robert E.
Peary's claim that he reached the North Pole in 1909. As part
of that effort, the Society has asked us to consider Dennis
Rawlins' recent sensational claims that new navigational
evidence -- a single worksheet relating to celestial
observations -- conclusively shows that Peary did not get
within 100 miles of the Pole and was aware of that fact.

Our review is well underway, and there is a great
deal of evidence, wholly apart from the worksheet that Rawlins
has publicized, that we are studying. We expect to take
several months to conclude that study. In the meantime,
however, Rawlins' analysis of Peary's worksheet, widely
reported in the press as fact, is creating a public impression
that Peary has been proved to be a fraud. Since we are
convinced beyond any doubt that the worksheet does not even
come close to proving any such thing, we are providing this
interim report analyzing the worksheet.

Rawlins assumes that the worksheet shows altitude
observations of the sun taken on April 7, 1909, when Peary
says that he was at the Pole. As explained in detail in the
attached report, Rawlins' analysis is clearly incorrect. The
numbers that Rawlins assumes are degrees, minutes and seconds
of <u>arc</u> can also be interpreted as hours, minutes and seconds

"The art of navigation incites those who follow it to learn the secrets of the world" —Christopher Columbus, 1501

of time (since both are written in the same sexigesimal system). Since the readings record half seconds, as sextant readings they would express a degree of precision far beyond the capability of the human eye or of the sextant vernier scale. Chronometer times, on the other hand, are easily read to accuracies of ½ second. Therefore, it is apparent that these values are times relating to the adjacent sextant values on the worksheet, which are clearly labelled as degrees and minutes. Further, Rawlins' analysis assumes several navigational techniques that are nonsensical, and his explanations of two key numbers on the worksheet (the sextant values) rests on erroneous calculations. The most obvious (although not the most serious) error in Rawlins' analysis can be appreciated by referring to Exhibit 2 to the attached report, which shows the faces of Peary's three watch-type chronometers. The prominent serial numbers on the faces of the watches also appear on the worksheet, and Rawlins "analyzed" them as a set of compass readings that supposedly confirmed Peary's erroneous view of the magnetic variation at the Pole.

Based on our study to date of Peary's navigational methods, our familiarity with the normal practices of celestial navigation in 1909, and our numerical analysis of the worksheet, we are satisfied beyond any doubt that it shows two sets of altitude observations called "time sights," i.e., celestial observations taken at a known location and used to determine chronometer error.[1] Before the availability of radio time signals, the "time sight" was the primary means of checking the chronometer. Knowing the chronometer error is essential to any method of longitude determination and to Peary's method of determining direction from the azimuth of the sun.

Our continuing study will, among other things, attempt to identify the precise dates and locations of the two time sights shown on the worksheet and identify the celestial bodies being observed. As explained in the attached report, because of the many unknown variables, the number of theoretical possibilities is enormous. At this point, we are checking out a small number of possibilities that appear to

_____

[1] Successive time sights were also used in surveying to measure longitude changes by using a portable chronometer to measure the difference in local mean time between two locations. Peary's 1900 survey of the Greenland coast shows that he was familiar with this technique. Peary could have considered an adaptation of this method as one means of checking for longitudinal drift.

fit well with what is known about Peary's movements about the times of his departures from land during his 1906 and 1909 treks over the polar ice cap.

Of course, this interim report does not reflect any ultimate conclusion on whether Peary did in fact reach the Pole. Our purpose is merely to expose Rawlins' purported "proof" to the critical scrutiny that it has so far escaped. Properly understood, the worksheet says nothing about whether Peary did or did not reach the Pole, although it does provide evidence that Peary was more careful about monitoring his chronometer error than some commentators have assumed.

We would be glad to receive any comments or answer any questions that the Society may have concerning this interim report.

Sincerely,

Thomas D. Davies
Rear Admiral U.S.N. (Ret.)
President

January 13, 1989

PEARY NORTH POLE PROJECT
INTERIM REPORT NO. 1

From the time that Rear Admiral Robert E. Peary
returned from his 1909 expedition in which he said he reached
the North Pole, there has been controversy surrounding that
claim. Those who dispute Peary's claim have argued that
Peary's claimed daily distances traveled by dogsled were
impossible; that Peary's navigational methods were inadequate
and could have resulted in his drifting hopelessly off course;
and that various anecdotal information demonstrates that Peary
faked his claim. Recently, Dennis Rawlins has made
sensational claims that new navigational evidence (a slip of
paper hereinafter referred to as "the worksheet") conclusively
shows that Peary did not get within 100 miles of the Pole and
was aware of that fact.

The National Geographic Society has asked The
Navigation Foundation to conduct a thorough review of all of
the navigational evidence available to determine what light
might be shed on the validity of Peary's claim. That review
is well underway, and there is a great deal of evidence,
wholly apart from the worksheet, that we are studying.
However, since Rawlins' analysis of the worksheet, widely
reported in the press as fact, is creating a public impression
that Peary has been proved to be a fraud, and since we are
convinced beyond any doubt that the worksheet does not even
come close to proving any such thing, we are providing this
interim report. Of course, this report does not reflect any

conclusion regarding the ultimate question whether Peary reached the Pole.

Summary

The worksheet is a single sheet of notes relating to navigational observations. The worksheet apparently was placed by Peary's wife in an envelope on which she wrote "Original Observations made by R.E. Peary, U.S.N. at 90° N. Lat. April 5 & 6, 1909."

Rawlins assumes that the worksheet shows altitude observations on the sun taken on April 7, 1909, when Peary claims to have been at the Pole. Rawlins' analysis is clearly incorrect. The numbers that Rawlins assumes are altitude observations are recorded with such precision that they can only be times. Further, Rawlins' analysis assumes several navigational techniques that are nonsensical, and his explanation of two key numbers on the worksheet rests on erroneous calculations. Finally, Rawlins completely missed the point of some portions of the worksheet that, although not critical to his analysis, provide an important clue to the proper interpretation of the worksheet.

Based on our study to date of Peary's navigational methods, our familiarity with normal practices of celestial navigation, and some tentative numerical analysis of the worksheet, we are satisfied beyond any doubt that it shows two sets of altitude observations taken as "time sights," celestial observations taken at a known location and used to

determine chronometer error.[1]/ Before the availability of
radio time signals, the "time sight" was the primary means of
checking chronometer error. Knowledge of the chronometer
error is essential to any method of determining longitude and
to Peary's method of determining direction from the azimuth of
the sun.

Our continuing study will, among other things,
attempt to identify the precise dates and locations of the
time sights and the celestial bodies being observed. As
explained below, because of the many unknown variables, the
number of theoretical possibilities is enormous. At this
point, we are checking out a small number of possibilities
that appear to fit well with what is known about Peary's
movements about the times of his departures from land during
his 1906 and 1909 treks over the polar ice cap.

Properly understood, the worksheet says nothing
about whether Peary did or did not reach the Pole, although it
does suggest that Peary was more careful about monitoring his
chronometer error than some commentators have assumed.

Rawlins' Analysis of the Worksheet

Rawlins assumes that the worksheet contains
information relating to sights of the altitude of the sun that
Peary took to determine his latitude at 1:00 a.m. Atlantic

1/   Such sights were also used in surveying to measure
longitude changes by using a portable chronometer to measure
the difference in local mean time between two locations.
Peary's 1900 survey of the north coast of Greenland shows that
he was familiar with this method, and he may have considered
an adaptation of this method as one means of checking for
longitudinal drift during the trip to the Pole.

Standard Time (AST) on April 7, 1909. Rawlins theorizes in his article in DIO #1 that Peary's observations showed a rapid rise in altitude, indicating that Peary was not on the meridian that he assumed and that he was very far from the Pole.[2] According to Rawlins, Peary realized, on the basis of these sights, that he could never reach the Pole and thereupon decided to fake his claim.

There are three reasons why Rawlins' analysis of the worksheet cannot possibly be correct. First, there is no number on the worksheet that can possibly be a value that Peary would have obtained for the observed altitude of the sun (double the actual altitude, since Peary took celestial sights by measuring the angle between a celestial body and its reflection in an "artificial horizon").[3] Rawlins is forced to assume that the numbers "12 17 15½," etc. on the left side

---

[2] Peary's method of determining latitude was in essence to take sights of the altitude of the sun as it crossed his meridian of longitude and compare the altitude with the altitude that the sun would have if he were at the North Pole (i.e., the sun's declination). The difference between the sun's altitude (after applying various corrections) and its declination is subtracted from 90 to obtain latitude.

As the sun crosses the meridian, it is neither rising nor setting, except at a very slow rate as a result of seasonal variation in the sun's declination. When the sun is not on the meridian, it rises or sets at a rate that increases with the observer's distance from the Pole.

[3] An artificial horizon is a small flat dish filled with mercury to provide a perfectly level reflecting surface. Because mercury is a solid at the low temperatures in which Peary was operating, he had to heat the mercury thoroughly before setting up the artificial horizon. To prevent wind ripples on the surface of the mercury, a glass roof is placed over the dish.

of the worksheet (see box 1 in Exhibit 1)[4] are observed altitudes of the sun, since these are the only numbers that are of approximately the correct magnitude. Thus Rawlins reads these numbers as, e.g., 12 degrees, 17 minutes, and 15½ seconds of arc. However, there is nothing on the worksheet that expressly identifies these numbers as measures of arc. Because both angular measure and time are expressed in the sexigesimal (base 60) system using minutes and seconds, these could just as easily be times.

The ambiguity is resolved in this case by recognizing that the numbers must be times, because it is simply not possible to read a sextant to a precision of anything close to ½" (second) of arc. The scale on a sextant (of that period) is designed to be read only to the nearest 10" of arc. That degree of precision is obtained by determining which of 60 pairs of closely spaced lines on vernier scales on the sextant's index arm and limb most nearly line up. The relative movement of the scales for a 10" change is about 2/10,000th of an inch. A small magnifier is attached to the sextant to permit the user to discern such a small interval.[5] It is inconceivable that anyone could discern an increment of ½" of arc -- twenty times smaller.

4/ Exhibit 1 is a sketch of the worksheet, not a photocopy. The worksheet is difficult to read and does not copy well. We are satisfied that we have accurately reconstructed the numbers.

5/ Modern sextants have a vernier that is easier to use, but still read angle at best only to the nearest tenth of a minute (six seconds) of arc.

Even if a sextant could be read to a precision better than 10" of arc, such a precise reading would be meaningless in view of the inherent limitations on the accuracy of a sight. Not surprisingly, records of Peary's other navigational observations do not show any instance of his having attempted to read a sextant more accurately than to the nearest 10 seconds of arc.

Second, Rawlins' theory assumes that Peary used a completely irrational method of taking celestial observations. Rawlins assumes that Peary, horrified to discover that the sun was rising rapidly, performed a complicated calculation to determine what altitude the sun would attain approximately four minutes later if the rate of ascent shown by the first three sights were correct, and then took a fourth sight at the predetermined time to see whether the sun did in fact rise to the predetermined altitude. This is a ridiculously circuitous procedure.[6] If Peary were trying to ascertain the rate of increase of the sun's altitude, he would simply have taken two observations far enough apart in time to minimize the effect of errors in the sights (preferably at least 15 minutes) and divided the change in altitude by the time interval.

_____

[6] Rawlins refers to this method as an "extrapolation-check," as though this were some kind of standard navigational practice. However, there is no mention of the method in the standard navigational reference of Peary's time (and the present), Bowditch's American Practical Navigator, or in any other text of which we are aware.

In any event, it is not clear why Peary would have been interested in determining the precise rate of ascent of the sun. There is no evidence that Peary knew of any method similar to the one that Rawlins developed in his paper to compute location from the altitude of a single body and its rate of change of altitude. Such a method was first developed by E.J. Willis in 1928, but was shown to be far too sensitive to sight inaccuracies to be of any real use to the navigator.[7]

Third, as discussed below in connection with our detailed analysis of the worksheet, most of the information on the worksheet is inconsistent with Rawlins' theory, and Rawlins is forced to adopt explanations of that information that are at best unfounded and at worst nonsensical and/or demonstrably incorrect.

What the Worksheet Shows

What the worksheet in fact shows is an incomplete record of two "time sights." These are observations taken from a known location of celestial bodies for which positions are tabulated in an almanac. Almanac data are used to determine the true time at which the observed altitude would have occurred at the known position of the observer, and that time is compared to the chronometer reading at the time of the observation to measure the chronometer error. The time sight

---

[7] See Mid. T.D. Davies, "Another Discussion of the Line of Azimuth Method," Naval Institute Proceedings (February 1937).

was a standard navigational technique, and one that Peary employed in connection with surveying work during his earlier polar explorations.

There is no reasonable analysis of the worksheet, as a time sight or otherwise, that can be reconciled with the characterization of the worksheet as observations on April 5 and 6, 1909 that appears on the envelope in which it apparently was kept at one time. In view of the fact that Peary himself did not write that description, and in view of the numerous possible explanations for an erroneous description,[8] we conclude that the characterization on the envelope is not accurate.

Our conclusion that the worksheet relates to time sights is based on the fact that the numbers starting with "12" on the upper left side of the worksheet (the numbers that Rawlins assumes are altitudes) can only be times. A chronometer, unlike a sextant, is easily read to a precision of $\frac{1}{2}$ second. In the lower left portion of the worksheet, Peary performs a subtraction and determines a difference of 14 seconds between what appears to be a computed time, 12h 18m 39s, and the average of the observed times, 12h 18m 25s.

---

[8] For example, Peary's wife could have written the note on the envelope long after Peary gave her the worksheet and incorrectly recalled what Peary told her; she could have misunderstood Peary's description of the worksheet; or the wrong slip of paper could have ended up in the envelope.

Further, as explained below, the numbers in the lower right of the worksheet are time comparisons between Peary's three chronometers (listed by serial number), again suggesting that the worksheet involves calculations relating to chronometer corrections.

The following analysis of each number on the worksheet further explains our conclusion that it reflects two time sights and demonstrates that each number is consistent with that view. Rawlins' analysis of each number is provided for comparison.

Our first clue that the worksheet related to efforts by Peary to correct his chronometers came from the numbers in the lower right of the worksheet (in box 6 in Exhibit 1). These show time comparisons among Peary's three watch-type chronometers. The numbers on the left are the serial numbers painted in large numerals on the face of these chronometers. See Exhibit 2.[9] The numbers to the right of the chronometer serial numbers show the determination of the differences among the times shown on the various chronometers. Thus at 1:12 the second chronometer was 10m 49s ahead of the first chronometer, and at 1:13 the third chronometer was 10m 37s ahead of the first chronometer.

Rawlins' analysis of the numbers in box 6 completely misses the mark. Rawlins assumes that the chronometer serial

_____

9/ Peary's chronometers are at the National Archives.

numbers in the left portion of box 6 ("306.320," etc.) are
compass readings, and notes that a "weighted average" of them
is consistent with Peary's estimate of the magnetic variation
of the compass at the Pole, which estimate Rawlins asserts was
incorrect. Having no real explanation for the times or
differences in box 6, Rawlins assumes that they relate in some
way to additional sun sights that Peary took or intended to
take, but did not record on the worksheet.

Boxes 1 and 2 in Exhibit 1 show two sets of sextant
observations. For each box, the numbers on the left are times
and the single number on the right is the altitude of the
celestial body being observed (a double altitude, since Peary
used an artificial horizon). The juxtaposition of the times
and altitudes is similar to the normal method of recording
sights. Only one altitude is shown corresponding to each set
of three times, because Peary was using a method for time
sights that involved presetting the sextant for three
altitudes and observing the times at which the celestial body
reached each preset altitude.[10] Since ultimately the three
times and the three altitudes will each be averaged, the
selection of evenly spaced altitudes saves a little work: The
average will be the second value, and only that value need be
recorded.

---

[10] This method is described in various texts of Peary's era,
including Bowditch's American Practical Navigator.

Since the motion of celestial bodies is essentially linear over short periods of time, the three times corresponding to three evenly spaced altitudes should also be evenly spaced. The three times in box 1 are very nearly evenly spaced at intervals of 1m 10s and 1m 9s. The times of the sights in box 2 are not quite as evenly spaced, at intervals of 1m 29s and 1m 26s. The 3-second difference would correspond to less than 10 seconds of arc error in estimating the altitude of the celestial body, a small error by the best navigator's standards.

Box 3 shows Peary's determination of the average time for the observations in box 1, and box 4 shows the scratch work for finding the average of the times for the sights in box 2 (1:01:57). In box 4, Peary first worked out the average time by totaling the first and last time and dividing by two. This calculation is scratched out, but the number 115 is the remainder (in seconds) after dividing the sum of the first and third sights by two. When the average of the first and third time did not equal the middle time, Peary added all three times and divided by three. (This time the remainder was 171½ seconds, as shown.) Peary calculated the difference between the second and third times (1m 29s, shown at the upper right of the worksheet), probably for the purpose of comparing it to the difference between the first two times (easily determined by inspection to be 1m 26s).

As discussed above, Rawlins incorrectly assumes that the times in box 1 are altitudes corresponding to the times in

box 2. Rawlins is then left with the problem of explaining
the two numbers in the right portions of boxes 1 and 2.
Rawlins' solution is that 19° 46' in box 1 is three times the
sun's declination at 1:00 a.m. on April 7, 1909, and 26° 23'
in box 2 is four times the sun's declination 20 minutes later.
Those conclusions are clearly erroneous.

First, Rawlins' suggestion that Peary would have had
any reason to calculate three (or four) times the sun's
declination is nonsense. Rawlins suggests that rather than
dividing the sum of the three observed altitudes of the sun by
three (to determine the average) and comparing the result to
the sun's declination, Peary would have found it simpler to
multiply the sun's declination by three and compare the result
to the sum of the three observed altitudes (and then divide
the resulting small number by three). However, even assuming
that there were some advantage to Rawlins' proposed method, it
simply does not work. The observed altitudes have to be
corrected for refraction before they are compared to the
declination. The refraction correction is nonlinear and can
be determined only on the basis of the actual observed
altitude -- not on the basis of double altitudes or the sum of
three double altitudes. The normal method for applying the
refraction correction (and the method used in all of Peary's
other sights) is to find the average double altitude (the step
that Rawlins suggests Peary could avoid) and then divide by
two. The resulting altitude is then used to determine the

refraction correction. Having thus determined the average, single altitude it is too late to benefit from the method that Rawlins suggests.[11]

Rawlins has even more trouble explaining the altitude of 26° 23' in box 2. Rawlins argues that this number is four times the sun's declination at 1:20 a.m. on April 7, 1909, when he assumes Peary made, or intended to make, four altitude observations of the sun that do not appear on the worksheet. Again, Rawlins' proposed method that would make use of four times the sun's declination simply does not work. Further, there is absolutely nothing on the worksheet to support Rawlins' suggestion that Peary made or intended to make four observations at or near 1:20. Rawlins assumes that the times shown in the lower right of the worksheet are somehow related to such observations, but as discussed above, those times are chronometer time comparisons, and not the times of any additional celestial observations.

---

[11] Peary could have determined the refraction on the basis of one of the observed altitudes as a reasonable approximation of the average. However, this would involve an extra step to divide the altitude by two.

More importantly, applying this correction at the end of the calculation that Rawlins suggests would require Peary either to add or subtract the correction depending on whether the altitude was greater than or less than the declination. (A similar source of error would arise when Peary applied the semidiameter correction, unless he multiplied it by three and applied it to the sum of the sights). Errors of this kind are avoided by adhering to the normal method of averaging the sights first.

Not only is Rawlins' explanation of the altitudes in boxes 1 and 2 nonsensical, it is wrong as a matter of arithmetic. As demonstrated in Appendix I, the sun's declination was approximately 6° 35' at 1:00 a.m. on April 7, 1909 and 6° 35' 20" at 1:20 a.m. on the same date. Multiplying by 3 and 4, respectively, gives 19° 45' and 26° 21' 20", respectively, not the numbers shown on the worksheet (19° 46' and 26° 23'). If greater precision is used in these calculations, the numbers are even further off.

Box 5 shows the comparison of the calculated time with the observed time for the time sight observation shown in box 1. The first value is the calculated time at which the celestial body would be observed at the altitude shown in box 2. That calculation does not appear on the worksheet, and may have been recorded on another slip of paper or in the margins of Peary's navigational tables. We are continuing to search for any remaining records of those calculations.

The calculated time is then reduced by 3m 56s. It is not clear what the 3m 56s correction represents. Perhaps coincidentally, this is almost exactly equal to the daily change in the sidereal time of noon, Greenwich Mean Time (GMT), which is one of the values used in the reduction of a time sight. This correction would have been required, for example, if Peary had inadvertently used the almanac entry for one day earlier than the date of his observations. It would also have been required if Peary had predetermined the time (by calculation or observation) for the day preceding the day of the observation.[12]

The final step in box 5 is the subtraction of the average of the times of the observations from box 1 from the calculated time. The difference shows the chronometer to be slow by 14 seconds.[13]

Rawlins explains the numbers in box 5 as an "extrapolation-check" to compare a fourth "altitude" with a precomputed increase of the previously observed "altitudes." As explained above, these are not altitudes, and the proposed technique would not make any sense.

The last two numbers on the worksheet (box 7) apparently show the application of the chronometer correction to the chronometer time differences from box 6.[14] Rawlins suggests that the numbers in box 7 are scratch calculations relating to the fourth and an assumed fifth "altitude."

12/ There is another explanation for the 3m 56s correction that would require a detailed explanation of the method of reducing a time sight. Since we hope to find the back up calculations that will pin down the precise explanation for the correction, we see no need to describe all of the hypothetical possibilities here.

13/ Peary writes this using the normal abbreviation for seconds of arc, rather than seconds of time ("). However, a number of Peary's other sights show the same misuse of this abbreviation.

14/ The correction of 14½s, rather than 14s, may be the result of an additional ½s carried over from the calculated time of the time sight but never written down. Alternatively, it may be attributable to the results of the second time sight, which do not appear on the worksheet.

Finally, the word "Betelgeux" on the worksheet is inexplicable under Rawlins' analysis, because on April 7, Rawlins' assumed date of the sights, Peary had full daylight 24 hours a day. Thus Betelgeux, a bright star in the constellation Orion, would not have been visible. Rawlins overcomes this obstacle by concluding that Peary wrote "Betelgeux" on the worksheet as an attempt to obscure its true meaning.

A more straightforward explanation is that Betelgeux is the star for which box 2 records altitude observations. As discussed below, that explanation makes sense in terms of the likely times and dates of the time sights.

Date and Location of the Time Sights

Trying to ascertain the dates and locations of the time sights shown on the worksheet is a laborious and, as yet unfinished, task. With respect to the left hand sight, we have the computed time of the observed altitude, i.e., 12h 18m 39s, and apparently the identity of the star, Betelgeux. With respect to the second time sight, we have neither the identity of the star (although the possible candidates can be reduced to a manageable number) nor the computed time for the sight, nor do we know which watch was used to determine the time of the observations. We do not have the date, assumed latitude, assumed longitude or sextant index error for either of the sights, although the first three of these parameters can to some extent be interrelated, given sufficient knowledge of Peary's movements, and the fourth is not likely to make much difference. We do not know whether the sights were taken during the 1909 expedition. Finally, we do not know whether the chronometers were being corrected to Atlantic Standard Time, Greenwich Mean Time or local mean time on any particular meridian.

With so many variables, the most logical approach is to try to find additional documentary information that will reduce or eliminate the uncertainty in these variables before trying to determine the dates and locations by exhaustive trial and error calculations. However, preliminary calculations do show that observations of Betelgeux in late February at various locations in the area between Cape Sheridan, the location of Peary's ship, and Cape Columbia, Peary's point of departure from land, produce results consistent with the numbers on the worksheet.

These would be logical dates and places for time sights. Peary's principal purpose in checking his chronometers would have been to be certain that his determinations of direction, based on the bearing of the sun at various times, would not be in error. It would be prudent to make this check just prior to the start of the trip across the ice. Further, since a chronometer check can be made only from a known position, it is more likely that the check would have been made on land, rather than on the ice.

Time sights are often taken in pairs (as appears to be shown on the worksheet), using two different celestial bodies, one as near as possible to due east and the other as near as possible to due west. Using two sights on opposite sides of the meridian reduces the effect of uncorrected refraction errors and minimizes the error that would result from an incorrect assumption of the latitude. The sight that appears to be an observation of Betelgeux, if taken in February or March in the area of Cape Sheridan and Cape Columbia would have been taken at an azimuth relatively close to due west.

Conclusion

Rawlins' published interpretation of the worksheet is completely erroneous. Details as to the actual or probable times and places of the sights shown on the worksheet cannot be specified at this time, but are the subject of further study. If these sights are shown to be from the 1909 expedition, they may demonstrate that previous conclusions that Peary might have been led off course by uncorrected chronometer errors were incorrect. In any event, they demonstrate that Peary was conscious of chronometer errors and knew how to correct them.

APPENDIX I

Rawlins' claim that 19° 46' is three times the sun's declination at 1:00 a.m. Atlantic Standard Time (AST) on April 7, 1909 is demonstrably false. The sun's declination is tabulated in Peary's almanac at noon Greenwich Mean Time (GMT) for each day, and hourly rates of change are provided for interpolation. One o'clock a.m. AST corresponds to 5:00 a.m. GMT, or 7 hours before noon GMT on April 7, 1909. Thus the value of the sun's declination tabulated for GMT noon April 7, 1909 (6° 41' 33.7") must be reduced by seven times the hourly increase in declination (56.46"). The calculation is as follows:

```
Hourly change (seconds)          56.46
Hours from GMT noon            x     7
Total change (seconds)          395.22

Total change (' ")           6'  35.22"

Noon declination        6° 41' 33.70"
Change                 -     6' 35.22"
1:00 a.m declination    6° 34' 58.48"
```

For navigational purposes, this result would typically be rounded off to 6° 35'. Peary made virtually the same calculation on the second page of a sight that he says he took on April 7, 1909 at 12:40 a.m., and arrived at a declination of 6° 35'.[1] Rawlins assumes that this value was determined for 12:40, the time of the sight, but inspection of Peary's

----

[1]   For some reason, Peary used the almanac data for Greenwich apparent time, rather than GMT. However, since apparent time was only 2m 18s ahead of mean time on that date, the difference is inconsequential.

calculation shows that he used the 1:00 a.m. value, ignoring the 20 minutes difference in time. This would be completely justifiable for a meridian sight, since the sun's altitude would not change significantly in that time.

Three times 6° 34' 58.48" is 19° 44' 55" (and three times the rounded figure of 6° 35' is 19° 45'). In comparison, the number on the worksheet is 19° 46'.

Rawlins' assertion that 26° 23' is four times the sun's declination at 1:20 a.m. on April 7, 1909 is similarly incorrect. Since the time is 20 minutes (1/3 of an hour) after 1:00 a.m., one third of the hourly increase in declination noted above must be added to the declination determined above. Thus the declination at 1:20 is:

```
Hourly change (seconds)        56.46
Hours                        x  .33
Total change (seconds)        18.63

1:00 declination       6° 34' 58.48"
Change              +         18.63"
1:20 a.m declination   6° 35' 17.11"
```

Multiplying by 4 gives 26° 21' 2", not 26° 23'.

Sketch diagram

- Bartlett again —

19°44'

① 12 7 15 (2
(8 25)
19
34½
15½
25½
55
15 18 12

③

⑦ 49
14½
34½

37
14½
22½

⑤ 22 35
3 56
18 39
25
14"

② -.30.
1.95
13.25

④ 5½ 11
17½
57
1.57
3 5 515½ 12½

3 25
55
69
23°
26°
23'

⑥ 0.10.37
0 10 49
1.22-494½   1.2.1.
1.3.-
1.2.37
306.320
307.310
306.320
306.309

Appendix B

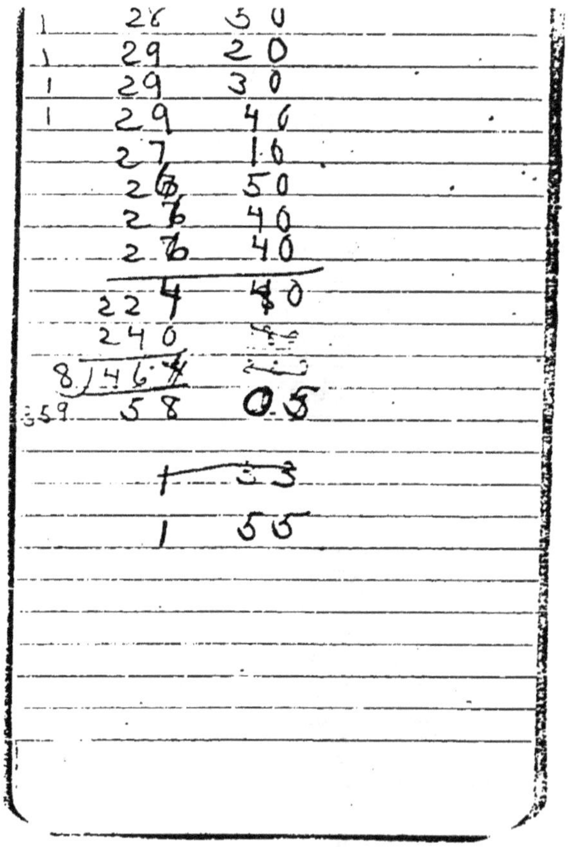

1	28	50
1	29	20
1	29	30
1	29	40
	27	10
	26	50
	26	40
	26	40
	4	40
	224	80
	240	
	8)467	
359	58	05
	1	53
	1	55

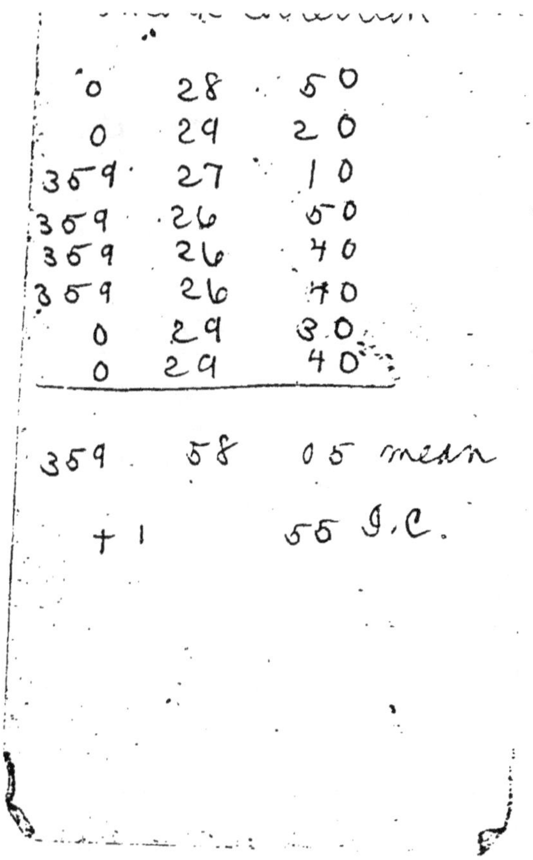

0	28	50
0	29	20
359	27	10
359	26	50
359	26	40
359	26	40
0	29	30
0	29	40
359	58	05 mean
+1		55 I.C.

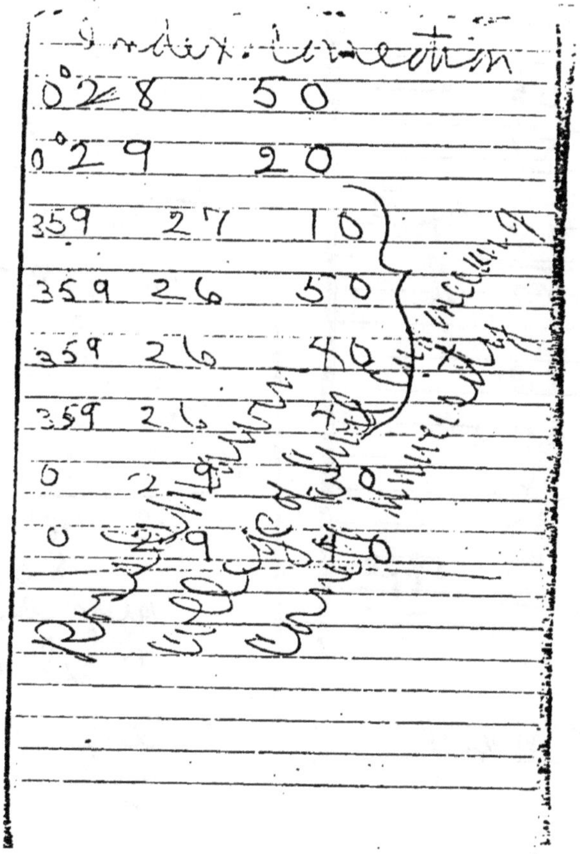

Index Correction

0°	28	50
0°	29	20
359	27	10
359	26	50
359	26	40
359	26	40
0	29	30
0	29	40

March 22nd, 1909
Temp -40° F   P.M.

F (10   27   00
  (10   24   30

  (9   21
R (9
  (9   21
  (
  (10   24   .5
F (
  (10   24   20

16?   24   50
16   24   30
16   24   30
16   24   20
9   21   20
9   21   50
9   21   10
9   21   00
_____
18 3 30
24 0
8) 42 3   3 6
2) 9   52   ~0:6
   4   56   05
_____
   1   55 + 9.C.

2) 9   5 3   43
   4   5 6   51
      / 9   30 — Ref
   4 / 47   21
          9 — +
   4   47   30 True alt

---

corrected Calculation

  9   52   56
      1   55   1C
2) 9   54   51
  4   57   25
      9   43   R+P
  4   47   42   h.

85   12   18
     29   24.2
      4   56.1
85   46   38
Cor for Ref   85   59.22
at -10°F   5
              6) 296.10
              4
85   48   03
Lat at Noon March 22
        1909

---

  9 — 52 — 56
+   1 — 55   I.C
2) 9 — 54 — 51
  4 — 57 — 25   alt.
        9 — 43   Ref + Par
— _____
  4 — 47 — 42   h

85 — 12 — 18   z
     29 — 24.2   dec
      4   56.1   diff for 5hr
_____
85 — 46 — 38
         85   Cor to Ref
+   for -10°F
_____
85°   48' — 03"   North
      85° — 48' North
signed,
Reeds marin,
College of Civil Engineering
Cornell University

Left note:
```
)    27   40
)    27   50
1    28   10
1    28   10
     26   50
     26   40
     26   20
     26   30
    218   10
    24  0
    458   10

     57   16

      2   44
```

Right note:
```
0    27   40
1.   27   50
1    28   1.0
1    28   10
    131   00
     27   57


0    26   50
0    26   40
0    26   20
0    26   30
          140

     26       35
     24
     21  4    25
    8)454
0     57   03    J. C.
                 2-57
```

March 25th, 1909

F 11   04   10
   11   04   30   }A
R 10   02
   10   02
   10   02
                          }B
                    20
F   04   50

---

11   04   10
11   04   30
11   04   20
11   04   50
10   02   00
10   02   10
10   02   30
10   02   20
      26   50
    246
10   266

10   4 4 2
10.   33   21
        2   57
2) 10   36   18
    5   18   09

---

5 - 18 - 09
       9   12
5 - 08 - 57 h.

84 - 51 - 03
      40 2
1 - 45 - 16
86 - 36 - 19
86 - 37 - 44

1 - 40 - 21
      455
1 - 45 - 16

58.99
    5
294.95

---

84 5 1   08
 1 45   15
86 - 36 - 24
            85
-10 deg 86 - 37 - 48
        86° - 38'

Lat at Noon March
25th, 1909,

1 - 40 - 20.9
      4 54.95
1 - 45 - 15.9

58.99
    5
294.95
  4

Computation

```
.  10 - 33 - 21
          2    44   I.C.
2/10 - 36 - 15
    5 - 18 - 07
         9 - 15   Ref + Par
    5 - 08 - 52   h'
   84 - 51 - 08   Z
    1 - 45 - 16   dec
   86 - 36 - 24
              85   Cor to Ref
              for -10° F'
+
   86 - 37 - 49
```

86° 38' North

signed,

Resselmawin,

College of Civil Engineering
Cornell University

Summary of results of observations, the original records and rough computations of which are contained on the preceding pages.

March 22 nd, 1909
Lat at Noon
            85° 48' North

march 25th, 1909
Lat at Noon
            86° 38' North

average distance made good in three marches
      16 2/3 nautical miles.

signed

Resselmawin,

College of Civil Engineering,
Cornell University

Arctic Ocean, April. 1.09.

Have today personally
determined our latitude to be
by sextant observations:—
Lat. in. 87.46.49 N

Return from here in Command
of the 4th Supporting Party.

    Have Commander Peary
with 5 men, 7 sledges with
full loads, and 40 picked
dogs.

Men & dogs are in good
condition, the going fair,
the weather good

At the same average as our
last eight marches
Commander Peary should
reach the Pole in
eight days

    Robert A. Bartlett,
Master, S.S. "Roosevelt".

1/2 alt. 13.09..0
7 6   +   4..0..0
     13 . 13 . 0 1

Refrac + Paral   3 . 55
     13 . 9 . 0 5

Semid   16 . 0 2
     13 . 25 . 07

Sun Cor — 10   33
2) 13 . 24 . 34
     6 . 42 . 1 7
     90
     83 . 17 . 43
     4 . 7 . 16
Lat — 87 46 47

R. in 57.9½
6) 19.55
    4 50

4 . 24 . 16

---

86 . 00 off +
28 . 00 on
2) 8 . 00
7.9. 4 . 00

original

this is how I
checked it—

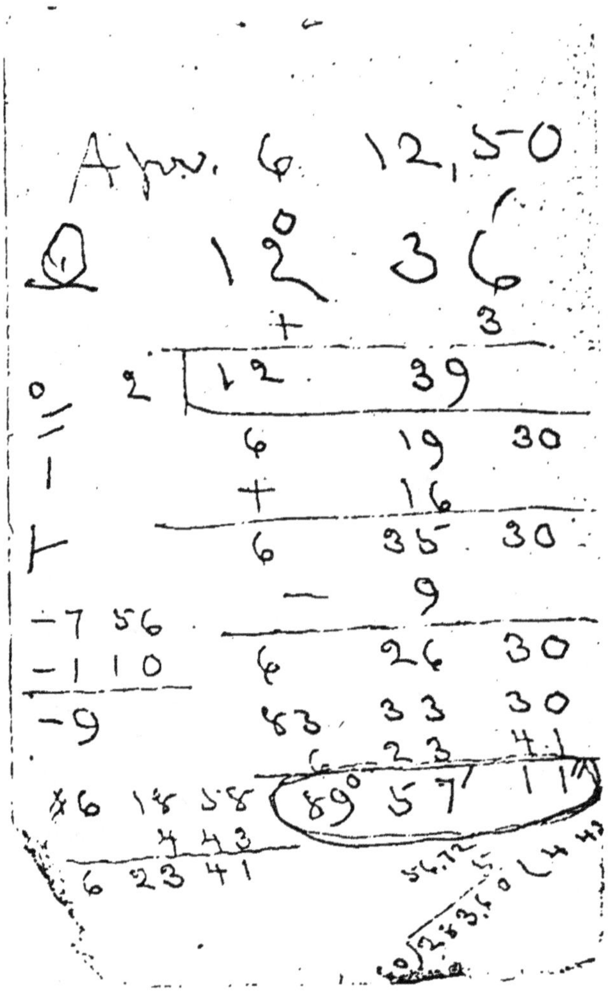

Apr. 7 12,40 am

☉ 13 14
☉☽ 14 18 20
☉ 13 14 20
☽ 14 18
_____
   55   4 40

T. −30°

4|55   4   40
  13 46   10
   +   1
2|13 47   10
   6 53   85
   −   8   20
   6 45   15
  83   1   45
   6 35
  (89° 79 75)

−7 20
−1
−8 20

              6 41 36
    56.44   − 6 35
        7
60)39 5·08 (5 35 5 1

Apr. 7 6,40 am

☉ 12 55 30
☽ 13 59
☉ 12 56
☽ 13 59 20
_____
   53 49 50

−30°

[am   30 } +2
  off 34]

4|53 49 50
  13 27 27
   +   2
2|13 29 27
   6 45 44
   −   8 30
   6 37   14
       2   46

−7 30
−1
−8 30

   6 41 36
   −   56
   6 40 40

Appendix B — 237

$$\begin{array}{rrr} 6 & 44 & 44 \\ - & 8 & 30 \\ \hline 6 & 36 & 14 \end{array}$$

$$\begin{array}{rrr} 83 & 23 & 46 \\ 6 & 40 & 40 \\ \hline 90^\circ & 4' & 26'' \end{array}$$

Continuation of 6:40 AM
computation .

Apr. 7   12 40
              true

① 13 18 20

① 14 21 30

② 13 18

① 14 21 50

4 | 5 5 19 40

On 30 } +2
Off 34

4 | 55 19 40
    13 50
  +   2
2 | 13 52
     6 56
         8 20
    6 47 40
   83 12 20

⟨89° 58' 37⟩

-7 20
-1
-8 20

1. Marvin I sights, 22 March 1909.

The sun's path as it passed thru culmination was compared with the set of sights Marvin took. The probability that this set matched the path of the sun at a given point was computed, with the following results:

Degrees before meridian transit	Prob. density exp. notation	Normalized Value
-4	0	
-3	1.707639E-05	.005357
-2	7.858931E-05	.024656
-1	3.551694E-04	.111426
0	6.972112E-04	.218733
+1	9.444937E-04	.296312
+2	7.623227E-04	.239161
+3	2.58901 E-04	.081224
+4	6.305988E-05	.019784
+5	1.067027E-05	.003348
+6	6.672997E-07	.000209
+7	0	

2. From these results we can say the sights matched the sun's culmination from the meridian to 2 degrees west, with a 75 % confidence level or from 1 degree east of the meridian to 3 degrees west, with a confidence level of 95 %.

3. Marvin II sights, 25 March 1909.

-9	0	
-8	4.179648E-06	.000664
-7	1.89265E-05	.003006
-6	9.569029E-05	.015199
-5	3.715315E-04	.059014
-4	8.922592E-04	.141725
-3	1.314279E-03	.208758
-2	1.567002E-03	.248900
-1	1.145991E-03	.182028
0	6.548917E-04	.104022
+1	1.7596E-04	.027949
+2	4.482794E-05	.007120
+3	1.016319E-05	.001614
0		

4. From these results we can say that the sights matched the sun's culmination from 3 degrees east of the meridian to 1 degree east, with a confidence level of 64 %, or from 4 degrees east to 0 degrees with a confidence level of 88 %.

5. Our conclusion is that these sights were in fact culminations and gave accurate latitudes. Marvin apparently commenced his first set slightly late and the second set slightly early. The spread of the "match" in directions is in general agreement with tables II-1 and II-2.

Computation of Marvin's observation of March 22th, 1909.

10°	24'	50"	
10	24	80	
9	21	20	
9	21	50	
9	21	10	
9	21	00	
10	24	80	
10	24	20	

9	52	56	Mean
	1	55	Index correction
9	54	51	
4	57	26	Apparent h
—	12	12	Refraction corr'n
+		9	Parallax
4	45	23	True h
85	14	37	True zenith distance (z)
+ 0	84	20	δ

85 48 57 = Latitude of point of observation, provided that the observer was on the 70th meridian west of Greenwich.

This latitude has had no ex-meridian or clock error correction applied to it. Together they amount to less than 1'.

COMPUTATION OF REFRACTION CORRECTION

Temperature : — 40° F.

$$\gamma \ldots = 1.2108131$$
$$\log \gamma = 0.08290$$
$$\lambda \ldots = 1.1289$$
$$\log (\gamma^{\lambda}) = 0.09817$$
$$\log a = 1.70949$$
$$\log \tan z = 1.06180$$
$$\log r = 2.86446$$
$$r = 782'' = 12' 12''$$

COMPUTATION OF PARALLAX CORR'N.

horizontal $p. = \pi = 8''.8$

$$\log 8.8 \ldots = 0.944$$
$$\log \sin z \ldots = 9.998$$
$$\log \text{parallax} = 0.942$$
$$\text{parallax} \ldots = 9''$$

MEAN TIME OF OBSERVATION

1 p.m. (60th meridian)
= 5 p. m. G. M. T.

$$\delta' = + \quad 0° \ 29' \ 24''$$
$$\Delta = + \quad\quad 4 \ 56$$
$$\delta = + \quad 0 \ 84 \ 20$$

Computation of Marvin's observation of March 25th, 1909.

11° 04′ 10″

11 04 80

10 02 00

10 02 10

10 02 80

10 02 20

11 04 20

11 04 50

---

10 33 21 Mean

2 44 Index corr'n

---

10 36 05

5 18 02 Apparent h

— 10 40 Refraction corr'n

+ 9 Parallax

---

5 07 31 True h

84 52 29 True zenith distan-ce (z)

+ 1 45 16 δ

---

86 37 45 = Latitude of point of observation, provided that the observer was on the 70th meridian west of Greenwich, and that the temperature was — 10° F.

A temperature of — 40° F. would make the latitude 51″ greater.

No correction for ex-meridian or clock error has been applied.

$\check{c}' = +$ 1° 40′ 21″ G. M. noon

Δ + 4 55

$\check{c} = +$ 1 45 16

$\pi =$ 8″.8, log = 0.944

log sin z 9.998

---

log parallax = 0.942

parallax = 9″

COMPUTATION

OF REFRACTION CORRECTION.

Temperature not recorded, but in his field computation Marvin uses — 10° F.; but on March 22 he also computes with — 10°, when his record was — 40°. This is because — 10° F. is the limit of his tables.

I. Using — 10° F. $\lambda = 1.1139$

log γ . . . . = 0.05307

log(γ^λ) . . = 0.05911

log α . . . . = 1.71473

log tan z . = 1.03261

---

log r . . . . = 2.80645

$r = 640″$ = 10′ 40″

II. Using — 40° F. (or C.)

λ . . . . . . = 1.1139

log γ . . . . = 0.08290

log (γ^λ) . . = 0.09234

log α . . . . = 1.71473

log tan z . = 1.03261

---

log r . . . . = 2.83968

$r = 691″$. = 11′ 31″

This value of r is 51″ greater than for a temperature of — 10° F.

44

Computation of Bartlett's observation of April 1st, 1909.

18° 09' 00" Observation on ☉

     4   Index corr'n

18 18 00"

 6 36 30   Apparent h of ☉

—   8 48   Refraction

+ 16 02   Semi-diameter

+   9   Parallax

 6 43 58 — True h of sun's center

33 16 07   True zenith distance (z)

+ 4 28 42 δ

87 44 49 = Latitude of point of observation provided that the observer was on the 70th meridian, and observed at local noon.

COMPUTATION
OF REFRACTION CORRECTION.

Temp. = — 10° F. (record not clear)

λ . . . . . . = 1.0825

$\log \gamma$ . . . . = 0.05807

$\log (\gamma^{\lambda})$ . . = 0.05745

$\log \alpha$ . . . . = 1.72925

$\log \tan z$. = 0.98610

$\log r$ . . . . = 2.72280

r = 528" = 8' 48"

Had the temperature been + 10° F a similar computation would give r = 8' 24", only 24" less than for temp. = — 10°.

COMPUTATION OF PARALLAX.

π = 8".8, $\log \pi$ . . . . = 0.944

$\log \sin z$ . . = 9.997

$\log$ parallax = 0.941

parallax . . . = 9"

IF THE SUN WAS OBSERVED CROSSING THE 70TH MERIDIAN.

δ' = + 4° 24' 12"

Δ = +   4 30

δ = + 4 28 42

CORRECTIONS TO LATITUDE FOR EX-MERIDIAN OBSERVATIONS.

The following table was computed from the formula given by Chauvenet (vol. 1, p. 233) for the reduction of ex-meridian observations for latitude, and the formula already given for the computation of latitude from observations on the meridian. These formulae are as follows:

$$\cos z \text{ (on meridian)} = \sin h + \cos \varphi \cdot \cos \delta, \left(2 \sin^2 \tfrac{1}{2} t\right)$$

and

$$\varphi = \delta + z$$

The quantities in the table are the corrections to the latitude (φ) as computed from the second formula given above. These corrections are all negative, decreasing the latitude as computed in the preceding pages.

Table of corrections to φ.

Ex-meridian distance	Corrections to computed latitude		
	At latitude 85° 48′ 57″ (March 22)	At latitude 86° 37′ 45″ (March 25)	At latitude 87° 44′ 49″ (April 1)
1°	2″	2″	0″
2	9	7	5
3	21	17	11
4	37	30	20
5	58	46	31
6	1′ 23	1′ 07	44
7	1 53	1 31	1′ 00
8	2 27	1 58	1 19
9	3 06	2 30	1 40
10	3 49	3 05	2 03
Length of 1° of the parallel in geographic miles.	4.4	3.5	2.4

From this table it is seen that in order to produce an error of 1′ in any one of the three computed latitudes just shown, the observer would have to observe the sun off his meridian by amounts of 5°, 6°, and 7°, respectively for the observations of March 22, 25, and April 1. In these latitudes, 5°, 6°, and 7° measured on the parallels would equal 22, 21, and 17 geographic miles respectively. This suffices to show, when considered in connection with the fact that the journey north was finished within 5 miles of the meridian of Cape Columbia, that none of the latitudes computed for March 22, 25, and April 1, can be in error by as much as 1′ due to the observer and the sun not being on the same meridian at the time of the observation.

GEOGRAPHIC POSITION OF CAMP JESUP.

The first observation obtained at Camp Jesup, was made at noon of April 6. This observation is imperfect (incomplete) and uncertain, having been made through clouds which prevented complete observations. It serves however as a rough check on the complete observations which were obtained 24 hours later.

The position of Camp Jesup is well fixed by two complete sets of observations on the sun, made on the date April 7th, at 6h 30m a. m. and at 12h 30m p. m., 60th meridian mean time.

In reducing these observations to a position the two co-authors of this paper followed different routes, obtaining thereby safe and satisfactory checks on the mechanical operations of the computations as well as on the theory of the problem.

Mr. Mitchell followed the method and formulae produced on page 260, volume 1, of Chauvenet's astronomy. His solution is given first.

Mr. Duvall, whose computation is placed immediately after that of Mr. Mitchell, used the s formula of spherical trigonometry, and by means of a series of approximations deduced a value for the latitude which satisfied the conditions imposed by the problem.

The problem is this: Two spherical triangles are considered; these triangles have for common vertices the pole and the zenith of Camp Jesup. The third vertex of each triangle is the position of the sun at the time of observation, namely, one is the position of the sun at 6h 30m a. m., April 7, 1909, and the other its position at 12h 30m p. m. of the same day. In these triangles we have the two sides corresponding to the two zenith distances (observed); the two sides corresponding to the two values of the co-declination of the sun at the two times of observation; and the difference of the two angles at the pole, which is equal to 90° and is the difference of the two hour angles of the sun. We have the further condition that the third side of the two triangles is common to both, and is equal to the co-latitude. By a series of approximations Mr. Duvall determined a value for this third side, the co-latitude, which would complete the two triangles and give values for the two angles at the pole differing by exactly 90°. The problem proved a determinate one, the difference in the two angles at the pole being very sensitive to small changes in the assumed co-latitude. Only the final approximation of this computation is shown here.

Peary's observations of April 6th, 1909, 12h 50m p. m. (watch)
at Camp Jesup.

12° 86' ☉

    3 Index correction

---

12 89

    6° 19' 30" apparent h of ☉

−   9 11 Refraction

+   9 Parallax

+ 16 00 Semi-diameter

---

  6 26 28 True h of sun's center

  6 26 28 = h on April 6th

      22 28 = change in δ for 23ʰ 50ᵐ

---

  6 48 56 = h on April 7 as computed from h of April 6.

  6 47 28 = h from observations on April 7.

COMPUTATION
OF REFRACTION CORRECTION

$T = -11°\ F.;\ \lambda = 1.0881$

$\log \gamma \ldots = 0.05403$

$\log (\gamma^\lambda) \ldots = 0.05879$

$\log \alpha \ldots = 1.72678$

$\log \tan \varepsilon\ . = 0.95580$

$\log r \ldots = 2.74082$

$r = 551''\ . = 9'\ 11''$

$\delta' = 6°\ 18'\ 55''$

$\lambda = +\ \ \ \ 4\ \ 25$

$\tilde{c} = 6\ \ 23\ \ 20$

The above computation and comparison is made to show that the single observation of April 6th at Camp Jesup, while imperfect, consisting of a single observation on the lower limb of the sun seen through clouds, still affords a rough check on the complete observations obtained 24 hours later at the same place. The agreement within less than 2′ is certainly a satisfactory check.

**Peary's observations at midnight, April 6-7th, 1909.
Made at a point 10 miles from Camp Jesup
in a direction away from Cape Columbia.**

18° 14'	COMPUTATION
14 18 20".	OF REFRACTION CORRECTION.
18 14 20	
14 18	Temp. = — 80° F.
—————	
18 46 10	log (γ^λ) . . = 0.07836
6 58 05 apparent h	log s . . . . = 1.78148
— 8 54 Refraction	log tan s . = 0.91814
+ 9 Parallax	—————
—————	log r . . . . = 2.72798
6 44 20 true h	$r = 534'' = 8'\ 54''$
6 34 30 = δ	log tan δ = 9.0616548
	log sec t = 0.0510248
	—————
	log tan D = 9.1127102

BY DEAD RECKONING FROM CAMP JESUP.

longitude = 140° 20' E.

D . . . . . = 7° 28' 10''

Time: 12ʰ 40ᵐ a. m. (60th meridian)

log sin h = 9.0694689

— . 10 watch correction

log sin D = 9.1090916

+ 4

log csc δ = 0.9411805

————

16 30   G. M. T.

log cos γ = 9.1197860

—   2 24

————

16 27 36 G. A. T.

γ . . . . . = 82° 25' 46''

24

————

7 32 24 = 113° 06'

$\Phi = D + \gamma = 89°\ 48'\ 56''$

as scaled off map $\Phi = 89°\ 50'.5$

$t = 140°\ 20' - 118°\ 06' = 27°\ 14'$

Peary's observations of April 7th, 1909, 12h 40m p. m. (watch)
at Camp Jesup.

18° 18′ 20″

14 21 30

13 18

14 21 50*

─────────

18 49 55   Mean

2   Index corr'n

─────────

18 51 55

6 55 58 Apparent h

—   8 44 Refraction

+   9 Parallax

6 47 28 True h

88 12 87 True z

COMPUTATION

OF REFRACTION CORRECTION.

Temp. $=$ — 25° F.; $\gamma = 1.16877$

$\log \gamma \ldots = 0.06772$

$\lambda \ldots\ldots = 1.0766$

─────────

$\log (\gamma^{\lambda}) = 0.07291$

$\log \alpha \ldots = 1.78179$

$\log \tan z = 0.91505$

$\log r \ldots = 2.71975$

$r = 524″ = 8′ 44″$

TIME OF OBSERVATION.

12h 40m p m. watch time

10   watch fast on 60th meridian M. T.

─────────

12 30 p. m. 60th meridian M. T.

$\delta' = + 6° 41′ 84″$

$\Delta + 4 14$

─────────

$\delta = + 6 45 48$

COMPUTATION OF PARALLAX.

$\pi = 8″.8$; $\log = 0.944$

$\log \sin z = 9.996$

─────────

$\log p \ldots = 0.940$

$p \ldots\ldots = 9″$

* This observation is on the upper limb, although it was recorded with the symbol for the lower limb.

Peary's observations of April 7th, 1909, 6h 40m a. m. (watch) at Camp Jesup.

12° 55′ 30″

18 59

12 56

18 59 20

---

18 27 27 Mean

2 Index corr'n

---

18 29 27

6 44 43 Apparent h

— 9 04 Refraction

+ 9 Parallax

---

6 35 48 True h

88 24 12 True z

COMPUTATION OF REFRACTION CORRECTION

Temp. = − 30° F.; γ = 1.18229

log γ . . . = 0.07272

λ . . . . . = 1.0800

---

log (γ^{λ}) . = 0.07854

log α . . . = 1.73036

log tan z = 0.92709

---

log r . . . = 2.73599

r = 544″ = 9′ 04″

COMPUTATION OF PARALLAX.

π = 8″.8; log π . . . = 0.944

log sin z = 9.997

---

log p . . = 0.941

p . . . . = 9″

TIME OF OBSERVATION.

6h 40m a.m. watch time

10 watch fast on 60th Meridian M. T.

---

6 30 a. m. 60th Meridian M. T.

δ' = 6° 41′ 34″

Δ = − 1 25

δ = 6 40 09

Computation of the geographic position of Camp Jesup
by Hugh C. Mitchell.

According to CHAUVENET, vol. 1, p. 260.

April 7, 1909.

$6^h\ 30^m$ a. m. ;	$h\ =$	$6°\ 85'\ 48''$		$\delta\ =$	$6°\ 40'\ 09''$
12 30 p. m. :	$h'\ =$	6 47 23		$\delta'\ =$	6 45 48

$\lambda/2 = 8^h = 45°$; $1/2\,(h + h') = $ 6 41 35.5 ; $1/2\,(\delta + \delta') = $ 6 42 58.5

$1/2\,(h - h') = -\,0$ 05 47.5 ; $1/2\,(\delta - \delta') = -\,0$ 02 49.5

$\log \sin 1/2\,(\delta - \delta') = 6.9147426n$	$\log \cos 1/2\,(\delta + \delta') = 9.9970094$
$\log \cos \lambda/2\ \ldots = 9.8494850$	$\log \sin \lambda/2\ \ldots = 9.8494850$
	$\log \sin C.\ \cos E\ . = 9.8464944$
$\log \sin C.\ \sin E. = 6.7642276n$	$\log \sin E\ \ldots = 6.9177830n$
$\log \sin C.\ \cos E. = 9.8464944$	$\log \cos E\ \ldots = 9.9999999$
$\log \tan E\ \ldots = 6.9177382n$	$\log \sin C\ \ldots = 9.8464945$
$E\ \ldots = -\,0°\,02'\,50''.67$	$C\ \ldots = 44°\,86'\,29''.4$
$\log \sin 1/2\,(\delta + \delta') = 9.0680091$	$\log \cos 1/2\,(\delta + \delta') = 9.9970094$
$\log \cos 1/2\,(\delta - \delta') = 9.9999999$	$\log \sin 1/2\,(\delta - \delta') = 6.9147426n$
$\log \sec C\ \ldots = 0.1475651$	$\log \sec D\ \ldots = 0.0059406$
	$\log \csc C\ \ldots = 0.1585055$
$\log \sin D\ \ldots = 9.2155741$	$\log \cos P\ \ldots = 7.0711981n$
$D\ \ldots = 9°\,27'\,18''.65$	$P\ \ldots = 90°\,04'\,03''.01$
$\log \sin 1/2\,(h + h') = 9.0665226$	$\log \cos 1/2\,(h + h') = 9.9970800$
$\log \cos 1/2\,(h - h') = 9.9999994$	$\log \sin 1/2\,(h - h') = 7.2265290n$
$\log \sec C\ \ldots = 0.1475651$	$\log \sec H\ \ldots = 0.0058995$
	$\log \csc C\ \ldots = 0.1585055$
$\log \sin H\ \ldots = 9.2140871$	$\log \cos Q\ \ldots = 7.3829640$
$H\ \ldots = 9°\,25'\,21''.28$	$Q\ \ldots = 90°\,08'\,18''.18$

$q = -\,0°\,04'\,15''.17$

(Continued on next page)

$\log \cos H \ldots = 9.9941005$ $\log \cos H \ldots = 9.9941005$

$\log \cos q \ldots = 9.9999997$ $\log \sin q \ldots = 7.0924089n$

$\log \cos \beta \sin \gamma = 9.9941002$ $\log \sin \beta \ldots = 7.0865044$

$\log \cos \beta \cos \gamma = 9.2140871$

$\log \tan \gamma \ldots = 0.7800181$ $\log \tan 1/2 (\delta + \delta') = 9.0709998$

$\gamma \ldots = 80° 34' 38''. 75$ $\log \tan 1/2 (\delta - \delta') = 6.9147428n$

$D + \gamma \ldots = 90° 01' 57''. 4$ $\log \tan \lambda/2 \ldots = 10.0000000$

$\log \sin \gamma \ldots = 9.9941005$ $\log \tan x \ldots = 5.9857426n$

$\log \cos \beta \ldots = 9.9999997$ $x \ldots = -0° 00' 20''$

$\log \cos (D + \gamma) = 6.7552892$

 115° 00' 11'' 115° 00' 11''

$\log \cos \varphi \cos \tau = 6.7552889$ $+ 20 + 20$

$\log \cos \varphi \sin \tau = 7.0865044$ $- 45 + 45$

$\log \tan \tau \ldots = 0.8812655$ 70 00 160 00

$\tau \ldots = - 64° 59' 48''. 78$ $+ 67 30 - 22 30$

or $\ldots$ 115 00 11. 27 $- 35 - 35$

$\log \cos \tau \ldots = 9.6259991$ longitude $= 187°$ west

$\log \sin \tau \ldots = 9.9572646$

 equation of time $= - 35'$

$\log \cos \varphi \ldots = 7.1292898$ 6 : 30 a. m. (60 M) $= $ 10 : 30 G.M.T.

$\varphi \ldots = 89° 55' 22''. 24$ $= - 22° 30'$

φ is the latitude of Camp Jesup.   12 : 30 p. m. (60 M) $= $ 4 : 30 G.M.T.

 $= + 67° 30'$

POSITION OF CAMP JESUP

LATITUDE $= 89° 55' 22''. 24$ north.   Azimuth of sun at 6 : 30 a. m.

LONGITUDE $= 187°$ west of Greenwich. $= 180° - 160° = 20°$ E. of N.

Computation of the geographic position of Camp Jesup

by C. R. Duvall.

April 7, 1909.

Watch time of observation ...... $=$ $6^h 40^m$ a. m.

Watch fast on 60th M. M. T. ..... $=$ 10

60th meridian M. T. .... $=$ 6 30 a. m.

Greenwich M. T. .... $=$ 10 30 a. m.

Astronomical date (G. M. T.) ..... $=$ 22 30 April 6.

Zenith distance of sun's center $= a' = 88° 24' 12''$

Polar distance of sun's center . $= b' = 88$ 19 51

Assumed colatitude .... $= c' = $ 0 04 37. 7

$$s' = 1/2\,(a' + b' + c') = 88\ 24\ 20.\ 85$$

$$(s' - b') \ldots\ldots\ldots = 0\ 04\ 29.\ 85$$

$$(s' - c') \ldots\ldots\ldots = 88\ 19\ 42\ .65$$

log sin $(s' - b') = 7.1158910$

log sin $(s' - c') = 9.9970492$

log csc b' . . . . $= 0.0029487$

log csc c' . . . . $= 2.8708500$

9.9867389

---

log sin $A'/2$ . . $= 9.9933694$

$A'/2$ . . . . $= 80° 00' 48''$

A' . . . . $= 160\ 01\ 36$

(Continued on next page)

April 7, 1909.

Watch time of observation . . . . . . = 12ʰ 40ᵐ p. m.

Watch fast on 60th M. M. T. . . . . . = 10

60th meridian M. T. . . . . = 12 30 p. m.

Greenwich mean time . . . . = 4 30 p. m.

Astronomical date (G. M. T.) . . . . . = 4 30 April 7.

Zenith distance of sun's center = a = 88° 12′ 37″

Polar distance of sun's center . = b = 88 14 12

Assumed colatitude . . . . = c = 0 04 37.7
_____

s = 1/2 ($a + b + c$) . . . . = 88 15 43.35

($s - b$) . . . . = 0 01 31.35

($s - c$) . . . . = 88 11 05.65

log sin ($s - b$) = 6.6462775

log sin ($s - c$) = 9.9989205

log csc b . . . = 0.0080828

log csc c . . . = 2.8706500
_____

9.5170808
_____

log sin A/2 . . = 9.7585404

A/2 . . . . = 34° 59′ 43″

A . . . . = 69 59 26

A′ . . . . = 160 01 36
_____

A′ − A . . . . . = 90 02 10

A previous computation based on an assumed colatitude of

0° 04′ 37″.5

gave

A′ = 160° 08′ 28″

A = 69 58 34
_____

A′ − A = 90 09 54

Hence it is easily deduced that a colatitude of

0° 04′ 37″.76

Will give A′ − A = 90° very nearly; therefore the

Latitude of Camp Jesup = 89° 55′ 22″.24

In the above A and A' are not azimuths, but hour angles.

Longitude computation — Camp Jesup — by C. R. D.

April 7, 6:30 a.m.

Hour angle of sun's center = local apparent time . . . . = — 160° = — 10ʰ 40ᵐ 00ˢ

Equation of time . . . . = +   2 19.37

Local mean time . . . . = — 10 37 40.63

Greenwich mean time . . . . = — 1 30 00

Difference in time = difference longitude =   9 07 40.63

                                = 137° west of Greenwich.

April 7, 12:30 p.m.

Hour angle of sun's center = local apparent time . . . . = — 70° = — 4ʰ 40ᵐ 00ˢ

Equation of time . . . . = +   2 15.41

Local mean time . . . . = — 4 37 44.59

Greenwich mean time . . . . = + 4 30 00

Difference in time = difference longitude =   9° 07′ 44″.59

                                = 137° west of Greenwich.

Azimuth. — It has been found by trial, and it is also evident *a priori*, that the azimuth of the sun in this latitude differs very little from the supplement of the hour angle of the sun. Therefore the azimuth of the sun at the time of observation, April 7, 1909, 6:40 a.m. (watch time) was 20° East of North. Likewise, assuming a longitude of 187° West of Greenwich, and a watch 10 minutes fast for the observation at supposed noon, April 6, 1909, the forward course derived from the sun was 70° West of North.

Appendix C

WILLIAM G. HYZER: Consultant in Engineering and Applied Science

136 S. GARFIELD AVENUE · JANESVILLE, WISCONSIN 53545   608-752-5581   608-754-7167

October 16, 1989

Admiral Thomas Davies
11025 Stanmore Drive
Potomac, MD   20854

Reference: Analysis of the North Pole Photographs

Dear Admiral Davies:

     This letter is a summary of my analysis of the methodology
employed in the analysis of the Admiral Peary 1909 photographs
and the Kobersteen 1986 photograph taken during those two expeditions to the North Pole. The three photographs you sent me
are identified as follows: 1) 1986 Kobersteen photograph, 2)
1909 Peary North Pole photograph, and 3) 1909 Peary Sounding
photograph.

     My analysis was conducted in three phases: 1) independ-
ently confirm the location of the vanishing point in the 1986
photograph; 2) verify the determination of the sun's elevation
in all three photographs based upon the data presented in your
report; and 3) conduct a controlled test to establish the validity of the above equations and methodology for determining
the sun's elevation angle from shadows cast by objects in the
scene under those conditions where the horizon can be located
in the scene and the focal length of the camera lens is known.

     The equations based upon camera lens focal length (F),
enlargement factor (E), and the measurements (X, Y, and Y')
were programmed into the computer to obtain the sun's elevation
angle (θ). The input and output data for this program are
tabulated on the enclosed two computer printout sheets.

     The 1986 North Pole photograph (with Mylar overlay sheet
removed) was independently evaluated by three professional engineers whose assignment was to determine the vanishing point
from shadows cast by various objects in the scene. The results
of this analysis are tabulated in the computer printout entitled
"Sunline". These analysts made no attempt to determine the
horizon line because of their unfamiliarity with the locale of
the photographs. The sun's elevation angles were computed on
the basis of these three independent measurements of the vanishing points and the location of the horizon line indicated in

WILLIAM G. HYZER

the National Geographic analysis of this same photograph. The mean elevation angle based on these three measurements is 15.786°. This is within 6' of the value you obtained. The mean value of all four measurements is 15°44'. The other entries in the table entitled "Sunline" are test conditions to determine the effect of variations in the measurements X, Y, and Y'.

The two tables entitled "Sunline .2" and "Sunline .3" are analyses of the two Admiral Peary photographs. Again, various values of X, Y, and Y' were introduced to determine the effect of these factors on the elevation angle. The table entitled "Sunline .1" is a summary of results obtained using your data for the three photographs.

A controlled test was set up in a tennis court to verify the accuracy of this methodology. A photograph is enclosed showing the set-up. The camera used in this experiment was a Hasselblad fitted with an 80mm lens. The lens was set at infinity for these experiments. The focal length was checked and determined to be 80.01mm. An artificial horizon was provided in the photograph by mounting the camera on a tripod with the lens at the same height as two reference posts in the background of the photograph. These background posts are distinguishable in the photograph by the white sphere (ping pong ball) mounted on the top of each post. A line drawn through the centerline of these spheres coincides with the height of the camera lens. The camera was mounted with the lens pointed down approximately 10°. Simultaneously with the making of the photograph, the length of the sun's shadow cast by an object a known height above the ground was measured. Also, the time was recorded. The results of analyzing the photograph are analyzed in the table entitled "Sunline .4". The value of θ obtained from measuring the shadows in the photograph is 32°56'. The sun's elevation measured at the scene at the same time that the photograph was taken was 32°50'. The small difference of 6 minutes of arc between these two measurements verifies the validity of this technique in measuring the elevation of the sun from photographs.

I did not attempt to perform any computations of the sun's elevation based on longitude, latitude, and time. This falls better into your area of expertise if you care to carry out these computations.

My experience in performing measurements from shadows cast

WILLIAM G. HYZER

by objects in sunlight indicates that the elevation angle
measured is closer to the top limb of the sun than to the center. The human eye usually tends to judge the terminus of the
shadow near the end of the umbra; not midway in the penumbra.
Therefore, the elevation angles to the center of the sun's disk
may be as much as 15' less than the angles measured from the
photographs or from direct visual observation of shadows on the
ground. I believe that any computations of the sun's elevation
angle based on the time and position of the tennis court
photograph will confirm this observation.

I am also of the opinion that the ± 15 minutes of arc error
value that you quote is a bit optimistic when applied to the
Admiral Peary photographs. I believe that an error of ± 20 to
± 30 minutes of arc is more realistic.

In conclusion, the methodology employed in analyzing the
photographs taken during the Admiral Peary 1909 expedition to
the North Pole has been carefully analyzed both analytically
and empirically and is considered to be a reliable method of
establishing the sun's elevation angle from shadows cast by
objects in the scene photographed.

Very truly yours,

William G. Hyzer, P.E.
Certified Photogrammetrist
No. 757 (ASPRS)

WGH:gj
Enclosures

WILLIAM G. HYZER

P.S. I am leaving for Australia on October 25th and will be out of the country until November 15th. I will be in North Palm Beach, Florida, from November 15th until November 30th and can be reached there at the following telephone number: (407) 626-4793. My address in Florida is 115 Lake Shore Drive, Apt. 1749, North Palm Beach, FL 33408.

If you wish to reach me by mail at the above Florida address, please be sure that it is dispatched to arrive after November 15th; otherwise, it will be forwarded to my home office here in Wisconsin.

WGH:gj

WILLIAM G. HYZER, P.E.
136 SOUTH GARFIELD AVENUE
JANESVILLE, WISCONSIN 53545
(608) 752-5581

Admiral Thomas Davies
11025 Stanmore Dr.
Potomac, MD   20854

Dear Adm. Davies:

The enclosed material plus the 1986 north-pole photograph
(without the mylar cover sheet) were dispatched to Donald
Graff today.

My analysis is just about complete. I have conducted an
error analysis based on three independent measurements of
the vanishing point performed by three different engineers
on the 1986 photograph. Using your measurements from the
1986 photograph of X = 62.3 mm, Y = 63.6 mm and Y' = 6.0
mm, I computed an elevation of 15° 41.4'. The average
computed elevation from the three independent measurements
is 15° 47.2' or a difference of only 5.8' of arc.

Y and Y' are the critical measurements and are subject to
errors of about 16' of arc per mm in the 1986 photograph.
The Y and Y' measurement errors in the Peary photographs
are 8.6' of arc per mm in the north pole (flag) photograph
and 10' of arc per mm in the sounding photograph. The Y
coordinates of both the horizon and the vanishing point are
critical to the accuracy of the elevation measurements.

I conducted a photographic test on a tennis court to
confirm the methodology under controlled conditions. As
soon as these photographs are analyzed, I can finalize my
opinion on this project.

Very truly yours,

William G. Hyzer, PE
Certified Photogrammetrist #757 (ASPRS)

12 October 1989

SUNLINE.4   TENNIS COURT TEST PHOTOGRAPH

F, mm	E	X, mm	Y, mm	Y', mm	PHOTO #	SUN'S ELEVATION Radians	Degrees
60.01	3.43	154.9	137.5	-51	PHOTO #6	.5746886	32.93723

SUNLINE.3 NORTH POLE PHOTOGRAPHS

F, mm	E	X, mm	Y, mm	Y', mm	PHOTO	SUN'S ELEVATION Radians	Degrees
170	1.993	31.242	28.448	-12.192	SOUNDING	.1192638	6.833315
170	1.993	31.242	29.448	-12.192	SOUNDING	.1221818	7.000499
170	1.993	31.242	27.448	-12.192	SOUNDING	.1163445	6.666049
170	1.993	31.242	28.448	-13.192	SOUNDING	.1222070	7.001944
170	1.993	31.242	28.448	-11.192	SOUNDING	.1163213	6.664721
170	1.993	30.242	28.448	-12.192	SOUNDING	.1192954	6.835124
170	1.993	32.242	28.448	-12.192	SOUNDING	.1192312	6.831447

SUNLINE.2 NORTH POLE PHOTOGRAPHS

F, mm	E	X, mm	Y, mm	Y', mm	PHOTO	SUN'S ELEVATION Radians	Degrees
170	1.993	198.12	66.675	20.32	POLE	.1164539	6.672319
170	1.993	198.12	67.675	20.32	POLE	.1189293	6.814147
170	1.993	198.12	65.675	20.32	POLE	.1139765	6.530372
170	1.993	198.12	66.675	21.32	POLE	.1138989	6.525925
170	1.993	198.12	66.675	19.32	POLE	.1190083	6.818674

SUNLINE.1 NORTH POLE PHOTOGRAPHS

F, mm	E	X, mm	Y, mm	Y', mm	PHOTO	SUN'S ELEVATION Radians	Degrees
170	1.993	198.12	66.675	20.32	POLE	.1164539	6.672319
170	1.993	31.242	28.448	-12.192	SOUNDING	.1192638	6.833315
27.93	6.924	62.3	63.6	6	1986	.2738289	15.68924

SUNLINE 1986 NORTH POLE PHOTOGRAPH

F, mm	E	X, mm	Y, mm	Y', mm	ANALYST	SUN'S ELEVATION Radians	Degrees
27.93	6.924	62.3	63.6	6	NAT'L G	.2738289	15.68924
27.93	6.924	62.6	63.8	6	MEAN	.2746089	15.73393
27.93	6.924	60.6	62.9	6	WGH	.2713304	15.54608
27.93	6.924	62.4	62.9	6	DWH	.2706497	15.50709
27.93	6.924	65.15	66.27	6	JBH	.2845923	16.30594
27.93	6.924	62.6	63.8	5	TEST	.2795322	16.01601
27.93	6.924	62.6	63.8	7	TEST	.2696842	15.45177
27.93	6.924	61.6	63.8	6	TEST	.2749948	15.75604
27.93	6.924	63.6	63.8	6	TEST	.2742185	15.71156
27.93	6.924	62.6	62.8	6	TEST	.2701242	15.47698
27.93	6.924	62.6	64.8	6	TEST	.2790810	15.99016

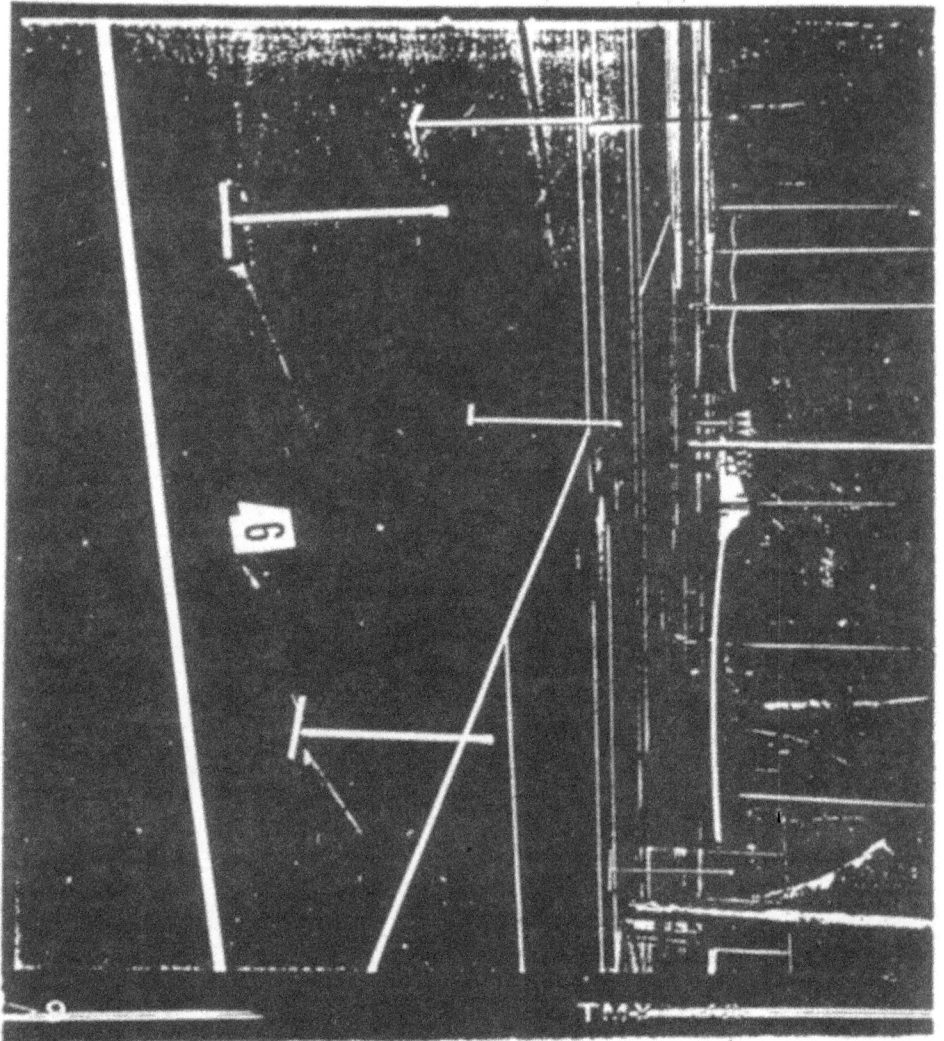

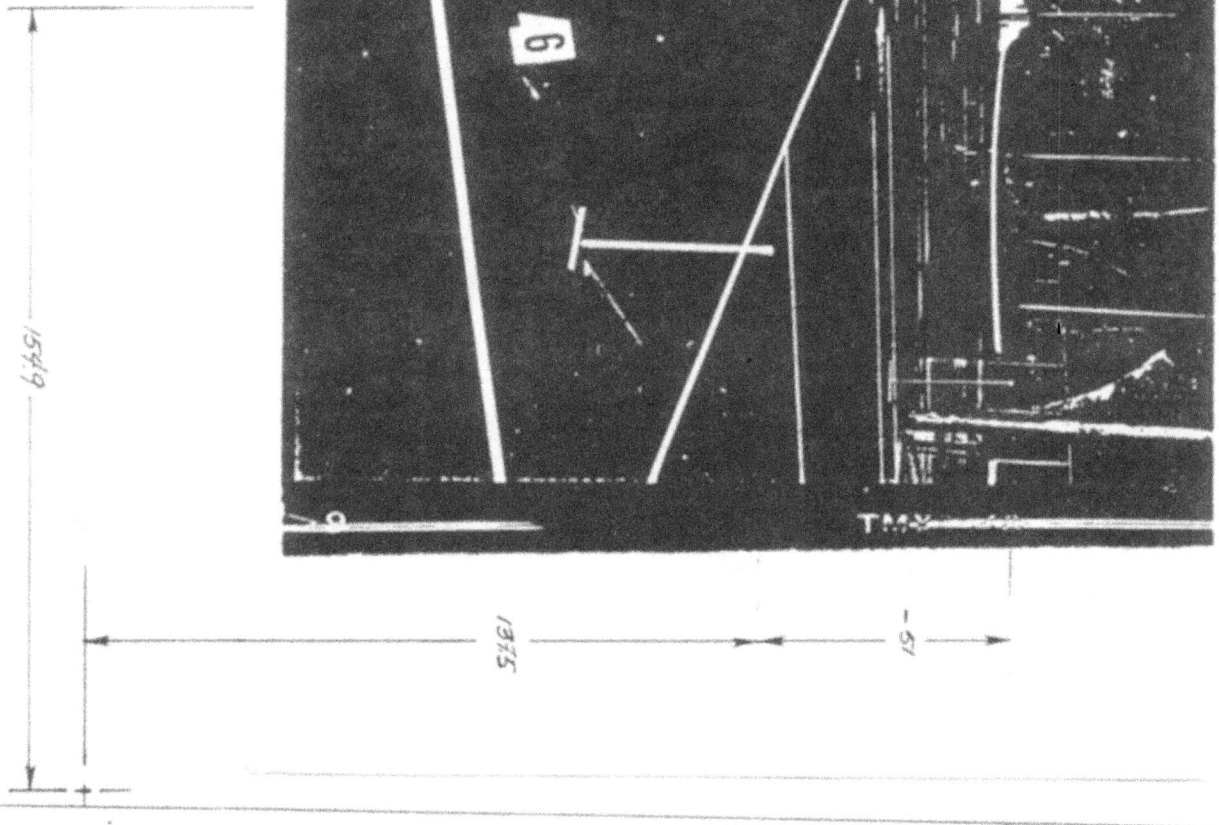

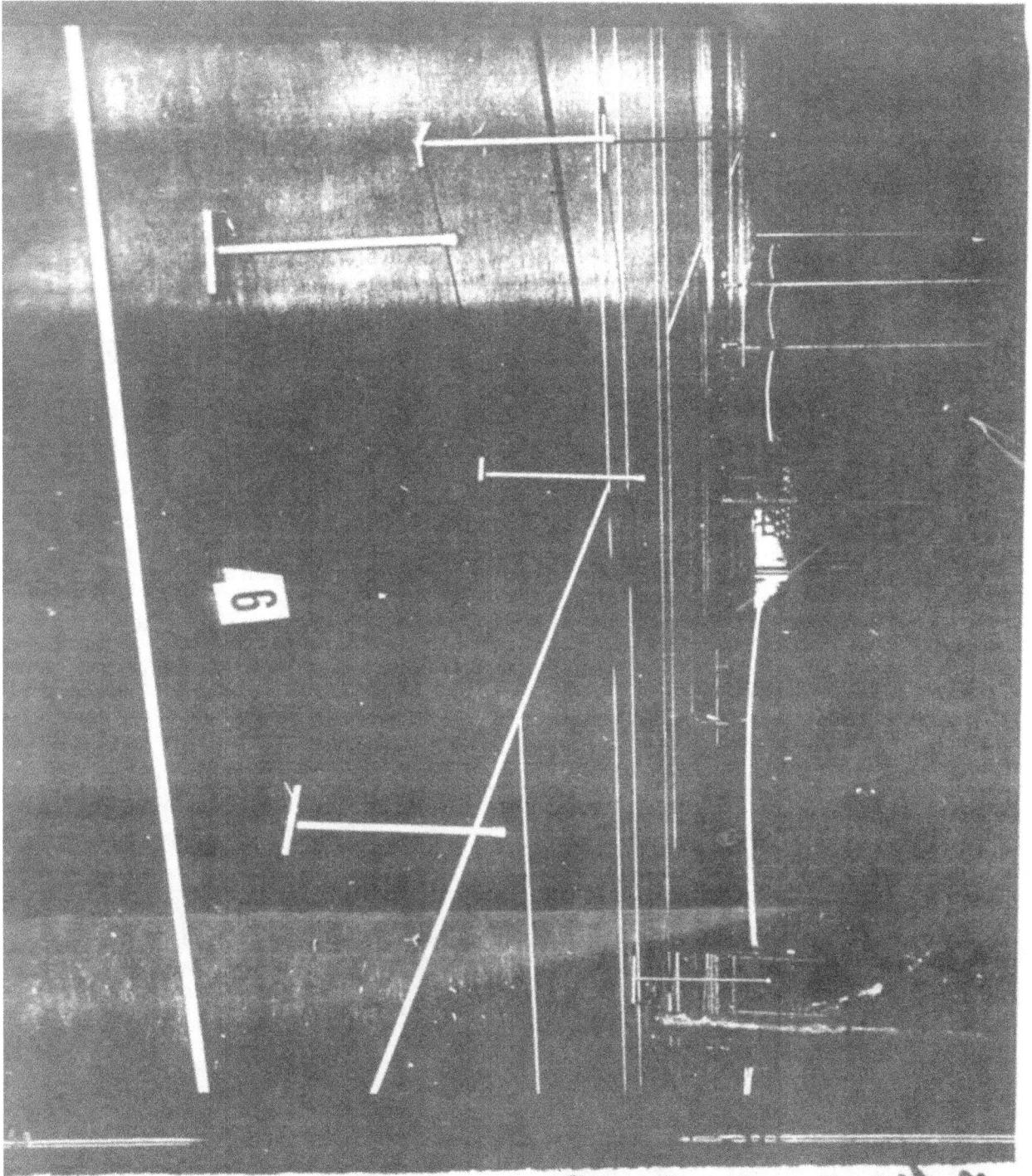

89.014 long.
42.691 lat.
0936 CST
F = 800 mm
F = 3.43
θ = 32° 56'
11 Oct 1989

D. R. GRAFF
Consultant in Surveying and Mapping

October 17, 1989

P. O. BOX 311
BEAVER DAM, WISCONSIN 53916

Admiral Thomas Davies
11025 Stanmore Drive
Potomac, Maryland 20854

Dear Admiral Davies:

This letter constitutes my report on the analysis of a photo taken at or near the North Pole on May 3, 1986.

I am in receipt of the above-mentioned photo and determined the altitude of the sun as follows:

The photo was overlaid with a piece of quality tracing paper. The principal point of the photo was estimated as the intersection of diagonals from the frame corners. The horizon line was located as the apparent horizon on the photo. Four objects and their shadows were found suitable for locating the vanishing point which represents the sun. These are:

1. The brow of the dog lying near the center of photo.
2. The thumb of the the left hand of the third man from the left.
3. The heel of the boot of the right foot of the fourth man from the left.
4. The bulge in the boot of the right foot of the first man from the right.

These four lines give 6 intersections, all of which are within a circle of about 2 mm in diameter.

Distances on the tracing paper were measured with a glass scale graduated to 0.100 mm. The results of the measurements are as follows (using the symbols from the six page writing entitled 'Shadows on the North Pole Photographs'):

Y1 = -3.66 mm
X (of vanishing point) = 63.0 mm
Y (of vanishing point) = -58.7 mm

The altitude of the sun was computed as 15.07 degrees using the formulation given on the following page. As developed, distances in the formulation should be taken as positive, which gives a positive altitude for the sun. I was unable to check the equations given on page 5 of 'Shadows on the North Pole Photographs'. Perhaps I am misinterpreting something. I do note the angle A (as defined by arctan (Y/D)) is not a vertical angle unless the tilt of the photo is zero or the point of interest lies on the principal line (imagine a photo pointed at the zenith).

As a rigorous error analysis does not seem justified, the following 'quick and dirty' method is used.

Variable	Assumed error	Change in measured altitude (plus or minus)
Principle distance	1 mm	.06 degrees
X	1 mm	.02 degrees
Y	1 mm	.26 degrees
X1	.5 mm	.14 degrees

If the assumed errors are reasonable, the error in the measured altitude is plus or minus 0.30 degrees or 18 minutes. Note that the Y dimensions give the largest uncertainties. These could be improved upon by repeating the exercise a number of times and using averages. Also, the use of image enhancement (edge detection in this case) would probably make objects and shadows more discernible.

Errors due to film shrinkage/expansion, lens distortions, mislocation of principal point, etc. are considered negligible for the purposes of this study.

The following corrections to the measured (observed) altitude should be applied:

Dip of the horizon	-2 minutes
Refraction	+13 minutes
Geocentric parallax	0 minutes

Applying the above correction, gives an apparent altitude of the sun to be 15 degrees 15 minutes at the time and place this photo was exposed.

I don't have a 1986 ephemeris of the sun and therefore I am unable to compare the altitude with the apparent declination. I would sincerely appreciate being advised as to the results of the comparison.

This has been an interesting exercise and if you have any questions or comments, please call or write.

I am returning the photo to Mr. William Hyzer on this date.

Sincerely,

Donald R. Graff, P.E.

Copy to: Mr. William Hyzer
          Janesville, Wisconsin

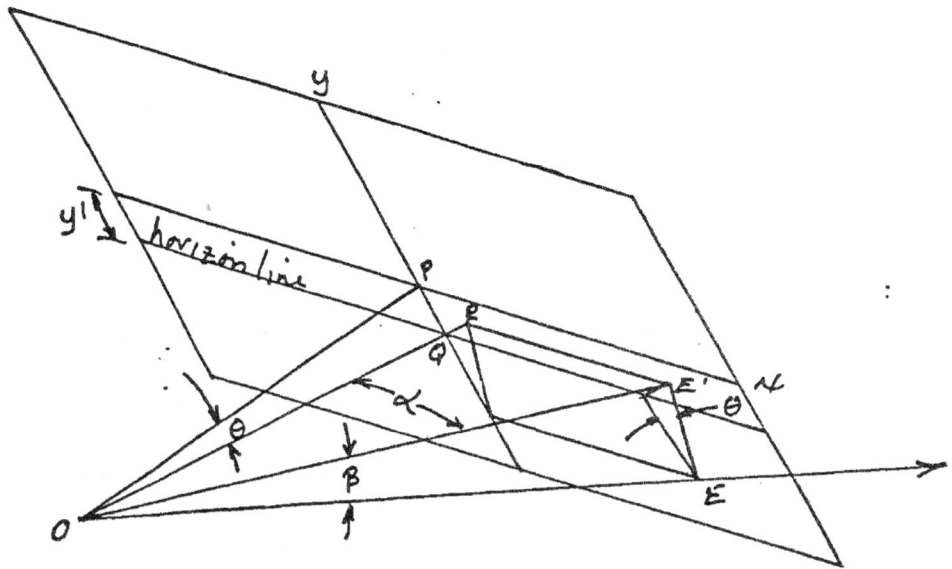

SKETCH OF TERRESTRIAL PHOTO TILTED UPWARD

Point O - perspective center
Point P - principal point (intersection of diagonals)
$\overline{OP}$ = principal distance = f
Point Q - intersection of horizontal line thru point O and y axis
Point E - point of interest
Point E' - intersection of vertical line thru point E with horizontal
        plane containing points O and Q
Point R - intersection of horizontal line thru E' with OQ extended
θ = inclination of optical axis with horizontal = $\angle$ POQ = $\tan^{-1}(f/y_1)$

Thus: points O, Q, R and E' lie in the same horizontal plane

       points O, E and E' lie in the same vertical plane

y_E' = photo distance from point E to horizon line.

α = horizontal angle to point $E = \angle QOE' =$

$$\tan^{-}\left(\frac{4E}{\overline{OQ} + \overline{QR}}\right), \quad \overline{OQ} = f/\cos\theta = f\sec\theta, \quad \overline{QR} = y_E' \sin\theta$$

or: $\alpha = \tan^{-1}\left(\dfrac{4E}{f\sec\theta + y_E'\sin\theta}\right)$.

β = vertical angle to point $E = \angle E'OE =$

$$\tan^{-1}\left(\frac{\overline{EE'}}{\overline{OE'}}\right), \quad \overline{EE'} = y_E'\cos\theta, \quad \overline{OE'} = \frac{\overline{OQ} + \overline{QR}}{\cos\alpha} = (\overline{OQ} + \overline{QR})\sec\alpha$$

or: $\beta = \tan^{-1}\left(\dfrac{y_E'\cos\theta}{(f\sec\theta + y_E'\sin\theta)\sec\alpha}\right)$

Bibliography

Amundsen, Roald. *My Life as an Explorer.* New York: Doubleday Doran, 1927.

Amundsen, Roald. *Our Polar Flight; the Amundsen-Ellsworth Polar Flight.* New York: Dodd, Mead and C., 1925

Astrup, Eivind. *With Peary Near the Pole.* London: Pearson, 1898.

Bartlett, Robert A. *The Log of Bob Bartlett.* New York: Putnam, 1928.

Borup, George. *A Tenderfoot with Peary.* New York: Stokes, 1911.

Cook, Frederick A. *My Attainment of the Pole.* New York; Kennerly, 1913, c1909.

Freuchen, Peter. *Arctic Adventure; My Life in the Frozen North.* New York: Farrer & Rinehart. c1935.

Freuchen, Peter, with Finn Salomonsen. *The Arctic Year.* New York: Putnam, 1958.

Greely, A. W. *True Tales of Arctic Heroism in the New World.* New York: C. Scribner's Sons, 1923, c1912.

Green, Fitzhugh, *Peary, the Man who Refused to Fail.* New York, London: G. P. Putnam's Sons, 1926.

Hall, Thomas F. *Has the North Pole Been Discovered.* Boston: Badger, 1917.

Henson, Matthew A. *A Negro Explorer at the North Pole.* New York: Stokes, 1912.

Herbert, Wally *Across the Top of the World.* London: Putnam, 1969.

Herbert, Wally *The Noose of Laurels: Robert E. Peary and the Race to the Pole.* New York: Atheneum, 1989.

Hobbs, William Herbert. *Peary.* New York: Macmillan, 1936.

Hunt, William R. *To Stand at the Pole.* New York: Stein and Day, 1981

Hayes, Rev. James Gordon. *Robert Edwin Peary, a Record of his Explorations, 1886-1909.* London: G. Richards and H. Toulmin, 1929.

Hayes, Rev. James Gordon. *Did Peary Reach the Pole?* London: Sherratt & Hughes, 1922

Lewin, Walter H. *Did Peary Reach the Pole?* London: Simpkin, Marshall, Hamilton, Kent & Co. Ltd., 1911.

Luigi, Duke of the Abruzzi. *On the Polar Star in the Arctic Sea.* New York: Dodd, Mead, 1903.

MacMillan, Donald B. *How Peary Reached the Pole.* Boston: Houghton Mifflin, 1934.

MacMillan, Donald B. *Four Years in the White North.* New York: Harper, 1918.

Markham, Sir Clements R. *The Lands of Silence.* Cambridge: University Press,1921.

Maxtone-Graham, John. *Safe Return Doubtful: The Heroic Age of Polar Exploration.* New York: Scribner's, 1988.

Morris, Charles (ed.) *Finding the North Pole.* Itro. by Adm Melville. Philadelphia: Scull, 1909

Mitchell, Hugh C. *Peary at the North Pole.* Annapolis: U.S. Naval Institute, 1959.

Nansen, Fidtjof. *Farthest North.* New York: Harper, 1897.

Rawlins, Dennis. *Peary at the North Pole; Fact or Fiction?* Washington: R. B. Luce, 1973.

Robinson, Bradley. *Dark Companion.* New York: McBride, 1947.

Stefansson, Evelyn S. B. *Here is the Far North.* New York: Scribner, 1957

Steger, Will. *North to the Pole.* New York: Times Books, 1987.

Sverdrup, Otto N. *New Land; Four Years in the Arctic Regions.* London: Longmans Green, and Co., 1904

Peary, Robert E. *Northward Over the "Great Ice."* New York: Stokes, 1898.

Peary, Robert E. *Nearest the Pole.* New York: Doubleday, 1907.

Peary, Robert E. *The North Pole.* New York: Stokes, 1910.

Shackleton, Edward. *Arctic Journeys: the Story of the Oxford University Ellesmere Land Expedition, 1934-35.* London: Hodder and Stoughton (n.d.)

Slama, Chester C. Editor-in-Chief. *Manual of Photogrammetry.* Falls Church, Va., American Society of Photogrammetry, 1980.

Stefansson, Vilhjalmur. *The Friendly Arctic.* New York: Macmillan, 1957.

Weems, John Edwin. *Race for the Pole.* New York: Holt, 1960.

Weems, John Edwin. *Peary, the Explorer and the Man.* Boston: Jeremy P. Tarcher, Inc.,1967.

Williams, John C. *Simple Photogrammetry.* London, New York: Academic Press, 1969.

Supplementary Materials

FOUNDATION FOR THE PROMOTION OF THE ART OF NAVIGATION

"THE NAVIGATION FOUNDATION"
A NON-PROFIT CORPORATION OF MARYLAND
P.O. BOX 1126, ROCKVILLE, MD

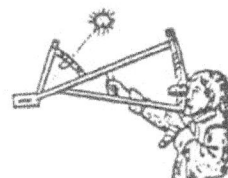

Dear Report Holder:

We are forwarding herewith the Supplemental Report to our basic report, Robert E. Peary at the North Pole. As you will see when you read the Supplement it was entirely unexpected and has added an unanticipated cost for both printing and mailing. Being a small non-profit organization with an all-volunteer staff, these expenses have taxed our limited resources. We therefore request that you contribute an amount of $3.00 to help with these expenses.

I know that you will find the new information in this supplement interesting and useful.

Sincerely,

Terry F. Carraway

"The art of navigation incites those who follow it to learn the secrets of the world." — Christopher Columbus, 1501

Robert E. Peary at the North Pole

A Report to the National Geographic Society by

The Foundation for the Promotion of the Art of Navigation

Supplemental Report

April 16, 1990

Dear Mr. Grosvenor:

I am pleased to submit herewith a supplemental report to the Navigation Foundation's report titled "Robert E. Peary at the North Pole", dated 11 December, 1989. The report has been written because of two new photographs from the Peary collection which we recently uncovered. In these two photographs the sun is clearly visible, as well as the horizon. Consequently the sun's altitude can be measured directly rather than through the indirect process of photogrammetry. The result so strongly confirms our photogrammetric measurements that we felt a supplement was desireable.

The supplemental report is being mailed to all 1000 holders of the basic report and will be bound into any future reprinting which may be required. In the supplemental we have also taken the opportunity to include germane comments on aspects other than the shadows on the photographs. I expect this to complete all work on the study.

In conclusion, let me again say that I believe that historians and students of this unique history are indebted to the National Geographic Society for underwriting this study.

Sincerely,

Thomas D. Davies, Rear Admiral, USN (Ret)
President

"The art of navigation incites those who follow it to learn the secrets of the world" —*Christopher Columbus, 1501*

Robert E. Peary at the North Pole

A Report to the National Geographic Society by

The Foundation for the Promotion of the Art of Navigation

Supplemental Report

In the months that have passed since the release of the original report last December, some previously undiscovered "North Pole" photographs have become available which back our conclusion that Robert E. Peary reached the North Pole on April 6, 1909. These pictures are so significant that we feel a brief supplement is desirable.

We wish to state at the outset that the conclusions in the report stand absolutely unaltered. In fact the newly uncovered photographs significantly narrow one of the bands of Peary's location and place him 5 miles closer to the Pole.

The Peary Photographs

About 6500 of the more than 7400 photographs in the "Peary Collection" were presented to the National Geographic Society in 1939 by Peary's daughter, Marie Peary Stafford. More photos were received from her in 1949. Her son, Commander Edward Stafford, sent approximately 250 lantern slides to be added to the collection in 1979 and 337 negatives in 1984.

In 1971 contact copy negatives were made of the old nitrate film which represented a fire hazard. These copies, fortunately, proved entirely adequate for our purpose. We discovered that the camera Peary used on his 1909 expedition made a characteristic line along each negative from top to bottom as the film was advanced. This was sometimes useful in identifying a picture or determining the dimensions of the negative. The "format" or exact dimensions of the negative were used to determine, with the help of the Eastman Kodak Museum, the camera used, and thereby the precise focal length, as described in the basic report.

The index of the Peary Collection is integrated into the computerized index of the entire National Geographic film library. The retrieval system depends on the use of "key words" as is the case in many other computerized systems. Thus to find the photographs taken in the vicinity of the Pole in 1909, we entered the system with a series of key words such as "north pole", "Peary", "flags", etc. Following the display of the negative

1

numbers and other data picked up by the key words, the actual picture is displayed for the viewer's examination by a video system.

The thirteen pictures used in the basic report were selected by this retrieval system. Choices for photogrammetric analysis to determine the elevation of the sun, and ultimately the location of the photographer, were made on the basis of potential suitability taking into account such factors as visible shadows beginning and ending within the frame, and the location of definable horizon lines. In applying these criteria, we considered the effect of any cropping or retouching done by Peary's publishers.

Once the pictures were selected, we utilized strongly overexposed (dark) enlargements to bring out shadows as clearly as possible. The basic report sets forth the method whereby shadows and vanishing points established by the angles of shadows were used to reveal the elevation of the sun. By consulting the Nautical Almanac, we then determined probable bands of position from which two distinct groups of photographs were taken on April 6 and 7. The values from these groups of pictures were averaged, and a composite of the bands defined an area in the near vicinity around the Pole that is the most likely location for the Peary party when the photographs were taken.[1]

For our purposes it was fortuitous that the pictures were taken at different times. Otherwise they would have simply given one band of probable location which extended indefinitely across the Pole in both directions. Such a single line passing through the Pole would be very strong evidence in support of Peary's claim but would not rule out the possibility that by sheer luck he took the picture when the sun was at exactly the right altitude. As described in the basic report (pp. 134-137) it can be determined from analysis of the photographs themselves that they were taken at different times, and thus afford intersecting bands of location.

Figure V-10 of the report (p. 142) gives the area of location we arrived at to place Peary within an approximate 20 mile radius of the Pole. The intersecting bands are analogous to the intersecting lines of position whereby a navigator obtains a "fix" in order to pinpoint his location.

The Additional Photographs.

After the publication of our report we continued to search for additional pictures from the polar series that the key word retrieval system might not have flushed out. We took enough time

_____

[1] If unlikely statistical extremes are considered the area would be somewhat expanded but not enough to alter our conclusion.

to manually go through the entire "Peary Collection" in the original albums. This was dog work, but it paid off. We turned up several pictures that were obviously part of the group taken in 1909 in the vicinity of the Pole that had been inadvertently indexed with pictures from Peary's 1906 "farthest North" expedition. They were identifiable by the tell-tale line made during the advance of the film, by the shape of a pinnacle showing in one, and by the number of cut-out patches on the flag flying from that pinnacle. It was Peary's practice to leave a scrap out of the flag his wife, Josephine, had made for him early in his career at each goal he later attained. Here the patches clearly visible in the properly-exposed prints ruled out the possibility that the photographs were taken during the 1906 expedition.

One of these new photographs shows the low arctic sun peeking from behind the very same pinnacle that features in several photographs in the basic report. The other shows the sun positioned in the center of a clear sky. Both offered the exciting prospect of permitting the calculation of the altitude of the sun to be done directly without reliance on angles derived from shadows.

On normal prints of these photographs the sun appeared as a large washed out area that was essentially useless for our purpose. We attempted to bring its image out clearly by overexposing the prints to the degree that almost everything was obscured except for the sun itself. The results were astounding. We now had two pictures (Figures 1 and 2) in which both the sun and a distant horizon were visible. The sun in each case was surrounded by a hazy bright area, but the area was clearly circular and its center could be accurately determined on the over-exposed print.

These pictures were superior to the thirteen analyzed in the original report because the altitude of the sun could be measured directly from the horizon to the center of the sun. Peary's own numerical designation of one negative and the sun's azimuth in the other tied both pictures to the group of six taken at about 8 to 10 p.m. on the 6th of April 1909. Our rectification of them thus gave us a reading on the degree of accuracy we had achieved in our previous work.

William Hyzer, of Janesville, Wisconsin, the certified photogrammetrist who reviewed our methodology for the basic report, undertook an independent analysis of these two new pictures simultaneously with our own. His measurements for the altitude of the sun were then compared with those obtained by separate analyses conducted by two members of the Navigation Foundation who had worked with the original photographs. The results are tabulated

3

below:

Photographs	Sun's Elevation in Degrees		
	Hyzer	N.F. 1	N.F. 2
Figure 1	6°-41′	6°-43′	6°-44′
Figure 2	6°-49′	6°-46′	6°-50′
Average	6°-45′	6°-45′	6°-47′

Mr. Hyzer's average value of 6°-45′ for the sun's elevation is well within the measurement of 6°-50′ plus or minus 13′ given in the report (Table V-6, p. 139). In other words our <u>indirect</u> measurement using the shadows gave essentially the same answer as the later <u>direct</u> measurement.

In his report[2] Mr. Hyzer estimates that the accuracy of these measurements is within 14.5′ for Figure 1 and 09′ for Figure 2. These combine to give an accuracy for the average altitude (6°-45′) of 08.5′. This means that the width of a probable location band based on these two pictures is no more than 17 miles instead of the 26 miles of the comparable band in Figure V-10 of the basic report. The use of this new value has the effect of shrinking the area from which the pictures must have been taken as shown in the replot in Figure 4.

The center of the band of Peary's probable location now moves 5 miles <u>closer</u> to the Pole. In the basic report (Figure V-10) it was centered at about 8 miles from the Pole; the new pictures center it at 3 miles from the Pole.

In addition to the two new pictures in Figures 1 and 2, we also have recently found an unretouched version of the photograph labelled Figure V-20 in the report. See Figure 3. The illustration is reproduced from one of Peary's glass slides provided us through

---

[2] We have attached Mr Hyzer's analysis of the two photographs hereto.

Hyzer described his participation in the study of the original Peary photographs in his column <u>Tech Talk</u> in the magazine <u>Photomethods</u> (March, 1990). There, under the heading "Only the Shadows Know", he reviewed the technique of photogrammetry applied to the original thirteen Peary photographs.

More recently, he presented the results of his analysis of the two new Peary photographs at a meeting of the American Academy of Forensic Sciences. These will be the subject of a future column.

4

the courtesy of Mr. Volkmar Wentzel from his private collection. The lack of any alteration of the picture is attested to by the familiar transport line made by Peary's 1909 camera, a line which here extends from the top to the bottom of the negative. As we were aware, in the picture reproduced from the National Geographic collection (Figure V-20) the sky had been painted over, as evidenced by the fact that the transport line extends only from the bottom of the picture to the apparent horizon.

The new print, which is very clear, shows that there is nothing visible beyond the dip in the horizon in the lower left background. In Figure V-19, as well as in Figure V-20 of the basic report, the horizon was conservatively assumed to be a short distance above the bottom of this dip, since the sky behind the bottom was obscured by paint. However, we can now see that the clear area behind the notch would show some evidence of ice cliffs if the horizon were as high as that used in our "worst case" assumption. A most probable horizon would be about 0.1 inch (on the 8x10) below that used in the report.

Applying our standard method of analysis to this new version of Figure V-20, still using the worst case horizon, gives an altitude of the sun of $7°-19'$, slightly higher but well within the standard deviation of $30'$ from the value of $7°-08'$ used in the report for that picture. Use of the more likely horizon mentioned above gives an altitude of the sun of $7°-00$.

Criticism of the Photogrammetry

We are pleased that the rectification of these three new photographs has confirmed the accuracy of our previous work, for the matter of the precision of our photogrammetric measurements has been the focus of critics who complain that the pictures are "fuzzy" and the horizons sometimes retouched. It should be noted in this connection that the illustrations in Figures V-11 through V-23 are half-tones of photographs, and as such, are inevitably "fuzzy." They were not intended to provide readers with anything more than a general idea of what the pictures with the superimposed lines used to determine vanishing points looked like.

The photographs utilized for plotting were, as explained above, heavily over-exposed; they were also were blown up to a considerably larger size than these half-tones to facilitate our work. We were aware that in some cases the accuracy of the shadow edges was more uncertain than was due solely to the sun's diameter (which we were able to correct for) and did a sensitivity analysis before assigning each standard deviation. Before compiling our report, we asked Mr. Hyzer to evaluate the accuracy of our procedures and he recommended a standard deviation of $20'$, about 0.3 degrees, which we used as our minimum on only two of the "best" pictures. Other deviations ran as high as $45'$ or 0.75 degrees.

5

In assessing each picture, we took the clarity or lack of clarity of the horizon into consideration and, as indicated with regard to V-20, adopted a pessimistic or "worst case" approach when in doubt. Since all but one of the original pictures were grouped in two time frames, as we have noted, it was possible to average the values of sun elevation of those in each group. Such averages are substantially more accurate than any value derived from a single photograph.

One critic of our photogrammetry, astronomer and long-time Peary detractor Dennis Rawlins, of Baltimore, has allegedly acknowledged to a news reporter that he is aware of one photograph that gives a "line of position through the Pole." Since he is convinced that Peary did not reach the Pole, he postulates that the explorer faked the picture, taking it from a position possibly 120 miles away after calculating the time at which the sun's altitude would be exactly correct for a person standing at the Pole. It is ridiculous to assume that Peary went to the trouble to set up a "staged" picture and then never used it, and indeed he never used this picture to "bolster" his case. Rawlins himself noted in his 1973 book <u>Peary at the North Pole: Fact or Fiction?</u> (p. 157) that "Especially crucial were the Camp Jesup [photos], since slight discrepancies elsewhere could usually be obscured by inexactitude about the local time. But at the Pole there is no local time, so a photo there is especially indicative." Now as he does with every other piece of evidence that supports Peary, Rawlins must dismiss this "crucial" photograph as bogus to sustain his case against him.

<u>Peary's Soundings Plotted on a Flat Chart</u>.

The three-dimensional computer-generated chart of the bottom of the Arctic Ocean in our basic report was not clear to some readers. To relieve their confusion we have added a plot of the same bathymetric data on a flat chart (Figure 5). Here we have focussed on the contour lines passing closest to Peary's reported positions and soundings. The areas of possible position shown on the three-dimensional charts (Figure IV-3 and IV-4, pp.122-123) are omitted for clarity. As mentioned in the report, modern submarine data from the Defense Mapping Agency indicates that the southern hook of the Lomonosov Ridge nearest Cape Columbia actually extends somewhat further to the west than the unclassified charts indicate; the chart of Figure 5 has been updated to agree with that data.

Even with the limitations attributable to breaks in Peary's sounding wire which resulted in some "no bottom" readings, the match between his readings and the true bottom is good enough to positively rule out guesswork or lucky accidents. While these soundings do not prove that Peary got to the Pole, they agree with his claimed track to the Pole. Moreover as the new chart clearly shows, the final sounding at "89°-55' no bottom at 2743 meters," rules out the position 55 nautical miles to the left of the Pole that Wally Herbert ascribes to him in <u>The Noose of Laurels</u>. In the

6

location Herbert has selected, the bottom contours are approximately 1500 meters over the Lomonosov Ridge. Thus Peary's sounding would have bottomed out at less than the 2743 meters his wire reached.

Further, the Defense Mapping Agency chart shows that the estimated position of Marvin's sounding of 567 meters at 85-23 north latitude, falls between the 500 meter and 1000 meter contours as it should. By contrast, Herbert's proposed track, which places Peary at least 20 nautical miles west of the 70th meridian at this latitude, lies between the 1000 and 1500 meter contours -- two to three times the depth recorded by Marvin. There is no data for 20 nautical miles west of the 70th meridian which supports Herbert's theory that at this juncture Peary had been carried by ice drift so far off his projected course.

Herbert's flat allegation in The Noose of Laurels that the only accurate soundings near Peary's route were made by the HMS Sovereign in October, 1976, flies in the face of the 1985 U.S. Naval Research Laboratory bathymetric map, the data provided us by the Defense Mapping Agency in 1989, and numerous scientific reports of soundings taken near and across the meridian since 1954. A check with the Defense Mapping Agency indicated that the classified Sovereign data had been provided to it by the British and that, after appropriate screening for navigational accuracy, it was incorporated in the data we used.

In sum, the significant proofs afforded by Peary's soundings should not be overlooked, as they have frequently been by commentators in reviewing our report. While in themselves they do not prove that he actually reached his goal, they put him in a position to have reached it, and they put the kibosh on the "ice drift" theory espoused by this leading modern-day critic.

As we explained in our basic report, Peary's noon latitude sights would have provided an indication of whatever drift occurred between Cape Columbia and the Pole and permitted him to take corrective action where he felt it was appropriate.

Comments on Recent Statements of Wally Herbert.

In the current (May) issue of the National Geographic Magazine, Herbert expresses his general disagreement with the report, observing at the outset that "not a single expedition that has attempted to reach the North Pole in the past 80 years has risked success by relying on latitude shots to give them a very rough heading." This observation misses its mark.

We do not question that later explorers -- with the benefit of Radio Time Signals, Radio Direction Finding, simple tabular methods of solving complex mathematics and bubble sextants -- have found other methods of determining their course more convenient and

7

accurate. However, polar explorers of Peary's day, including Commander Cagni, who led an Italian attempt at the North Pole in 1900, did not have these aids available and relied on the "homing" method used by Peary. This method got Amundsen to the South Pole where intervening mountain ranges complicated navigation by requiring major deviations from the direct course; there is no reason to assume that it was inadequate to get Peary to the North Pole on a more direct course across the Arctic Ocean.

Herbert's statement is tantamount to saying that no modern day trans-Atlantic flier would risk crossing the Atlantic ocean in the fragile single engine "Spirit of St. Louis" equipped with only the most rudimentary navigation devices. Of course none would. Yet the plane carried Charles A. Lindberg safely from New York to Paris, taking off from Roosevelt Field, Long Island, at 7:42 A.M. on May 20, 1927, and landing at Le Bourget at 10 P.M. Paris time on the evening of May 21st. Lindberg's success, like Peary's, was due to a combination of meticulous planning, true grit, and good fortune insofar as the weather was concerned.

We do not accept at face value Herbert's assertion that in his September 1988 National Geographic article and his book, he "hoped to introduce into the polar controversy a more practical and sympathetic understanding of this great explorer." A careful reading of The Noose of Laurels shows quite the opposite. While repeatedly claiming to give Peary the benefit of the doubt because of his profound respect for the man's courage and tenacity in the face of adversity, he does anything but that. He overlooks information in expedition member George Borup's book which conflicts with his own theory that Peary was carried far off his course by a westerly ice drift soon after leaving Cape Columbia; he overlooks Peary's notation of wind shifts which countered a slight drift to the westward at this early stage of the journey; and he ignores means that Peary had for correcting for ice movements during the course of the polar trek. As to Peary's sledging distances, he first inflates them by an inappropriate detour factor. Then, after saying that even the inflated values were possible on smooth ice, he proceeds to ignore the evidence of the smooth ice Peary and other explorers encountered and reluctantly concludes the distances were impossible of attainment. This is "sympathetic understanding?"

Herbert further charges that "in place of the practical issues and the complex character of Peary himself, [readers] are asked to accept as proof the evidence of shadows." We find this assertion astonishing in view of the fact that in addition to photogrammetric data we introduced (1) evidence of the reliability of Peary's navigational techniques (as Peary himself vainly attempted to describe them before the Congress); (2) statistical data in support of his claimed speeds and distances (attested by perhaps the greatest modern day dog-sledger, Will Steger, conqueror of both poles, as well as other earlier and contemporary sledgers); (3) the

8

best available technical data regarding the ocean contours along the 70th meridian to show that the contours agree with Peary's soundings and verify his track; and (4) a minute analysis of the celestial observations Peary brought back from the Pole (which both Rawlins and Herbert have, without analysis, dismissed as "faked") that strongly indicates they are genuine. As our report made clear, we reached our conclusion that Peary attained the Pole in the light of all the foregoing evidence <u>taken together with</u> that afforded by the photographs when analyzed in accordance with professionally approved techniques. In addition, we considered and dismissed as without merit the so-called "suspicious" factors that Herbert and other critics have construed as an indication of dissembling on Peary's part --the detached diary page on which he wrote "The Pole at last!!!", the incomplete entry on the diary cover, and his seeming depression upon his return to the <u>Roosevelt</u>. If these are not "practical issues" just how would Herbert define the term?

In dealing with Peary's "complex" (translate as "sinister") character, Herbert shows astonishing creativity and an alarming disregard for documented facts. The British explorer utilizes what appear to us to be innocuous entries in the explorer's diary to portray his predecessor as a "weather beaten fanatic," driven to lie and cheat by his "deepening obsession with fame." [3]

---

[3] An example is the manner in which he ascribes a sinister meaning to an entry reading "The first day of 'dark'" that appears in a typewritten transcript of Peary's 1906 diary, for which much of the original is missing. Herbert correctly notes that "dark" has no astronomical significance and concludes that it must have a metaphorical significance. Apparently he never heard of a "typo." The transcript includes numerous blanks and obvious transcription errors and was certainly not a proof-read final paper. A reading of the sentence in its context indicates that Peary must have written "The first day of <u>dash.</u>" The entry noted the beginning of his attempt to establish a new "farthest North" record with a skeletal party after reluctantly abandoning his logistic support and any chance of reaching the Pole. Moreover, a simple examination of Peary's handwriting on the extant original pages of the diary reveals that he did not close the small letter "s", making it almost identical with an "r," and that the same was frequently true of his small "k," making it resemble an "h." Thus common sense tells us that the world "dark" should have been transcribed as "dash."

But Herbert, seeking to impute to Peary some sinister meaning, utilizes the ominous phrase "The first day of 'dark'" as a subheading for one of three chapters devoted to an attempt to establish that the "farthest North" expedition was a fraud.

It will be recalled that in our original report we analyzed a photograph taken at the explorer's most northerly position in

9

Disregarding the careful preparations Peary made for his journey, and his many years of sledging in the arctic regions, Herbert claims with a straight face (p.272) "he set out on that crowning achievement of his polar career with apparently nothing more than the certain direction of his destiny to guide him across the drifting pack ice to his goal." "And where was his proof he had been to the Pole?" the author asks rhetorically, "The answer - he had none."[4]

But when Herbert poses the last of many rhetorical questions -- "What was the price he paid for ...fame? The burden of knowing that he had not reached the Pole, or his bitterness at being doubted when he was telling the truth?" -- his answer hinges on Peary's allegedly deficient navigation:

> He had only 133 miles to go from the point where Bartlett turned for home. He had the best men, the strongest dogs, and most of all, the need to reach it. How tragic then the irony that north had not been Peary's heading and in spite of all his effort, his courage and persistence he failed to reach the Pole.

In short, despite his assertion of having thoroughly and objectively appraised the man and his mission after being given access to his papers by the Peary family,[5] Herbert ends up with a

---

1906 which indicated that he had achieved his claimed record-breaking latitude of 87-06 or possibly exceeded it.

[4] Compare Herbert's demand for "proof" on Peary's part with his description of his own attainment of the Pole (Across the Top of the World, page 267). "We were dog-tired and hungry. Too tired to celebrate our arrival on the summit of this super mountain around which the sun circles almost as stuck in a groove. We set up our cameras and posed for some pictures -- thirty six shots at different exposures. We tried not to look weary, tried not to look cold; tried only to huddle, four fur clad figures, in a pose that was vaguely familiar -- for what other proof could we bring back that we had reached the Pole?"

[5] As we noted in our original report, the Peary family had much earlier made the same material available to the explorer's biographer, John Edward Weems. Weems' Peary, The Explorer And The Man (1967), and Herbert's The Noose Of Laurels (1989) share one feature in common -- each tells Peary's story largely in the explorer's own words, drawing upon his diaries, his letters to his mother and Josephine, and his several books. As Weems tells it, however, the story is one of a hard won victory achieved by a courageous straight-shooter after successive failures. Herbert's is a sordid tale of repeated failures and continual deceptions by a man whose craving for fame dominated every aspect of his life.

10

single string to his bow -- Peary did not reach the Pole when every factor was in his favor, he reasons, because he was carried off his northerly course by a westerly ice drift due to his failure to take longitude observations. Having disposed of the fallacious "ice drift" theory, we believe we have shot down Herbert's case.

In sum although Herbert, wrapping himself in the mantle of the polar explorer, belittles our documented determination that Peary reached the Pole as "armchair theory," he provides no credible data whatsoever to sustain his own theory that he did not.

<u>Summary</u>

Our conclusion that Peary attained the Pole remains unaltered, reinforced by our measurements from the newly acquired photographs which more than reaffirm our analysis of the original thirteen with their revealing shadows. Any critic who advances a contrary theory, whatever his tenet, has the burden of overcoming this crucial photographic evidence.

11

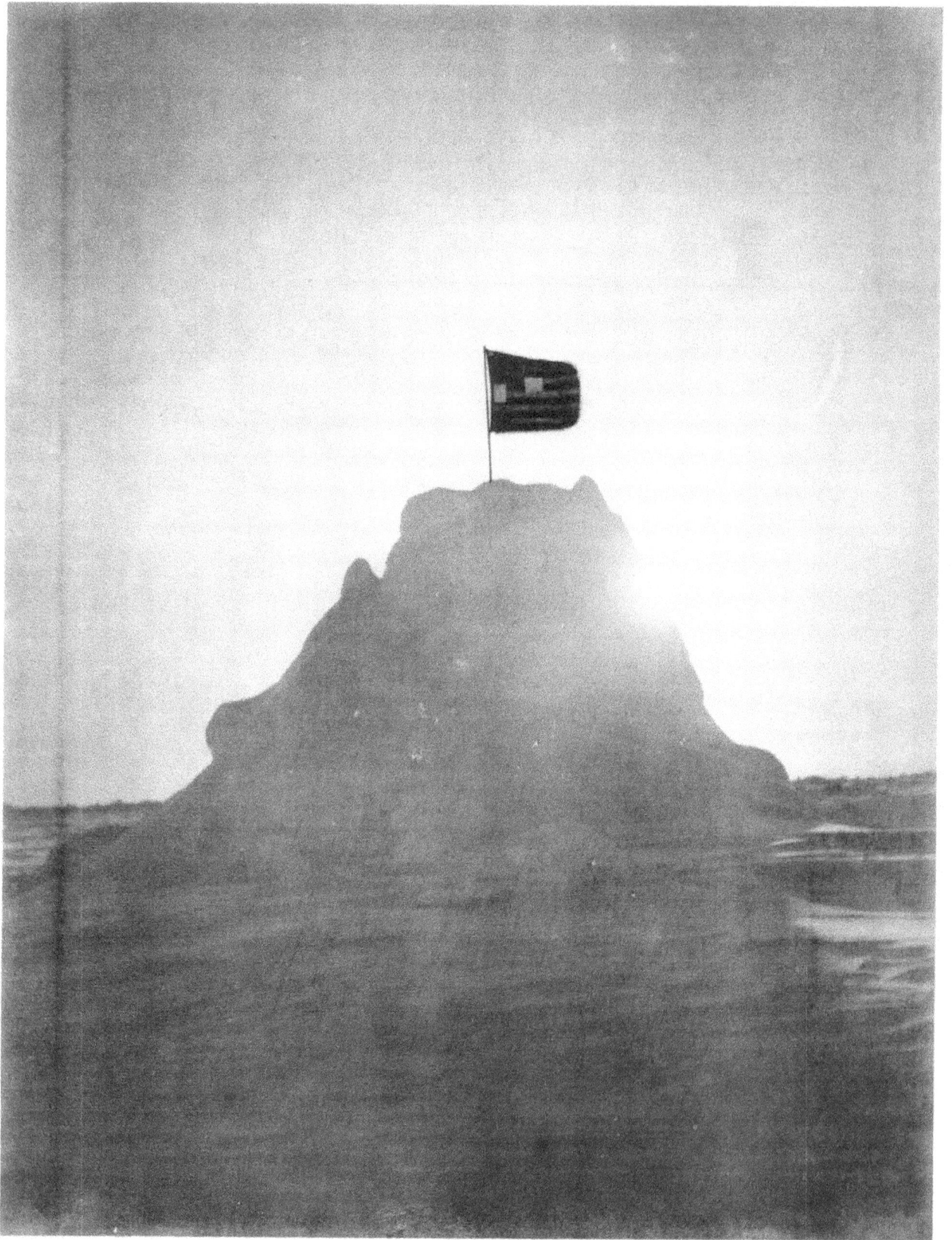

Figure 1

290 — Robert E. Peary at the North Pole

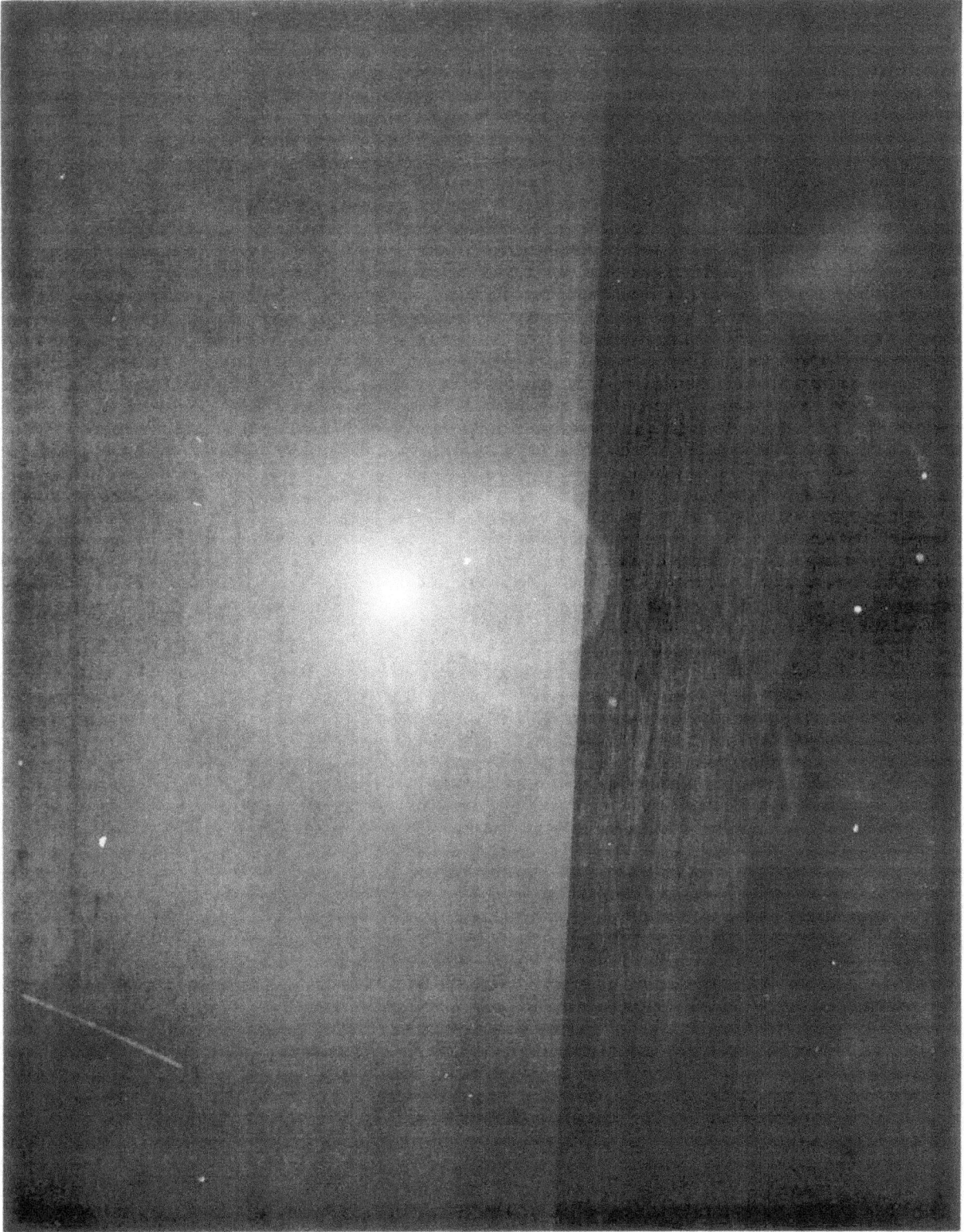

Figure 2

Figure 3

292 — Robert E. Peary at the North Pole

PLOT OF THE AREA OF INTERSECTION OF THE BANDS OF LOCATION

Revised to incorporate data from Figures 1 and 2

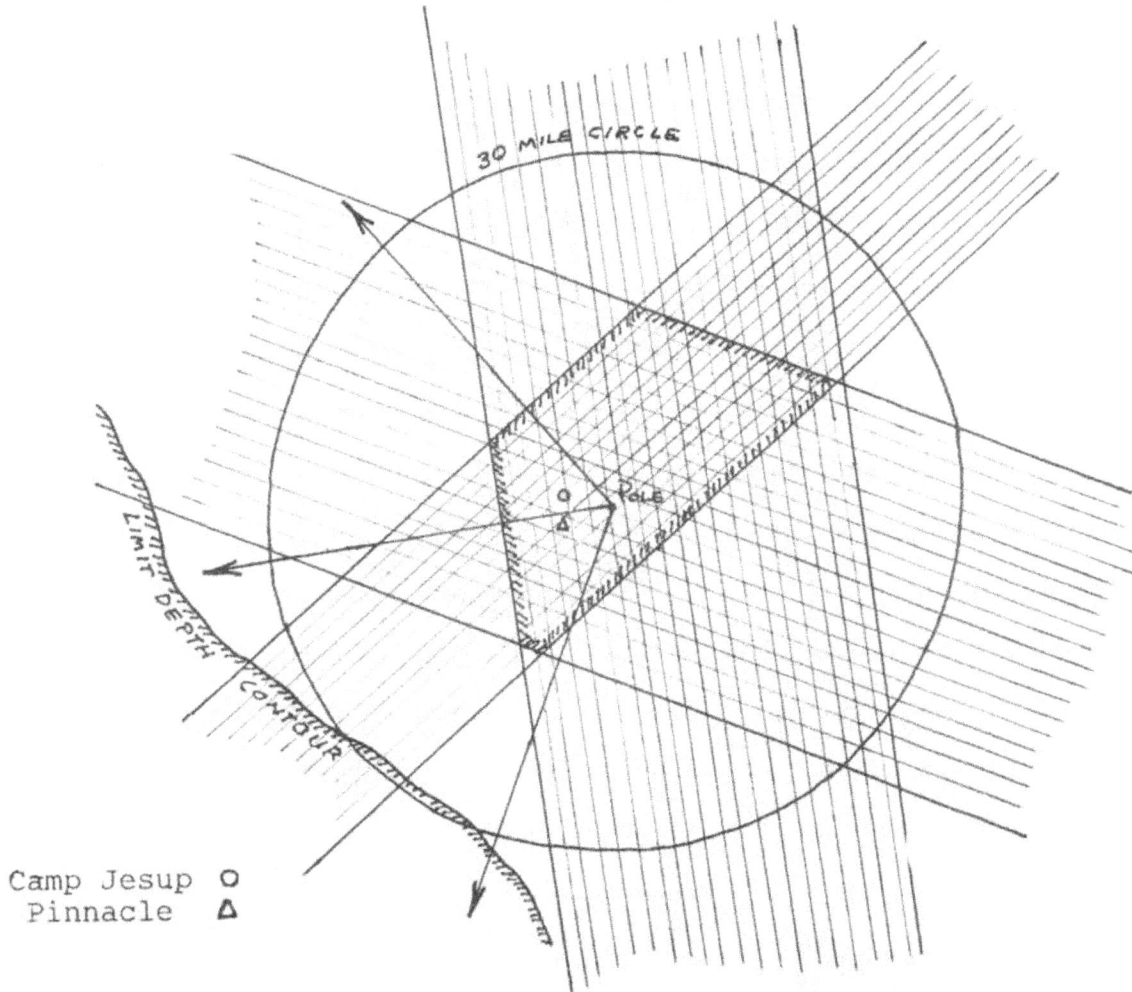

Figure 4.

COMPARISON OF PEARY'S SOUNDINGS WITH A MODERN CHART
OF THE ARCTIC OCEAN BOTTOM
(Updated from Submarine Soundings)

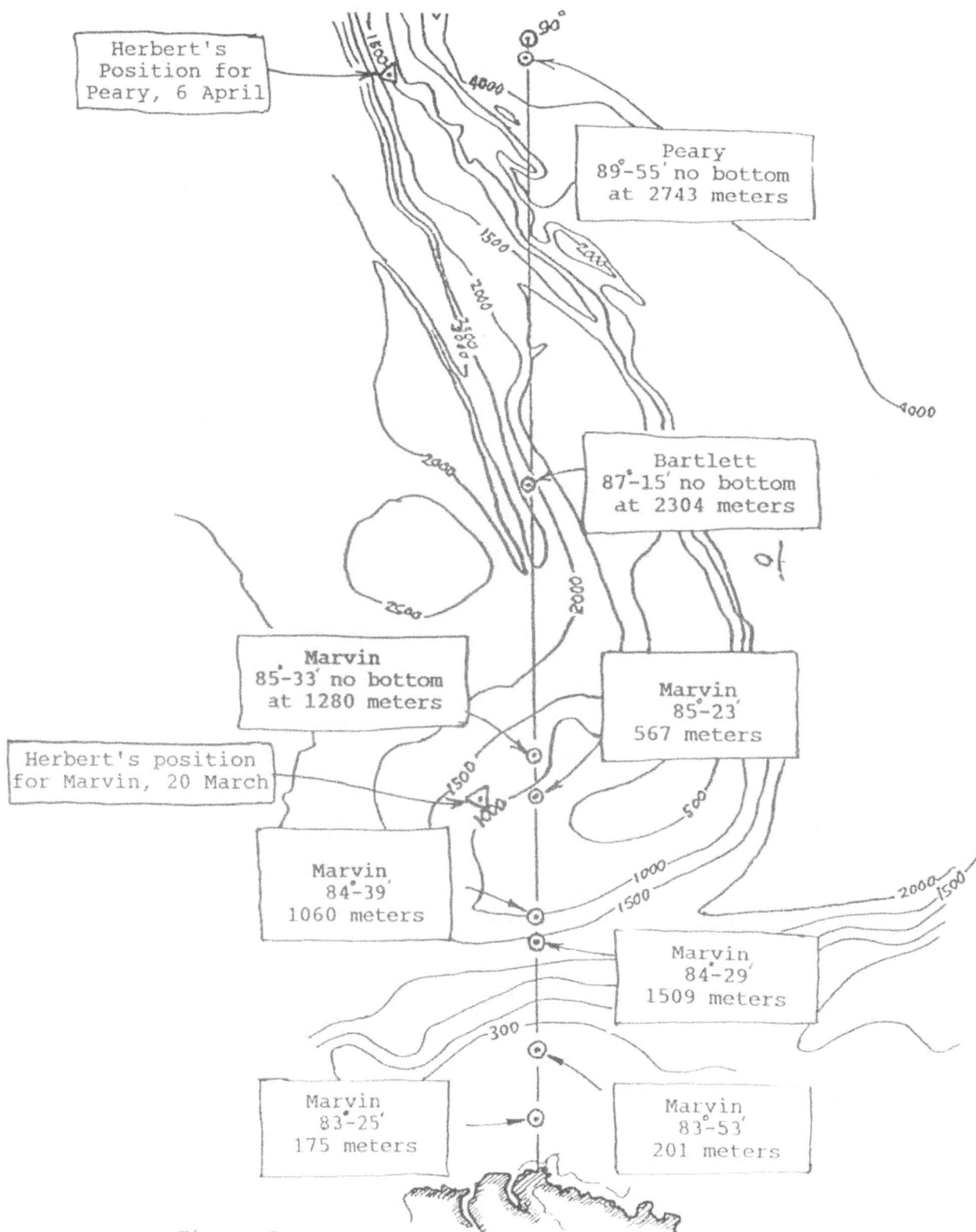

Herbert's
Position for
Peary, 6 April

Peary
89°-55' no bottom
at 2743 meters

Bartlett
87°-15' no bottom
at 2304 meters

Marvin
85°-33' no bottom
at 1280 meters

Marvin
85°-23'
567 meters

Herbert's position
for Marvin, 20 March

Marvin
84°-39'
1060 meters

Marvin
84°-29'
1509 meters

Marvin
83°-25'
175 meters

Marvin
83°-53'
201 meters

Figure 5

294 — Robert E. Peary at the North Pole

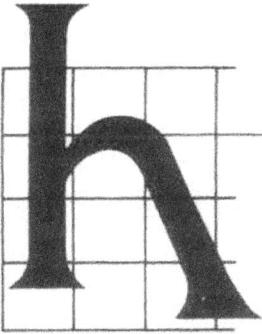

WILLIAM G. HYZER: Consultant in Engineering and Applied Science

136 S. GARFIELD AVENUE · JANESVILLE, WISCONSIN 53545 · 608-752-5581 · 608-754-7167

28 February 1990

Admiral Thomas Davies
The Navigation Foundation
11025 Stanmore Dr.
Potomac, MD   20854

Dear Adm. Davies:

This letter is a summary of my analysis of two photographs
from the Adm. Robert E. Peary collection in which images of
the sun's disc are recorded. The first photograph shows the
sun peeking around a snow pinnacle. I refer to this
photograph as number X1. The second photograph, numbered E5,
shows the sun above a vast snow field. Both the sun and the
horizon line are very well defined in E5. The horizon line in
the 8 x 10 print is taken as a line 0.071 inches below the
top of the ice ridge that separates the ice from the sky.
Part of the sun's disc is obscured by the snow pinnacle in X1
and the horizon line is less distinct than in E5, but it is a
good photograph for analytical purposes.   Both E5 and X1
were available to me in the form of contact prints and 8 x 10
inch enlargements.

First, the optical centers of the photographs were defined in
both contact prints. Next, the print enlargement ratios were
determined by dividing the scale of each enlarged print by
the scale of its corresponding contact print using a Gurley
glass scale graduated in 0.1 mm divisions.   Then the
positions of the optical centers were transferred from the
contact prints to the enlargements.

The X and Y coordinates of the center of the sun's disc and
the Y' coordinate of the horizon line relative to the optical
center of the image were measured to the nearest 0.1 mm in
each enlargement using the Gurley glass scale.

WILLIAM G. HYZER

-2-

The elevation angles (A) of the sun's center above the horizon were then computed using the following equation:

$$A = \tan^{-1}[Y/(F^2 + X^2)^{1/2}] - \tan^{-1}[Y'/(F^2 + X^2)^{1/2}]$$

where F = Effective Focal Length obtained by multiplying the actual focal length by the print enlargement factor.

The results of these analyses are tabulated on the attached page. The sun's elevation angle was found to be 6° 41' in photograph X1 and 6° 49' in photograph E5. The accuracies of these measurements are estimated to be within 14.5' in X1 and 09' in E5.

Very truly yours,

William G. Hyzer, P.E.

ANALYSIS OF PHOTOGRAPHS X1 AND E5

SUN ELEVATION ANGLE COMPUTATION FROM PHOTO #X1 (SUN PEEKING AROUND PINNACLE):

Camera Lens Focal Length, in.	6.74
Assumed Focus Setting	Infinity
Print Enlargement Ratio	1.973
Effective Focal Length, in.	13.298
X, in.	1.553
Y, in.	0.179
Y', in.	-1.388
Sun's Elevation, degrees of arc	6° 41'
Accuracy, degrees of arc	0° 14.5'
Maximum Sun Elevation, degrees of arc	6° 56'
Minimum Sun Elevation, degrees of arc	6° 27'

SUN ELEVATION ANGLE COMPUTATION FROM PHOTO #E5 (SUN OVER FLAT SNOW FIELD):

Camera Lens Focal Length, in.	6.74
Assumed Focus Setting	Infinity
Print Enlargement Ratio	1.900
Effective Focal Length, in.	12.806
X, in.	0.100
Y, in.	0.685
Y', in.	-0.839
Sun's Elevation, degrees of arc	6° 49'
Accuracy, degrees of arc	0° 09'
Maximum Sun Elevation, degrees of arc	6° 58'
Minimum Sun Elevation, degrees of arc	6° 40'

2/28/90

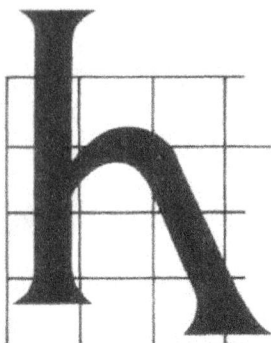

5 March 1990

Admiral Thomas Davies
The Navigation Foundation
11025 Stanmore Dr.
Potomac, MD   20854

Dear Adm. Davies:

This will confirm our conversation of this morning in which I
informed you that my analysis of the Peary photographs is
being performed as an independent evaluation and that I am
not being paid by the Navigation Foundation, the National
Geographic Society or any other organization. This is what I
told Rensberger of the Washington Post when he called me last
Wednesday to alleviate any "hired-gun" criticisms that were
definitely in the back of his mind.. As far as Rensberger
and any other reporters are concerned, my final conclusions
conveyed in my last report to you will be kept confidential
until the report you are now preparing is released to the
press by the National Geographic.

Please send a copy of the Washington Times article.

If there is anything further I can do to contribute to this
project, please don't hesitate to ask.

I am enclosing the slides you loaned me.   Please note that
several of the cover glasses were broken in shipment to me.

Very truly yours,

William G. Hyzer, P.E.

The Following article is reproduced with permission from Navigation: Journal of the Institute of Navigation, Vol. 37, No.1 Spring 1990. This article and related studies of celestial navigation and arctic exploration are included on the Institute of Navigation's custom Celestial Navigation CD, available at www.ion.org/publications. This CD was produced in cooperation with the Navigation Foundation. It is a highly recommended primary resource for all matters relating to celestial navigation.

NAVIGATION: *Journal of The Institute of Navigation*
Vol. 37, No. 1, Spring 1990
Printed in U.S.A.

The Institute's Professional Forum

ANALYSIS OF WHETHER PEARY EMPLOYED AMUNDSEN'S METHOD OF OBTAINING COMPASS HEADING

Both Peary and Amundsen admitted that they took no transverse sextant sightings for longitude on their expeditions to the Poles. Amundsen's claim to the South Pole has never been questioned; Peary's claim to the North Pole has. The Navigation Foundation maintains photographic and other evidence proves Peary was at the Pole, and it is logical, therefore, to assume both used the same method of navigation. This assumption is fallacious.

Amundsen had only two methods available for determining heading: one was the transverse sighting crossed with a latitude sight; the other was to note carefully the transit of the noon sun with his sextant, which would give him latitude and a heading simultaneously. The former required tedious spherical trigonometry and plotting on a chart under adverse conditions. The latter was a lengthy process, but required only addition and subtraction and no plotting. Amundsen chose the latter method. Peary had an ocean horizon; Amundsen did not. The ocean horizon gave Peary three additional ways to obtain course and heading. Each of these three methods was easier than either of the two methods available to Amundsen.

The Navigation Foundation called their version of Amundsen's noon-sight method the "time sight." The ease and simplicity of this method, according to the Navigation Foundation's theory, made it the logical choice for both navigators.

It is not possible to obtain heading by the "time sight" method as originated by the Navigation Foundation and described and illustrated by Admiral Davies in his January 1990 article in The National Geographic Magazine.

At noon transit time from 86 deg N, the altitude of the sun varied only 9 arcsec in 15 min. Peary was obtaining latitudes from 1 to 12 days after vernal equinox. At this time of year, the declination of the sun was increasing 14+ arcsec in 15 min (7 arcsec additive before transit and 7 arcsec canceling after transit). Peary's party was observing the sun at altitudes of 5 and 6 deg. However, on page 61 of Admiral Davies' and the Navigation Foundation's report on the Peary trip is the following:

> At the latitude and time of Marvin's sights the altitude of the sun when on the "prime vertical" for a longitude sight would have been about 1.75 degrees ... arctic refraction variability is such at low altitudes that the sight would have been virtually worthless [1].

When the sun is only 3.25 deg higher, refraction variability does not disappear. The sun randomly moves up and down several arcsec as its rays pass through various configurations of atmosphere. If one were lying prone on the ground with one's eye on the sextant eyepiece and one's hand holding a sextant, simply inhaling or exhaling would move the sextant a few arcsec. If a gust of wind hit the mercury artificial horizon, it would move a few arcsec. The ice floe

113

the observer was lying prone upon would be floating and moving with the winds and tides, which could cause a few arcsec movement of the sextant. Under these conditions, it is completely impossible to hand-hold a sextant, observe the sun moving up and down 9 arc sec in 15 min, and determine that transit has occurred.

Amundsen obtained heading on his 1911 trip to the South Pole by using a sextant to observe noon sun transit. He was traveling in late November and December, close to the summer solstice. At this time of the year, the declination increases only 1 or 2 arcsec/h. Amundsen was also observing the sun at altitudes greater than 20 deg, where the random up and down movement of refraction is greatly reduced. His procedure would have been to take a sextant altitude every 1 or 2 min for at least 30 min, most probably longer, in order to average out the vagaries of refraction and other factors. By close examination of the data, an estimate could be made of when transit might have occurred. Very skilled work with the sextant could obtain longitude within about ±5 nmi at best. Amundsen described obtaining heading and longitude in this manner by using a team of four men and two sextants [2].

On Peary's trip, in 30 min of time, the altitude of the sun varied only 32 arcsec at transit. Facing a much greater refraction problem, an observer in Peary's situation could take a sextant reading every minute for 30 min and be unable to detect a definite rising and descending of the sun. In fact, the data might indicate a small rising of the sun when in actuality the sun was descending, or vice versa. The resulting heading error could be quite large. Because of the large vagaries of refraction, a sextant altitude would have to have been taken every minute or two for at least 40 min or longer in order to detect the rising and descending of the sun at transit. Saying this could be done in 12 or 15 min reveals considerable misunderstanding of the limits and capabilities of the hand-held sextant. It would not have been possible for either Amundsen or Peary to hand-hold a sextant steadily enough to watch the phenomenon of transit occur.

According to the Navigation Foundation's report to the National Geographic Society, Peary obtained a good compass heading on 5 March when the sun just barely cleared the southern horizon for the first time since the previous October. His next heading checks were when, as Peary wrote, "The sun setting due E & W on 21 and 22 Mar. gave us an accurate check on our compasses" [3]. Ross Marvin is alleged to have performed the first "time sight" for heading on 22 March. On this date, the Peary party had allegedly been traveling 16 days without a heading or longitude check. Marvin would have had to begin observing the sun at least 30 min before expected transit time in order to allow for the fact that he could be off course some distance. At the time of Marvin's sights, Peary specifically noted that the temperature was −40 °F [3]. One wonders why Marvin would attempt to perform this lengthy sextant procedure for compass heading when, just 6 h earlier, Peary had gotten an "accurate check on our compasses."

Peary could not have obtained an "accurate check on our compasses" on 21 or 22 March without knowing his longitude at the time. Without a compass check, allegedly for 16 days, it is obvious he had already discovered his longitude (and thereby heading) by some method other than the "time sight."

In the unnumbered Section B of the Navigation Foundation's report to the National Geographic Society is a probability analysis of Marvin's sights. Computerized analysis of these sights, to six decimal points, has produced a set of figures purportedly showing that the 22 March sextant sights agree with culmination with a confidence factor of 95 percent; this means merely that they do not disagree with culmination. This result could be expected. What these figures do not show is that the computer has yet to be designed that could prove, with a confidence factor greater than 50 percent, that it was impossible for these sextant sightings, differing by as much as 30 and 40 arcsec, to have been made 30 nmi off the transit meridian.

According to the Navigation Foundation's analysis of Peary's navigation, Peary was never concerned with his longitude, only his heading. By obtaining a series of heading checks, he could have "homed" on the Pole with his compass without regard for longitude. While this is true enough (provided he obtained compass checks by some logical means), Peary was a consummate navigator who would concern himself with his course and longitude. Peary said that the fathom soundings could be presumed to have been taken on the 70th meridian [2].

In support of the argument that Peary obtained his heading by the "time sight" method, the experience of Umberto Cagni (predecessor of Peary) was cited by the Navigation Foundation:

> . . . We find him recording the taking of meridian altitudes. . . . that he was getting directions from these culminations is clear. . . . At latitude 86–34 N, where the party decided to turn back . . . the first longitude sight was taken. This makes sense because the use of meridian altitudes alone would have taken him south . . . but probably not to his specific destination [1].

This might make sense to the Navigation Foundation, but it does not to the author. If Cagni was determining transit for heading, why did he not look at his watch and determine his longitude at the same time? That Cagni took a transverse sextant sighting for longitude is evidence that he was obtaining latitude, but neither heading nor longitude from the meridian altitudes.

Amundsen had no ocean horizon to work with as did Peary. Amundsen was obliged to determine noon transit or use tedious spherical trigonometry for heading and longitude. He chose the former [1]. Peary was not obliged to choose either.

It is concluded that Peary could not use the "time sight" method for heading in the manner explained by Admiral Davies. It is also concluded that Peary would never bother to use Amundsen's lengthy and what for Peary would be a very difficult and inaccurate method when, with an ocean horizon, he had available to him the very easy and far more accurate methods explained in my recent article for this journal [4].

It should be made clear that the central issue of the Navigation Foundation study is not in dispute. I am in full agreement with their conclusion that Peary did indeed reach the North Pole.

REFERENCES

1. Davies, T. D., *Robert E. Peary at the North Pole,* A Report to the National Geographic Society, 1989, pp. 59, 61, 62.
2. Neider, C., *Antarctica,* New York: Random House, 1972, p. 209.
3. Peary, R. E., *1909 Diary,* National Archives, Entry for 22 March.

4. Molett, W. E., *Analysis of Admiral Peary's Trip to the North Pole*, NAVIGATION, Journal of The Institute of Navigation, Vol. 36, No.2, Summer 1989.

William E. Molett, Lt. Colonel, USAF (Ret.)
Frankfort, Kentucky

COMMENTS ON COL. MOLETT'S ANALYSIS

To fully appreciate the Navigation Foundation's view of all aspects of Peary's 1909 trip to the Pole, one must really read the report. Colonel Molett has postulated an ingenious and possible method for Peary to have used for *staying on a meridian,* which he communicated to me by letter early on. In our research, we diligently sought any indication that Peary actually used this method. Instead, we came across several items that supported the view we eventually adopted—that he did *not* attempt to stay precisely on the meridian, but considered the compass courses from the approximate direction he got from his necessary LAN latitude sights. This method was good enough to get him close enough to the Pole so that the transverse sights taken, when he estimated that he had arrived, would give him his true location and permit "nailing it" by whatever additional run was necessary. This navigational scheme was apparently used by the Italian Cagni before Peary and by Amundsen after.

In the above article, Colonel Molett begins and ends by discussing the determination of heading in the context of Amundsen versus Peary. Our report says that Amundsen did not take longitude sights. Molett says the reason Amundsen did not do so was that he did not have "an ocean horizon" and that Peary did; therefore, Peary must have used one of three other methods available to him, which include the method Molett had postulated in his previous article.

In fact, both Amundsen and Peary used similar (surveyor's) artificial horizons and thus had equal availability of a "horizon." Photographs are available of each using these horizons.

Molett says the Navigation Foundation called our version of Amundsen's noon sight method a "time sight." He is confused, and he continues this confusion throughout his article. The report makes reference to the classical Time Sight only in terms of a method Peary *would have used* if he had had to take a longitude sight on the return trip. Anyone familiar with the Time Sight knows that it is best taken on the Prime Vertical, not at LAN as were all of the sights Molett refers to as Time Sights.

Molett quotes a paragraph from our report that refers to the effect of arctic refraction on very low-altitude (longitude) sights, making these sights "virtually worthless." However, he omits the relevant statement contained in a footnote (footnote 19, page 73), which says, "We hasten to point out that atmospheric refraction has no effect on the determination of *direction* from observations."

Molett's discussion of the difficulties of determining the culmination under arctic conditions is somewhat exaggerated. He seems to believe that rotating the sextant slightly ("simply exhaling or inhaling") produces an angular error in the results. Of course this is not the case. Nonetheless, the observer took every means to brace his sextant/hand (against tremor and fatigue), as well as his artificial horizon. Further, the artificial horizon was protected by a glass cover, and the entire setup was protected by an ice block wind wall. The effect of the changing of the sun's declination was accounted for in the report.

The report contains tables that illustrate the probable accuracy of the determination of direction and its effect on the error of arrival at the Pole. For example, at 88 deg north (the last sights before the Pole), the error can be as high as ±5.2 deg, but that produces an arrival at the Pole only 11 mi in error. Marvin was a competent surveyor (as was Peary), well experienced in the use of his instruments, and the fact that his results were the average of eight sights adds to the credibility of his direction.

Molett's conclusion from his discussion of the computerized analysis of Marvin's sights in Appendix B of the report (". . . the computer has yet to be designed . . .") is incomprehensible. These analyses relate the individual sights to the calculated altitude of the sun throughout the run, and probabilities are expressed to six decimal places so that a reasonable probability-density curve can be derived. There is no implication that the sights are read to six decimal places. The confidence levels expressed are that Marvin's sights matched the culmination of the sun within 4 deg of azimuth at a confidence level of 95 percent in one case, and within 4 deg of azimuth at a confidence level of 88 percent in the other. Our conclusion was that Marvin's latitudes were therefore accurate, but also that he had to be oriented approximately south when he was taking the sights.

Molett's discussion of Peary's navigation says that at the time of Marvin's first sights, they had been traveling for 16 days without a heading. On the contrary, they made a careful compass check before leaving Cape Columbia (Bartlett's letter, page 54) and used this heading during that period. The compass direction changed only about 7 deg during those 16 days, according to the magnetic information for 1909. Peary's notes indicate that they had an update 5 days out on the ice from the sun showing over the horizon.

Molett also concludes that Peary must have determined his longitude by some means to have been able to get an accurate check on his compasses when the sun was setting due east and west on March 21 and 22, as he reported. Peary was simply referring to the fact that the sun's declination was approximately zero on those days, and therefore rose and set on the Prime Vertical, *regardless of longitude.*

Thomas D. Davies, Rear Admiral, USN (Ret.)
The Navigation Foundation, Rockville, Maryland

9 780914 025207